NATIONS DIVIDED

NATIONS DIVIDED

AMERICAN JEWS AND THE STRUGGLE OVER APARTHEID

Marjorie N. Feld

palgrave
macmillan

NATIONS DIVIDED
Copyright © Marjorie N. Feld, 2014.
Softcover reprint of the hardcover 1st edition 2014 978-1-137-02970-6

All rights reserved.

First published in 2014 by
PALGRAVE MACMILLAN®
in the United States—a division of St. Martin's Press LLC,
175 Fifth Avenue, New York, NY 10010.

Where this book is distributed in the UK, Europe and the rest of the world, this is by Palgrave Macmillan, a division of Macmillan Publishers Limited, registered in England, company number 785998, of Houndmills, Basingstoke, Hampshire RG21 6XS.

Palgrave Macmillan is the global academic imprint of the above companies and has companies and representatives throughout the world.

Palgrave® and Macmillan® are registered trademarks in the United States, the United Kingdom, Europe and other countries.

ISBN 978-1-137-02971-3   ISBN 978-1-137-02972-0 (eBook)
DOI 10.1057/9781137029720

Library of Congress Cataloging-in-Publication Data

Feld, Marjorie N., author.
   Nations divided : American Jews and the struggle over apartheid / Marjorie N. Feld.
       pages cm
   Includes bibliographical references and index.

   1. Anti-apartheid movements—United States. 2. Apartheid—South Africa—Public opinion. 3. Jews—United States—Attitudes. 4. Jews—United States—Attitudes toward Israel. 5. Zionism—Israel—Public opinion. 6. Social justice—South Africa—Public opinion. 7. Social justice—Israel—Public opinion. 8. South Africa—Foreign public opinion, American. 9. Israel—Foreign public opinion, American. 10. African Americans—Relations with Jews. I. Title.

E183.8.S6F45 2014
323.1680973—dc23   2014002964

A catalogue record of the book is available from the British Library.

Design by Newgen Knowledge Works (P) Ltd., Chennai, India.

First edition: July 2014

10 9 8 7 6 5 4 3 2 1

Contents

Acknowledgments		vii
Introduction: Apartheid and American Jews		1
1	Postwar Conflicts over Racial Justice	9
2	American Zionism and African Liberation	21
3	Jews or Radicals?	41
4	"South Africa Needs Friends": Cold War Narratives and Counternarratives	63
5	Jewish Women, Zionism, and Apartheid	87
6	New Agendas: The Organizational Jewish Response to Apartheid	107
7	"Our South Africa Moment": American Jews' Struggles with Apartheid, Zionism, and Divestment	127
Notes		155
Bibliography		209
Index		223

Acknowledgments

A few months after the publication of my first book, a biography of Lillian Wald, I went hunting for local archival resources about Jews and apartheid. I planned to write an article about American Jewish antiapartheid activism in the 1980s. After a decade researching the Progressive era, I embraced the chance to study a more recent era and actually interview those who participated in this global movement.

Although my sisters and I danced to the "Sun City" music video, which I write about in chapter 6, I had little personal contact with the antiapartheid movement. I arrived at SUNY Binghamton in 1989, a few months after I had had my orientation in the student union's Mandela Room. The SUNY Board of Trustees had divested all of the University's funds from South Africa four years before I arrived. In high school and then again in college, I missed the movement and the building of shantytowns I here describe.

As I dug into archival sources and as the Durban Review conference began to appear in the news in 2009, the story grew far larger and wider than just one of American Jews in the antiapartheid movement in the 1980s. I knew that the story of American Jews and apartheid would reach back to the Second World War and stretch through the debates over apartheid in Israel/Palestine still occurring today. In connecting these debates across time, this study taps into urgent controversies. While I earnestly thank all those who assisted me in completing this study, I alone am responsible for its conclusions.

An early conversation with Michael Staub, a longtime friend and mentor, convinced me of the viability and importance of this topic. Kevin Proffitt at the American Jewish Archives in Cincinnati provided invaluable research assistance for what became the foundation of this book. He also connected me to Adam Mendelsohn at the College of Charleston, who generously shared his superb thesis with me.

All historians rely on skilled archivists and librarians. I want to thank the following experts with whom I worked: Amanda Seigel, in the Dorot Reading Room of the New York Public Library; Sharon Howard of Schomburg Center for Research in Black Culture at the NYPL; Gail Malmgreen, Jan Hilley, Rachel Schimke, and Kate Donovan of Tamiment Library at New York University; Kate Hutchens at University of Michigan; Susan Dayall of Hampshire College; Richard Knight at the African Activist

Archive Project; Dr Nancy Isserman, Coordinator of the Feinstein Center for American Jewish History at Temple University. In Manhattan, Haya Luftig ushered me into the offices of the Jewish Council for Public Affairs and allowed me access to the papers of the National Jewish Community Relations Advisory Council. Ezra Nepon gave me a good orientation to the New Jewish Agenda records. In addition to offering expert advice, Jim Rosenbloom and Nancy Zibman in the Judaica Reference room of Brandeis University always made me feel welcome and at home. Downstairs, I relied on the smart assistance of University Archivist Maggie McNeely.

At conferences and in casual conversations, colleagues offered me helpful feedback and advice. I offer my thanks to: David Hostetter, Vickie Langhor, Pam Brooks, Alex Lichtenstein, Elizabeth Goldberg, Zengie Mangaliso, and Jeff Melnick. Meenakshi Khanna offers me friendship and laughter along with brilliant and invaluable commentary. At Babson, my fellow feminists in the Center for Women's Entrepreneurial Leadership offer their good will; thanks to Susan Duffy, Joan Whalen, Heatherjean MacNeil, and Linda Woods. Mary Driscoll, Sheila Dinsmoor, Susan Chern, and Barbara Kendrick also provided crucial support. My chair, Blake Pattridge, cheered me at every turn. Without my even asking, Stephen Deets kindly traveled to an archive that I could not access. Kevin Bruyneel, Jon Dietrick, and Amir Reza make Babson a great place to work.

I also want to thank the activists whose inspiring stories proved so central to this narrative: George Houser, Cora Weiss, Gordie Fellman, Diana Aviv, Rabbi Sharon Kleinbaum, Melanie Kaye/Katrowitz, Eleanor Roffman, Delores Wilkenfeld, Leonard Fein, Alison Bernstein, Ellen Cantarow, Marlene Provizer, Herb Magidson, Rabbi Arthur Waskow, and Ruth Messinger. Tasha Calhoun sent me sources just in time, and Ariel Moritz continued to pose my questions to Ruth Messinger long after my interview. My own rabbi, Rabbi Toba Spitzer of Congregation Dorshei Tzedek, gracefully connected me to Rabbi Brian Walt, who shared his stories with me. Alisa Solomon sent me a trove of documents from the early years of Jews for Racial and Economic Justice, and Marjorie Dove Kent worked with me to include them in this book. To Peter Weiss I owe a great debt for his camaraderie, guidance, and feedback. When I traveled to Manhattan to visit with him it was either freezing cold or blisteringly hot. Yet he always met me and spoke openly about his own lifelong dedication to struggles for justice.

This project began during a sabbatical afforded in part with a grant from the Babson Faculty Research Fund. I am grateful to the BFRF for their support. I am also grateful to Chris Chappell of Palgrave Macmillan, who shepherded this manuscript through to publication.

Finally, I thank my family. Michael Fein offered me the time, support, inspiration, and editing I needed to finish this book. After 17 years of equal partnership, I am still finding new things about him to love. To him and to our wonderful sons, Isaac and Nathan, I dedicate this book with love and gratitude for the joy that sustains me.

Introduction: Apartheid and American Jews

In June 1990, New York City prepared for a triumphant visit by Nelson Mandela, the deputy president of the African National Congress (ANC), who had recently been released from his 27 years in prison for working to end apartheid in South Africa. New Yorkers welcomed the hero of human rights and saw his visit as the culmination of decades of global antiapartheid activism that helped to end 45 years of apartheid rule and more than 300 years of segregation in South Africa. Movement leaders emphasized that their struggle drew strength from the core American values of dignity, equality, and freedom.[1] In working against apartheid, American Jewish organizations wedded these ideals to the Jewish imperative of justice, and they spoke of their activism in language that linked the lessons of the Holocaust and Black liberation.

Beneath the outward veneer of celebration, however, American Jewish leaders engaged in fierce debates over how to greet Mandela. These debates highlighted long-standing tensions over American Jews' loyalty to Israel, and, specifically, over Mandela's relationship with Yasser Arafat, leader of the Palestine Liberation Organization. Shortly after his release from prison, Mandela was reported to have "embraced" Arafat, explicitly paralleling the antiapartheid struggle in South Africa to Arafat's struggle against "a unique form of colonialism" in Israel.[2] To those who considered Arafat's struggle a threat to Israel's existence, this sounded alarm bells. Large ads in the *New York Times* accused "liberal" Jews and non-Jews alike of choosing Mandela over Israel, of prioritizing the liberation campaign for Black South Africa over Jews' liberation ideology of Zionism, and even of promoting anti-Semitism.[3]

Nations Divided reviews the high stakes of these conflicts over South Africa and apartheid for American Jews, from the end of the Holocaust to the present day. As they played out in the English-language media and within Jewish organizational meetings, correspondence, and literature, these conflicts revealed fundamental disagreements over how to define Jewish interests and values. They also raised questions about what role American Jews should play in the world Jewish community and what global causes Jews should ally themselves with *as* Jews.

After World War II, American Jews increasingly saw their own Jewishness fractured through the prism of domestic and international liberation struggles. Following the Civil Rights, women's, and gay rights movements, many American Jews—especially the younger generation born after the war—joined the fight against apartheid, often tying their feminist and anti-colonialist positions to their Jewishness. During these same decades, many American Jewish organizational leaders linked the legacies of the Holocaust to a more narrow definition of Jewish interests, embracing agendas built around staunch support of Israel and fears of declining religiosity. The stage was set, then, for heated, intracommunal disputes over "Jewish positions" on Civil, women's, and gay rights, and on Israel, Palestine, and South Africa.[4]

This study, the first to examine American Jewish encounters with apartheid, examines how women and men balanced particularist and universalist commitments in working against apartheid *as Jews*. Through the analysis of key moments in American Jewish debates over apartheid—debates among themselves and with African American leaders, United Nations officials, and other leaders and laypeople—this study advances scholarly conversations across multiple fields.

First, it integrates new narratives into American Jewish history. Scholars in that discipline too often claim historical actors so as to celebrate Jewish contributions to the women's movement, or Civil Rights, only to conclude with the return of those actors "home" to organized Judaism and the American Zionism of mainstream Jewish communal organizations. *Nations Divided* examines the voices and actions of Americans who granted Jewish meaning to their antiracist commitments at home and then sought to apply those commitments to global struggles against colonialism. Scholars often fail to examine how the whole of Jewish activists' worldviews refract back on race and privilege, belonging and inclusiveness in the United States and beyond.

This study records the lives of those who drew from their Jewish identities in taking positions on apartheid and Zionism that dissented from those of mainstream Jewish organizational leaders, as historically the two issues came to be inextricably linked decades before Mandela's U.S. visit. Feeling forced to choose between Jewish particularism and universalist anti-colonialist campaigns, these activists founded their own Jewish institutions or departed Jewish life altogether. Their stories, captured as brief biographies in these pages, demonstrate the distance between some American Jews' priorities and those of the organizations that were to represent them. This study, then, alerts us to the key role apartheid played in intracommunal contests over Jewish priorities and values. It draws attention to the ways in which antiapartheid activists shaped and were shaped by conversations about these priorities and values in American Jewish life and beyond.

Second, this work situates the study of American Jewish history within a global framework that extends beyond examinations of American Jewish responses to the Holocaust, Israel's statehood and wars, and campaigns to free Soviet Jewry.[5] It builds on Hasia Diner's pioneering examination of American Jews' commitment to Civil Rights, a study that revealed a broad spectrum of American Jewish political commitments, along with newer studies of American Jews' racial identities, and domestic alliances among African Americans and Jews.[6] It builds, too, on Stuart Svonkin's analysis of American Jewish antiracist activism.[7] In broadening its focus globally, it follows the lead of Michael Staub's work in documenting American intra-Jewish debate over the war in Vietnam, when both doves and hawks drew from Holocaust consciousness and prophetic Judaism to support their positions as Jews.[8] It builds on the research of Michael Galchinsky, which examines Jewish contributions to global human rights struggles, and Sasha Polakow-Suransky, whose study reveals the close Cold War relationship between South Africa and Israel.[9] In line with the internationalization of history, this book explores the diasporic relationships among Jews—in the United States and South Africa—and the interplay of national and ethno-religious alliances in the historic struggle against apartheid.[10] It utilizes communalist and dispersionist approaches, in locating Jewish antiapartheid activists within and (at times) outside of Jewish organizations.[11] Above all, *Nations Divided* looks closely at the careful and contested construction of boundaries of Jewish belonging in order to build bridges between American Jewish history and the history of American race, politics, and liberation movements.

American Jews and the Struggle over Apartheid follows the lead of scholars who draw from postcolonial theory in studying global diasporas, specifically scholars of African and African American Studies.[12] These studies began the examination of the personal and political connections between the Black populations of the United States and Africa, focusing on the transnational dynamics of race and racism, of liberation ideology and struggles for justice. Scholars who place women in the center of these movements for social change offer particularly instructive models for thinking about the dearth of women's voices in early organized Jewish antiapartheid efforts in the United States.[13]

This book also joins pressing and timely conversations about global, anticolonialist struggles during the Cold War. Scholars have begun to look more closely at the connections between domestic and foreign policies during the Cold War, revealing the multiple ways in which international conflicts pressed national leaders to pay greater heed to the interplay of race and democracy.[14] This project frames struggles for racial justice in a wide lens, situating its analysis of Jewish antiapartheid activism within this global setting. Importantly, the rich histories of South African Jewish antiapartheid activism serve as far more than a comparative backdrop; the connections among American and South African Jewry—including the key roles in the American antiapartheid movement played by South African Jewish immigrants to the United States—are a crucial piece of this unfolding narrative.[15]

Finally, *Nations Divided* addresses a gap in scholarship of the American antiapartheid movement. Policy makers and their students wrote the first studies of the relationship between South Africa and the United States.[16] This study of Jewish antiapartheid work will join an emerging second wave of historical literature that looks broadly at the motivations, agendas, and experiences of antiapartheid activists.[17] Adopting this emphasis on social history, *Nations Divided* highlights the role of members of a particular ethno-religious group in combating injustice. The experiences of Jewish activists reveal the often decisive role that religious, ethnic, and national identity played in defining citizen movements during the late twentieth and early twenty-first centuries. Like other studies of the antiapartheid movement, this project demonstrates the ways in which single-cause protests become focal points for larger inter- and intracommunal debates over domestic and global commitments—and indeed for debates over the very meaning of group identity. American Jewish leaders and laypeople debated apartheid, Civil Rights, Israel, and their own global responsibilities; they also debated what the "authentic" Jewish position was on these and other pivotal issues in the postwar era. All of these debates continue in our own day.

The study begins in the 1950s, when the World Jewish Congress (WJC) prioritized Jewish unity in its organizational work, and spoke of that unity as a response to the Holocaust. Fearful that American critiques of apartheid would jeopardize WJC efforts to court South African membership—and thus jeopardize Western Jewish unity—top officials prohibited any public antiapartheid statements from their American colleagues. This prompted fierce and long-running arguments with American Jewish activist leaders, such as Rabbi Joachim Prinz, who had close ties to Civil Rights and anticolonialist movements. In chapter 1, analysis of these arguments challenges the timeline of scholars who locate the origin of intracommunal debates over Jewish human rights commitments only after 1967.[18]

Chapters 2, 3, and 4 gauge the rising temperature of these disputes during the 1960s and 1970s. In these years, marked by the rise of both Black Nationalism and new, inward-focused agendas in mainstream Jewish communal organizations, debates raged within and between members of African-American and Jewish communities over South Africa's relationship to Israel. Sharp exchanges over the measure of American Jews' support for Israelis, Palestinians, and the antiapartheid movement appeared widely, testing the ties of group belonging and of Black/Jewish alliances. In the arena of international diplomacy, Jews throughout the world vehemently protested the United Nations' General Assembly's 1975 passage of the Zionism is racism resolution, the language of which appeared first at a UN women's conference. As global sympathy slowly shifted to Palestinians' self-determination, and criticisms of Israel's Occupation became more widespread, Jews wrestled with their own sense of Jewish belonging in the midst of Third World liberation movements, including South Africa's.[19]

In the 1980s, activists in the women's movement, on college campuses, and in Jewish organizations encountered the incredible force of the global antiapartheid movement. Chapters 5 and 6 focus on the diverse responses of Jewish activists in these spaces, how they negotiated their relationship to South African apartheid and Israel/Zionism in the face of the American Cold War alliances among South Africa, Israel, and the United States.

The final chapter of *Nations Divided* traces the broad outlines of these debates through Mandela's 1990 visit to the United States, the collapse of apartheid, and into the twenty-first century, as American Jews continue to negotiate particularist and universalist commitments to racial and economic justice. To that end, it historicizes recent and controversial invocations of apartheid in debates over Israel and Palestine. Thus the project concludes as it began, with a discussion of loyalties in the tension between the workings of the WJC and that of the United Nations. The United Nations 2001 World Conference on Racism in Durban, South Africa, was the first such conference to address issues of racism and colonialism in a nation now free from apartheid. An early draft of the Durban Declaration described Israel's policies in its Territories as "a new kind of apartheid," and though delegates voted the language out of the document, it revived the explosive equation of Zionism with racism. Ultimately, it led to the boycotting of the conference by the United States and Israel.[20] Similar currents—fears of anti-Zionism and anti-Semitism—led to the American and Israeli boycott of "Durban II," the Durban Review Conference held in Geneva in April 2009.[21] The WJC lobbied vigorously for this boycott. Other nations' representatives walked out when Iran's president, Mahmoud Ahmadinejad—known as an authoritarian ruler, human rights abuser, and Holocaust denier—delivered the opening speech of the conference, attacking Israel and "spewing venom" which "promoted a spirit of intolerance" that "ran counter to the spirit and dignity of the conference."[22]

Emotional debates within the Jewish community marked these events, as leaders and laypeople alike accused each other of betraying Jewish priorities or global justice. Much like the debate over South Africa's membership in the WJC in the 1950s, each side in the Durban debate insisted that the other had blinders on and could not see what was truly important. These debates bookended the firestorm that surrounded the publication of former President Jimmy Carter's book, *Palestine: Peace Not Apartheid* (2007). Tensions rose, once again, to the boiling point, and individuals' responses to the book were seen as litmus tests of Jewish loyalties. Adopting a "long view," this chapter analyzes the controversies over Durban and Carter's book and situates them in the context of long-standing debates over ethno-religious unity and social justice.

This chapter also includes an analysis of the Boycott, Divestment, and Sanctions (BDS) movement, and the related Israel Apartheid Week, whose followers model their movement on the activism that brought down South African apartheid. The target of the modern BDS movement, however, is Israel, and its aim is "[t]o strengthen and spread the culture of Boycott as a central form of civil resistance to Israeli occupation and apartheid."[23] With millions of dollars in resources, the Jewish Federations of North America formed the Israel Action Network (IAN) to respond to the BDS movement by "defining and confronting delegitimization—which at bottom is an effort to isolate Israel from the family of nations." The IAN warns that the BDS movement "utilizes various tactics, ranging from economic sanctions, including efforts to boycott Israeli products, to negative messaging campaigns, such as equating Israel with apartheid South Africa."[24] Both movements claim that they are working toward peace for Israel and its neighbors. At this moment in history, the stakes are very high in this war of words and ideas, and apartheid stands in the middle of the battlefield.

Like members of other dispersed peoples, American Jews have felt the pull of their diasporic identity, perhaps especially in times of crisis.[25] In their encounters with each other and with these other groups, American Jews have demonstrated a broad array of ways to make sense of that identity. *Nations Divided* chronicles debates behind Jewish contributions to the social movement that ended apartheid, and reveals how a people's contested loyalties continue to shape its commitments to the principles of liberation. This story demonstrates the shifting priorities of American Jewish communal leaders as they increased their power and visibility in the postwar world. It unfolds in the context of Israel's shifting relationship to Black Africa and to Western nations during and after the Cold War.

In studying intracommunal debates, this book examines how American (and some South African) Jews linked their positions on apartheid to their Jewish identities. Crucial studies have recorded and analyzed the pioneering contributions of African Americans to anti-colonialism and to African liberation struggles, mapping the boundaries of solidarity in struggles against oppression.[26] Placing white American Jews' relationship to the system of apartheid at the center of its analysis, this study takes seriously the activists' notions of the links between their ethno-religious identity and their activism, and measures the impact of those ideas on contemporary boundaries of belonging in the Jewish community.[27]

A study of activist networks in the Global North, this study in no way seeks to supplant the importance of studies of liberation movement networks in the Global South; importantly, it also does not purport to be comprehensive on the controversial topic of American Jews and apartheid.[28] Many Jews who fought against apartheid—and indeed, those who opposed involvement in that battle—do not appear in these pages. Because the issue of inclusion posed a challenge to the study, included here are Jewish figures who linked their activism to their Jewishness. The Cold War, oil embargoes, nuclear weapons arsenals, and global capitalism all play important roles in this study; as with significant moments in the histories of the United States, Israel, and South Africa, they are mentioned in the context of Jewish struggles over responses to apartheid.

Nations Divided presents key moments in a long history of one group's struggles with the terms of belonging—to the Jewish community in their nation of residence, the United States, and to global struggles for liberation since World War II. Concentrating closely on how and why American Jews encountered these conflicts as Jews, this study provides a critical historical lens to make sense of one community grappling with competing global commitments and with its own identity.

1

Postwar Conflicts over Racial Justice

Political histories of the relationship between the United States and South Africa in the postwar era focus on the cementing of a Cold War alliance. American leaders saw in South Africa an important ally and trading partner. They were drawn to its growing economy, its wealth of minerals, its strategic location, and the zealous anticommunism of its leaders, the architects of apartheid. For these reasons, the United States supported South Africa at the United Nations.

Western Jewish leaders' desire for an alliance with South Africa emerged out of their quest for Western Jewish unity after the destruction of the Holocaust. Many of these leaders felt an urgent duty to unify world Jewry, to perpetuate Western Judaism now that its cultural homeland in Europe had been viciously destroyed. Organizations like the World Jewish Congress (WJC) emerged from the war with new priorities. Founded in 1936 to meet the increasingly urgent need for a unified, representative body to coordinate, support, and defend Jewish interests in Europe, the WJC sought to represent Jewish interests in international and regional organizations; its leaders formulated creative plans for vital Jewish communal life outside of Europe and, too, outside of Palestine/Israel after the war. Its goal was also to strengthen the bonds among Jewish communities throughout the world.

Any history of the United States and South Africa in this era must account for the explosive racial situations in both nations, as American and South African citizens engaged in courageous acts of defiance to protest state-sanctioned white supremacy. South Africa's African National Congress (ANC) galvanized protests to apartheid, "moving from moderation to militancy" in the late 1940s and 1950s. While working fervently toward Civil Rights in the fires of the Cold War at home, liberal African American leaders were forced to accept "the U.S. foreign policy of fighting against communism, not colonialism." These leaders spoke of their opposition to apartheid in anticommunist terms, or in terms that evoked clear analogies with evil: they compared apartheid to Nazism, white regime leaders to Hitler.[1] While these analogies had a special resonance for American Jews, it was a complicated road to their own apartheid protests.

The WJC sought the membership of South African Jewry, and this pursuit mandated taking a stand on South African apartheid. While the WJC's international work only reinforced the already strong concept of Jewish solidarity, it also shed light on the different and uneven development, on the diffuse commitments and ideologies, of Western nations' diverse Jewish communities.

At times, the pursuit of unity placed Jewish leaders like those of the WJC at odds with world organizations that strove to draw universalist lessons from the destruction of both World Wars—organizations like the United Nations, whose members also struggled to balance commitment to individual nations' sovereignty with a professed commitment to universal human rights for all world citizens.[2] Jewish leaders' vision of a unified world Jewry also proved to be at odds with those who took positions on domestic and global liberation struggles. This chapter first examines the postwar debate within the WJC, and concludes with a discussion of Fritz Flesch, a Holocaust survivor and American union activist. His correspondence over Jews and South African apartheid opens a window onto the diverse responses of American Jewish leaders to apartheid, as they wrestled with the live question of how Jewish organizations and individuals might balance what they saw as best for the particular interests of world Jewry with their positions on universal crusades for justice.

* * *

The war, the founding of the United Nations, and the gradual rise of South African apartheid set the scene for critical debates over this question. A decade after the founding of the United Nations, South African legislators began to strengthen apartheid laws for "separate development," restricting nonwhite residence to specific areas, controlling social interactions with nonwhite South Africans, limiting their movement as well as their access to education, jobs, union membership, land and business ownership, and governmental participation. Although the ideologies stretched back to the beginning of white settlement in the seventeenth century, the rise of the Afrikaner Nationalists in South African politics after 1948 marked the start of the codification of apartheid. These new laws further entrenched the white minority's control over South African land and resources.

India attempted to place South Africa's poor treatment of people of Indian origin on the agenda of the United Nations General Assembly. As the number of members of the General Assembly grew with recently decolonized nations, and as groups such as the Council on African Affairs began lobbying the United Nations and drawing worldwide attention to oppression in South Africa, the United Nations began to criticize apartheid.[3] Unhappy with the pressure placed upon it by the United Nations, the South African government later chose to withdraw from the United Nations Educational, Scientific, and Cultural Organization (UNESCO) and downgrade its representation at Assembly meetings.[4] In December 1950, the United Nations formed its Commission on the Racial Situation in the Union of South Africa. Four years later, it issued a Resolution urging nongovernmental organizations (NGOs) to "eradicate prejudice and discrimination" and to work with them on "promoting a peaceful settlement" in South Africa.[5]

As an NGO, the WJC received this resolution.[6] With its main leadership and constituency in the United States, the WJC had already developed a productive relationship with the United Nations. Its leaders worked with the United Nations to draft the language of 5 of the 30 articles in the Universal Declaration of Human Rights. These articles dealt with the international treatment of national laws that restricted human rights and issues of asylum. "We had learned our lessons from the Nazis," wrote one WJC leader, celebrating the passage of the Declaration in 1948.[7] Although limited by Cold War political alliances, the United Nations became a forum for global awareness around issues of human rights and offered the antiapartheid and other anticolonialist movements the opportunity to use the language of human rights to appeal to a legitimate higher authority.[8] These limits proved especially powerful for African Americans, as scholar Carol Anderson documents: American governmental leaders sought to mute the United Nations' investigations into South Africa's human rights abuses so as to "escape national scrutiny of the 'negro problem'" within their own borders.[9]

The WJC had a complex and tangled relationship with South Africa's organized Jewish community, whose primary instrument was the South African Jewish Board of Deputies (SAJBD).[10] This Resolution presented yet another tense moment in that history. Since the years immediately following the war, the WJC had courted South African membership. With the SAJBD as members, the WJC would gain credibility over the British Board of Deputies, with its long-standing ties to South African Jewry, as the leaders of world Jewry. Indeed, the WJC would emerge as the main Jewish NGO at the United Nations. The WJC also faced a tremendous fiscal crisis, and hoped to benefit from the immense wealth and historic philanthropic generosity of organized South African Jewry. Ultimately, prior to the United Nations resolution, the WJC reached an agreement with the SAJBD that stopped just short of formal affiliation: the WJC received a moderate sum from South Africa each year and also gained the loyalty of the organized South African Jewish community. But the temporary nature of the arrangements gave the SAJBD significant leverage over the WJC. The promise of a more permanent, future affiliation was regularly used to fend off any criticism of South African Jews, especially over apartheid.[11]

But leaders of the WJC differed over how to respond to the United Nations 1954 resolution regarding South Africa. The white South African government continued to respond to nonviolent protests of apartheid with repressive measures, meeting the Defiance Campaign, in which Nelson Mandela rose to leadership, with massive arrests and curfews. South African Jewish leaders continued to debate formal membership in the WJC. How might the WJC best balance the organization's commitment to uniting world Jewry—building on their valuable connection to South African Jewry and negotiating its relations with other Jewish organizations—with its responsibility to speak out against injustice in an affiliated nation? Did it, indeed, have that responsibility?

British Rabbi Maurice Perlzweig, who became head of the WJC's New York office, served as a strong advocate of Jewish solidarity in this debate. He informed the board that it must ignore the United Nations request: though his regret was "deep and genuine," he saw this as "inevitable in view of our relationship with the South African Board of Deputies."[12] To the president of the WJC, Perlzweig was even more direct: "It would manifestly be a very foolish thing for us to send a highly critical document on South Africa to the U.N., and it would certainly wreck the hope of doing anything in regard to affiliation." Using language indicative of his powerful feelings of allegiance to world Jewry, Perlzweig asserted that Simon Kuper, chairman of the SAJBD, "would rightly regard it as a betrayal."[13] With family in South Africa, Perlzweig had intimate knowledge of the political position of the SAJBD, and his feelings of a strong diasporic identity, a Jewish family in diaspora, was doubtless informed by this.

David Petegorsky, an executive board member of the WJC since 1948, responded to Perlzweig's memo with "vigorous protest." He replied as a leader in the American Jewish Congress, founded by East European Jewish immigrants in 1918 as a more democratic, less elitist alternative to the American Jewish Committee. "The refusal of the WJC to reply to a communication from the Secretary General on one of the worst cases of racial segregation in the world cannot be regarded simply as a matter of expediency," Petegorsky wrote. "It seems to me to go to the very heart of the principles for which we stand." Although Petegorsky acknowledged the difficult position of the WJC with regard to South African Jewish leadership, he insisted that a "dignified reply" could be made without jeopardizing South Africa's affiliation. In his final paragraph, Petegorsky inserted a reference to the American Civil Rights movement and to Jewish organizational involvement in a pivotal event within US borders in 1954, the case of *Brown v. the Board of Education of Topeka, Kansas*:

> You may not be aware of the fact that last year, the AJCongress filed a brief amicus in the segregation case before the Supreme Court. A delegation of three Jews from the South came to New York to visit Dr. Goldstein [Israel Goldstein, head of the American Jewish Congress from 1951–1958]…to demand that we withdraw our brief and threatened that if we did not…we would be denied allocations from Welfare Funds in the South. Dr. Goldstein promptly told them that while he had no idea how we would be financially affected, this was to us a matter of basic principle and we could under no circumstances yield to any such demands.[14]

Many mainstream American Jewish organizations supported Civil Rights in the postwar era, drawing from a "unitary concept of prejudice" which meant that "anti-Semitism, white racism, and all other forms of bigotry" were inseparable. To defeat white supremacy, then, was to defeat anti-Semitism. These groups saw a direct connection between their "wartime struggle against fascism and their postwar dedication to intergroup relations," including Civil Rights.[15] The American Jewish Congress specifically viewed the adoption of a liberal, universalist worldview, intentionally linked to both Zionism and to Jewish communal solidarity, as a means to "save American Jewry from assimilation."[16] In these years, Petegorsky and other AJCongress leaders saw no conflict between a commitment to universal ideals and to Jewish particularism. Indeed, taking a stand against apartheid marked the global extension of their dedication to pluralism and inclusive democracy at home—and not incidentally, aligned Jewishness, even Judaism, with these forces in the postwar, modern world.

Struggling against Perlzweig's notion of solidarity as consensus, Petegorsky continued to press the issue. He asserted that he was "not insensitive to the peculiar problems which an international organization faces." But to him, Perlzweig's argument for silence on the issue of South African apartheid rested on weak evidence. From an organizational standpoint, Petegorsky noted that the AJCongress's "actual allocation from the Southern part of the U.S. is far greater than the sum which the South African Board contributes to the WJCongress." Thus the risk the AJCongress took in speaking out against American segregation was, by his measure, far greater than the WJC faced. Nevertheless, they were "outspoken" on the issue of African Americans' Civil Rights. Moreover, he wrote, the problem of segregation in South Africa was not solely a domestic issue: "Evidently the United Nations did not think so when it set up its commission."[17]

In 1960, activists in the United States and South Africa focused new attention on the evils of white supremacy. Thousands of Black South Africans marched in response to the calls from South Africa's Pan-Africanist Congress (PAC) for nonviolent protests against the pass laws that severely restricted their movement in designated "white" areas. At a march in Sharpeville, 35 miles from Johannesburg, government troops killed 69 people and wounded 186. Police shot protesters in the back as they fled. After the Sharpeville Massacre, the South African government declared a state of emergency, banning the PAC and the ANC and arresting their leaders.[18]

South Africa appeared in headlines throughout the world. For the first time, the United Nations Security Council discussed South African apartheid.[19] The event's brutality and visibility placed it squarely on the radar, and agendas, of American Civil Rights groups.[20] Liberal and radical Black presses, as well as African American leaders such as Benjamin Mays, president of Morehouse College, and Mary McLeod Bethune, Civil Rights leader and educator, and many others had long drawn attention to the evils of South African apartheid.[21] Importantly, 1960 was also the year African American Civil Rights student activists David Richmond, Franklin McCain, Ezell Blair Jr, and Joseph McNeil began the sit-in movement at segregated eating establishments in the Southern United States. Thousands of activists followed their leadership in challenging American white supremacy while keeping their eyes fixed on South African apartheid as well.

Despite the charged and polarizing nature of these events, the WJC's Perlzweig remained hopeful that a Paris meeting—attended by Western Jewish leaders, including a South African delegation—could produce a working consensus and present a united Jewish front on issues of international concern. For, as he wrote, even apart from the constitutional rules of the WJC, his personal priorities were to respect "the obligations of courtesy and of Jewish solidarity."[22]

For Perlzweig and many other Jews across the world, the Holocaust's lessons lay in a desire for unity and solidarity; in keeping with this line of thought, deep sensitivity to any anti-Semitism or element resembling Nazism required a united front. For Petegorsky, too great an insistence on unity threatened to deny Jewish organizations the opportunity to confront moral questions embedded in issues of racial injustice. These threats presented their own opportunities to assert a distinctively Jewish worldview, one consistent with anticolonialist positions.[23]

Even as Perlzweig pursued his goal of Jewish solidarity, he held up the very different Jewish communities of South Africa and the United States to acknowledge their differences. The South African Board of Jewish Deputies, he wrote admiringly, was a "genuinely representative body, including all shades of opinion."[24] Although criticized by Jewish and non-Jewish liberals and radicals in South Africa and throughout the world, the strict policy of the SAJBD was one of noninvolvement in "controversial questions of national policy."[25]

In contrast, Perlzweig lamented the free marketplace of American Jewish organizational life. Jewish organizations competed there, and that competition sharpened the distance between their carefully defined views. "There is something that they do not have to lose, because they do not have it," Perlzweig wrote, "and that is Jewish unity." By his own lights, he found it "curious" that some respectable Jewish organizations believe "that Jewish organized unity cannot be achieved, and would in any case be bad and undemocratic."[26]

Perlzweig's curiosity emerged out of his belief that Jewish survival depended on unity and carefully maintained consensus. To his mind, democratic, liberal competition in American Jewish organizations only served to fracture American Jewry along the lines of ideology, religious interpretation, and observance. While some Western Jews appreciated this cacophony of views, seeing it as a healthy reflection of American pluralism and democracy, Perlzweig saw it as a threat to Jewish survival. Compromising Jewish solidarity, he believed, endangered Jewish continuity.

Perlzweig's words echoed those of one of the founders of the WJC, Dr Nahum Goldmann, who served as president from 1948 to 1977. During a meeting called a few years earlier to discuss the expansion of the WJC, Goldmann responded to Jews in many nations who held reservations because they felt that any expansion would compromise their autonomy in dealing with their own national Jewish communities:

> Let us say a few words about America. Nearly half of the Jewish population of the world lives in the United States. Take away the popular response to Hitler and Nazism; take away the popular response to the support of the State of

Israel. What will remain to sustain the Jews in America? Have you forgotten the Gallup poll among the Jewish students who wrote that they considered themselves Jewish "because they do not wish to insult their parents?" What are the instruments in America for the fight for Jewish survival? They are, quite frankly, ridiculous, if you face up to the immense problem of sustaining the 5½ million Jews in the U.S.A. as Jews, living and acting as Jews in the years to come....We of the WJC know that we have absolutely inadequate means to try to fill the dangerous vacuum which is growing rapidly around us, and we appeal to you, telling you plainly and clearly that unless you see the historic necessity to defend with united forces the Jewish life and future you are taking a great historical responsibility.[27]

For Goldmann, fears of assimilation and anti-Semitism were not sufficient to sustain a Jewish future; nor were the forces of Zionism or sympathy for Jewish suffering and loss. The urgency of these statements makes plain the conviction behind Perlzweig's remarks. Perlzweig sought Jewish continuity through diplomacy toward Jewish unity; Goldmann dedicated much of his life to Jewish continuity through Jewish education. Together, global Jewish communities gave meaning to Jewish belonging, and together they could fight the disappearance of the Jewish people.

From Perlzweig's perspective, if Americans attended the Paris meeting and spoke out against apartheid, they would endanger South African Jews and thus, Jews everywhere. Perlzweig considered these Jews to be in a precarious position, represented by a government including many who actively supported the Nazi cause during the war.[28] And in this, he was not alone: Jewish organizations outside of South Africa often depicted South African Jews as "victims of rampant anti-Semitism, implying that it was the natural ancillary of apartheid racism." These reports served as useful explanations for the lack of vocal resistance to apartheid on the part of the SAJBD, who "tread carefully lest it sound like it was making excuses for the apartheid regime."[29] Ultimately Perlzweig agreed that the WJC owed South African Jewish leaders a meeting, at which they could discuss the possibility of making a public antiapartheid statement. But he feared "an outbreak of competitive righteousness" from the AJCongress, and later admitted that his anxiety over whether the American leaders would break their silence even took a toll on his health.[30]

Perlzweig's trepidation over supporting public antiapartheid statements and his warnings to world Jewish communities over the loss of unity did not sit well with Rabbi Joachim Prinz. A towering figure among American Jewish religious leaders and also among American Jews in the Civil Rights movement, Prinz had recently conducted a sit-in at the Woolworth's on New York's Fifth Avenue, drawing attention to the practices of racial segregation at its Southern stores. Just as British and French Jews have the right to "criticize the United States for its failure to implement the Supreme Court decision on segregation in the public schools," he reasoned, American Jews can speak out about apartheid. He called it "a matter of deep Jewish concern," and cited his own experiences in Germany, when American Jews spoke out about Hitler. "We will not be silent in the face of any injustice that we feel is being committed."[31]

Despite WJC resistance, the AJCongress issued a resolution on apartheid in 1960. The WJC influence was powerful enough, however, to convince Prinz to see "that this should not be communicated to the press." The AJCongress announced the passage of resolutions, disseminated only internally to its membership and allies, in the following order: (1) they voiced their support for the sit-in movement, and pledged to call on American businesses to end the "undemocratic and outdated" practices of discrimination; (2) they condemned apartheid in South Africa; (3) they urged the United States to use its influence to end apartheid in South Africa; (4) they pledged support for legislation that would end discrimination in the Southern and Northern United States. Perlzweig was pleased not only that Prinz did not leak the antiapartheid resolution to the press, but also that in his opening remarks he limited himself to talking generally about support for Black Africans.[32]

Indeed, to South African Jewish leaders, Perlzweig explained that the AJCongress's outspokenness grew out of its close ties with African American organizations, and the fact that "there are places in the American South where active anti-Semitism and resistance to integration are closely tied."[33] Organized South African Jewry's silence on apartheid best served Jewish interests, as it avoided making the Jewish community vulnerable to anti-Semitic attacks that threatened their well-being and their white privilege.[34] American Jewish activism served Jewish communal interest by dismantling anti-Semitism itself. Perlzweig saw little room for Jews to embrace universalist causes outside of direct, urgent concerns for their own peoplehood.

These heated exchanges over South African membership in the WJC have received little scholarly attention.[35] Those who mention the ordeal date this conflict to the mid-1960s or 1970s.[36] But Jews' struggle over apartheid has deeper roots. It began with the early struggles of the United Nations to define its authority to protect universal human rights. It deepened as the American Civil Rights movement grew in strength, and as the passage of harsh apartheid laws sparked greater conflict in South Africa. Immediately after World War II, the realpolitik of Cold War alliances began to take shape, and that proved an enormous barrier to American and South African Jewish condemnations of apartheid. For Jews in both nations, the barriers were particular to their own experiences in the war, their own visions of peoplehood, belonging, and self-definition.[37] These events are crucial to understanding the shifting relationships among and between African Americans and American Jews in this period; they are also crucial to understanding the evolving nature of American Jewish commitments to unity and universalism, to liberation struggles and to their own particularist agendas in the decades following World War II.

Fritz Flesch: Cui Bono?

Few examples present so clear and decisive a connection between the Holocaust and Jewish attitudes to apartheid as the correspondence of Fritz Flesch. Flesch was a Holocaust survivor and a union activist. He began working in the Detroit auto industry and joined the United Auto Workers (UAW) in 1940, after he left his native Austria by way of England. In the 1950s, he began gathering material about Jews—mainly from South Africa and the United States—and their responses to South African apartheid. He collected obsessively, cutting out articles from presses across the world, taping them together and making multiple copies. He mailed his 228 pages of "documentation," titled "Jews in South Africa," to the University of Cape Town Library, the New York Public Library, and the Detroit Public Library, along with other libraries in Austria, England, and the Netherlands.[38] By the 1950s, he began distributing these materials to political figures such as New York Senator Jacob Javits and former First Lady Eleanor Roosevelt, as well as Jewish leaders across the world.

Flesch wrote that the "TOP REPRESENTATIVES of Judaism in South Africa...act like 'gleichgeschaltete' 'German Christians' under Hitler" (literally translated as "conformists"). He blasted Jewish leadership in South Africa for not cooperating with United Nations investigations, and Jewish leadership outside of South Africa for backing South Africa in those efforts. He was angry, he wrote, at the "silence of the world."[39] Alternating quotes in German and Hebrew, Flesch asserted a clear responsibility for Jews to speak out against apartheid after the Holocaust, and even drew attention to Jewish theology by asking Jewish religious leaders to "act in the name of the Lord."[40] Those who remained silent about apartheid were "traitors to JUDAISM."[41]

Although scholars dismiss his actions because of his obsessive tendencies, Flesch connected the Holocaust and South African apartheid in compelling ways that cut through the debates occurring simultaneously among WJC members.[42] On most materials he distributed, he handwrote the words "Cui bono?" that translates as "to whose benefit?" Citing his experiences at Dachau in the late 1930s, Flesch demanded accountability for a system he saw as analogous to Nazism. He linked the murderous fate of Jews under Nazism to the unexamined privilege of Jews under South African apartheid, insisting on a sense of peoplehood and historical belonging that demanded moral action. Flesch's sense of Jewish solidarity mandated action against injustice.

Recipients of Flesch's clippings had mixed responses to his ideas. Some were dismissive, while others gave his concerns more credence. In 1958, Eleanor Roosevelt passed along her letter from Flesch to the American Zionist leader Israel Goldstein, who led the AJCongress and had taken a firm stand on American desegregation in 1954. Goldstein laced his reply to Flesch with references to prophetic Judaism's imperative to dismantle white supremacy in the United States and South Africa. "No doubt there are Jews in South Africa," he wrote, "just as there are some Jews in our own Southern States, who take an attitude which we think to be wrong and utterly incompatible with the teachings of Judaism." He noted the many South African rabbis who work "with great courage" to resist the policies of the apartheid regime. And of his own credentials, and those of American Jews overall,

Goldstein claimed that American Jews were the "principal supporters" in the struggle for "full emancipation and equality" for African Americans.[43]

Only one year before his writing to Flesch, on December 10, 1957, Goldstein had signed the Declaration of Conscience of the American Committee on Africa (ACOA), which called on the government of South Africa to honor its "moral and legal obligations to the United Nations Charter by honoring the Declaration of Human Rights." Activists founded the ACOA in 1953 to support African struggles against colonialism, including the ANC's early campaigns against apartheid.[44] Goldstein belonged to that group of American Jews whose Judaism inspired their involvement with global political struggles for justice. Several American Jews also served on the board of the ACOA.

Rabbi Eugene J. Lipman responded to Flesch with far less faith in American activism to affect global change. His organization, the newly-established Commission on Social Action of Reform Judaism, was "on record as opposing the policies of the Government of South Africa." But he disagreed with Flesch that American Jews should get involved in South African affairs. Replaying the debate among members of the WJC, Lipman wrote that "we have no moral right to ask or to demand of Jews in South Africa that they become heroes and martyrs." He wrote that American Jews should take "leadership in the solving of racial integration in our own country. Our record is not so good that we can smugly ask others to speak out courageously."[45]

Although he did not play a leading role in the American debates over South African apartheid—and though American activists sidelined his correspondence and claims—Flesch filled the mailboxes of several leaders with documentation of Jewish responses to apartheid. His letters can be found in the files of the American Committee on Africa, and the Reform Movement of American Judaism's Religious Action Center. As he was a UAW activist, they lie, too in the Walter Reuther Archive (named for the UAW president) in Detroit. Flesch disseminated these documents to inspire reflection, redemption, and action. These leaders' responses offer a window onto the diverse perspectives of Jewish leaders on the connections among white supremacy in the United States, South African apartheid, and the Holocaust. They demonstrate, most clearly, how individuals followed their own moral instincts and their own sense of what connected Jews throughout the world.

Importantly, Flesch's lifelong labor affiliations provided a solid foundation to his ideas about liberation and his steadfast commitment to fighting apartheid. Certainly labor leaders and laypeople in South Africa and throughout the world joined Communists and others on the left to play pivotal roles in fighting colonialism and white supremacy. Flesch's activism foreshadows the commitment of American Jewish labor to the antiapartheid movement in an era when other Jewish communal organizations edged away from universalist commitments, prioritizing instead issues internal to American Jewish life. Although engaged in bitter racial conflicts at home, Jewish labor often remained committed to the global struggle against apartheid into the 1960s and beyond.

This chapter chronicles the encounters of American Jews with anticolonialist campaigns in the 1950s. Those seeking to support anticolonialism as Jews were confronted with reluctance to prioritize racial justice, a universalist crusade, ahead of the particularist interests of Jewish unity and consensus. These were competing agendas, divergent strategies, perhaps, for how to keep Jewishness and Judaism relevant in an age of rising assimilation, mobility, and power for most American Jews. In the decades that followed, activist American Jews faced an even greater struggle, as Cold War domestic and foreign policy commitments further divided the community. Israel's growing alliance with South Africa, and emerging parallels between Israeli "apartheid" and South African apartheid, ensured that apartheid would continue to play a decisive role in the politics of Jewish belonging in the United States.

2

American Zionism and African Liberation

Relations between African Americans and American Jews in the 1950s were tightly bound up in the Civil Rights movement, the Holocaust, and the rise of South African apartheid, just as they were intricately connected to the Cold War and to liberation movements in African nations.[1] Indeed, it is impossible to separate the evolution of African American and American Jewish identities—and too the evolution of a Black/Jewish alliance—from global events in this era.

In the 1950s, and even through the early 1960s, American Jews continued to link Jewish particularism to universalist concerns in the United States and in Africa, as Fritz Flesch and other activists continued to urge Jews to do. Motivated by prophetic Judaism, interpretations of the lessons of the Holocaust, and other currents, many American Jews held deep commitments to Civil Rights, civil liberties, antimilitarism, anticolonialism, and other liberal and left causes—including fighting anticommunism.[2] They relied on an "approach to Jewish identity that preached an intimate interconnection between personal behavior and political action" that was for many Jews "the wellspring" of their activism for causes at home and abroad.[3]

Several scholars have noted the high price paid by mainstream and liberal Jewish groups for their adoption of Cold War worldviews. As Cheryl Greenberg, historian of modern American Black/Jewish relations, observes:

> The unwillingness [of Jewish organizations] to work with communists meant more than a loss of colleagues. It also meant the loss of their emphasis on the structures of oppression. Recognizing early on the institutional benefits white skin provided, communists offered an important critique of the presumption that black and Jewish experiences, and therefore agendas, were the same.... Had the liberal Jewish community heeded...warnings earlier, it is possible the divisions of the 1960s might have played themselves out differently.[4]

Scholars Stuart Svonkin and Michael Staub have also written about the deleterious effect of liberal anticommunism on the Jewish left. Staub found that it had a "crippling impact on grassroots leftist Jewish anti-racist activism."[5] Others have noted the profound impact of the Cold War on the Civil Rights, labor, women's, and other American social movements.[6] Its impact is also clear when one looks at the Black/Jewish alliance in the 1960s, as those who embraced Zionism and African liberation in the United States often came face-to-face in painful conflicts.

This chapter begins with a discussion of three events: the 1959 observance of Africa Freedom Day, the Emergency Action Conference on South Africa in 1960, and a 1961 conference on "Africa and the Jews." It concludes with an analysis of correspondence between American and South African Jewish leaders during the mid-1960s. The tensions in these moments and in these relationships foreshadowed what was to come. Riding the tide of Cold War anxieties, leaders of many American Jewish organizations embraced a sense of Jewishness that left little room for dissent on Israel or, importantly, for links to universalist concerns. At the same time, Black Nationalist leaders promoted Third World Solidarity as a response to the tenacity of white supremacy and colonialism in South Africa, in the United States, and around the world. Finally, Israel shifted its allegiances from Black Africa to South Africa's apartheid regime.

Scholars have analyzed the seismic shifts in the Black/Jewish alliance in this period. They focus especially on Jewish responses to the rise of Black Nationalism and to the anti-Semitism that emerged within that movement and in the New Left more broadly.[7] Yet the role of South Africa in these developments has yet to be explored. As the flashpoints studied here illustrate, tensions over South African apartheid had profound and lasting effects on Black/Jewish relationships and on the internal politics of American Jewry.

* * *

Africa Freedom Day originated with the Conference of Independent African States in Accra, Ghana, in April 1958. At this meeting, the ANC successfully lobbied for African support for an economic boycott of South African products. The Pan-African Conference took this campaign still further, and soon groups around the world lobbied for the boycott as well.[8]

One year later, the ACOA sought to raise awareness of independence movements in Africa by observing Africa Freedom Day with speeches and celebrations, in New York and around the United States.[9] Key to these celebrations was a visit from Tom Mboya, chairman of the All-African People's Conference and head of his native Kenya's trade union movement. A hero to global anticolonialist activists, Mboya visited the United States on a five-week tour, his second American tour sponsored by the ACOA. Speaking to major American press outlets, along with students, scholars, laypeople, and leaders in American politics, labor, activism, and philanthropy, Mboya conveyed revolutionary messages about African ingenuity, modernity, and independence as he analyzed both the African and United States contexts. "The United States loses great moral effectiveness in the international community because of her domestic disease of segregation," he observed, asserting the "natural feeling of kinship" between African Americans and Africans.

South Africa remained a key topic in every conversation with Mboya, as he drew attention to the pivotal role of Africans and African exiles in building the transnational antiapartheid movement.[10] He predicted that South Africa's future would be "Black."[11] The ACOA's coverage of his tour linked freedom struggles in all African nations, calling attention to the "saddest" observance of Africa Freedom Day in South Africa, where the government refused speech permits for a freedom march, and where demonstrators stood silently in commemoration.[12]

As anticommunism had a decisive impact on all world events, including the shape and agendas of anticolonialist and Civil Rights organizations, the Cold War also played a role in all of Mboya's talks. Addressing keen fears and frequent accusations of communist infiltration in the ACOA and in African movements, he offered a pragmatic statement on Africans and communism: "[W]hether Africa may go Communist or not depends partly on the attitude of the West toward African peoples, partly on whether the present African leadership can satisfy the legitimate desires of a people. You cannot talk ideology with someone who wants a pair of shoes, or a blanket, or a piece of soap. The people want performance, not promises."[13]

Mboya gave the keynote speech at the Africa Freedom Day celebration in New York's Carnegie Hall, sponsored by the American Committee on Africa. It commemorated the "efforts of all African people in their strivings for self government." The African American Students Foundation (AASF) also played a role in planning the event. Americans and Africans committed to the causes of anticolonialism and Civil Rights first founded AASF. Some, like Reverend George Houser, an activist and cofounder of the Congress of Racial Equality, and Cora and Peter Weiss, were involved with both the AASF and the ACOA. The AASF was privately funded, and Mboya toured the United States in part to "drum up support" for its main mission: to airlift students from East African nations to United States colleges and universities.[14] Like Mboya, these students defied racist stereotypes of African citizens as "uncivilized." They trained abroad—as colonial educational institutions in their own nations were closed to them—in preparation for returning home to take leadership positions in their own independent nations.[15]

The Carnegie Hall celebration of Africa Freedom Day marked the first large ACOA–AASF fundraising event. Packed to capacity, the hall filled with 2,700 people. The American Federation of Labor and Congress of Industrial Organizations (AFL–CIO), the Brotherhood of Sleeping Car Porters, diplomats, and foreign leaders attended and sent greetings to the gathering. In addition to Mboya, and an address by Michigan Governor G. Mennen Williams, the inspiring program included the poetry of Langston Hughes and the music of Harry Belafonte.[16] Dr Martin Luther King, Jr co-chaired the event. Ted Kheel, a Jewish labor mediator, real estate developer, and leader in the National Urban League, introduced "several honored guests sitting in the audience," including Eleanor Roosevelt, Jackie Robinson, the Israeli-Consul-General in New York City, and National Association for the

Advancement of Colored People (NAACP) leader Daisy Bates, a central figure to the desegregation of Central High School in Little Rock, Arkansas in 1957. These guests attested to the firm links between African and African American liberation, between the freedom struggles in the United States and in the nations of Africa. The inclusion of the Israeli-Consul General was especially significant, as at this time Israel actively sought alliances with Black African nations. Many American Jews were present in the audience and had done organizational work for the day itself.

It appeared outwardly to be a peaceful celebration, a happy consensus on the rising tide of independence movements in Africa. Written accounts of the event place it securely in the context of Mboya's triumphant visit: the 40 scholarships he had secured from American colleges and universities; the huge, sympathetic crowds; audiences with presidential candidates Richard Nixon and John F. Kennedy, among many other leaders.[17] But tensions between Israel and Africa disrupted the day at two important junctures. The rippling effect of these tensions registered with activist American Jews in the audience, as well as those who read and commented on it in the days that followed.

The first moment of tension occurred early in the day, at the Waldorf Astoria, when United Nations delegations of the nine independent African nations celebrated together. While at first the celebration's official committee had planned to invite all UN delegates to join with them in celebration, some Arab representatives objected to Israel's invitation. These representatives viewed Israel as a close ally of colonial powers because of its alliance with French colonialists in Algeria, and also because of Israel's alliance with Britain and France in invading Egypt during the Suez Canal conflict of Fall 1956.[18] The Soviet Union supported Egypt in that conflict, and thus the event played a central role in the building up of Cold War allegiances. The Suez conflict proved immensely powerful for its import in anticolonialist movements, too, as the success of President Gamal Abdel Nasser of Egypt in nationalizing the canal represented, to many, a decisive victory over Western colonialism.[19] The same powerful association of Israel with Western colonialism prevented Israel from receiving an invitation to a conference of independent Asian and African states in Bandung, Indonesia, in 1955, as the Suez conflict heated up.[20]

Multiple audiences remained riveted by the Suez conflict. Eyes focused on the United Nations Emergency Force (UNEF), formed expressly at the suggestion of UN Secretary General Dag Hammerskjold to maintain peace along the lines agreed to in the armistice. Those forces escorted the departing French and British troops and remained until the Six-Day War of 1967. The second UNEF later formed in response to the armistice of the Yom Kippur War in 1973. Tensions over the terms of these international forces' work added to an already strained relationship. The Suez served as a flashpoint not only in the Cold War, then, but also in the war of words over the mission, responsibility, and neutrality of the United Nations.

The Suez Crisis pressed into the coming months, raising tensions and fears. President Nasser continued to block Israel's ships (along with any cargo bound for Israel) from using the Suez Canal, and Hammarskjold and UN Representative Dr Ralph Bunche stepped in to intercede. US President Eisenhower remained neutral in the conflict, outraged that France and Britain had not told him of their intentions. He was motivated, too, by his "desires for increased economic opportunities in Africa." He urged Britain and France to withdraw.[21]

American Jews, including Zionists on the left, supported Israel, decried Nasser's "intolerable blockade," and urged the United Nations and the world to force Nasser to comply with his pledge of an open canal.[22] After the United States refused funding for Egypt's Aswan Dam, Nasser sought Soviet support. Among his Cold War allegiances, he also counted many African nationalist movements. Indeed, Cairo housed the offices of the ANC, outlawed in South Africa after the Sharpeville massacre in 1960. In these same years, Khrushchev too began to support Third World liberation movements such as the struggle against apartheid.[23]

Jews across the world took positions on the Suez Crisis, some continuing to argue that allegiance to their own Jewish community, to Jewish unity and to Israel, meant a disavowal of anticolonialist sympathies. Two South African-born Jewish writers living abroad, for example, had the crisis as the backdrop to their debate over the responsibility of the SAJBD, and all Jews in South Africa, to take a stand against apartheid. Author Dan Jacobson attacked the idea that South African Jews had a communal responsibility to speak out against apartheid. Ronald M. Segal, antiapartheid activist and editor of *Africa South*, assailed the "one-eyed morality" and "hypocrisy" of South African Jewish leaders who "casually commended" the apartheid regime even while "pleading with the world to acknowledge at last the cruelties of the Nasser regime," the poor treatment of the Jews in Egypt by his edict. Segal felt that Jewish history gave Jews a "sharpened sense of the difference between right and wrong, between oppression and liberty." He also noted that Jewish "heritage" instilled a "fear of authority, a reluctance to fall out with those in power unless it absolutely necessary to their continued existence as a community." Segal urged South African Jews to recognize this necessity, for anything less would be, he asserted, an "abdication of their moral place in history." Dan Jacobson responded to Segal by calling out any comparisons between South African Jews and other religious groups: group belonging is defined by a group's common interests, Jacobson noted, and "to put it crudely, I do believe that had there been black Jews the Jewish religious leaders would have put in their protests along with the others—who were obligated to do so."[24]

These conflicts also divided African Americans and American Jews. Black Communist leaders split over supporting Egypt or Israel in the Suez; Jewish comrades accused Egypt-supporters of anti-Semitism.[25] These wounds were undoubtedly still fresh one year later when Israel did not receive a UN invitation to celebrate Africa Freedom Day on American soil.

More trouble came at the official opening of the Africa Freedom Day program at Carnegie Hall, when the flags of African nations, including that of the FLN, the Front de Liberation Nationale, Algeria's liberation movement, were placed on the stage. In response to the FLN flag's presence, the Israeli representatives walked out.[26] Israel received arms from France, which was fighting Algeria's independence movement (and thus the FLN).[27] Most of those in attendance felt sympathy for the FLN, as the war to wrest Algeria from colonial control had become the "primary symbol of Third World Unity" and a "key reason for the radicalization of Third World anti-colonialism."[28] M'Hammed Yazid, a leader in the FLN and later in Algeria's Provisional Government, drew global attention to his nation's struggles, as he successfully garnered international recognition for the cause of Algerian independence at the United Nations and at the Bandung conference.[29]

"By the time it was over, no one recalled the walk out," noted Cora Weiss, executive director (and on the board) of AASF and an activist with the ACOA.[30] But this early display of divisiveness revealed a fissure among Jewish activists that would widen over the decade. Israel's alliances and positioning would prove key to this fissure, as would the growth of the Third World Solidarity movement and the divisive politics of American Jewish life.

While the Israeli walk out went unrecorded in public memory, the same could not be said of the UN gathering's exclusion of Israel. The Jewish Labor Committee (JLC) raised a firestorm of protest. Founded in 1934 by recent Jewish immigrants with deep roots in the labor and socialist movements of Central and Eastern Europe, the JLC was first and foremost a secular, American antifascist organization that came to the aid of Jews and other victims of fascism across the world. It played a crucial role in aiding refugees and survivors of the Holocaust. While initially its members were hostile to Zionism, emphasizing the struggle for pluralist, socialist societies all over the world, the JLC came to embrace Labor Zionism after the establishment of Israel in 1948.

In the 1950s, the JLC worked with American labor and Jewish organizations in pioneering Civil Rights work.[31] Many of its activists attended the Carnegie Hall celebration, and later protested Israel's exclusion from the UN gathering in a memo that noted the presence of colonizing nations and the apartheid nation of South Africa at that same gathering:

> How outrageous this action is can be seen by the fact that the UN delegation of every other country in the world was invited—even the countries against which these nations have had to fight, sometimes with arms, in order to achieve their freedom, such as France, England, Belgium, and Portugal. And even the Union of South Africa was included...[where] at this very moment a tiny white ruling minority is depriving the overwhelming African majority of what little rights, freedoms, representation they had achieved![32]

The JLC's argument—which compared Israel's alliances with those of other nations—would later be used by many Jewish communal organizations to defend Israel's ties to South Africa: why "single out" Israel for its ties to the apartheid regime, the argument put forward, when so many other nations (including African and Arab nations) do business with South Africa on a scale even larger than Israel does? Perhaps more importantly, many JLC members, like others on the liberal/left in American Jewry, saw Israel itself as the product of the liberation ideology of Zionism, with Israel a positive, democratic, tolerant influence in the Middle East that emerged from the ashes of Jewish genocide. Later, they would frequently refer to Israel's assistance to Black African nations as proof of its altruism, as evidence that equations of Israel's actions with those of colonial nations were ill-fitting, even absurd.

Importantly, other groups used their deep ties to Israel, and especially to the Labor Party and movement in Israel, to *criticize* Israel's actions that led to its exclusion from the 1959 Africa Freedom Day gathering. A May editorial that year in *Israel Horizons*, the monthly periodical for the socialist Zionist organization of HaShomer Hatzair (which translates as the Youth Guard),[33] examined "The Africa Day Snub of Israel" and stated flatly that "we do not wish to absolve Israel completely in the matter." Also noting the "hollowness" of the celebration demonstrated by the exclusion of Israel but not France, Britain, Belgium, Spain, Portugal, and even South Africa, the editors pointed out Israel's need for France's support given the Cold War *realpolitik* at play: "France, and France alone...supplies Israel with her jet planes to match the air power of Nasser's Russian MIG's." Yet they urged Israel's leaders to consider the "snub," led by Nasser's Egypt, as a crucial harbinger, "a symptom of the awakening of a continent long kept in the dark." The editors saw Israel as approaching an important decision:

> Israel can either be part of the awakening or excluded from it, and further isolated. The answer is not entirely in her hands, but enough of it is to make imperative the effort to break out of entanglements in the Cold War generally and specifically with the colonial powers—the enemies of her friends.[34]

The editors of *Israel Horizons* had long condemned colonialist oppression in Africa, including the rise of South African apartheid. In the spirit of universalism, they linked apartheid to oppressive campaigns against Jews and people of color across the world nearly a decade before Israeli leaders connected their nation to Africa and African liberation movements. As early as 1950, members of HaShomer Hatzair offered a stinging critique of the leadership of South African Nationalist Party Parliamentary Speaker Daniel F. Malan, architect of apartheid and supporter of Hitler during World War II, and linked his oppressive colonialism to anti-Semitism across the world. As the AJCongress and later Rabbi Joachim Prinz argued for the connections among Nazi fascism, apartheid, and American white supremacy, *Israel Horizons* editors wrote that "the South African Nationalists are persecuting the African people on the false grounds of racial superiority. But 'white v. black' is merely the thin end of the wedge, as American Jewry know to their cost." They drew from the lessons of the Holocaust in attacking apartheid: "There is a straight and not very long road between sneering at 'n-----s' and gassing Jews," they wrote, lamenting that "many leading South African

Jews, judging from their nauseating praise of Malan, seem as yet unaware of this elementary truth."[35] Like Fritz Flesch, HaShomer Hatzair had a worldview grounded in the politics of labor. From this event in 1950 to the snub of Israel in 1959, its leaders drew from that worldview in consistently criticizing Jews—including leaders of Jewish South Africa and of Israel—for allying with imperialism and racism.[36]

In 1959, such critiques were absent in mainstream presses like the *New York Times*, which joined the JLC's protest in editorializing that the UN gathering showed "a singular lack of . . . . statesmanship in pointedly omitting invitations to Israeli representatives. Africans, like all of us, must realize that freedom is not divisible."[37] In a letter to the editor of the *Times*, the ACOA chairman, Rev. Donald Harrington, distanced his organization from the UN event, making it clear that *only* the UN gathering had excluded Israel; that at Carnegie Hall, "representatives of the Israeli government were present as both box holders and as guests" of the ACOA. He expressed his regret at the exclusion from the earlier gathering, noting that the ACOA "believes in the right of sovereign national existence of all peoples, whether they be the people of Egypt, of Kenya, of Algeria or of Israel."[38] Including Algeria and Israel side by side in his apology, he (also) made no direct mention of the walk out of Israeli representatives over the presence of the Algerian Freedom Fighters' (FLN) flag.

At the Africa Freedom Day celebration in Carnegie Hall, in the meeting rooms of the Waldorf Astoria UN gathering, the stage was set for intense confrontations among those who cared deeply about liberation struggles. Many felt as Harrington described: "freedom was not divisible." For many Zionists, Israel stood for freedom; they defined Zionism as a liberating expression of nationhood for Jews across the world. Some Zionist activists on the left used their faith in Israel's historical commitment to liberation to criticize its alliances and to urge its leaders to choose a future path that was, in their words, "beyond reproach."[39] They saw in Israel and in anticolonialist struggles an opportunity—or an imperative—for Jews and Jewishness to be aligned with (what they saw as) forces of liberation in the new, postwar world. But the displacement of indigenous Arabs from the land that became Israel in 1948, the treatment of non-Jews within Israel's state borders, the tense relationship between Israel and its Arab neighbors, the alliances of Israel with colonial powers: these became rallying cries for anticolonialist groups that lined up to oppose the position of the JLC, the *Times*, and others. Indeed, within the United States, some African American organizations began criticizing Israel and building alliances with Arab Americans.[40]

The 1959 celebration of Africa Freedom Day became—at least in part—mired in the conflicts that would soon strain American Jewish unity and too the alliance between African Americans and American Jews. Many American Jewish leaders felt that Zionism met an urgent need for a Jewish future. They did not welcome criticism of any of Israel's doings. Their allegiance was reflected and cemented by the United States alliance with Israel as a bulwark against Soviet influence in that part of the world, especially after "nascent alliances" formed "between Moscow and radical Arab nationalist regimes" (as by 1956, Egyptian President Gamal Abdel Nasser had turned to the Soviet Union for aid).[41]

As Jewish progressives articulated their positions on Israel in the fires of the Cold War—some softening their criticism of Israel, some explicitly advocating anti-Zionist stances—their positions on South African apartheid became central to their approach to Third World liberation, anticolonialism, and ultimately to Israel itself. Jews' positions on colonialism, apartheid, and Israel, then, became central to their relationships and alliances with African Americans. This was especially true as Israel shifted its allegiances away from Black Africa and toward South Africa's apartheid regime. In 1960, however, even with recent, and very public, conflicts between African American and Jewish progressive leaders, it was still possible to balance liberal Zionism[42] and allegiance to American and global anticolonialist struggles.

* * *

The year 1960 was the year of the Sharpeville Massacre, when South African troops opened fire on nonviolent protests over the pass laws. For African Americans, the events surrounding Sharpeville "took on high meaning" as the domestic sit-in movement spread to 54 cities in 9 states, and as activists founded the Student Nonviolent Coordinating Committee (SNCC).[43] Black churches and other organizations, including the Negro American Labor Council, demanded equality at home as they protested brutality in South Africa: they picketed in front of South African consulates and urged boycotts of South African goods. The African American press praised the strength of South African activists. The National Association for the Advancement of Colored People issued strong statements and attempted to influence US policy toward South Africa.

Yet American foreign policy barely registered the Sharpeville massacre of 1960. Indeed, the Eisenhower administration, blind to human rights abuses in developing nations and dedicated to America's anticommunist trade alliance with apartheid South Africa, worked to soften the UN resolution condemning South Africa after Sharpeville. Importantly, the African American press also highlighted the hypocrisy of a government that would add its name to a "mild resolution" condemning the oppression of Black Africans and yet ignore the racism and violence within its own borders. The *Chicago Defender*, for one, "made clear its own view that the administration followed a double standard, pointing out that no comparable expression of outrage had come forth while blacks had been molested and jailed for peacefully demonstrating against inequality and injustice in the American South."[44]

Despite the outcry of other South African religious communities, South African and global Jewish organizations such as the WJC stood silent in the wake of the Sharpeville massacre and the subsequent crackdown on protests of all kinds.[45] Organized South African Jewry focused its attention internally, on their sense of their own precarious whiteness; externally, it extended exclusively to Israel, as organized South African Jews were more devoted to Zionism—in terms of organization building, monetary donations, and ideology—than perhaps any other Jewish community in the world.

American anticolonialist organizations like the ACOA mobilized strong responses to Sharpeville. One month after its annual "Africa Freedom Day" celebration, the ACOA called an Emergency Action Conference for May 31 and June 1, 1960. Cosponsors included AMSAC (American Society of African Culture), the NAACP, Americans for Democratic Action, the JLC, Amalgamated Clothing Workers of America, International Ladies' Garment Workers' Union (ILGWU), and United Auto Workers (UAW) Region 9 (Western and Central New York, which was separate from the region of Fritz Flesch). Oliver Tambo, Deputy-President of the ANC, was to offer the keynote address to an audience of over 300 people; because of a delay in obtaining his visa, South African exiles Professors Absalom Vilakazi and Mlahleni Kjisane addressed the crowd.[46] Three hundred academics, activists, business and labor leaders, and journalists offered workshops, which began with the reading of a background paper engaging the themes of "The Boycott of South African Goods," "U.S. investment in South Africa," "U.S. Policy Toward South Africa," "American Action Against Apartheid," and "Defense and Aid to Opponents of Apartheid."[47]

And so the very same week that Perlzweig and Prinz debated questions of morality and loyalty, debated whether Jewish solidarity prevented Western Jews from speaking out against South African apartheid, and the very same week that the Histadrut, Israel's trade union organization, decided to boycott South African consumer goods because of apartheid, the JLC continued its commitment to antiracism and anticolonialism by cosponsoring the Emergency Action Conference on South Africa.[48] The AJCongress, though vocal in support of domestic Civil Rights, remained silent on Sharpeville because of pressure by Perlzweig in the WJC. Its leaders expressed regret but felt bound by the WJC's quest for South African formal membership. Criticizing the SAJBD for its "neutral" stand on apartheid would jeopardize that membership.[49]

One year before, the tensions regarding Israel's exclusion from the Africa Freedom Day celebration in New York City had roiled JLC members. Their sponsorship of this conference, however, demonstrated their continued commitment to fighting apartheid. The JLC located its allegiances with South African workers, and thus approached the question of international justice through labor rights, drawing from Jewish currents of social justice as well as the solidarity of workers around the world.

The "Summary of Resolutions Adopted by the Emergency Action Conference on South Africa" called for consumers and investors to boycott South African goods, and included suggestions for American policymakers as well as labor unions. Conference goers discouraged "tourists, athletes, artists, and intellectuals" from traveling to South Africa. In future years, antiapartheid and other activists—including members of the twenty-first-century Boycott, Divestment, and Sanctions movement for Palestinian rights—would employ many of these tactics. One scholar writes that "the workings of this conference helped pave the way for antiapartheid efforts in the years to come."[50]

Several of these recommendations bore the imprint of union leadership, some specifically that of the JLC. No doubt UAW, ILGWU, and JLC leaders penned the recommendation that American labor unions were to "study the possibility of an industrial boycott of South African goods through refusing to unload ships from South Africa and other handling of South African products." The JLC had worked diligently to enforce a similar boycott of German machinery and other goods during World War II. And the JLC, following its Cold War sensibilities and in line with its long history of aiding refugees from fascism, probably encouraged the adoption of the recommendation to "aid escapees from South Africa and South West Africa in a manner comparable to U.S. aid given Hungarian refugees," a reference to those who streamed out of Hungary after a failed 1958 attempt to topple the Soviet-backed Communist government.[51]

Even prior to the Emergency Action Conference, the JLC lent its voice to an "appeal to free trade union organizations" to boycott South African goods through its membership in the European-controlled, noncommunist International Confederation of Free Trade Unions (ICFTU). Following the lead of the Conference of Independent African States, which called for a boycott of apartheid South Africa in Accra in 1958, the ICFTU's Sixth World Congress in Brussels in December 1959 decided on the boycott in order "to protest against South Africa's racial policies and denial of trade union rights to millions of African workers." Identifying their policies as "what amounts to slave labor," the JLC and other trade groups encouraged unionists to "strike your blow for freedom in South Africa now!"[52]

While the JLC joined African American leaders in condemning apartheid, their domestic work was not immune from the tensions that plagued all facets of the Black/Jewish alliance in the United States, as the Africa Freedom Day celebration made clear. Indeed, Cheryl Greenberg writes that the labor movement "proved one of the most bitter battlegrounds."[53] Tensions in the Black/Jewish labor alliance related to African Americans' frustration with white and Jewish paternalism and condescension, and a broader frustration with liberalism as a strategy for liberation. Indeed, the JLC worked with the ICFTU and cosponsored the Emergency Action Conference with the NAACP despite the heavy weight of a conflict earlier that year. In that conflict, this was clear: while the JLC willingly lent its voice to a coalition criticizing colonialism and white supremacy abroad, African American trade union leaders and later the NAACP felt that the JLC in fact defended discrimination in domestic union practices.[54]

Of the earliest years of the American Jewish labor movement, Tony Michels writes that:

> From the start the Jewish labor movement—and the broader Yiddish culture it fostered—contained its own tensions and conflicts. How could it have been otherwise? Socialists espoused universal principles yet created a movement

consisting entirely of Yiddish-speaking Jews. The Jewish labor movement's dual character—its universalism and particularlism—wrestled with itself constantly.[55]

Although decades later than the era Michels here describes, the JLC's anti-apartheid activism, like its Civil Rights activism, represented its universalist commitments. Within the borders of the United States, the JLC's commitment to Civil Rights was imperiled by a host of developments both in and outside of its control. These included racist paternalism, Cold War liberalism, a divergence of liberation strategies on the part of African Americans and Jews, American Zionism, resistance to Zionism in the anticolonialist movement, anti-Semitism on the left, and the desire of American Jews to accent their difference amidst the ethnic revival period in the latter half of the 1960s. Deeply invested in seeing themselves as apart from the white power structure, American Jews remained deeply invested in an integrationist paradigm—even as they benefited from white privilege. African Americans' very real frustration with the lack of progress while relying on that paradigm meant, for many, a new vision of Jewish contributions to the Civil Rights movement.[56] But if the JLC's moral vision was clouded, complicated, or compromised in the United States, their eyes focused clearly on the universalist moral question of South African apartheid. They continued to wrestle with the "dual character" of their work, and (yet) prioritized global workers' solidarity and thus their antiapartheid work.

In desiring visibility and accenting their difference as Jews, many members of the JLC embraced a worldview that placed Israel and Zionism in line with Black liberation movements in the United States and in Africa. In this they were not alone. In fact, across much of the political spectrum, American Jews and their allies drew very visible parallels between Zionism and Black African liberation movements. Israel's outreach to Black Africa, the nation's building up of ties to Black Africa, contributed to these parallels.[57] When Israeli representatives walked out of the African Freedom Day celebration because of the presence of the FLN's flag, they offered evidence of a new definition of Zionism, one that countered the idea that Zionism was liberation. Although that walkout did not make the news, Israel's assistance to Black Africa appeared frequently in the mainstream and Jewish presses. Indeed, Jewish leaders would later use these efforts to demonstrate Israel's antiracist and anticolonialist credentials.

The tensions at the two celebrations of Africa Freedom Day belied a vigorous diplomatic effort on Israel's part, as Israel exchanged agricultural experts and medical teams with newly independent African nations. In 1960, Israeli Foreign Minister Golda Meir spoke at a tribute dinner held by 15 African nations to honor Israel's programs of technical assistance to Central Africa. There, she "drew a parallel between the 'common history' of Jews who have been subject to persecution and various forms of prejudice and the sufferings and prejudice encountered by the colored people of Africa."[58]

Observers of Israel's work in Africa noted that Israel's political neutrality—its independence from colonial powers, and indeed the successful struggle it waged against Britain as a colonial power—made it an ideal ally for Black Africa. (South African leaders who crafted alliances with Israel would later draw similar parallels as means toward a very different end.) Hope Yomekpe, Ghana's delegate to the United Nations, agreed that Israel offered historical parallels to Africa in rising to specific challenges: "In our eyes Israel is a small country that freed itself from colonial imperialism and achieved much, in a very short period, in conquering the desert and mixing the tribes—problems that are in some way or other basic problems of Africa."[59] Also, Israel stood as a model of "development through cooperative and publicly-owned enterprises."[60] Israel extended its positive, democratic approach—some would say its socialist approach to social welfare and economic organization in kibbutzim—from the Middle East to Africa.[61]

In line with its outreach to Black African nations, Israel made visible, diplomatic efforts to show its strong disapproval of apartheid beginning in the early 1960s. It joined an antiapartheid censure initiative in the United Nations in 1961, repeated that vote in 1962, and in 1963 withdrew its diplomatic delegate from South Africa. The first censure earned Israel a "Bravo!" from the left Zionist organization HaShomer Hatzair. Editors of the organization's newspaper, *Israel Horizons*, praised Israel for being "on the side of the angels" and later noted that "a Jewish State, the haven of so many refugees from the worst Holocaust a people has ever known, cannot condone racial discrimination anywhere."[62]

In response to Israel's antiapartheid position, South Africa's white leaders subsequently froze the transfer of funds to Israel. Israel's censure and this action placed organized South African Jewry in a difficult and anxious position. Gideon Shimoni notes that "the issue of Israel's condemnations of apartheid compounded and, indeed, overshadowed the acute dilemma of the Jewish leadership over the Jewish attitude to the apartheid order itself." Although support for Zionism did not significantly weaken, leaders remained largely silent, criticizing neither Israel nor their own government.[63] Many felt that a rise in anti-Semitism grew out of Israel's stands. Helen Suzman, a Jewish Progressive Party member in the South African Parliament who took stands against apartheid—and who from 1961 to 1974 was Parliament's sole Progressive Party member—noted that "when Israel did not vote against anti-South African resolutions at the United Nations, I came in for a goodly dose of abuse, all of it anti-Semitic."[64]

Scholars of the bonds between Israel and Black Africa offered divergent interpretations for Israel's outreach into Black Africa. They cite Israel's condemnation of apartheid. Many touted the "humanitarian and altruistic factors" at work in Israel's early efforts in Africa, dismissing the claim that Africa was simply "a battleground for political support and votes."[65] Some assessed these alliances in terms of the Cold War, and saw Israel's overtures to Africa as unabashed Cold War moves, as bulwarks against communism on that continent. Others saw these overtures as attempts to persuade African nations to take Israel's side in the Arab/Israeli conflict.[66]

African American activists who touted Israel's work in Black Africa often met with intense criticism from this Cold War vantage point. Bayard Rustin, for example, was an American Peace and Civil Rights activist and a leader in the ACOA who cited Israel's ties to Black Africa as part of the justification for his long-standing support of Zionism.[67] Making use of popular conspiracy theories, radical African American lawyer and activist William Lorenzo Patterson later accused Rustin of not seeing the forces at work in Israel's actions:

> Bayard Rustin states that Israel "has established ambitious programs of cooperation with, and aid to Asian and African nations. Part of this help comes in the form of economic and military aid." It is better to be more specific. The military training is in preparation to fight guerrillas and is more helpful to Portugal and the neo-colonialist of the West than to the African liberation movement. The unity of the Arab countries and Black Africa is historically necessary for the defeat of neo-colonialism. One must ask: What price economic aid from Israel? Israel is giving Black Africa anti-Arab, and particularly anti-Soviet, ideological indoctrination. It acts as the agent of the imperialist forces that established it—the major cost of which is paid by world Zionist agencies and U.S.A. imperialism.[68]

Patterson endorsed a Third World Solidarity movement that opposed Israel and any support for Zionism; like other African American and white leaders on the left, he linked American imperialism to Zionism and to domestic white supremacy, and saw each as bolstered by the policies of Cold Warriors.

In his study of Israel's ties to South Africa, foreign policy historian Sasha Polakow-Suransky terms this era "Israel's Honeymoon in Africa." Israel's relationship with the United States was not yet strong, and in the absence of an alliance with a major Western power, Israel needed friends. Polakow-Suransky notes that behind Golda Meir's moving testimony on the redemptive ties between Israel and independent African nations, Israel's "charm offensive" in Africa was a concerted effort to form close ties with nations "just beyond the hostile Arab states surrounding it" in order to check Egyptian leader Abdul Nasser's pan-Arabism and Soviet influence.[69] These nations also offered Israel "prestige and a positive image." After the alienation that followed exclusion from the Bandung conference, Israel was buoyed up by the strong support of Black African countries at the United Nations, where for the first time, "Israeli delegates were elected to executive–administrative posts as representatives of the Afro-Asian world."[70]

In February 1961, continuing these conversations about Zionism and Africa, the Theodor Herzl Institute of the Jewish Agency, a Zionist organization, held a conference titled "Africa and the Jews." Here, observers and experts sounded notes of caution that echoed the broader tensions among African Americans and American Jews in the Civil Rights movement. Rabbi Andre Ungar was among those who attended. Ungar's years in South Africa were marked by antiapartheid activism. As a pulpit rabbi he had been castigated by the Jewish community for that activism.[71] Fritz Flesch admired him deeply and corresponded with him at length; the WJC regretted his influence on Rabbi Joachim Prinz in the 1960s, fearful it would lead to Prinz's speaking out publicly against South African apartheid. To the conference audience Ungar gave "a rousing indictment... of the leadership of the South African community for its failure to oppose *apartheid*."

Claiming deep kinship and inspirational bonds between the newly developing nations of Israel and those within Black Africa, remarks by Arieh Eilan, Israeli representative to the United Nations, set the tone of the conference. He said that Israel brought African nations "technical skills" but also an "infectious" spirit and an important message: "if we could do it, so can you." Although he "decried the 'exaggerated flood of publicity' about Israeli aid to African states and stressed that Israel's contribution was at best modest," he encouraged his audience to assess that aid "not so much in terms of volume but in terms of quality."[72] He also took pains to note that Israel was selling "a political philosophy" through their kibbutzim: that you can have "collective farm life without communism."[73]

While Professor Hugh Smythe, an African American anthropologist from Brooklyn College, also delved into Cold War alliances, he noted the tension within Black African nations over Israel's racial politics. He reported on "What Africans Think about Israel." (The editor of the progressive magazine *Jewish Currents* asked, parenthetically, "Why were Africans not invited to speak for themselves on this subject?") Prof Smythe noted that African states, fearful of "Nasser's expansionism," turned to Israel for assistance. But these nations had some reservations. "Because Africans are extremely sensitive to all race prejudice, anti-Israel attitudes develop when they hear reports from Israel about prejudice against Israeli Arabs or Jews from North Africa."[74]

Those engaged in anticolonialist struggles across the world watched Israel's domestic *and* foreign policies closely. Golda Meir continued to use strong moral language that united the Jewish experience of anti-Semitism with Black Africans' experiences of colonialism and apartheid; she equated Israel's existence with Jewish liberation in ways that paralleled Black African liberation movements.[75] Yet already, Israel's alliances with colonialist forces had cost Israel the faith of left-leaning African Americans, Jews, and others. As this conference program testified, Israel's official position with regard to South Africa's government, along with mainstream South African Jewry's silence on apartheid, continued to provoke debate.

Many Jews around the world continued to hold Jewish solidarity paramount, as Maurice Perlzweig did within the WJC, and they protested positions within world Jewry that stood in the way of that goal. Indeed, organized South African Jewry reacted with alarm when Israel supported United Nations sanctions against their government in 1961 and 1962. They felt anger, frustration, and deep fear about the implications of that position for South Africa's treatment of them (as Jews) and of Israel.[76]

South African Jewish leaders grew wary when they read an article in a Johannesburg paper about a resolution of the American Negro Leadership Conference on Africa (ANLCA) supporting sanctions against South Africa, and the article mentioned American Jewish support for Israel. Prominent African American Civil Rights leaders, including Dorothy Height, James Farmer, Dr Martin Luther King, Jr., A. Philip Randolph, Roy Wilkins, and Whitney Young had founded the ANLCA that very year in order to bring American attention to African affairs.[77]

When South African Jewish leaders read about the successes of the elite Black leadership of the ANLCA, and noted the references to American Jews and Israel, they assumed that the article referenced the idea that African Americans would try to pattern their support for Black South Africans on American Jewish support for Israel. "On the other hand," wrote Gus Saron, general secretary of the SAJBD, "it might mean that the American Jewish community is inaugurating a campaign to secure support for Israel's attitude against South Africa." Although he doubted that this was the case, he urged his American colleague to write a quick reply to his note. A second note, written the following day, asked generally about "any reactions within the American Jewish community in regard to Israel's vote at the U.N."[78]

The quick reply of Sam Spiegler of the National Jewish Community Relations Advisory Council (NJCRAC), the umbrella group of mainstream American Jewish organizations, assuaged the fears of South African Jewish leaders. The parallel drawn by the Associated Press in the article was about the organization of Jewish public opinion for Israel, nothing more. Further, Spiegler went on to say that American Jews paid little attention to Israel's antiapartheid position: the UN vote "occasioned no reaction in the Anglo-Jewish press in this country, nor does there appear to be any special interest in the vote."[79]

The Saron/Spiegler exchange placed a spotlight on African Americans' antiapartheid work, which often found activists triangulating Israel, South Africa, and American Jews (though not within the ANLCA). It also highlighted South African Jewish leaders' abiding fears of Jewish criticisms of apartheid, which were soon to be realized.

Indeed, while American and South African Jewish leaders corresponded regularly about global anti-Semitism and events in Israel, the issue of apartheid continued to strain relations—especially after Sharpeville. The SAJBD grew more defensive about its refusal to take a position on apartheid, as a series of letters between Gus Saron and Saul Joftes of America's B'nai B'rith make clear. In 1962, Saron was responding to an article under review by B'nai B'rith in the United States, one that focused on South African Jewry and apartheid.[80] Recognizing that the American perspective was quite different, Saron insisted that his own words reflected the "vantage point" of all those who served as officers on the Board. Saron's sentiments toward the strident antiapartheid stance of the article's author are telling.

To begin with, Saron wrote, he felt the piece "oversimplified" apartheid. "The author proceeds on the assumption that everything about apartheid is evil—that any form of segregation or racial discrimination is wrong—and reflects little or nothing of the real complexities in the relationship between a white minority and a large non-white majority, differing greatly in their standards of civilisation, etc."[81]

Specifically with regard to the SAJBD's stand on apartheid, Saron wrote again that the author did not pay due heed to the "grave difficulties that would face a representative Jewish body if it were to take up a position in permanent opposition to the Government on the most vital political issue of the country." Parenthetically, Saron noted that the Board of Deputies "has been unable to sift out the moral from the political aspects of racial policies" in South Africa.[82] He presented South African Jewry as precariously positioned, and rested his arguments on the urgency of prioritizing the Jewish community's health and well-being. He rejected the article as he rejected the moral positioning of its author.

Many activists objected to Saron's insistence on apartheid's complexity, his aside about "sifting" moral from political aspects of apartheid. They felt that such phrasing denied the close ties forming between white South African leaders and the organized Jewish community. That Jews were safe in South Africa owed much to common support for Israel among those leaders and among most Jews. As in the United States, the sides in the conflict came into relief, though more quickly and more sharply because of the proximity to the evils of apartheid. South African Jews who supported Israel and supported (or condoned) apartheid lay on one side. Jews who opposed Israel's existence and/or its policies and who fought apartheid lay on the other. Many who fit into this latter category were communist antiapartheid activists with Jewish backgrounds, some of whom considered themselves Jews.[83]

In the Cold War era, Zionist Jewish leaders in South Africa accused antiapartheid activists of multiple kinds of betrayal: betrayal of nation, in working against white South African leaders; betrayal of Jewish belonging, in working against the SAJBD and in rejecting Zionism; betrayal of Jewish interests, in drawing attention to the Jewish community simply by being Jewish and joining with Black Africans in fighting for a cause they saw as just, moral, and deeply intertwined with white supremacy, colonialism, violence, and unequal distributions of power. This was especially true after the Rivonia trial of 1963–1964, when 13 activists of the ANC were tried for crimes against the apartheid state, including Nelson Mandela, who after the trial began his nearly 27 years in prison before his 1990 release. Displaying this divide within South African Jewry, six of the whites arrested were Jewish, as was the chief prosecutor.[84]

Saron appealed to American Jews with pleas to consider the complexity of inequality, but he also spoke to the organized, South African Jewish community's investment in the status quo of inequality. Grappling with commitments to universalism and justice on the one hand, Jewish unity and an unjust system on the other, Saron sought understanding from the American Jewish community that he saw as wrestling with those same commitments.

The following year, the SAJBD appealed to the American Jewish community with a direct query about balancing those commitments. The Board asked about the American Jewish response to the Civil Rights movement in their own quest to improve South African Jewish public relations, in order to "examine afresh our own policies towards South African racial issues."[85] "It is our purpose to ascertain whether the experience of American communities, especially those in the South which in some respects have analogous problems, can assist us in our own particular situation."[86]

Saron qualified his request with an acknowledgment of the vast differences between the government, populations, and state-sanctioned white supremacy in South Africa and the United States. His appeal, and the long-running connections and correspondence between South African and American Jewish leaders, proves important to this story: beneath the organizational and individual struggles to make sense of the decolonizing world, there lay this consistent attempt to find common ground and unity.

Buoyed by its Cold War allies, including the United States, the South African economy was strong as the Rivonia trial ended in June 1964. But there were harbingers of the movement that would isolate South Africa on the world stage. For even as attention turned toward domestic Civil Rights in the United States, African American and other US antiapartheid leaders and organizations continued to press the cause with demonstrations. On his way to accept the Nobel Peace Prize in December 1964, Dr Martin Luther King spoke to a meeting in London of "the deadly struggle for freedom in South Africa," linking it to "the struggle for freedom and justice in the United States."[87] The courageous work of these individuals and groups meant a growing momentum for anticolonialist movements, and greater success. As South Africa felt increasingly alone in the world, South African Jews would turn to American Jews far more directly in a search for friends.

* * *

As this chapter reveals, prior to 1967, American Jewish activists pushed back against the priorities of WJC leaders, revealing the possibilities of a stronger Jewish response to apartheid that seemed unimaginable in the immediate postwar period. In those same years, Israel's work with Black Africa provided a historical moment in which Jews in the United States and elsewhere could see Israel as a product of Jewish liberation *and* a committed contributor to Black liberation.

Yet these alliances began to shift, and the global Third World movement had a deep and lasting impact on how citizens across the world viewed them. To cite just one example: Israel's exclusion from the 1959 Africa Freedom Day celebration in New York City was grounded in Israel's alliance with France during that nation's bloody war against Algerian independence. In 1962, when Algerians won their independence, both Nelson Mandela (in Morocco) and Yasser Arafat (in Algiers) participated in the celebration.[88] Jewish encounters with the liberation movements of Black South Africans as well as Palestinians meant that they had to work out their positions on apartheid and Zionism, often simultaneously.

As the next chapter in this history demonstrates, the Six Day War of 1967 forever altered the terms and context of this debate, ushering in a hard and fast American Zionist "consensus" among many Jewish leaders. American Jews with diverse positions on Israel and Zionism who wanted to protest apartheid, who felt allied with global and domestic anticolonialist movements *as Jews*, were left with few places to go.

3

Jews or Radicals?

In the early 1960s, members of the anticommunist Jewish liberal/Left were able to hold universalist and particularist commitments, more or less, in balance: those who saw themselves as Zionists expressed both praise and criticism of Israel, and many walked alongside African Americans in anticolonialist campaigns, including those against South African apartheid. When they spoke of these interracial alliances, American Jews continued to use the language of prophetic Judaism and cite the lessons of the Holocaust. Several large global and American Jewish organizations had passed resolutions against South African apartheid—the World Union for Progressive Judaism (an umbrella organization for Reform, Reconstructionist, Liberal, and Progressive congregations) in 1960, and the American Jewish Congress in 1964.[1] American Jews followed the leadership of African Americans in the Civil Rights movement in these years, and both groups praised Israel's strong antiapartheid position. Indeed, Black newspapers recorded fear among African Americans that the apartheid regime's leaders would harm South African Jews, who might suffer reprisals for "Israel's undisguised and unflagging opposition to South Africa's brutal segregative practices."[2]

But the narrative of Black/Jewish relations in the United States shifted gradually in the late 1960s. Many studies in American Jewish history lay the blame for this shift exclusively on the rise of militant Black Nationalism. They focus on the anti-Semitism that emerged within some Black nationalist ideology and rhetoric, as criticisms of Israel veered into blatant anti-Semitism. Certainly this elision occurred throughout the Left. The promulgation of such ideas in African American organizations particularly alienated liberal Jews, as did the purging of whites, including Jews, from Civil Rights coalitions. While most scholars agree that the 1967 Arab–Israeli war constituted a decisive turning point in this history, a complex and protracted departure from universalism had begun prior to 1967, rooted in a series of domestic and international factors underemphasized or ignored by many studies of Black/Jewish relations. Prioritizing Jewish unity and security had challenged Jewish antiapartheid protests, for example, beginning immediately after World War II.[3]

Other scholars provide a more nuanced understanding of this change in relations. These analyses often focus more heavily on the roles of South Africa and Israel. In 1997, historians Paul Buhle and Robin D. G. Kelley introduced their study of African Americans and Jews on the left by noting that, while "the emergence of a particular brand of Black nationalism in the mid-1960s and Israel's policies toward the Middle East and apartheid in South Africa deeply damaged Black-Jewish relations within progressive circles...the story is far more complicated" than past historical narratives have allowed.[4] Focusing on Israel, along with Jews in South Africa and the United States, this chapter expands upon a portion of this "more complicated" story. It draws out how and why these pressures and fissures undermined political alliances between African Americans and Jews and divided American Jews themselves, preventing a more unified Jewish response to apartheid.

One crucial and overlooked force acting on the Black/Jewish alliance in this era, intricately connected to the politics of South Africa and Israel, was the new, inward-facing agenda of mainstream American Jewish organizations. As scholar Stuart Svonkin explains, the intergroup relations project that occupied the energies of these organizations immediately after the war had explicitly linked the struggle against Nazism to struggles against all kinds of prejudice. The Civil Rights work of Prinz and Petegorsky for the American Jewish Congress and their protests against South African Jews for their silence on apartheid drew as much upon Prinz and Petegorsky's particularist Jewish loyalty as it did from their liberal, universalist commitments. By the 1960s, however, the "paradigm of intergroup relations established during the 1940s and 1950s was no longer adequate."[5] Socioeconomic mobility brought many American Jews closer to the privileged majority, so the case for a shared fate with disadvantaged groups weakened. Increased assimilation made Israel central to American Jewish visibility in ways that had a profound impact on the brands of Zionism American Jews embraced in the following decades.

Many young American Jews who had lived through the antiwar and liberation movements that challenged American political leadership also rejected the priorities of American Jewish organizational leaders. They issued strong critiques: of overwhelmingly male leaders who resisted change and endorsed rigid organizational structures; of these leaders' agendas that embraced assimilation and middle-class lifestyles but did not sufficiently engage pressing world issues.[6] These young Jews felt increasingly isolated from mainstream, organized Jewish life *and* from the New Left's anti-Israel, anti-Semitic influences. In the words of Bill Novak, editor of the Jewish countercultural journal *Response*, the younger generation was "turned off...by an organized Jewish Community which is neither Jewish nor Community—only organized."[7]

Jewish activists began to view organized Jewish life as part of "the system" and, in response, founded a Jewish counterculture that encompassed politics, education, and religion. Drawing from the Black Power movement and the rise of identity politics, Jewish countercultural activists created new spaces and diverse organizations, some feminist, some inclusive of gay and lesbian members, others wrestling with domestic and international issues. These largely decentralized Jewish countercultural organizations and congregations aimed to reinvigorate Jewish particularism, Jewish culture, and Jewish religious and communal life.[8] Importantly, though, while members of the Jewish counterculture rejected the authority and formality of much of Jewish life—synagogues, rabbinical and mainstream organizational leaders, for example[9]—many of these activists remained dedicated to Zionism.[10] They approached Zionism from diverse political perspectives, alongside their other political commitments; they defined Zionism as Jewish liberation and saw its ideology as central to Jewish difference.[11]

The impact of the 1967 war in Israel on all American Jews—whether in mainstream Jewish life or in the Jewish counterculture—cannot be overstated, perhaps especially with the defining, even urgent postwar quest for Jewish unity among Jewish leaders. "The fateful period before, during, and immediately following the Six Day War in June 1967," writes historian Jonathan Sarna, "jolted the American Jewish community from [its] universalistic agenda" of social justice and militarism, of fighting for Civil Rights and against the war in Vietnam.[12] As Arab troops massed on Israel's borders, Jews around the world experienced tremendous anxiety over that nation's future, invoking the Holocaust as they expressed their fear of another "abandonment of the Jews."[13]

Many American Jewish leaders felt betrayed by colleagues in the Civil Rights, antiwar, and interfaith movements who did not speak out on behalf of Israel in this period. The ensuing feelings of alienation and isolation reinforced the shift away from universalism that had begun before 1967, because of the historical trends mentioned earlier: a new, militant Black nationalism; the new agendas of the mainstream American Jewish community. Still, scholars note the import of 1967 on American Jews' self-perceptions and the politics of their worldviews.[14]

In the wake of the war, many mainstream American Jews reconfigured their theological and political commitments. Increasingly, they expressed their Jewishness through religious observance and support of Israel while dismissing those who linked the prophetic tradition in Judaism to social justice, antiwar, Civil Rights, and anticolonial campaigns. Liberal and left American Jews who continued to embrace these campaigns as Jews faced accusations: they were traitors to the Jewish community, consumed by self-hatred, harbored communist sympathies, and were unconcerned with the future of the Jewish people. "By the late 1960s," writes historian Michael Staub, who documents this turn comprehensively, "[i]t was scarcely possible to speak in an uncomplicated way about the direct relationship between Judaism and justice."[15]

Human rights scholar Michael Galchinsky also argues that the 1960s marked the end of the "honeymoon between Jews and international human rights." Suburbanization contributed to this move "away from their traditional liberal stance toward conservatism," as did the increasingly vocal international criticism of Israel by global human rights bodies, which came to see Israel's policies as outgrowths of colonialism. "Since the 1970s," Galchinsky writes, "Jews have found repeatedly that they have had to choose between commitments to human rights and Israel."[16] As human rights groups came to link Israel and South Africa in the same global critiques, American Jews had to choose sides in their struggles with apartheid.

Countercultural Jews likewise felt this pressure to choose, with Cold War alliances playing a key role. Many Zionist activists in the Jewish counterculture felt betrayed by those in the New Left who likened Israel's victory in 1967 to another Vietnam, with Western powers supporting an illegal occupation and oppressing the land's rightful inhabitants.[17] And importantly, the Soviets had switched sides. After recognizing and supporting Israel since its founding in 1948, the Soviets began backing Arab nationalism in 1954.[18] Such a move aimed to secure the allegiance of post-colonial governments and limit the West's access to Middle Eastern oil. It also positioned Nasser as a hero of postcolonial revolutions, and for many made Zionism synonymous with colonialist imperialism.[19] New Left and human rights activists who rejected Western capitalism and imperialism saw Israel as aligned with those forces, and this alienated Jewish Zionists on the left.

From the late 1960s onwards, struggling to balance their New Left political radicalism with a Jewishness grounded in Zionism, members of these organizations departed Civil Rights groups and coalitions. Editors of left and liberal Jewish journals dedicated a shrinking amount of space to anticolonialist campaigns; left and liberal Zionist organizations of American Jewish life reconfigured their priorities, placing support of Israel over other commitments, such as Black African liberation and South African apartheid. As "outsiders to America and outsiders to [the New Left's] alternative vision of America," they truly felt presented with a staggeringly difficult choice, "unable to be both Jews and radicals."[20]

Although scholars have studied these trends, they have not considered American Jews who rejected this choice altogether. These Jews held fast to their commitments to liberation campaigns, allying with the growing Third World movement and strongly criticizing Israeli policies and Zionism—or rejecting them outright. Historian Odd Arne Westad argues that Western members of the Third World movement often saw the Third World as "the future—in political and moral, if not economic terms." Their radical critiques of colonialism and their alliances with developing nations served as "mirror[s] for the criticisms that [they]...had of their own countries as undemocratic, racist, and elitist."[21] Certainly African Americans had long seen the struggle for domestic Civil Rights as part of a global campaign, unfolding in the United States and in the African Freedom movements, including the antiapartheid campaign in South Africa.[22] American Jews in the antiapartheid and other anticolonialist movements held up a mirror to domestic white supremacy and to American involvement in the Vietnam War; many appraised the organized American Jewish community and found that it also perpetuated racist, ethnocentric, patriarchal, homophobic, and inward-focused models that felt to them outmoded and unjust. These American Jews tried to carve out spaces for themselves in American Jewish organizations. When faced with the either/or choice, they opted to remain in Civil Rights and anticolonialist campaigns, continuing to speak of their involvement as motivated by their Jewishness.

This chapter and the two that follow find these Jewish activists in the labor movement and in the liberation movements of the 1960s and 1970s. Instead of citing only Israel's ties to Black Africa, these progressive American Jewish women and men often recalled Israel's alliance with France in its war against Algerian independence, spoke out against Israel's treatment of Palestinians in its new territories, and began to take note of Israel's ties to South Africa. Because they did not cease to count their Jewishness as key to their activism—including their antiapartheid activism—they present a distinctive expression of late twentieth-century American Jewishness.

Historian Adam Mendelsohn writes with skepticism of American Jews' antiapartheid statements in the late 1960s. He considers the alliances between Jews and the antiapartheid cause a "bubble":

> Much of the hot air that inflated this brief bubble dissipated as the civil rights alliance deflated. The souring of the alliance removed much of the impetus for pronouncements on South Africa. Interest in apartheid proved to be transient. In the absence of dramatic developments it was displaced by other distractions—Black Power, the Vietnam War, and Israel. This waning of interest was temporary, reviving a decade later in the service of new political needs.[23]

Mendelsohn's assessment neglects the steadfast political commitments of those American Jews who continued to fight apartheid *as Jews*, who saw antiapartheid as the logical, global extension of their Jewish commitment to American antiracism. This "brief bubble" of the late 1960s, then, can be seen less as the strategic, opportunistic positioning of Jews within the Black/Jewish alliance than as a fleeting moment of coalescence of liberal and left Jews within organized American Jewry. Afterward, the Jewish voices against apartheid remained—but largely outside of most mainstream Jewish organizations. The divides within and among American Jewry grew more pronounced. In fact, they appear more significant when historians account for the presence of American Jews who saw their Jewishness as intricately bound up in their antiapartheid activism.

In this era, American Jews contested the lessons of the Holocaust in ways reminiscent of the early debates over South Africa's membership in the WJC, and too of debates over early Jewish involvement in American antiracist activism. How should Jews express their Jewishness, and what are the most pressing "Jewish" priorities? What methods would prove most effective in preserving Jewish difference, belonging, and communal life for future generations? Could campaigns for justice create meaningful Jewish communal belonging that would stand the test of time? These debates begged the broader question: who speaks for American Jews when it comes to South Africa and Israel? These three national and communal histories were intricately connected. As American Jews worked out their positions on South African apartheid, they were also determining their positions on Israel.

* * *

The horrors of the Holocaust cemented the idea of the dire need for a Jewish state. Many Jews saw in Israel a beacon of freedom for the refugees of the war; the possibility for democracy in the Middle East; a solid, even revolutionary, foundation on which to build a modern meaning for Jewishness, for Jewish difference, for Jewish identity. They pointed to Israel's strong labor movement. Israel's aid to Africa, beginning in the 1950s, provided still more evidence of that nation's positive, democratic influence on the world, and especially on Africa and the Middle East.[24]

"Jewish nationalism is revolutionary," wrote academic, journalist, and Jewish leader Leonard Fein in his essay contribution to the 1971 collection *The New Left and the Jews*. At its best, it shows us how to reconcile "the two contradictory impulses of the modern temper," particularism and universalism.[25] The promise of Israel, he wrote, is not only of its "rejection of the assumptions of universalism" (in that it is a nation created for Jews) but also its "useful precedent and helpful insight" into how the "typically reactionary consequences of particularist nationalism may be avoided."[26] The "idea of Israel," Fein asserted, is "a society parochial in structure but universal in ideology."[27] Even as Fein and others on the left often criticized Israeli leaders for heading toward "destructive parochialism," they spoke of Israel as a liberal, tolerant influence, a home for the Jews at a time when Auschwitz and the 1967 war were not distant memories. All residents of Israel would benefit from its experimentation with democracy, its strong labor and kibbutz movements. Although they argued vociferously about Palestinian nationalism, anti-Semitism, and anti-Israel sentiment, they held fast to their faith in Israel, which to them represented "progressivism."

How then did those ideas intersect with Jewish approaches to apartheid? Immediately after the war, when Israel again joined other nations in condemning South African apartheid, *Israel Horizons* praised Israel for doing "its annual painful duty." As editors of an English-language newspaper linked to the left-wing Meretz Party in Israel, they focused liberal/left American Jews' attention on the ways in which Israel crafted its condemnation. They quoted Joel Barromi, Israeli Representative at the United Nations, who continued to use Golda Meir's language in analogizing Zionism, Civil Rights, and anti-colonialism. Barromi quoted Theodor Herzl, founder of modern Zionism, as well as scholar and Civil Rights leader Dr W. E. B. Du Bois: "The African movement means to us what the Zionist movement must mean to the Jews," he asserted. As late as 1967, then, lessons of the Holocaust still served as the foundation to the alliance between Jews and Black Africa, in support of Black independent nations and in opposition to all forms of prejudice: "For us, the Jews," he said, "the question of apartheid is first and foremost a matter of principle and of conscience. It is a facet of our impassioned condemnation of each and every form of racial discrimination." The editors agreed that Israel "cannot do otherwise." "Apartheid is wrong," they wrote. "To fight it is an imperative."[28]

The editors of *Israel Horizons* also gauged the impact of the war on South African Jews. Government officials again allowed funds to flow freely from South African Jews to Israel, reinstating the arrangement that they had put in place in 1948—and then removed in 1962 and again in 1967, amidst the controversy over Israel's condemnation of apartheid and "so many Jews'" involvement in South Africa's antiapartheid movement.[29] But Israel's actions also imperiled South African Jews, creating a backlash that included "loyalty tests," because apartheid's leaders feared that all South African Jews agreed with Israel's antiapartheid stand.[30]

After 1967, however, the likelihood of encountering unconditional African and African American support of Israel rapidly diminished. The differing positions of Martin Luther King, Jr, in the 1950s Suez Crisis and in 1967 speak to this shift specifically within African American liberation struggles. In 1956, many individuals in anticolonialist movements had supported Egypt's nationalization of the Suez Canal from British and French interests; despite this, King took the side of Israel, which allied with Britain and France against Egypt. "There is something in the very nature of the universe which is on the side of Israel in its struggle with every Egypt," he wrote in 1956.[31] Days before the 1967 war, King signed a letter printed in the *New York Times* calling on Americans to support the "independence, integrity, and freedom of Israel."[32] Yet King did not take a public position on the Six Day War itself, much to the dismay of mainstream Jewish organizations.

The leadership of the National Association for the Advancement of Colored People, too, struggled to adopt a position on the 1967 war. Andrew Weinberger, a Jewish member of the NAACP Board of Directors, appealed to Roy Wilkins, executive director of the NAACP, to issue a public statement at a Washington rally on June 8, the third day of deadly fighting in the Middle East. They noted that labor and Civil Rights activist A. Philip Randolph spoke out publicly "immediately following the outbreak of the hostilities," saying that "Israel must be supported."[33] Conflicted, Wilkins sent a telegram to his board, asking for a "return vote by wire" on whether or not the NAACP should take a formal position in support of Israel. "Since the NAACP did not issue any official statement pro or con Vietnam," Wilkins wrote, "I have been reluctant to assume individual responsibility on a grave matter on which there is no guiding policy."[34] Maintaining a domestic focus for his organization, Wilkins nonetheless thought the call from American Jewish leaders worthy of consideration.

Although the majority voted *for* that support—the tally was 20 for, 14 against—the replies were telling.[35] Henry Lee Moon, an activist and journalist, replied with these words:

> While I personally agree with your statement in support of Israel, I recognize that there is an Arab side. Here in the U.S.A., the Negroes are closer to the

Jews than to the Arabs. However, in a world sense, Negroes are much closer to the Arabs than to the Jews. I am convinced that your statement as it now stands will evoke angry denunciations from the Black Nationalists and Black Muslim crowd in this country.[36]

The emerging Third World Solidarity among African American organizations and individuals, Soviet support for Arab nations, Israel's alliances and domestic policies: these meant that many in the Freedom struggle viewed Israel as an imperialist power. King, the NAACP, and other African American leaders had to contend with that perspective in taking a position on the war. King remained supportive of Israel until his death in April 1968, but not until two months after the 1967 war ended did he reaffirm his commitment to Zionism in an article in the *Saturday Review*.[37] Indeed, King "smarted from criticism that he had abandoned non-violence" by signing the *Times* letter in support of Israel. His most visible Civil Rights and anti-Vietnam Jewish ally, Rabbi Abraham Joshua Heschel, also faced harsh criticism from peace activists for his support of Israel's war; testifying to the conservative turn among American Jews, Heschel's Jewish colleagues at the Jewish Theological Seminary in Manhattan, meanwhile, "further ostracized [him] in their zeal for both wars."[38]

Just as many American Jewish Zionists stood deeply disappointed with King's position, wishing him to be far more visible and vocal in his support for Israel, so too were they increasingly defensive of Israel's actions within the Civil Rights movement after 1967. Many on the left felt dismayed that anticolonialist activists now rejected Zionism and instead favored movements and governments they saw as hostile to Israel's existence: "Now it is the Arab side that has the aura of being a national liberation struggle and a people's war," wrote Jewish activist Sol Stern in the New Left journal *Ramparts*, "with the attention of the international left being focused on the Palestinian guerillas, not on the reactionary Arab governments." For Stern too, with his Jewishness inextricably bound to Zionism, this "shattered for me the unspoken assumptions that there was no conflict between being a Jew and a radical."[39]

American Jewish communal leaders increasingly sought to erase any visible ties between American Zionism and radical left critiques. In 1968, for example, mainstream Jewish leaders invited the members of the socialist Zionist group Hashomer Hatzair to lead New York's Independence Day parade. While members remained lukewarm on the symbolism of the parade, considering it "a bland imitation of the St. Patrick's Day Parade" with participants who "barely knew where Israel was," the group was still emerging from the "outcast status" it held as socialists during the McCarthy era. They felt pleased to showcase "pioneering Israel on the stuffy pavements of Fifth Avenue." But when young members of Hashomer Hatzair decided to march with a red banner to demonstrate their opposition to the Vietnam War, the parade marshals insisted they remove it:

> The shomrim [guards of Hashomer Hatzair] protested that the Betar movement [a right wing student Zionist organization] were marching with rifles,

and they surely could march with their banners. To no avail. The shomrim refused to back down, and at the last minute were taken out of the line of march. The movement attempted to convince the Zionist establishment that it was important to show people that Jews of varying social ideologies could join in support of Zionism, and that it was not a monopoly of mainstream Jewish notables. The message did not get across and the movement was censured for its actions.

While Hashomer Hatzair too struggled to "walk the thin line between criticism of the policies of the Israeli government and the anti-Zionist rhetoric of the New Left," its members issued strong criticisms against those who would not tolerate dissent from the American Zionist "consensus."[40] They rejected the idea that their support for Zionism be unqualified, and also that their Zionism remain exclusive of progressive positions on urgent issues such as the war in Vietnam.

A similar dynamic was at work in mainstream South African Jewish organizations, as seen through their own relationship to South African chapters of Hashomer Hatzair. Funded by South Africa's Zionist Federation beginning in 1935, Hashomer Hatzair's leaders dedicated themselves to socialist Zionism, preparing South African Jewish youth to live on kibbutzim. At first these ideas and practices aligned well with the larger, mainstream Jewish community. Members of the movement believed that the socialist struggle for social justice was to be fought in Israel, supporting collectivism through the kibbutz movement. But the apartheid system presented an abiding challenge to these individuals. The choice was this: "to be Zionists and socialists or to remain in South Africa and join the revolutionary struggle of the blacks [sic] against their white oppressors."[41] The radical teachings of the movement meant that they "slowly learned to relate to the blacks [sic] as equals."[42] But members of the mainstream South African Jewish community began to look askance at the movement, which they felt was tainted by the communist influences of the ANC.[43]

Those on the Zionist left had long lamented the increasing conservatism of South African Jews. Nearly a decade earlier, *Israel Horizons* editors observed the "increasing number of South African Jews" who "appear to be changing their political loyalties...to the National pro-apartheid party."[44] By 1970, South African Jewish leaders saw Hashomer Hatzair as outside the consensus of the community, and closed its doors in South Africa for good.

In addition to their impact on American and South African Jewry, developments of the late 1960s had profound implications for Israel's relationship with apartheid South Africa. Scholar Sasha Polakow-Suransky carefully documents Israel's fall from international favor after the Six-Day War and its subsequent quest for new allies. The decision of Charles De Gaulle of France to cool relations with Israel played a crucial role in motivating that quest.[45] The closure of the Suez Canal for eight years following the war, as Israel and Egypt continued to fight in the Sinai Peninsula, deprived East African nations of large amounts of revenue while it benefited the trade of South Africa. This too created deep tension and resentment, and led many

Africans and African allies to blame Israel for what they saw as its colonialist stance.[46]

Cold War alliances also pushed Israel toward closer relations with apartheid South Africa. Israel was seen as an "outpost of the West" in an "unstable" area under threat from Soviet influence. "For some time Israel's policy of cultivating [B]lack African nations was resented," wrote Cyrus Leo Sulzberger, longtime foreign correspondent for the *New York Times*, in 1971. "Now this has been forgotten in the belief that Israel's stand against Russia and Russian proxies at this continent's extreme north helps prepare a position for a similar stand, if need be, when the day for such comes to the extreme south." Preparing for the "hot" war to follow the Cold War's alliances and tensions, South Africa cultivated Israel as an ally.

Sulzberger was also quick to point out that this alliance served South Africa in another way: "Among foreign critics of South African policy there are many Jewish voices, especially in the United States and Britain. South Africa therefore feels that if Israel is sympathetic this will help its own international standing."[47] According to Sulzberger, South Africa's alliance with Israel served in part as a public relations move intended to counterbalance a conspicuously large Jewish presence in the global antiapartheid movement (though mostly outside of Jewish organizations).

Organized South African Jewry sought this same counterbalance through another means: by seeking out friends among American Jews through public relations work. In late 1966, for example, Gus Saron, general secretary of the SAJBD, delivered lectures on a tour of major American Jewish organizations; he returned "gratified by the universally sympathetic reception given to his explications of the South African community's situation and the Board's policy."[48] As Israel and the United States formed a Cold War alliance with South Africa, affiliated Jews in South Africa began to cultivate Jewish friends in the United States in order to bolster their own image. As discussed in the following chapter, South Africa needed friends. As affiliated American Jews withdrew from universalist commitments, they accepted these overtures of friendship in the name of Jewish unity.

The final implication of the Six-Day War related to Jewish encounters with apartheid, then, was that it prompted fiercely emotional debates within the American Jewish community. Opinions about Jewish unity and continuity often divided along the lines of politics and generation. American Jewish organizations had their own anxieties about making friends and indeed members out of younger American Jews. The liberation movements of the 1950s and 1960s, along with class mobility, assimilation, and shifting Jewish organizational priorities, contributed to the alienation of Jewish youth from mainstream Jewish organizations. The growth of the Jewish counterculture stood as testimony to that, as did the fears of declining numbers of young Jews in Jewish organizations.

Mainstream Jewish groups could see the writing on the wall with these developments. They feared the Jewish communal world would "lose" this younger generation. In September 1968, the umbrella organization of American Jewish organizations, the NJCRAC, held a "Reassessment Conference on Combating Anti-Semitism Today." Jewish leaders took seriously anti-Semitism in the New Left, and feared its implications for young Jews, especially in light of their anticolonialist activism. Black Nationalism, Israel, the Soviet Union, and Arab nations' influences all factored into a distressing portrait:

> Among some on the New Left and in some militant Negro circles credence is given to the Soviet and Arab propaganda that American Jews control the government of the United States, which at their bidding maintains Israel as an outpost of American imperialism, threatening the independence of Asian and African nations. The charge is compatible with the general thesis of the New Left that America is embarked upon a course of aggressive capitalist imperialism and all its policies are supportive of that aggressive design. Jews are viewed—even by some of the Jewish young people who are adherents of the movement—as part of the structure of political and social power that supports that design.

These leaders took note of "the efforts of Communist and Arab propagandists to foment anti-Semitism in the United States by seeking to create sentiment against Israel." New Left anti-Semitism arose from an acceptance of the "Arab propaganda view of the role of Israel on the world scene and of the relationship of American Jews to that role."[49]

By their lights, young, Jewish members of the New Left were in a precarious position if they grew to reject the "unique relationship," the "spiritual tie" of American Jews to the fate and welfare of Israel. With Zionism central to the mission of American Jewish leaders, they deeply feared a "generation gap" that would make Zionism and their own organizations irrelevant to a new generation of American Jews.

Their suggestions amounted to listening to these young Jews, allowing them to discuss their criticisms of Israel and imperialism—referencing Israel's ties to South Africa only indirectly. The generation gap "can be bridged in part by welcoming and involving young people into the structured activities of the Jewish community," the study's authors wrote, "affording opportunities for dissent, in the course of which their views are given attentive hearing." The "summary of major findings" of this conference focused mainly on latent anti-Semitism in the United States. Given near-equal attention, however, was the "heightened polarization on many issues," the fact that "Jewish young people, in their alienation, are caught up in the radical antagonism." For "the advancement of Jewish continuity," the "entire Jewish community must be involved in the community relations effort."[50]

Other experts in the Jewish community attested to this same desperate need in this new era.[51] For as Stuart Svonkin writes, after World War II, "Jewishness and Americanism were equal and [complementary] commitments" for Jewish activists of all ages balancing their Jewish affiliations with commitments to civil liberties and Civil Rights. The Jews of the 1960s protest movements, however, encountered a very different landscape, with Jewish agencies focused, in the main, almost exclusively on issues internal to Jewish life. Some found these agencies out of touch and irrelevant to their own lives. Some turned their energy toward expressions of Judaism and liberation on their own terms in the Jewish counterculture, or in the case of Jewish women, in Jewish feminist groups that could embrace feminism and Zionism as ideologies of liberation. Others remained a part of broader, global liberation campaigns. Svonkin contends that the "Jewishness" of these later activists was "subsumed or marginal to their 'American' politics."[52] Svonkin and other scholars conclude that Jews who remained in anticolonialist campaigns—now seen as compromised by anti-Zionism and anti-Semitism—did not link their Jewishness to their activism.

Missing from these accounts, however, are the words of antiapartheid activists who saw their activism as expressions of Jewish values and their own Jewish identities. They are difficult to find in Jewish agencies' publications in the late 1960s, and they virtually disappeared from those publications by the 1970. In the eyes of Jewish leaders who stressed Jewish unity and consensus, these were American Jews who chose universalism—as antiapartheid activism—over Jewish particularism and loyalty.

Brief biographies of antiapartheid activists here and in later sections of this study demonstrate alternative narratives of American Jewish history. In these narratives, American Jews engage global issues—including apartheid and Zionism—as Jews. Forced to choose between antiapartheid and Jewishness, they remain committed to both. These narratives demonstrate the distance between American Jews' priorities and the priorities of mainstream American Jewish organizations, just as Jewish encounters with apartheid continued to reveal the unresolved tensions between Jewish particularism and universalist campaigns for justice.

Arthur Waskow

Born in 1933, Arthur Waskow grew up in what he refers to as a "Jewish ghetto" in Baltimore, surrounded by parents and grandparents whose liberal political consciousness was profoundly shaped by the Holocaust. They were activists and unionists. Waskow wrote his doctoral dissertation on the history of the 1919 race riots and shortly after joined the Civil Rights and peace movements. He worked for the antiapartheid movement through his membership in Students for a Democratic Society (SDS), which critiqued American racism and imperialism domestically and globally. In 1965, SDS began targeting Chase Manhattan Bank for its loans to the apartheid regime in South Africa, loans that aided the government in recovering from its isolation after the Sharpeville Massacre. Collaborating with students from the Union Theological Seminary, Waskow and other SDS members—with Waskow as "probably the oldest member of SDS at the time"—protested on the steps of the bank in that year.[53] Police came and arrested the group, marking Waskow's second of a career's worth of police arrests at protests for justice.[54] Members of the American Committee on Africa, sponsors of the

Africa Freedom Day discussed in chapter 2, then coordinated a broader campaign against banks that provided loans to South Africa, and they invited Waskow onto the board. He remained a part of the antiapartheid movement until 1969, when he turned his attention largely to progressive currents in the American Jewish religious world.[55]

Although Waskow never considered himself a Zionist, like many Jewish activists, he departed from the New Left at the 1967 National Conference for New Politics, after several leaders adopted an anti-Israel resolution proposed by the nationalist Black Caucus. He later traveled to Israel, as well as the Occupied Palestinian Territories.

Throughout this period, Waskow's ties to the Civil Rights movement remained strong. After the assassination of Dr Martin Luther King in April 1968, with his hometown of Washington DC "occupied" by the United States army, Waskow authored the *Freedom Seder*, a book of ritual for the Jewish holiday of Passover that linked the Jewish liberation in ancient Egypt to the liberation of African Americans and other oppressed peoples throughout the world. The New Left journal *Ramparts* first published the text. Waskow recalls that 800 people attended that first Freedom Seder, held in the basement of Reverend Channing Phillips's African American church on the first anniversary of King's assassination: 400 white Jews and 400 Christians, about half of them African American.[56] Phillips coofficiated the seder with Rabbi Balfour Brickner of the Reform Movement, a Civil Rights, antiwar, and antiapartheid activist.[57]

By the mid-1970s, Waskow began to devote himself full time to the Jewish Renewal movement, an alternative to mainstream, denominational Judaism that seeks to transform it through its "distinctive blending of spirituality and a liberatory political vision." Waskow links prophetic Judaism explicitly to the many movements for social and racial justice to which he remains dedicated.[58] He continues to refer back to that 1969 gathering as a sign of a continuing Black/Jewish alliance, despite the pressures and tensions brought to bear by both local and global developments. Although his positions on issues have earned him biting criticisms from other Jewish leaders—especially his early embrace of a two-state solution to the Israeli/Palestinian conflict in the progressive organization New Jewish Agenda—he still sees his Jewishness as "absolutely at the root" of all of his activism.[59]

Peter Weiss

Peter Weiss first invited Arthur Waskow onto the board of ACOA. Like Waskow, he was a vocal critic of those who argued that Jewish allegiance required departing the Civil Rights movement after 1967. A progressive Jewish leader active in Civil Rights and African independence work, Weiss challenged the idea that American Jews should "abrogate or reduce" their "historical commitment" to the Civil Rights movement.[60] In late 1967, editors of the American Jewish Congress newsletter invited him to write about the state of the Black/Jewish alliance. As someone with a foot in the worlds of Jewish life and international development in Africa, Weiss offered an informed perspective on this issue.

Born in 1925, Weiss grew up in a Zionist household in Austria. His father was a member of Kadima, an early Zionist student organization. After briefly joining the right wing Zionist organization Betar as a teenager—this in 1941, when his family moved to the United States—Weiss veered leftward, to the socialist Zionist movement of Hashomer Hatzair. He attended Yale Law School and practiced law from 1955 to 2006, dividing his time between representing multinational companies, specializing in trademark law, and doing *pro bono* work in the fields of human rights, constitutional law, and nuclear weapons law. One of the founders, and later president, of the American Committee on Africa, Weiss founded and was then executive director of the International Development Placement Association, a precursor of the Peace Corps.[61]

With deep connections to the Civil Rights movement, Weiss began his piece in the American Jewish Congress 1967 newsletter by roundly dismissing the idea that Jews should abandon the Civil Rights movement because some of its leaders took anti-Israel positions. He termed this "patently absurd," "politically unwise and morally indefensible." But Weiss elaborated by deliberating on the arguments presented by American Jews wishing to abandon the Movement. He began with a balanced assessment of the turn to militancy among some Black leaders—quite logical, he concluded, given the inability of the nation's "'power structure' to deal with the basic problem of inequality in America." These failures, Weiss asserted, meant that Jews "have a duty to continue, if not redouble, their efforts to achieve justice for all Americans."

Responding to those who saw all critiques of Israel as pernicious and threatening, Weiss termed it "a misleading equation" to say that anti-Israel attitudes were one and the same as anti-Semitism. He identified himself as a Zionist, and then noted the many criticisms he himself had leveled at Israel: of its "Cold War alignments, her treatment of Arabs and black Jews, her reluctance to go further than she has in making concrete proposals for the settlement of the refugee question." And then asked: "Am I anti-Semitic?" Here Weiss echoed the formulations of other liberal and left Jews such as Leonard Fein who tried to guide Israeli policy toward a realization of full democracy. Drawing once again on Israel's progressive credentials—as a haven for refugees, a beacon of democracy in the Middle East—Weiss saw Israel as the nation that responded to independent Africa's requests when much of the West would not grant these nations a hearing.

Weiss also explicated the turn to Soviet power and influence among African and African American leaders who had attempted to work with the West to no avail. It is "garbled morality," Weiss states, to "turn against the black movement because it is looking for allies in unapproved places."[62] He likened that logic to the "garbled morality" that underpinned American Cold War foreign policy: "'Ask not whether a man's cause is just, ask only whether he is with us or with them.'" He also likened it to the logic that underpinned the silence of Jews and Jewish groups on the Vietnam War, as they feared that speaking out on Vietnam might cause the president to "vent his displeasure on Israel."[63] In the same breath, then, Weiss criticized the Cold Warrior logic that gave no heed to complicated, realpolitik contexts and the American Jewish tendency to prioritize Israel above all other pressing global concerns. In short, he rejected the either/or proposition given to American Jews who worked for radical causes. His own relationship to the African American community, to Civil Rights, and anticolonialism, demonstrated that rejection.

Weiss's friend Ossie Davis, actor and activist, took the long view of the Black/Jewish alliance in a 1969 speech to an audience of liberal and left Zionists who saw Israel as the product of Jewish liberation.[64] Davis spoke of the passing of the old alliance of African Americans and Jews, which was based on the belief "that this was a good and wonderful country which could be reformed, which could be manipulated, which could be appealed to, to solve the problems and pressing needs of a crying community of dispossessed peoples." Like Weiss, he pointed to the fact that "the appeals went basically unheeded; [and] we have not solved the problems."

Davis explained the ebbing of the Black/Jewish alliance even as he drew urgent attention to the signs that a "new alliance" was needed in a "new context" in which a nation "makes a great deal of money in a war which is despised by more and more of its people...lets its inner cities rot and deteriorate...[and] in which more and more votes in its elections [are] for men like George Wallace." In a nation such as this, Davis asserted, young activists turned away from an alliance with the middle class and toward an alliance with the Third World; and then these activists embraced a new definition of Zionism, seeing Israel as a "representative, or as a friend, or as a member of the inner-club, the capitalist club."

Instead, Davis expressed his admiration for an older definition of Zionism, linking Black liberation to Jewish liberation with the founding of Israel. He universalized the persecution and liberation of Jews and other peoples across the world. He expressed his earnest admiration for Jews who had found their Jerusalem, had found "out of their vast experience and their suffering" the place that marked "the end for which history set us in motion thousands of years ago." Using spiritual language, Davis urged Jews to see the forces that had oppressed both their community and that of African Americans. "We, too, seek our Jerusalem," he said, and made a plea for understanding the passion, the "ruthless and brutal" treatment given "to those who we think stand in the way, to those who would not understand." Underlying those sentiments, Davis explained, was deep "pathos." He urged his Jewish audience to have the "pity, have the forbearance, to remember that you were Jews longer than we were."[65]

Taken together, Weiss and Davis's writings offer arguments informed by passionate commitments to struggles for justice. The treatment both received in those years testified to the very dynamics, the divergent definitions of Zionism, which made a continuing and effective Black/Jewish alliance increasingly untenable.

Weiss's politics also made his position in mainstream Jewish organizations increasingly untenable. He thought of himself as "always on the fringes" of the Jewish community, though he "never felt any problems" in embracing Zionism and working to end apartheid simultaneously. But by the late 1960s, he had been removed from the speakers' list of the American Jewish Congress: "Golda Meir had me fired," he recalls, "because I was using the term 'Palestinian' prematurely."[66]

In 1960, Milton Himmelfarb famously asked if the American Jewish Congress was "a Jewish organization with a civil rights program or a civil rights organization whose members are Jews." [67] By the late 1960s, though the characterization may have still fit, leaders of the liberal AJCongress would not grant space for critiques such as Weiss's. Weiss could no longer serve as one of its public representatives. Soon after, he stopped working with the AJCongress altogether, as they began to work from the perspective of "Israel: right or wrong," with no room for opposition to Israel's policies.[68] In 1992, after several years as a member of the Israel-based International Center for Peace in the Middle East, he joined Americans for Peace Now, an American Jewish Zionist organization founded as the sister organization to Shalom Achshav, Israel's peace movement. Weiss sits on the board with Leonard Fein and others dedicated to Israeli-Palestinian and Israeli-Arab peace.

Ossie Davis was an outspoken advocate of Civil Rights and anticolonialism movements, including antiapartheid. Years later, he joined his wife, actor and author Ruby Dee, along with Harry Belafonte, Arthur Ashe, Tony Randall, Gregory Hines, and others to form Artists and Athletes against Apartheid.[69] For speaking out in favor and occasionally in defense of American Jews and Israel, Ossie Davis was viciously attacked as a tool of whites (including organized Jewry) in the pages of *Liberator*, a Black Nationalist magazine.[70]

As leader of the ACOA, Weiss also soon found himself in a controversy that cut right to the heart of debates over the role of Israel in the Black/Jewish alliance, and indeed over each community's set of priorities. It placed Israel and South Africa, Jewishness and apartheid, at the center of a raging debate among African Americans, American Jews, and liberal activists of all backgrounds.

On June 28, 1970, a full-page advertisement in the *New York Times* sparked a tremendous firestorm among and between African Americans and American Jews. Titled "An Appeal by Black Americans for United States Support to Israel," the ad listed the signatures of seventy African Americans who called for American support for Israel—specifically in the form of military jets. The signers included leaders of the National Association for the Advancement of Colored People, the National Urban League, Congressional and other political leaders. Bayard Rustin, Civil Rights leader and the chief organizer of the 1963 March on Washington, initiated the advertisement, describing it as holding "extraordinary moral and political significance." Citing Jewish support for the recent African American nominee for Lieutenant Governor of New York State, Rustin asserted that "the traditional Negro-Jewish alliance for social justice still prevails." "Blacks should support Israel's right to exist for the same reasons that they have struggled for freedom and equality in this country."[71] While activists now introduced Israel and Zionism into the Black/Jewish equation, then, South Africa was not yet invoked.

Although Rustin and his allies saw the appeal as a moral act, respecting a long-standing alliance by supporting a Jewish liberation movement in Zionism, Black Nationalists in the United States expressed their anger at what some called "an unforgivable act of treason against our people."[72] Calling the signers opportunistic, a leader of the Pan African Congress responded to the ad in the pages of *Liberator*: "Any Black man anywhere in the world who advocates the support of Israel is advocating support for the enemies of all African people." Like many in Third World movements, he drew parallels among Israel, the United States, and South Africa, as each one was an "artificial white settler state." Above all, he claimed solidarity with Arab peoples, displaced from Israel, as with Africans, displaced and "enslaved" in South Africa.[73]

Frustrated with the pace of change in the American Civil Rights movement and with continuing inequality, distressed at the alliances between Israel and South Africa, some African Americans outside of Black Nationalist organizations also articulated these perspectives. One of them was Charles Hightower, Washington director of the American Committee on Africa. Hightower caused a crisis in his organization when he sent a letter on ACOA letterhead, using his ACOA title, to some of the signers of the appeal for Israel, criticizing their actions. "This is to express my profound opposition and outrage brought about by your signature to the statement," Hightower began. He vigorously protested the idea that Israel was "related" to the "world-wide movement for social justice."

Hightower's anger testified to the shifting sympathies of American radicals, especially African Americans, and reached back to Dr King's silence on Israel's victory in 1967 and the opposition of several NAACP board members to supporting Israel in that war. As his first piece of evidence, though, Hightower invoked information relatively new to public conversations about Israel that would have a profound effect on American Jews and their Cold War encounters with apartheid and Zionism: he cited "the fact that Israel is supported by South Africa." He listed Israel's treatment of people in its Occupied Territories, its "social exploitation" of "dark-skinned Sephardic Jews of Oriental heritage." Hightower wrote of his admiration for the "Arab revolution," which he identified as "a movement to improve the social, economic, and political existences for these peoples."[74]

Some of the ACOA board members objected to Hightower's stand and insisted that he write to each recipient of his letter, clarifying that he spoke for himself and not for the organization. As head of the steering committee, Peter Weiss responded to Hightower. He began with what he termed a "parenthetical" statement, noting that he too thought the ad was "inaccurate, stupid, and not helpful either to the cause of Israel or to that of peace in the Middle East."[75] He found the letter far too strident in its unqualified support for Israel.[76] Weiss was deeply connected to Civil Rights and anticolonialist movements. Indeed, he served as the contact to Bayard Rustin on the matter,[77] and wrote of his personal familiarity with an Israeli politician mentioned by Hightower in his letter of protest.[78] Weiss (on behalf of his fellow board members) advised Hightower to write to each recipient of his original letter and clarify that his statements reflected his views alone—not those of ACOA. Three days later, Hightower sent off these letters of clarification.[79]

The board called a special meeting to discuss the topic. Professor Richard P. Stevens of Lincoln University, who wrote about Israel and Zionism, sat on the ACOA board, but because he could not attend the special meeting he composed a thoughtful letter grounded in his research about Israel, South African apartheid, and the African American Freedom struggle. For Stevens, Hightower's letter raised issues that "must be explored" by the ACOA and other likeminded groups, especially the tendency among younger Blacks to "insist on carrying forth in a more total way the identification of forces which seem to stand in the way of Black liberation everywhere." With his letter to the ACOA, Stevens sent two essays he published in 1969 under the title "Zionism, South Africa and Apartheid: The Paradoxical Triangle." He pinpointed the Zionism of South African Jews as the primary reason for their silence on apartheid, and documented the growing closeness between Israel and the ruling South African regime. Stevens suggested that this might lead younger Black men and women in the Movement to "single out" Jews and Israel "for attack."[80] Tapping directly into the long-standing tension between American Jews' particularist unity and universalist commitments, Stevens cautioned the ACOA not to dismiss the powerful sentiments that threatened liberal white opinion, and especially the American Jewish/Black alliance.

Stevens sensed a road diverging, and felt that the ACOA, like other organizations, might have to choose between any sympathy with Zionism on one hand, and broader Third World alliances on the other. He called out what he saw as hypocrisy on the part of the original letter's signers. "I find it personally incredible that it should appear in June 1970 that the concern of Black American 'leadership' should be Israel and not Africa," he wrote, "Could we expect the Zionist organization of America to take out an advertisement condemning Britain for arming South Africa? If so, then Black Americans might have adequate reason to support Zionism; if not, should the concern of Blacks move in support of Israel? Young militants are asking these questions."

Like leaders of many social groups, including American Jews, Stevens had detected a "generational and ideological gap" between leaders and "the younger element": "Among younger Blacks, the inclination to view their struggle more in terms of 'liberation' and 'Third World' identification is more pronounced." Addressing leaders of the ACOA, including Peter Weiss, Stevens said that the ACOA ignored these issues at their peril. The stakes of the choice were high, he admitted: "We need Black community support," he wrote. "We also need money. Perhaps we cannot have both; if not, we all stand to lose."[81]

* * *

Stevens's observations spoke to a growing rift between African Americans and Jews, as political sympathies diverged and leaders prioritized new agendas after 1967. Ultimately ACOA leadership acknowledged that conditions in Israel and South Africa had severely strained older Black-Jewish alliances already imperiled by the everyday, neighborhood experiences of African Americans and Jews in urban encounters, in merchant-customer and landlord-tenant relationships. Jewish ACOA board members Waskow and Weiss offer a snapshot of Jewish contributions to the antiapartheid movement, of those who did not withdraw their commitments to anticolonialism, to Civil Rights and antiapartheid, after 1967. They held on to those commitments alongside their critiques of, and dedication to, Israel.

These Jewish activists further stressed American Jewish intracommunal relationships already strained by Civil Rights and the Vietnam War. One telling example lies in the American Jewish Congress's petition to the American government to deny American landing rights to South African Airways because of apartheid. Although rejecting anticolonialist critiques of Israel such as those offered by Peter Weiss, the AJCongress felt safe on this global, anticolonialist platform, and wrote to support the recommendation of Representative Charles C. Diggs of Michigan. As chair of the House Foreign Affairs Subcommittee on Africa, Diggs had "pressed the Civil Aeronautics Board to re-examine its decision to give South African Airways" landing rights in the United States. The Black press voiced its support for Diggs's recommendation: "South African Airways: The tourism you promote is racism. Racism is not welcome here."[82]

The new air route flew between Johannesburg and New York via Rio de Janeiro—and would later aid the SAJBD in flying American Jews to South Africa to court their friendship and political support. But Rabbi Joachim Prinz, who decades earlier protested South Africa's membership in the WJC, now protested the State Department's decision to ignore Rep. Diggs's recommendation. Prinz declared it "self-evidently against public policy to grant an economic reward to an airline which is an agency of the South African government and thereby inescapably implicated in official policies of racial discrimination and persecution."[83]

This move sparked further controversy among American Jews. Although now in an entirely new context—no longer the immediate postwar world, but now one of the American ethnic revival, the Cold War, Vietnam, and other global liberation struggles—these controversies engaged rivals in an old battle of universalism and particularism, of moral campaigns for racial justice and calls for Jewish solidarity and unity.

Samuel Wang, a Holocaust refugee, Orthodox American Jew, Zionist leader, and later a resident of Hebron, Israel, spoke out in a *New York Times* advertisement he bought. He denied that the AJCongress was "a Congress"—as it was "self-appointed"—and said further that it was "in essence, not Jewish." Specifically, he accused the Congress of acting "contrary to Jewish interests" because it placed South African Jewry in peril. "The South African Jews who are noted for their devotion to the cause of Jewry and who are in the forefront with their contribution to Jewish world needs, surely deserve more concern from responsible Jewish organizations."[84]

Finally, in an increasingly popular attempt to unveil the hypocrisy of the Congress in singling out Israel, Wang linked the Holocaust and the Cold War to Jewish interests by invoking the plight of Soviet Jewry:

> Whatever the wrongs of "Apartheit," there can be no gainsay that no one has a right to play noble at the expense of others as you did with your anti-South African appearance. It is distinctly puzzling why you singled out the Union of South Africa for an attack and ignored the ruthless dictatorship of Soviet Russia and its brand of oppression, practicing spiritual genocide against Russian Jewry. Why did you fail to petition the U.S. not to grant landing rights to the Soviet's Aero Flo[a]t? As an organization, you are, of course, entitled to appear as champions for and against all causes. But in the name of ethical responsibility, and Jewish conscience, please do not wrap yourself in a Jewish banner when you indulge in campaigns which may harm Jews.[85]

Both Prinz and Wang felt they were acting on Jewish interests, out of Jewish values. These debates had as their foundation the WJC membership controversies of the 1950s: who speaks for world Jewry, for American Jewry, and what responsibility do global Jewish communities have for one another and for other populations?

Indeed, in that same year the WJC renewed the debate about South Africa's becoming a full-fledged member. Once again, as in the 1950s, the debate became one over South African apartheid and the mandate of the United Nations. But this time, as Adam Mendelsohn writes, "the political price of chaperoning the Board [the South African Jewish Board of Deputies] vastly increased as the anti-apartheid movement gained momentum. Association with South Africa became a potential liability."[86]

Maurice Perlzweig, representing the WJC, remained steadfast in trying to have his organization represent "the whole of organized Jewry," and saw that desire as "doing no more than adopting to our own situation the doctrine of universality which is becoming increasingly influential in the United Nations." But he saw adhering to that doctrine as difficult in light of particularist commitments to Jewish survival: this meant that the WJC must "seek to protect the rights and status of Jewish communities, as well, of course, the Jewish State, but that it must seek to make a Jewish contribution to the advancement of humanity as a whole in its striving for peace, justice, and freedom. We cannot overlook the fact that this second principle may superficially come into conflict with the first." The "moral difficulties" of the WJC emerged, he wrote, because in seeking South African Jewish membership, its leaders had to acknowledge that "silence is itself an act." Invoking a popular equation, he wrote that Soviet and Arab representatives accused the WJC of "engaging in political work in support of apartheid," and that accusation threatened the status of the WJC as an NGO.

Still, Perlzweig believed that considering South African membership in the WJC was "a risk which in my opinion we ought to take."[87] Even as South Africa grew more isolated on the world stage, desperately needing friends, Perlzweig prioritized Jewish communities and Jewish unity, seeing it as the most effective strategy toward a healthy future for modern Jewish life.

In the postwar era, and especially after 1967, choices motivated by the goal of Jewish particularist unity produced, perhaps ironically, more divisiveness within American Jewry. This chapter suggests the broad outlines of local and global events that shattered the sort of alliances that might have led to a more decisive response to South African apartheid among American Jews. The cost of an indecisive response was indeed quite high: it created tensions and ruptures between African Americans and Jews, between Jews and the New Left, and among Jews of all ages and on all parts of the political spectrum. Importantly, the shifting alliances described in this chapter also further complicated American Jews' views on Israel.

The chapters that follow will chronicle the impact of other local and global events, forces, and movements that rippled through the American Jewish community in the years of the Cold War. American Jewish positions on South African apartheid continued to shape and be shaped by these developments, as apartheid played a pivotal role in the Cold War politics of American Jewish organizations and individuals.

4

"SOUTH AFRICA NEEDS FRIENDS":
COLD WAR NARRATIVES AND
COUNTERNARRATIVES

In his study of the Iran hostage crisis of the 1970s, historian David Farber writes that an exclusive focus on Cold War politics meant that many involved in the crisis "saw Soviet Red and not Islamic Green." Farber convincingly argues that the United States paid a heavy price for such a narrow vision of global events, in which, as Peter Weiss noted in the previous chapter, nations were either with us or against us. Blinded to the full context in which this struggle unfolded, Reagan and other leaders allowed Islamic fundamentalism to grow unchecked.[1] Shortsighted American Cold War politics proved pivotal to the Middle East and to South Africa. President Ronald Reagan justified continuing American support of apartheid South Africa, for example, because he viewed that nation as a bulwark against communism. In addition, given that South Africa's apartheid regime became increasingly linked to Israel, debates over support for Israel, both financial and spiritual, hinged on approaches to South Africa. Indeed, the very painful history of the 1975 United Nations resolution equating Zionism with racism cannot be divorced from these Cold War battles and alliances; nor can the responses to the 1976 visit of South African Prime Minister John Vorster, former Nazi supporter, to Israel. Utilizing a litmus test that lasted for decades, many American Jews saw any discussion of Israeli or Jewish engagement with Palestinian rights or with the Palestine Liberation Organization (PLO) as a clear sign of communist influence, Jewish self-hatred, and danger for Israel's and Jews' existence. Indeed, these accusations led to the demise of several liberal and left Jewish organizations. They also complicated the American visit of South African Anglican Archbishop Desmond Tutu, in 1987, and nearly derailed Jewish celebrations of Nelson Mandela's visit with New York Jewish leaders as late as 1990.

Those events highlight the powerful impact of apartheid and Middle East/African politics on the Black/Jewish alliance, as both diasporic groups struggled to balance their priorities in the Cold War era.[2] Some scholars see this controversy as the high point of tensions long brewing over other issues: foreign assistance to Israel at the cost of domestic antipoverty programs that had profound effects on African Americans, who were disproportionately represented in poor America; growing disagreement between Black and Jewish Americans over affirmative action and quotas; and, importantly, Israel's commercial and military ties to South Africa.

Indeed, from the perspective of Jews combating apartheid, the rise of Cold War militarism not only strained—some would say broke—the Black/Jewish alliance, but poisoned mainstream Jewish support for the United Nations, further divided American and other Western Jews, alienated many Jewish feminists and other activists, and made a peaceful resolution to the Israeli/Palestinian conflict feel ever more out of reach.

Since World War II, Western Jews spoke of Jewish unity and the Jewish future as primary, motivating concerns that at times kept them from taking strong stands on issues like Civil Rights and apartheid. Perlzweig and others who came to use this language cited the Holocaust, arguing that the Jewish future depended on Jews' working together—and that meant not criticizing each other across national boundaries, and often not criticizing Israel at all. Ultimately, and perhaps ironically in this period, those who spoke of Jewish unity gave voice to blistering criticisms of other Jews. Their language reveals the very high stakes of these disagreements, as many felt they had to choose between Israel and Jewish invisibility, between undiluted Jewish loyalty and universalist campaigns for justice.

This chapter travels to the world stage, aiming to see the impact of global Cold War battles at home. South African apartheid had long proven to be its own litmus test for American Jews' willingness to link their identities as Jews to universalist crusades. Immediately after the war, these debates occurred among a small group of elite, white, male Jewish leaders, and focused on Western Jews'—and especially American Jews'—relationships with apartheid South Africa. Apartheid remained intricately tangled up in questions of Jewish loyalty, but now these questions engaged Jews throughout the world in their connection to Israel. As Israel's ties to South Africa grew more visible, more left and liberal American Jews spoke publicly about their fidelity to the state of Israel and their opposition to the oppression of Black South Africans and Palestinians.

* * *

ISRAEL AND SOUTH AFRICA, JEWS AND AFRICAN AMERICANS

After 1967, when Civil Rights and Third World movement activists spoke of American support for Israel, they increasingly mentioned Israel's support of apartheid through its commercial and military ties to South Africa. They measured the policies most beneficial to Black Americans and Black Africans up against Israel's policies and found a wide chasm of separation. Apartheid and support for apartheid South Africa thus loomed large in the growing critiques of America's Cold War foreign policy commitments.

In November 1970, in response to the June "Appeal by Black Americans for United States Support to Israel" published in the *New York Times*, prominent African American leaders published a counterletter in the same paper, titled "An Appeal by Black Americans Against United States Support of The Zionist Government of Israel." Union leaders, activists, artists, and educators—including the ACOA's Charles Hightower, whom Peter Weiss had reprimanded for his personal responses to the initial June letter—expressed "complete solidarity with our Palestinian Brothers and Sisters who like us, are struggling for self-determination and an end to racist oppression." Asserting that they were "anti-Zionist" and "not anti-Jewish," the signers viewed Israel as "an outpost of American imperialism." They linked South Africa to other sites of anticolonialist struggle, seeing Vietnam, Laos, and Brazil as in line with "anticolonial revolution" struggles in South Africa and Zimbabwe/Rhodesia; they also linked Israel to South Africa as "privileged white settler states" tied by arms trade and military training.[3]

South Africa grew increasingly central to conversations about Israel after Israel faced another military attack in 1973. Egypt and Syria's full-scale military assault against Israel, in which these nations attempted to retake territories lost in 1967, caught Israel off guard on Yom Kippur, the holiest day of the Jewish calendar. After two days of serious losses, Israel received over twenty thousand tons of weaponry from the United States and went on to win the war. American Secretary of State Henry Kissinger and his Soviet counterparts negotiated the ceasefire in Moscow on October 21. Kissinger later negotiated an end to the Oil Embargo, begun by Arab members of the Organization of Petroleum Exporting Countries (OPEC), which reduced and then cut oil exports to the United States and other nations in protest over support for Israel in the war.

In the words of Sasha Polakow-Suransky, the 1973 Yom Kippur War in Israel brought about "The Rise of Realpolitik" as Israel "realigned" itself with South Africa. Although Israel attempted to hold onto its Black African allies after 1967, critics of these alliances increasingly likened support for Black African nations with support for Arab leaders and for communism, and thus with the forces that sought to destroy Israel.[4]

Leaders now cited new historical analogies, the emerging counternarratives to Meir's comparisons of Black African nations' liberation with Zionism, as the foundation of the new bonds between Israel and South Africa. Both Israel and white South Africa had defeated an imperial power, with "terrorist infiltration across the border" and "enemies bent on their destruction."[5] Israel's closure of the Suez Canal, which greatly angered Black Africa and its allies, transformed South Africa into a crucial trade location. In the 1970s, the United States had a few moments when its support of Israel lagged—most notably in 1975—leaving Israel feeling vulnerable and setting the scene for its growing partnership with South Africa.

Finally, Israel and South Africa traded arms in the name of defeating the Soviet threat. "After the Six-Day War, Israel's alliances throughout black Africa had been tenuous," writes Polakow-Suransky. "After the Yom Kippur

War [in 1973]...the African strategy so carefully crafted by Golda Meir and Abba Eban was left in tatters."[6] Those in the budding Cold War alliances among newly independent Black and Arab states and the Soviet Union opposed the American-supported military actions of Israel. The sum total of these actions left Israel's overtures to Black Africa in the distant and irretrievable past.

Like the Six-Day War of 1967, the impact of the Yom Kippur War on debates over apartheid among Jews in South Africa, Israel, and the United States cannot be overstated. Dedicated Zionists in a nation where group identity was paramount, affiliated South African Jews felt pleased with the post–Yom Kippur War alliance. Knowledge of the vast trade in weapons went largely unheeded, as "uncovering the full extent of Israel's military cooperation with the forces upholding white supremacy under apartheid would have created intolerable cognitive dissonance."[7] South African Jewish and governmental leaders warmed to Israel as a new ally.[8]

As in the United States, political fault lines in South Africa often fell along generational divides during the 1970s. Some Jewish college students protested the priorities of the established Jewish community, in this case objecting to the SAJBD's silence on apartheid. In 1972, representatives of the National Jewish Students' Association walked out of the Board's National Congress when Congress members refused to pass a resolution that "denounced all forms of discrimination based on race, color, or religion." That summer, Jewish students at Cape Town University used their magazine, *Strike*, to publish a call for "our representative communal organizations...to take a stand on moral issues in South Africa." Their research dispelled the myth that members of the Jewish community treated Black South Africans better than other whites did—that Jewish employers gave Black workers better wages, better terms of employment.[9] Many young South Africans began to identify less with the Zionism of Jewish particularism and more with the universalistic language of the antiapartheid movement. In that movement, there were older, radical activists of Jewish descent who had long since cut ties to the Jewish community and whose anti-Zionism was grounded in their dedication to class politics, anticolonialism, and antinationalism. Many of these adult South African Jewish antiapartheid activists embraced radicalism and not Jewish affiliation, rejecting the silence of organized South African Jewry on apartheid and downplaying particularism in their work for economic and racial justice.

Calls for united South African Jewish opposition to apartheid, fought over since the 1950s, grew louder in the 1970s, as young Jews challenged the SAJBD's divide between "moral" and "political" issues.[10] The stakes remained very high, as some felt that white privilege would be the price for standing against the government. "As with most whites," wrote one scholar in 1980, "the [South African] Jew is unwilling to surrender his economic and political future."[11] Intracommunal divides grew deeper. Only in the late 1970s and early 1980s did organized South African Jewish leadership begin to speak out against apartheid, as the urgency of the situation forced them to question their own place in what would be a new, majority-ruled, post-apartheid nation. After years of marginalizing radical Jewish activists, this leadership then began to lay claim to the activists' work to undo apartheid. The Zionist and Jewish left in the United States in the 1970s, meanwhile, continued to follow the work of these radical Jewish activists, who worked with Black Africans in the liberation struggle.

American Jews followed the events in Israel, too, where voters elected to replace the old guard of leadership, including Golda Meir (whom many blamed for the surprise attacks of 1973), with new, more militant leaders who were not invested in "Meir's dream of a staunchly Zionist African continent." Some observers were quick to point out that Israel's alliance with South Africa did not imply "Israeli approval of the internal policies of the Republic."[12] And yet this new guard "saw Israel's security as paramount, and they were willing to make moral compromises in order to ensure it." According to Polakow-Suransky, "It was precisely this worldview that gave birth to the alliance with South Africa."[13] Indeed, as he notes, one year before the Yom Kippur War, in September 1972, Israel signaled this new perspective at the United Nations, when its delegates abstained from a vote to grant United Nations observer status to the ANC and other Black liberation movements.[14] According to South African Jewish historian Gideon Shimoni, "the Yom Kippur War precipitated the collapse" of Israel's alliances with Black African nations, as these nations cut ties with Israel in "an avalanche of diplomatic ruptures" that sent Israel into the "all-too-willing arms of South Africa," which had supported Israel throughout the war.[15] Debates within Israel continued over Palestinian land and the building of Jewish settlements in the Occupied Territories.

The Yom Kippur War proved pivotal to American Jewish debates over apartheid, as political differences over Israel's policies repeatedly connected back to South Africa. American liberal and left Jews continued to face pressure to choose: struggling to remain supportive of Israel with its growing ties to South Africa, they also sought to remain in Civil Rights coalitions that critiqued Israel for allying with—and, by some assessments, now approximating—an apartheid state. The decade began with a statement by Prime Minister John Vorster, whose state visit to Israel would later create tremendous controversy, in which he referred to Israel's "apartheid problem—how to handle its Arab inhabitants."[16] Here was the ultimate counternarrative: Israel's experiences were no longer seen as liberating, paralleling the struggles of Black African nations against colonialism; now, Israel's policies of Occupation (and later even its domestic policies) were seen as in line with colonialism and apartheid.

In the 1960s and through the early 1970s, most American Jewish Zionists saw their support for Israel mirrored in United States foreign aid to its Cold War ally, as there was a "growing convergence between the special relationship paradigm and the national interest orientation."[17] Michael Staub documents the rightwing drift of American Zionism in the period following 1967 and the growth of Breira: A Project of Concern in Diaspora-Israel Relations (translation, "alternative"). Breira was an American Jewish organization that took a progressive position in Israeli politics, founded after left and liberal Jews grew disillusioned with mainstream Jewish responses to the Yom Kippur War. Its first public statement noted the need for Israel to make territorial concessions and recognize the rights of Palestinians; its members also wrote that they "deplore those pressures in American Jewish life which make open discussion of these and other vital issues virtually synonymous with heresy."[18] For four tumultuous years, Breira struggled to voice support for a bi-national solution to the Israeli/Palestinian conflict. Its members urged Israel to consider what ally Leonard Fein says was at the time "unthinkable, scandalous, unheard of": to enter a dialogue with members of the PLO.[19] Breira's members criticized Israel's Occupation of the West Bank as imperialistic. Interestingly, Breira funding came from two individuals with ties elsewhere in this narrative: Sam Rubin, of Faberge cosmetics, father of peace and women's rights activist Cora Weiss and father-in-law of Peter Weiss of ACOA, and a major philanthropist creating and supporting Israeli cultural and community institutions; and from Nahum Goldmann, former president of the World Jewish Congress and the World Zionist Organization.[20]

With rabbis and communal leaders alongside members who were "outside of the Jewish establishment," some Zionist and some anti-Zionist, Breira counted on the voices of two "members of an older American Zionism...[that] had promoted the cause of antiracist activity in the Jewish community."[21] These were Rabbis Joachim Prinz and Balfour Brickner, both of whom also appear in these chapters as strong voices from within the American Jewish community for Civil Rights and against apartheid. Leaders such as Prinz and Brickner had long tied their Jewishness and their Zionism to universal campaigns for justice, pushing back against those who argued that their activism diminished Jewish loyalty. In addition to calling for a Palestinian state alongside of Israel, both also protested the lack of "free speech" in American Jewish life.[22] Prinz, Brickner, and other Breira members called for more democracy and equality—including gender equality—among American and Israeli Jews.

For longtime critics of apartheid in South Africa, taking stands that compromised "Jewish unity" felt decidedly familiar. They had long rejected the idea that these criticisms imperiled American, South African, or other communities of Jews around the world. They saw their political choices as bound up in an alternative definition of Jewishness, one that prioritized universalist stands—for Civil Rights, against apartheid, for Palestinian self-rule and security. Although one should not overstate the role played by Prinz and Brickner in these campaigns, their multiple allegiances make clear that as American Jews worked out their feelings toward South Africa and its apartheid regime, they were also gradually working out their positions on Israel.

Indeed, activists and political leaders alike began to see Israel and South Africa through the same, apartheid lens, as the definition of apartheid expanded. They likened the oppression caused by Israel's policies toward its

Palestinian population to that created under South African apartheid. The growing intensity of the global antiapartheid movement, then, intensified criticisms of Israel's policies in human rights campaigns. On the other side of that development, the power of the universalist antiapartheid movement also muted critiques of apartheid among particularist Jewish leaders.

The anticolonialist work of Prinz and Brickner, along with other left and liberal American Jews, kept alive some Black/Jewish political alliances. Like their progressive Zionist Jewish counterparts, some African Americans continued to see Israel as a manifestation of Jewish universalist commitments to human progress and social welfare. Indeed, for many African Americans this view formed the foundation of their commitments to Israel. As the previous chapters make clear, until the late 1960s, editors in the African American press praised Israel's "undisguised and unflagging opposition to South Africa's brutal segregative practices."[23] The African American press also covered antiapartheid programs and speakers in the Jewish community, such as when Rabbi Andre Ungar, expelled from South Africa because of his opposition to apartheid, spoke at the American Jewish Congress.[24]

Even into the 1970s, support for Israel continued in some segments of Black union leadership. On October 23, 1973 a letter appeared in the *New York Times* titled "An Appeal from Black Trade Unionists: Support Israel." From unions across the United States, the signers praised the "egalitarian spirit" of Israel, ruled by a labor government that "breathes the spirit of democracy" with a strong trade union organization, the Histadrut. They cited the universal lessons of historic Black and Jewish oppression as they called on Arab nations to make peace with Israel. "We have learned in our struggle for dignity and equality that no minority is safe if any minority is threatened, that democracy is not the special privilege of some people, but the inalienable right of all people."[25] Two years later, two of the signers, A. Philip Randolph, retired leader of the Brotherhood of Sleeping Car Porters, and Bayard Rustin, Civil Rights leader and director of the A. Philip Randolph Institute, formed the Black Americans to Support Israel Committee, BASIC.[26]

Younger, radical African Americans began to challenge the worldview of BASIC's largely older generation of leadership, including their heroization of Israel for its strong labor movement. Their counternarratives linked the liberation of Black Africans and African Americans instead to Palestinian liberation. They assailed the fact that Israel's influence on the American labor movement only reinforced its longstanding ties to white supremacy and fervent anticommunism:

> One can only say of the Afro-Asian Institute of which Rustin glowingly speaks...was headed by Eliahu Elath, former Israeli Ambassador to the United States. The Institute was set up with money from the AFL-CIO and the training is of the Meany-Lovestone variety which has kept the unions of the U.S.A. split along the color line.[27]

Referencing the virulently anticommunist policies of Jay Lovestone and George Meany, Cold War leaders in the American Federation of Labor who alienated leftist, antiracist allies of labor, radical African Americans offered up these partisan analyses of Jews' profiting from white supremacy at home and abroad. They challenged the labor foundation of the Black/Jewish alliance and outwardly rejected the idea that support for Israel flowed inevitably from their shared pursuit of social justice. As Israel's relationship with apartheid South Africa grew more visible, the challenges to that support grew more vigorous.

Within the United States, then, apartheid played a key role as activists and leaders began to re-envision Israel during the Cold War 1970s. Anticolonialist activists, including many Civil Rights leaders, increasingly spoke of Israel and apartheid South Africa in the same breath, seeing both as imperialist states. Many Jewish leaders saw these condemnations as akin to Arab and communist threats in endangering Israel, just as Jewish leaders came to tie American Jewish visibility increasingly to unquestioning unity around Israel and its policies. In 1975, two events in the world of global politics and diplomacy had a seismic impact on these groups, widening the chasm between them still more. Both events linked Israel and South Africa.

Israel, South Africa, and the United Nations

In 1975, United Nations delegates called for the ouster of both South Africa and Israel: South Africa for its resistance to calls to end apartheid; Israel for its policies of Occupation. The Organization of Nonaligned States considered whether or not to apply sanctions to Israel and to withdraw its membership in the United Nations. Ten of the 17 members of the Congressional Black Caucus wrote a letter urging United Nations officials not to expel Israel, arguing that such a move would reduce American commitments to the United Nations and thus would increase harm to vulnerable areas such as developing nations in Africa and around the world.[28] Other African American leaders were also critical of proposals to oust Israel from the United Nations. The African American *Chicago Defender* and the *Philadelphia Tribune* both echoed that such a move would threaten American support of the United Nations. The *Tribune* spoke too of the character of other UN member nations, their tremendous inequality and ruthless, oppressive state policies, asking why Israel was singled out and held to a higher standard.[29]

A journalist for the New York *Jewish Week* pondered the possibilities of this historic proposal in May of that year. He quoted UN representatives who argued that because "Israel's 'transgressions' were not in the same league with South Africa's [they] should not have the same treatment."[30] By June, editors at the *Jewish Week* worried more loudly over the UN General Assembly's Third World-Arab-Communist majority. Supporting US Ambassador to the United Nations Daniel Patrick Moynihan, emerging as a vigorous ally of Israel, the editors positioned Israel as a solid Western ally and South Africa as a state "belonging to a minority" that was in great danger of falling victim to "communist designs":

> There is also the problem of South Africa. The Third World states are eager to ostracize South Africa, but our administration feels that the UN would destroy its usefulness if any majority were to make a practice of ousting states belonging to a minority, no matter what the issue.... The real objection to Moynihan's blunt warning reflects the desire of the administration to persuade the Third World nations, through Arab mediation, to desist from ousting South Africa. That is a more difficult chore than preventing the ouster of Israel, since the Third World nations would support such a move only to obtain Arab and Communist backing for their designs on South Africa.[31]

With a watchful eye on the United Nations, American Jewish Zionists had reason to feel vulnerable. For seven months in 1975, in the wake of Israel's refusal to remove their troops from the Sinai Peninsula, the United States withdrew economic aid and reduced military aid to Israel.[32] South Africa stepped into this breach.[33] And by 1975, South Africa was excluded from all organs of the United Nations and thus faced its own, far longer, period of international isolation.[34]

Born of a United Nations mandate, Israel continued its fraught relationship with this international body. As discussed in chapter 1, active participation in the 1948 Declaration of Human Rights was followed by tensions between supporters of Jewish unity and those who wished to speak out against injustice on the part of Jews. If "Never Again" served as the bedrock to twentieth-century human rights discourses, seeking to protect all "Jews"—a universal stand-in for victims—from genocide, then the implications for Israel were twofold and opposing. On one hand, linking Israel's existence to the Holocaust made Israel's actions exempt from the protections of human rights discourses (i.e., Israel must do what it has to do to prevent another Holocaust, including joining forces with apartheid regimes and abusing the human rights of Palestinians and others). On the other hand, Israel's claim to victimhood also encouraged individuals to hold Israel to a higher standard of conduct (i.e., Jews have learned their lessons firsthand about oppression and oppressors, and now must not stand in for Nazi oppressors in abusing any group or people). South African apartheid brought this tension into sharp relief, and played a crucial role in conversations about Jewishness and Zionism throughout the world.[35]

As early as 1965, Soviet delegates to the Third Committee of the General Assembly of the United Nations—the Social, Humanitarian, and Cultural Affairs Committee, which examines human rights and other issues—tried to include Zionism with Nazism and Apartheid as forms of discrimination to be condemned in the draft of the International Convention on the Elimination of All Forms of Racial Discrimination.[36] Two years later, delegates attempted to include Zionism in a draft convention on religious intolerance.[37] While these efforts met defeat, their ideas and language lived on. In 1973, the

United Nations passed resolutions calling for the end of apartheid that explicitly linked it to Zionism. Immediately following a condemnation of states that provided apartheid South Africa with military equipment and cooperation, the General Assembly's Resolution 3151 condemned "the unholy alliance between Portuguese colonialism [in neighboring Mozambique], South African racism, [Z]ionism and Israeli imperialism."[38] The Soviets used the resolution to express their antagonism toward the West and toward Israel, while positioning themselves as an ally of Black Africa. This resolution put the Soviet/Arab/Black Africa alliance, begun in the 1950s, on par with South Africa's assistance to Mozambique, which, along with American support, later led to 15 years of Civil War in that nation.

Two years later, in 1975, the United Nations commemorated and celebrated the power of the global women's movement by holding a United Nations World Conference on Women in Mexico City. There, delegates passed another resolution stating that "international cooperation and peace require the achievement of national liberation and independence, the elimination of colonialism and neocolonialism, foreign occupation, [Z]ionism, apartheid and racial discrimination in all its forms." (The profound impact of this resolution on Jewish women who attended the conference, and on the women's movement broadly, is discussed in the following chapter.) Later that summer, the Organization of African Unity declared that "the racist regimes in Occupied Palestine and the racist regimes in Zimbabwe and South Africa have a common imperialist origin, forming a whole and having the same racist structure and being organically linked in their policy aimed at the repression of the dignity and integrity of the human being."[39] Following UN procedure, Mexico City's World Plan of Action, resolutions, and Declaration traveled to the General Assembly, where members engaged in heated debates over Zionism.

Resolution 3379, passed by the United Nations General Assembly in November 1975, built on this history and these documents and declared Zionism "a form of racism and racial discrimination." Cold War historian Thomas Borstelmann observes that this resolution "reflected similar international anger at what was seen as another unjust 'white settler' state in the Third World (and the United States defended Israel much as it did South Africa)."[40] Historians view the resolution as an outgrowth of the Cold War alliances among the United States, Israel, and South Africa, and of the growing power of Asian and African states.[41] And indeed, the United States lagged behind sweeping international sentiment against South Africa, as American support for the apartheid regime lasted well into Ronald Reagan's presidency in the 1980s. American conservatives, including many white southerners, rallied support for apartheid South Africa that countered the loud and visible global antiapartheid movement.[42] American support for apartheid South Africa and for Israel angered the Soviets as it angered non-Western nations engaged in struggles against colonialism.

Support for Resolution 3379 grew out of Soviet hostility to Israel, as well as that nation's aim to sidestep a public condemnation of Soviet anti-Semitism and to protect its "carefully cultivated image" as an enemy of colonialism and a "protector of minority rights."[43] The Resolution was also the product of increasing acceptance of the PLO, globally and specifically at the United Nations, and Arab hostility to Zionism and to Israel's treatment of Palestinians. The Resolution can be seen as emerging from the newly powerful group of Third World countries in the United Nations: they disliked the effect of Western capitalism on their own nations, and saw Israel as a settler state, an outpost of Western capitalism and imperialism in the Middle East.[44] In addition, the resolution was the product of broad anger toward the United States over Vietnam.

Attempts to discredit the resolution, or oversimplify its origins, often ignore its roots in American and Israeli support for apartheid South Africa. Those roots contributed to the resolution's long life span, as activists used it to make sense of and oppose systems of state oppression of which South African apartheid was the clearest, most visible example. In future, even post–Cold War gatherings of nations, American support of apartheid South Africa and Israel, along with Israel's historical support of apartheid South Africa, would prove to be touchstones for those continuing to protest state oppression. For its Western origins, for its claims to democracy, for other complex reasons enumerated earlier, Israel came to stand in for state oppression and apartheid because of its treatment of Palestinians. Indeed, Resolution 3379 later served as pivotal to the agenda of the 2001 Durban, South Africa World Conference against Racism, Racial Discrimination, Xenophobia, and Related Intolerance, as some delegates demanded its reinstitution so that Israel's policies could be formally labeled apartheid.

In 1975, critics of Resolution 3379 feared that it would diminish charges of racism the world over, and distract nations from the battle against South African apartheid. Indeed, 28 African American "scholars, educators and other intellectual leaders" urged that the anti Zionist resolution be rejected, for, as they saw it, "The prospects of a concerted United Nations drive against African apartheid has been effectively thwarted by an amendment which introduces an extraneous issue to a worthy United Nations undertaking." The leaders were fearful that "concern for the anti-Semitic implications of this amendment, however legitimate will heavily compromise African hopes of expunging apartheid from the world conscience."[45]

Jewish and African American liberals struggled mightily to try to maintain common ground in the face of the explosive response to 3379. To that end, BASIC's November 23, 1975 *New York Times* letter also referenced Israel's aid to Black Africa in its rejection of the Zionism is racism resolution. Its signers endorsed Israel's right to exist and also Palestinian self-determination. As OPEC continued to utilize the oil embargo as a political weapon for profit, the signers also noted its negative impact on Black Africans. The Jewish Labor Committee issued a mailing in the fall of 1976 to affirm its commitment to Israel and to "the cause of Black freedom in Rhodesia and South Africa." The impact of these efforts can be gauged from criticisms of BASIC by younger, radical African American activists, and by the relatively small role of Civil Rights in the work done by the JLC and other Jewish organizations in the

1970s. Their efforts did little to counter the growing chasm between the two communities.

Zionist critics of the Resolution feared for the broad and long-standing impact of Resolution 3379 on Jews across the globe, as it "fused long-standing anti-Semitism with anti-Americanism."[46] They presented the Israeli/Palestinian conflict as one of racial, rather than national, conflict. According to historian and columnist Gil Troy, those who cast it as a racial conflict "implicitly sanctioned Palestinian terrorism, given the immorality of racial tyranny…[and] linked the United States and Israel as the sinning successors to South Africa's apartheid regime in leftist demonology."[47]

Importantly, there were critics of Resolution 3379 on the left as well, including Noam Chomsky and Edward Said.[48] Scholars felt that the resolution took away from authentic accusations of racism, tapped into hypocritical accusations of human rights abuses (among the Soviets and among Arab nations), and diminished faith in—and the potential of—the United Nations. Many critics across the political spectrum noted that the Resolution failed to differentiate between the ideology of Zionism and the policies of the Israeli government.

Still others on the left, Jews and others active in anticolonialist movements, used the Resolution to bolster their claims that Israel was indeed a racist, colonial, settler state. The Resolution contributed to their worldview, their critique of Western imperialist alliances among the United States, South Africa, and Israel.

From 1975 through the 1980s, this anti-Zionist resolution proved to be a deeply painful touchstone for American and other Jews. It provided what they believed was incontrovertible evidence of deep, global hostility to a movement and a nation central to their identity and visibility. Racism was the scourge of the Western world, and now that stain blotted what they saw as the liberation movement of Zionism. Many Zionist Jews and other allies labeled the resolution Soviet propaganda, and spoke of the United Nations and its subsequent conferences as having been hijacked by Arab and Soviet states. Thousands protested outside the United Nations and around the world in November 1975. They felt in peril. Many assailed the United Nations for singling out Israel's policies with no mention of the Arab terrorism in that region.

Broadly, then, the Resolution also contributed to Jewish unity amidst abiding fears of invisibility inextricably tied to the Holocaust.[49] American Ambassador Daniel Patrick Moynihan attacked the Resolution at the United Nations by defining Zionism as a national liberation movement, and was immediately lionized by Jewish organizations throughout the world.[50]

For many, this Resolution cemented the idea that the Soviets and their Arab allies, the sponsors of this resolution, were the "new Nazis," that Jews again faced a true threat. In many ways, these developments made it easier for mainstream Jews to label all criticisms of Israel as illegitimate, as inspired by communism or Arab propaganda or both. Although American Jews now often stopped short of identifying with the South African Jewish community, they expressed sympathy for its precarious position. For example, both communities pointed to the Resolution to explain their increased vigilance to anti-Israel and anti-Semitic ideas. Indeed, some argued that the Resolution made clear why Israel *needed* South Africa's aid in such a hostile global climate.

How Zionists were to respond to the association of racism with Zionism was a live question. Across the world, Jews devoted ample resources to discrediting the Resolution. The American Jewish Congress, long a liberal voice in the American Jewish community with regard to domestic issues, turned to Israel's work in Black Africa in the 1950s and 1960s as specific evidence of Israel's commitment to undoing racism. Congress leadership saw this work as affirming the "Jewish passion" that united Zionism and Judaism, "the age-old Jewish passion for justice, the quest for peace." Of the UN's resolution, the American Jewish Congress Research Director Moshe Decter, wrote: "Zionism has...been equated with racism. Under intense pressure at the United Nations, many Black African states—to their shame—supported the Soviet-Arab initiative at the United Nations, which proclaimed that evil doctrine in November of 1975. But the Africans know better—from their very own experience with Israel."[51]

Focusing on Israel's foreign policies rather than its domestic affairs, editors at the New York *Jewish Week* noted the importance of South Africa's Cold War relationship to Israel to the "Zionism is Racism" equation. How, for instance, was Israel to respond when it was called "apartheid's ally," in order to counter the idea that Israel was itself acting in racist ways? The editors pointed out that "the Israelis obviously were well prepared for the apartheid debate, having done considerable research, and whenever a country raises any questions about Israel's trade with South Africa, Israeli Ambassador [to the UN Chaim] Herzog digs into his briefcase and comes up with a complete dossier of that state's own deals with the country it professes to despise."[52] Israel and its allies continued to use this strategy throughout the 1970s and 1980s, arguing for the minute nature of Israel's trade with South Africa compared to other nations, and rejecting the idea that Israel, under siege from its enemies, should be held to a higher standard than these other nations. The singling out of Israel, these leaders argued, rested on an unfair standard. If Israel's and Zionism's racism lay in its ties to South Africa, the argument that Israel should not be singled out was to undo those racist accusations by implicating other nations—including those of Black Africa.

* * *

Sasha Polakow-Suransky begins *The Unspoken Alliance: Israel's Secret Relationship with Apartheid South Africa* with South African Prime Minister John Vorster's April 1976 visit to Yad Vashem, the Holocaust Memorial in Jerusalem, on his official state visit to Israel.[53] People around the world saw this visit as crucial evidence of Israel's growing ties to South Africa's apartheid regime. The visit turned the Holocaust analogy on its head: a former Nazi supporter, architect of South African apartheid, visited Israel's Holocaust memorial, Yad Vashem, to crystallize South Africa's trading partnership with Israel, born in the aftermath of the Holocaust. Vorster's visit prompted visceral responses from activists across the world. It also elicited great introspection in Jewish communities: whither Israel?

Tying Vorster's visit so intimately to Holocaust memory brought to the fore the opposing ideas about Israel's existence and its leaders' policy decisions: was it acceptable to criticize Israel for forming Cold War alliances with racist rulers who once supported Jewish genocide? Or were Israel's rulers to be supported when they insisted that these alliances were necessary for Israel to survive? To quote Moshe Decter in his report on Israel and South Africa for the American Jewish Congress: "the world somehow expects Israel to behave better than other states," and in Israel's pursuit of its "national interest," there exists a "pervasive double standard" as a result.[54]

Polakow-Suransky interprets Vorster's visit to Israel as a move toward pragmatism. "By the time Vorster set foot in Jerusalem," he writes, "the idealism of Israel's early years had been replaced by hardened self-interest." Further, the visit "gave South Africa a surge of self-confidence and helped relieve its feelings of growing isolation."[55] Strained or broken relations with Black African nations, who now allied with the Arab world, led Israel to a "new set of international circumstances." South African trade stood to "shore up the sagging economy in Israel."[56] For South African Jews (and others) who worked against apartheid, the visit prompted nothing short of disgust.

Although only a small group of powerful Israeli leaders supported the apartheid regime, the complicated relationship between Israel and South Africa grew harder to ignore after Vorster's visit. To Israel's allies *and* critics, Vorster's visit offered evidence, or further confirmation, of Zionism's connection to racism.[57] The *New York Times* recorded the strong criticism of the Dutch Government, which said "that the visit would complicate the efforts of Israel's friends abroad to persuade the world that there is no connection between Zionism and racism." The Organization of African Unity, the Arab League, and the Soviet Party paper *Pravda* also "predictably" condemned the visit.[58] The Middle East Research and Information Project proclaimed "Vorster Visit Marks New Israel/South Africa Ties."[59] An editorial in the *Ghanaian Times* read: "Israel's active cooperation with South Africa makes it impossible for any African country which is committed to the African Liberation Movement to extend sympathy to its cause in the Middle East."[60] Eastern bloc and African nations consistently drew attention to Israel's ties to apartheid South Africa, to Israel's military, commercial, and economic ties to their strongest enemy on the continent.[61] Vorster's visit to Israel made their criticisms still louder, more urgent, and more powerful.

To individuals and groups around the world who were committed to the independence, integrity, and stability of Black Africa, these links—between Palestinians and Black South Africans, between Zionism and apartheid/racism—grew harder to ignore. African American presses reprinted a *Time*

Magazine article on the "blossoming relationship between South Africa and Israel"[62] even as they printed the American Jewish organizations' defensive arguments over this relationship: their insistence that other nations' trade with apartheid South Africa was far more noteworthy, and that "the singling out of Israel" for wrongdoing was unjust.[63]

African American journalists also pointed out that not all Black African leaders harkened back to Israel's aid to their nations as they worked out their feelings toward Israel and Zionism. Instead, they lived with the present reality of Moynihan's attack of Resolution 3379 at the United Nations: "Ever since Daniel Patrick Moynihan attacked the African countries en mass in the United Nations as racist bigots because of their vote against Zionism, the Third World bloc has been smoldering with resentment," said the editors of the *Tri-State Defender*. "It hasn't helped that their hated enemy, Prime Minister Vorster of South Africa, paid a state visit to Israel recently and was warmly received there."[64]

American Jewish responses to Vorster's visit to Africa fell along predictable lines. The left-Zionist journal *New Outlook* editorialized the visit as "both wrong and stupid," asserting that such an alliance cuts against Israel's "long range interest" and its "true interests" in the "development, survival, and well-being of the peoples of Asia and Africa, all opponents of the South African racist regime."[65] In the progressive journal *Jewish Currents*, Columbia College student and Zionist activist Sheldon Ranz published a piece that he insisted had been rejected by his own Zionist student organization's publications. Ranz began by asking why American Jews had not responded in kind to the BASIC signers' gesture—why they had not begun "condemning the racist policies of apartheid in South Africa while affirming that we are Zionists that strongly disagree with the visit made by South Africa's prime minister to Israel." He encouraged American Jews to articulate their feeling "that the announcement that closer ties are being developed between the two countries is shocking."

Ranz labeled these developments as the "skeleton in the closet" of American Jews and blamed Rabbi Arthur Hertzberg, president of the American Jewish Congress. Ranz cited Hertzberg as giving voice to the increasingly common logic that Israel could not afford to "ignore sources of economic cooperation with other countries no matter how execrable their governments may be." According to Ranz, speaking out against apartheid and cutting ties with South Africa would benefit all concerned: Israel would appear "less racist," and become less isolated, "since we judge nations by the friends they keep"; the South African Jewish community would be safer, as South African Jews might likely become seen as "Vorster's 'little helpers'" in a new, majority-ruled, Black South Africa. Moreover, he concluded that Israel would pay a high price for the hypocrisy of allowing Vorster to lay a wreath at the memorial for Jews murdered during the Holocaust. Given the loud conversations linking Zionism to racism, the faltering support for Israel among Black African nations, Israel could not afford "to lose the support of people like those in BASIC."[66]

Later in that same issue, *Jewish Currents* editors carefully reprinted the exchange between Hertzberg of the AJCongress and Bayard Rustin, laying out the argument that the world held Israel to an unfair, higher standard for its trade with South Africa. Rustin had elsewhere voiced his "distress" that any nation—Israel or those of Black Africa—should be "compelled by economic necessity to trade with any repressive countries."[67] They cited too a letter from UN Ambassador from Malawi, J. T. X. Muwamba, who accused critics of Israel of "double-faced hypocrisy" and "political gimmickry."[68]

Liberal Zionists and their allies stopped short of apologizing for Israel's ties to South Africa in arguing that the survival of a once-persecuted group of people (i.e., Jews) was now contingent on Israel's continued existence in the dangerous Cold War political world. Some observers felt that they effectively distanced supporters of Israel—and thus Zionism itself—from liberation struggles across the world. Likewise, those who used the rhetoric of anticolonialism to offer unqualified critiques of Zionism, paying no heed to its ties to the Holocaust, also presented support for Israel and support for human rights campaigns as an either/or choice for Zionists. By their lights, Zionism was not compatible with anticolonialism, with antiracist, antiapartheid work.

Choices only grew starker in the late 1970s. Mainstream American Jewish periodicals began to place all those who linked Israel to South Africa into the category of "enemies of the Jews and Israel," leaving little room for conversation or complexity about contexts or alternatives. Meanwhile, Yasser Arafat, head of the PLO, demonized by American Jewish mainstream leaders and by American foreign policy, tied Palestinian liberation to the antiapartheid struggle. In 1977, for example, the New York *Jewish Week* followed Arafat to the meeting of the Organization of African Unity, where they quoted him as denouncing "the unholy alliance between South Africa, Rhodesia, and Israel."[69] Portraying Arafat as dangerous and an enemy of the Jews, akin to Hitler in his aim of Jewish genocide, mainstream Jewish leaders were also silencing those who invoked Israel's ties to South Africa.

And indeed, when African American ministers Joseph Lowery and Walter Fauntroy led a Southern Christian Leadership Conference (SCLC) delegation to meet with Arafat on a "mission of reconciliation" in 1979, mainstream American Jewish leaders called the visit "morally reprehensible" and "politically foolish." Lowery was president of SCLC, led the 1965 Selma to Montgomery March, and cofounded the Black Leadership Forum, which began protesting South African apartheid in the mid-1970s. Fauntroy was one of the original members of Rustin's BASIC, a friend and ally of Dr King in SCLC, Washington DC's Congressional delegate beginning in 1970, and a founding member of the Congressional Black Caucus. He would later be a cofounder of the Free South Africa Movement in the United States. After their visit with Arafat, both ministers became "personas non grata in most Jewish circles." Sheldon Ranz's predictions continued to be realized, as the Black/Jewish alliance further deteriorated, American Jews lost allies in the

Black community, and donations from American Jews to Civil Rights groups like those of Lowery and Fauntroy declined drastically.[70]

While members of the older, Black/Jewish Civil Rights coalition made overtures to Arafat in the hopes of healing breaches abroad, radical Black activists made more aggressive claims. They tied Israel to South Africa and translated what American aid meant to the depressed state of the American poor. Communist, Civil Rights activist, and union organizer Ishmael Flory noted that Israeli weapons oppress and murder Black Africans and Indians in southern Africa, and that support for Israel at home comes at the expense of the "unemployment and deprivation" of "black people, poor people, and working people."

In a 1976 column in the Black press, Flory described South African Prime Minister John Vorster's state visit to Israel as the symbolic centerpiece to an array of wrongful actions and priorities. For Flory, Israel's visible ties to South African racism, oppression, and suppression, combined with its treatment of Palestinians, confirmed the equation of Zionism and racism. Flory blamed the "imperialist backers and business interests of the United States, Europe, and Japan" for the global buildup of militarism and the danger of war. He blamed American Zionists for giving "money for Israel for war to hold the lands of the Arabs, while our people suffer from unemployment, inflation, and deprivation." Repeatedly, he urged: "We should protest." "Israel's relations and collaborations with the racist government of South Africa, tantamount to support for racism and against black and democratic forces everywhere in the world, we should protest."[71]

Flory's linking Zionism to unequivocal support for South Africa, and, by extension, to global imperialism and white supremacy is, to be sure, an oversimplified reading, resting on an implied right-wing Zionist consensus, perhaps even conspiracy. There were Zionists—in South Africa, Israel, and throughout the world—who expressed dismay over Vorster's visit and trade between Israel and South Africa. Yet Flory's rhetoric reveals the way in which the analogue of apartheid was gaining wider use, seen not just as one state's policy but as an ideology of oppression applicable to Israel and other "imperialist" states.

Importantly, American Jews were also wrestling with if and how they might divide the ideology of Zionism from Israel's policies in the face of the UN resolution, Vorster's visit to Israel, and the deteriorating relationship between African Americans and Jews. In an issue dedicated to "Chauvinist Politics and Politicized Religion," left-Zionist *New Outlook* contributors examined the growing global schism on the issue of Zionism. Reform Rabbi Anson Laytner asked "Why Does the Third World Oppose Zionism?" He concluded that "two absolutely contradictory definitions of Zionism" existed. First was the ideology that Moynihan spoke of in the UN General Assembly, the foundation of Golda Meir's explanation for Israel's aid to Black Africa. This was a definition of Zionism as a "national liberation movement." For Jews and their allies who embraced this definition, the UN resolution evoked "outrage" because Zionism was the response to "centuries of Jewish suffering that culminated in the Holocaust."

The second definition of Zionism lay in the "sum total of the policies practiced by the Israeli government." Israel's Occupation of its Territories, its failure to address the plight of Palestinian refugees, its defiance of UN resolutions ("the very body that was responsible for its creation"): Laytner enumerated these as defining Zionism for millions throughout the world. For the "Afro-Asian countries," he wrote, "one analogy comes to mind: Zionism is to Israel as apartheid is to South Africa." He strongly cautioned against seeing 3379 as "Moynihan, Israel, and hysterical American Jewish leaders have painted it"—as "universal degeneration into moral depravity, inhumanity and anti-Semitism." He viewed it, instead, as an opportunity to deliberate on these diverging definitions.

For Laytner saw danger of a different sort in the future for Israel and world Jewry. If Israel does not change its approach to Palestinians, he warned, the divide between those who hold opposing definitions of Zionism will only grow. Israel's "intransigence" must be met with condemnation; Israel must be "judged for its deeds." Nothing short of "revolutionary change" in Israel's policies would succeed in redefining Zionism for the growing segment of the world population who see it as racism. Only with "radical change" will Israel find "acceptance in the world community," and only then can it reclaim the "raison d'etre" for the Jewish state's existence.[72]

According to Laytner, analogies to racism and apartheid endangered Israel's legitimacy in world affairs. Israel's leaders could reassert legitimacy only by contradicting all elements of that analogy, undoing its oppression of Palestinians, and cutting ties with apartheid South Africa. Vehement disagreements over Jewish unity, and now Zionism and Israel, contributed to the destruction of alliances essential for a Jewish response to South African apartheid. Because some American Jewish Zionists felt vulnerable in the face of increasingly strident criticisms of Israel, they cited Jewish unity to explain why they edged closer to South African Jews in their worldviews. To Jews on the left, these actions were tantamount to betrayal, a surrender to strains of Jewish identity and Zionism that would only deepen the indictment of both in the court of world opinion.

South Africa Needs Friends

In May 1976, amidst the painful intracommunal American Jewish debates about Israel, Zionism, and South Africa, about Israel and the PLO, the organized South African Jewish Community launched a public relations campaign designed to build on the recent visit of South African Prime Minister John Vorster to Israel. The SAJBD, along with the South African Tourist Bureau, SATUR, and Pan American Airways, brought the editors of 14 major American Jewish newspapers to South Africa as guests. The aim of this outreach was to highlight the growing bonds between South African and American Jews.

Traveling via Brazil, the guests utilized the flight path of South Africa Airways that had opened up in 1969 under protest from Representative Charles C. Diggs and the American Jewish Congress's Rabbi Joachim Prinz, among others. Upon their return, these editors wrote pieces about the Jewish community of South Africa, focusing especially on the parallels between American and South African Jews' devotion to Israel. Above all, they encouraged tourism to South Africa as a means to build tighter links between two significant world Jewish communities.

American editors were impressed with their tour. Some who cited apartheid—Philip Slomovitz of the New York *Jewish Week* wrote that South Africa was "racially suspect," and called apartheid "repellent" and a "menace"— were assuaged by the SAJBD's endorsement of a plan for "separate development." Slomovitz concluded the article by noting the deep commonalities of American and South African Jews: their firm anticommunism, their equal dedication to Israel. His hosts assured him that the kind hospitality received by the editors "awaits our fellow Jews who choose to visit with us." Echoing the words of World Jewish Congress leaders two decades prior, Slomovitz wrote of the "oneness of the Jewish people and the urgency for the understanding of the aims of the various communities, no matter how distant."[73]

Philip Hochstein, editor of the New York *Jewish Week*, known for his conservatism and red-baiting of liberal and left Jews, also praised the Pan Am tour. Hochstein saw South African Jews as a "vital link in the evolving new policies" of their nation. He dedicated much of his piece to the Cold War tensions in Africa, to the pivotal and positive role that South Africa played in what he called the tensions of East and West. As Jews were of "great economic importance to South Africa," as so many were members of the middle and upper classes, Hochstein recognized that the South African/American Jewish connection may be a route to improving public relations. To drive that point home, he emphasized the careful attention South Africa paid to American public opinion. He consistently cited his ignorance on the "race situation" in South Africa, even after his tour. Indeed, his portrait of a typical South African Jew presented the situation as difficult to understand:

> The extreme complexity of the South African condition is perhaps best illustrated by the fairly prevalent attitude of Jews who combine their outspoken sense of Jewish identity with both intense South African patriotism and frank skepticism about apartheid.[74]

Still, by Hochstein's lights, with a common enemy in Russia, and a common friend in Israel, South African and American Jews had much in common.

Addressing an item of concern to Jews in the United States and elsewhere, the editors of American Jewish newspapers interviewed Israel's ambassador to South Africa, Yitzhak Unna, about the growing closeness between Israel and South Africa. In explaining and defending that relationship, Unna also turned a long-cited analogy on its head. For decades, Golda Meir and others had tied the fates of world Jewry to Black Africa, citing Israel and free African nations as analogous in their struggles for freedom. In his counternarrative, Unna spoke instead of the common struggles of Afrikaners and Israeli Jews: their "common Biblical heritage"; the similarities between the Great Trek of the Afrikaners away from the British to the Transvaal and the Jewish Exodus from slavery in Egypt; finally, the feeling that they are in the "same boat" in that South Africa, like Israel, is a "small community surrounded by a preponderance of hostile neighbors." Unna even mentioned the scientific exchanges between the two nations, recalling similar exchanges between Israel and Black Africa heralded by liberals in the 1950s and 1960s. About Israel's relations with Black African nations, Unna said that Israel received signals that some of these nations (which he left unnamed) regretted that they "surrendered to the Arab blackmail" and cut diplomatic ties with Israel in 1973.[75] Still, he noted that Israel's commercial trade with Black African nations continued to grow.

Irwin Stein, coeditor of Chicago's Jewish weekly the *Sentinel*, pursued one of the agendas of the voyage in asking Unna if, because of the special relationship between South Africa and Israel, the Jewish communities of "Israel, America, or anywhere else" have an "obligation" to "look favorably on South Africa." To that leading query, Unna would say only that the editors should return home and report back to their readers about the "honest look" they have had at South Africa. To do that, Unna concluded, would be to do a service to South African–Israeli relations, South Africa itself, and also to "your own intellectual integrity."[76] Following the trip, Pam Am began advertising tours of the Jewish communities of Brazil, South Africa, and Israel. The New York *Jewish Week* proclaimed: "All the Jewish communities are anxious to be visited by American Jews."[77]

But a crisis preempted those visits. On June 16, 1976, 15,000 schoolchildren gathered in Soweto, the Black "homelands" southwest of Johannesburg, to protest the government's ruling that half of all classes in nonwhite secondary schools must be taught in Afrikaans, the language of South Africa's seventeenth-century Dutch settlers. Police opened fire, killing hundreds. Nelson Mandela writes that "the events of that day reverberated in every town and township of South Africa." The "spirit of mass protest" against state oppression spread, gradually eroding the power of the apartheid government.[78] Archbishop Desmond Tutu began advocating for an economic boycott of South Africa. Global outrage at the massacre translated into protests across the globe. In the United States, African American activist leaders set the stage for the founding of TransAfrica, the "most important lobby for Africa and the Caribbean ever created by African Americans."[79]

In South Africa, the minority white government initiated still more repressive tactics, including assassinations, against the grassroots, violent protests that continued for months, gradually eroding apartheid. Radical Jewish activists, many of whom were exiled or arrested, continued their work with Black activists. The SAJBD, along with more Orthodox leaders, remained silent. Rabbis in the Reform movement in South Africa, however, called the

South African Union for Progressive Judaism, were "outspoken" in their opposition. Rabbi Richard Lampert, for example, took his conscience to the pulpit at Temple Emanuel in Johannesburg, most famously on Kol Nidrei in 1976, at the start of the Yom Kippur holiday. To his 1,500 congregants he distributed an adaptation he'd written of the "Al Chet" prayer, which referred to "the sin we have committed by forgetting we were oppressed" and the "sin we have committed by keeping silent in the face of injustice." "It created a furor," he recalled. "There was criticism, some people protested afterwards." Authorities raided his home several days later and confiscated works that were considered seditious. Shortly after, Lampert emigrated from South Africa.[80]

Writing in *Hadassah Magazine*, Denis Diamond, executive director of the SAJBD and a key figure in the Pan Am tour for American Jewish editors, carefully and shockingly cast the Soweto riots as "one of the most tragic episodes in the history of urban interrelationships in South Africa." Describing the "polyglot" urban Blacks who travel to Johannesburg, Diamond described "the language problem" as "compounded by the multitude of native tongues" of Black South Africans. He lamented that the riots came at a time when "the prospects for ending racial discrimination had never been better." Addressing the global condemnation of apartheid, the movement for sanctions and divestment, he asserted that "one thing is for sure: [a peaceful solution] will not be determined outside this country."[81]

Diamond quickly transitioned to his ultimate focus, the South African Jews who hoped to win allies of guests on the Pam Am tour. Playing "only a peripheral role" in the peacemaking process, South African Jews were sometimes active in politics as individuals, according to Diamond. Beginning to lavish praise on that population, Diamond asserted that it was in "civic involvement" that they "have stamped their mark" on Johannesburg. In cultural institutions such as museums, ballet, drama, and music, Diamond told his audience, "except for New York, there is no city outside of Israel quite as Jewish as Jo'burg." He went on to praise the "vital, and in many ways, complementary Jewish communities" of the United States and South Africa, and to celebrate the Pan Am tour in the context of South Africa's strong Zionism. Straying from any sustained mention of apartheid, Diamond suggested an intimate connection among the three nations of Israel, South Africa, and the United States.

But for whom did Diamond and the journal speak? Liberal and radical Jews in the United States criticized the Pam Am public relations tour of South Africa. *Jewish Currents*, edited by communist, historian, and educator Morris Schappes, called out the tragedy of what Diamond and other Jewish authors had done: identifying and mourning only Dr Melville Leonard Edelstein, an antiapartheid sociologist and one of three whites and the only Jew killed in the riots compared with hundreds of Black Africans. The editors noted the building up of military ties between Israel and South Africa, and dismissed the statement made by an Israeli cabinet minister that said "There is no ideological significance to our trade relations." Most strongly, they stated succinctly and finally: "Whatever diplomatic reasons Israel may have, U.S. Jews should resist being sucked into South African tourism or weakening opposition to apartheid."[82]

Joining Schappes, in August 1978, Berkeley student David Hammerstein wrote a smart, frank assessment of Israel's relationship with South Africa in *The Jewish Radical*, published by students in the left-leaning Radical Jewish Union at University of California at Berkeley. The issue's subjects linked many of the progressive currents running through the American Jewish world in that moment, with articles on "Marx and the Jewish question," "Judaism and Feminism," "Israel Should Agree to Meet PLO" and "Begin's Palestinian Bantustan" (a reference to the South African "Bantustans" where the apartheid regime "relocated" Black South Africans).

In the year since Schappes's writing, Menachem Begin's surprising upset victory in 1977 meant that a broader agenda of ethnic nationalism was at work in Israeli politics. According to Polakow-Suransky, Begin and other members of his Likud Party were willing "to tolerate xenophobic and racist ideas" if they served that agenda. Echoing Unna's narrative, Polakow-Suransky sees a direct parallel in Begin's Zionism and Afrikaner nationalism: using "military force to ensure national survival."[83]

Hammerstein began his piece by evoking precisely the same historical moment as begins Polakow-Suransky's study: South African Prime Minister John Vorster's April 1976 visit to Yad Vashem, the Holocaust Memorial in Jerusalem, on an official state visit to Israel.[84] Both authors chose this moment to document the dramatic and striking parallels between Nazi racialism and that of the apartheid regime in South Africa, as well as the growing alliance between the two nations in the 1970s. "Israel, a country founded upon the ashes of Jewish victims of racism, has, in the last ten years, dramatically strengthened its diplomatic, commercial, and military ties with the most racist country in the world, South Africa. At a time when much of the world has begun to disengage from ties with South Africa, Israel is basing a major part of its future on an alliance with the apartheid regime."[85]

Following these statements, Hammerstein reviewed the history of Israel's commercial, military, and diplomatic ties to South Africa. He emphasized each nation's growing isolation: Israel because of the 1973 War, and South Africa because of the iron grip of apartheid. Hammerstein concluded by reminding his audience of American Jewish students of their own role in this new calculus. "South Africa Needs Friends," he explains, "especially in the U.S. where the Carter Administration is under growing pressure by antiapartheid groups and the black community to sever ties with South Africa." "If South Africa hopes to broaden its U.S. public support beyond right-wingers, the organized Jewish community might be a prime hunting ground."[86] The Pam Am tour, he asserted, clearly served as part of this hunt.

Some parts of the mainstream American Jewish community followed through on Hammerstein's predictions, defending Israel's trade with South

Africa by insisting that it was necessary and also comparatively small, relative to other nations. By 1978, when Hammerstein authored this piece and drew attention to this search for friends, radical critiques of these friendships such as his were few and far between. The editors of *Jewish Currents*, for example, continued to pay attention to the growing ties between Israel and South Africa—not only through tourism, but also military aid. The voice of the journal had come to adopt the response of the mainstream Jewish community: asserting that Israel alone should not be "singled out" for its trade with South Africa, when so many other nations—and many from Black Africa— likewise traded with the apartheid regime. Many of these assertions served as responses to anger in the African American community over Israel's ties to South Africa.[87]

Events the following year only deepened that anger. In 1979, Andrew Young, American Ambassador to the United Nations and the first African American in that post, was forced to resign because he had held a secret meeting with a representative of the PLO, despite the fact that United States policy banned contact with any organization that did not recognize Israel's right to exist.[88] Although only one American Jewish organization, the American Zionist Federation, publicly demanded Young's resignation, many African Americans accused American Jews of working behind the scenes, of demonstrating paternalism in pressuring President Carter to remove Young. They "charged Jews with blocking all programs for improving the lives of nonwhite people anywhere in the world."[89] The response to this event represents another point of the narrative arc of the 1970s: a decade that began with two opposing letters in the *New York Times*—one supporting, one rejecting African American support of Israel, with South Africa mentioned only in the latter—the decade ended with an esteemed Civil Rights organization, the National Association for the Advancement of Colored People (NAACP), explicitly citing Israel's links to South Africa as a key obstacle to Black/Jewish relations in the United States.

Two hundred African American leaders gathered at the headquarters of the NAACP to talk about the Black/Jewish "split." They released a series of talking points that they called "our Declaration of Independence"—from the Black/Jewish alliance, from Jewish contributions to African American organizations. They listed Israel as their number one issue. Jewish leaders condescended to African Americans when they warned them to stay out of Middle East policy, the leaders asserted; African Americans considered the Palestinian cause a human rights issue, in which they had a deep interest.

Second on the Declaration list was Southern Africa. Mainstream presses took note. *Time Magazine* recorded that:

> The black manifesto demanded that Jews bring pressure on Israel to halt "its support of those repressive and racist regimes" in South Africa and Zimbabwe/ Rhodesia. Israel does in fact maintain a flourishing trade with South Africa ($120 million last year), and it provided military assistance that has been used

against black guerrillas. Ties between Israel and South Africa started when both nations needed whatever allies they could find. Israel also used to help black Africa until the Africans themselves broke off these relations in order to take a more pro-Arab position.[90]

Other organizations followed the NAACP's lead in linking Israel's treatment of Palestinians to its ties to South Africa, and then to criticism of American Jews for not pressuring Israel to change its position on both. TransAfrica, an African American lobbying group that later led effective antiapartheid protests outside of the South African embassy in Washington DC, issued a statement immediately following the NAACP conference. Under the headline "Black American Lobby Backs Palestinian State," the *New York Times* reported that the group spoke for its 10,000 members in blasting Israel for its treatment of Palestinians, and too for the "growing intimacy between Israel and the state of South Africa."[91]

With this declaration, African American Civil Rights leaders sought independence from American Jews, listing Israel and apartheid, along with other tensions, as prime motivators for that quest. With the Pan Am tour, South African Jewish leaders sought friends because the global antiapartheid movement increasingly alienated their minority rule government. Poised between these two quests, American Jews navigated the perilous 1970s with attention to global conversations about Zionism and local condemnations of Jewish dissent about Israel's policies.

In the 1970s, apartheid's definition expanded, used by leaders and laypeople alike to refer to oppressive state ideologies anywhere in the world. From South African Prime Minister John Vorster to American President Jimmy Carter, political leaders of these years would come to use the term to call out the conditions in Israel's Occupied Territories. As the apartheid analogy took on a power of its own, American Jewish leaders consistently circled back to the United Nations resolution and to their own definition of Zionism as a liberatory vision. They fiercely defended Israel in the face of these growing critiques.

American Jewish leaders' positions on these issues in the 1970s contributed to the destruction of alliances with African Americans, alliances that would have aided the building of a unified Jewish response to South African apartheid. Their positions also created bitter debates in spaces often seen as sites for social experimentation and cultural critiques. The following two chapters chronicle the response to Zionism is racism in some of these spaces: in the women's movement, on American college campuses, and in old and new Jewish organizations.

5

Jewish Women, Zionism, and Apartheid

Many American Jewish women first encountered "Zionism is racism" at the world conference of the International Women's Year in Mexico City, the first United Nations Conference on the status of women. For Zionist and non-Zionist women in the women's movement, this first encounter held great significance. One communal Jewish leader described the feeling at the conference as "scary, disruptive, and chaotic," with women feeling "scarred and disappointed."[1] The sense of disappointment was as deep as the excitement had been in the lead up to the conference. Activists in many nations had celebrated the United Nations' recognition of the profound impact of the international women's movement with the planning of Mexico City and two subsequent conferences as part of its UN Decade for Women from 1975–1985.[2] In the United States, as the women's movement gained tremendous momentum, white women and women of color anticipated unprecedented opportunity for unity on pressing issues.

The Mexico City conference had many successes. It led to more data collection and analysis specifically about women. As feminist writer and scholar Devaki Jain notes, this "demand that member states review their procedure of data collection ... helped reduce some of the invisibility of women's work and contributions to society." The conference drew attention to the goal of women's equal access to all parts of society, establishing institutions in many nations to plan programs around women's international development. Broadly, Mexico City provided the foundation for a new partnership between the United Nations and women's groups.[3] As human rights scholar Niamh Reilly writes, the International Women's Year moved women's rights and gender issues "from the margin to the centre of key UN agendas."[4]

Yet Cold War and other tensions took a toll on the conference. Issues of concern divided women of the Global North and South. Women from the North, "where feminism was taking hold," were concerned about "male-female relations and opportunities." For delegates from the South, "fresh from colonial domination, issues such as apartheid, the global economy, and Palestinian rights were integral to improving the status and situation of women."[5]

As delegates to the conference later observed, political concerns of the Middle East and Southern Africa consistently divided delegates. "Virtually all" delegates stood opposed to South African apartheid. But not all delegates agreed that they should lend support to "the struggle of peoples in Rhodesia, Namibia, South Africa, and the occupied territories." Among the most rancorous debates were those over Israel and Palestine. Indeed, when Israel's chief delegate rose to speak, Arab delegations walked out in protest of Israeli policies. Israel's delegate "calmly responded that the walkout had no place in a conference on women's issues."[6] Yet those in attendance reached no consensus on this point either.

Later, the UN "Zionism is racism" Resolution 3379 traveled to the UN General Assembly, where it passed despite "strenuous Western opposition." The impact on American women's roles in the international women's movement was profound: "U.S. support for the UN immediately declined," commentators note, "just as International Women's Year (IWY), one of the most successful UN-sponsored years, drew to a close and just as Americans were pressing for their own IWY conference."[7]

For many Jewish women with deep investments in Zionism and Israel, Mexico City's inclusion of Zionism is racism proved utterly disappointing, even disorienting. Zionism and apartheid proved important to the aftermath of this resolution globally and locally, and the women's movement provided Jewish women with a space to work out their positions on both. They struggled with a schism in Zionism's definition in international diplomatic dialogues: some embraced Zionism as a liberation ideology realized in the State of Israel; others saw it as oppressive, a product of imperialism, and sympathized with Palestinians as its victims. In the women's movement, Jewish women (among others) had to reckon with this new language and a new set of ideas—all refracted through the lenses of apartheid, race, and colonialism— about what Zionism and feminism meant to them as individuals.

Before 1975, there is a nearly-complete silence on apartheid among Jewish women as recorded by mainstream Jewish organizations, likely because there were so very few women in leadership positions.[8] The dearth of women's voices on apartheid, then, mirrors the patriarchal arrangements in Jewish organizational and traditional religious life. Buoyed up by the women's movement, and mobilized in part by the Zionism is racism resolution, Jewish women found their voices in Jewish and secular organizations in the 1970s and 1980s, at UN Women's Conferences and beyond.[9] In these years, many Jewish women worked out their positions on Zionism and racism, apartheid and colonialism, within the women's movement and outside of it.

Scholars of African and African American women's struggles against apartheid locate their protests at the intersection of racism and sexism, the white supremacy and patriarchy embedded in colonialism and its legacies. In the 1970s and 1980s, self-identified Jewish women activists with the many privileges of whiteness protested apartheid as they struggled too with the power distribution and patriarchy in traditional religious Judaism and Jewish organizational life. These women moved within and outside of

Jewish organizations according to their vision of Jewishness, of how Jewish power and influence should be used in the postwar world.[10]

At least a decade before Zionism is racism, exclusion from a patriarchal religion left some Jewish feminists with the urgent need to redefine Judaism for themselves. Jewish women began building feminist Jewish institutions in the early 1970s.[11] Some created new religious homes for themselves in the Jewish counterculture: in havurot (Jewish prayer or discussion groups), in Jewish feminist, Zionist, and liberal/left organizations. Others participated in the Jewish roots movement, inspired by the liberation movements of the 1960s and 1970s, by Black Power, and by the new brand of Zionism in post-1967 America. Many of these women felt discomfort with Jewish assimilation and with what they saw as anti-Semitism within the global women's movement. Their sense of being under siege from anti-Israel, anti-Zionist, and anti-Semitic attacks—and indeed from anticolonialist activists whom they felt unfairly conflated Zionism with racism and imperialism—had profound implications for their roles in the antiapartheid movement. As Jewish women challenged gendered hierarchies in the Jewish and secular worlds, they also engaged in painful contests over definitions of Zionism and of Jewishness itself.

Still other Jewish women left the organized Jewish world altogether, still seeing their individual Jewishness as bound up in global, universalist work toward justice. Yet another group of Jewish women defined themselves as women first and foremost, without reference to Jewishness at all, and disentangled all of their political choices from debates over Jewishness. For nearly all of these women, defining their relationships to Jewishness and protest hinged on their perceptions of the American Jewish community: its global politics (especially its support of Israel and South Africa) as well as its politics of nationalism, sexuality, gender, and class.

Scholars have extensively documented the shortcomings of a movement whose language embraced the liberation of all women and men from rigid constructions of gender, yet that fractured along the lines of class, race, ethnicity, sexuality, age, ability, and religion. Zionism and increasingly the practice and concept of apartheid proved to be divisive issues that painfully split sisterhood, dividing women and preventing coalition building on crucial issues—including South African apartheid. The fact that this decade of women's liberation movements overlapped with the building momentum and the growing reach and urgency of the global antiapartheid movement lent even greater significance to these lost opportunities. From the perspective of some Zionist Jewish women, the anti-Israel, anti-Semitic political rhetoric and positions of antiapartheid activists at key moments, such as UN conferences, proved prohibitive. These activists created an exclusivity that did not allow for Zionist Jewish women to join with them in working for women and against colonialism.[12] From the perspective of some anti-apartheid activists, allegiance to Zionism as a liberation movement denied the impact of Israeli Occupation on the Palestinian population, and ignored Israel's role in South African apartheid; further, it alienated women of color and their allies as they sought to link colonialism and oppression across the globe.

This chapter begins with an event discussed in chapter 4: the United Nations Zionism as racism Resolution 3379, whose roots can be traced back to the first United Nations conference on the global status of women. It charts the long-standing impact of that resolution and its language on American Jewish women by focusing first on the varied, at times divergent, responses to the UN Women's Conferences of 1975, 1980, and 1985. To capture the diverse experiences of Jewish women in the women's movement, the chapter then moves from encounters with global diplomatic discourses to more local, grassroots American encounters with apartheid. To that end, as in a previous chapter, this one includes brief biographical portraits that illustrate the lack of consensus among Jewish women about how to respond to the challenges of apartheid and Zionism in these years. The final section of the chapter presents brief biographical sketches of famous South African Jewish women activists. For the purpose of this study, their approaches to apartheid, Zionism, and Jewishness in South Africa help to bring American Jewish struggles with apartheid into sharp relief.

American Jewish women's historians dedicate the majority of their analyses to Zionist Jewish women. By shedding light on Jewish women's contests over what constitutes Jewish values and Jewish activism, by integrating Jewish women with diverse approaches to Zionism and to apartheid, this chapter presents an analysis of the broader contours of Jewish struggles over apartheid and Jewishness itself. It invites new chapters and new approaches in American Jewish women's history and United States and global women's history, asking questions about the limits of coalitions, identity politics, and pluralism, and also about what the women in these pages took with them out of these struggles over apartheid.

JEWISH WOMEN, ZIONISM, AND APARTHEID: THE "GRAVEYARD OF THE WOMEN'S MOVEMENT"[13]

Israel's growing alliance with South Africa in the 1970s, along with the Zionism is racism resolution, introduced great controversy to the women's movement. As discussed in the previous chapter, the resolution grew out of Cold War politics, Arab and other nations' hostility to Israel, Israeli policies of Occupation, and the growth of the Third World movement, which allied itself with Palestinian liberation. Some Jewish women felt that these controversies laid bare their most important identities and loyalties, reinvigorating their Jewish selves and making them into Jewish feminists.[14] The resolution propelled these feminists into self-consciously *Jewish* feminism and engagement with African American and other feminists over issues like Israel's ties to South Africa.

For feminists like activist, journalist, and author Letty Cottin Pogrebin, cofounder of *Ms. Magazine* in 1971, the initial language of "Zionism is racism" proved transformative. She writes, "although it was ostensibly the

Israelis who had been attacked as racists, I knew the arrow was also meant for me....[T]o feminists who hate Israel I was not a woman, I was a *Jewish* woman. The men of the minyan (Jewish prayer group) might not consider me a Jew among Jews, but to many of those delegates in Mexico City, that's all I was."[15]

Pogrebin took part in the "roots movement" of the 1970s, which drew women back to Jewish belonging and then to Zionism. The search involved "not simply a rediscovery of Jewishness but also of anti-Semitism, and, in anti-Semitism, proof of the need for a Jewish homeland."[16] Indeed, Pogrebin spoke of Zionism and feminism in the same breath, seeing both as liberation movements: "Zionism is to Jews what feminism is to women," she wrote in her classic Jewish feminist text, *Deborah, Golda, and Me*, in 1991, "a source of solidarity, pride, and unity." She adamantly rejected "Zionism is racism": "I know Zionists who are racists, just as I know racist feminists, but that didn't make Zionism racism any more than a few bigoted women made feminism racism," she wrote. "At the heart of the matter," she concluded, "Zionism and feminism are directly analogous in that both movements are fueled by the fires of self-determination."[17]

Radical Zionist, American feminist, antiwar, Civil Rights and gay rights activist Congresswoman Bella Abzug agreed. Abzug had attended the camps of Hashomer Hatzair as a child, and championed Zionism as a liberation movement for the Jewish people. She mounted a fierce defense of Israel in Mexico City and again at the second UN women's conference in Copenhagen, Denmark, in 1980. Abzug observed that the anti-Zionist statement could be traced back to the fact that the UN conference had been "organized by men of the United Nations and therefore had all the faults and prejudices of the United Nations." She took credit for the American delegation's vote of no, as they had originally planned to abstain from the vote.[18] As Pogrebin writes, when "an American black woman rose to accuse our delegation of deferring to the Jews [because] she couldn't understand what was wrong with saying Zionism is racism," Abzug stood up. She gave voice to her definition of Zionism as a "liberation movement for a people who have been persecuted all their lives and throughout human history."[19]

Abzug and Pogrebin's definition of Zionism stood at odds with those of other, non-Zionist women in the global women's movement, and with the Third World's definition of Zionism as described by Layntner in 1976. Those disagreements had profound implications for the global women's movement and for the fight against South African apartheid. At the 1980 mid-decade conference for women in Copenhagen, links between South Africa and Israel were just below the surface of fierce debates over Zionism that divided feminist delegates there and for years afterward. Pogrebin noted this dynamic in her controversial 1982 article in *Ms. Magazine*, "Anti-Semitism in the Women's Movement." In it she tells the story of an exchange that occurred one month before the UN Copenhagen conference. She invited an African American friend to join her in signing a petition that might prevent "Zionism is racism" from derailing the Copenhagen conference on women's issues, as many felt it had in Mexico City. "My friend told me the Copenhagen conference was a hot topic in the black community. Trade-offs were being negotiated; an antiapartheid resolution might be passed in return for American blacks' compliance on a Palestinian agenda item. 'Please understand,' said my friend, 'I can't afford to sign.'"[20]

Not only did votes on apartheid and Zionism serve as a currency of exchange, a dynamic that would be repeated in future attempts at reconciling conflicting agendas. In international diplomatic circles, apartheid came to be synonymous with intolerable state oppression. Zionism's definition splintered, and the Third World definition relied on the analogy, later the equation, of Israel's policies of Occupation with apartheid.

Some Jewish feminists pushed against the elision of Zionism and apartheid. Indeed, they compared the hostility they felt from Palestinian women and their allies to the racism of apartheid. "Many Jews believe that pro-PLO women in America are expressing their anti-Semitism as surely as pro-Afrikaner whites in South Africa are assumed to be expressing their racism," Pogrebin wrote, noting that "the average Palestinian woman would wish me dead."[21] Thus she concluded that these dynamics left her cut off from the political possibilities of universal sisterhood: "As much as I might wish for a world of universalist values and de-emphasized differences, I would no longer tolerate a women's movement in which Jews are the only group asked to relinquish their own interests while other women were allowed to push their private agendas and subvert feminist ideals when it suited them. I would no longer assume all women were my sisters." She now embraced a "pluralist feminism founded on a mutual respect for each other's 'identity politics,' which include the particularities of culture, peoplehood, and history."[22]

The feminist Jewish magazine *Lilith*'s report on the Copenhagen conference illustrates how Cold War alliances, identity, and global politics linked Israel and apartheid, alienating Zionist women. "Israel was insulted at every channel," they reported, because the PLO dominated. "Whenever the microphones were opened for questions from the floor," they reported, "the PLO was there. Equality? 'We can't have equality without having a country.' Apartheid? 'Vorster was a Nazi, and now Israel is South Africa's best friend.'"[23] The following year, *Lilith* lamented that "The virulent anti-Semitism expressed at the August 1980 U.N. Mid-Decade Conference on Women in Copenhagen–sometimes, but not always, masked as anti-Zionism–has not yet been discussed in the women's movement. Particularly shocking to many of the Jewish women there was the lack of support on this issue from other women."[24] Jewish women felt that anticolonialist and pro-Palestinian activists could not engage in a discussion of apartheid and imperialism without including Zionism. So long as this remained the primary rhetorical strategy, they could not participate.

In Copenhagen, delegates engaged in fierce arguments about Zionism and racism. Their alliances reflected increased American isolation at the United Nations, and the increasing power and visibility of Asian and African nations. There was a growing group of nations hostile to Israel and its policies, and on that issue America stood increasingly alone. That fact had been on display with the passage of Resolution 3379. Ultimately, due to paragraphs linking Zionism with racism (categorized with imperialism, colonialism, and apartheid as "obstacles to women's equality and participation"), the United States (along with Israel and Canada) voted against the Programme of Action adopted at the conference's conclusion.[25]

The Copenhagen conference was a pivotal moment in the women's movement, as it "helped legitimize women as an issue not just for the West but for the world."[26] Indeed, many women found the UN Conferences of the Decade for Women opening up possibilities for unity. Especially for women from developing countries, Jain writes, it "was the first time they realized that women around the world struggled with the same issues and had similar interests."[27] Zionist Jewish women and their allies found that their own unity around the issue of Zionism prevented them from feeling a sense of belonging to the global women's movement, which strove—with limited success—to build bridges among women in all nations.

There were fleeting moments in which it seemed possible to build bridges. Abzug worked to create a caucus of Jewish and Arab women that met one morning at 6 o'clock, one hour before the Copenhagen conference program began. Feminist activist Robin Morgan "had some credibility among the Arabs" due to her Third World activism, and she collaborated with Abzug in bringing the women together. "We did not solve the Middle East [crisis]," Morgan reported, but the women told stories, and "that magic happened, where people embrace and cry."[28]

These moments did not distract women on all sides of the Zionism issue from feeling betrayed by the women's movement. Gail Lerner, who attended as a representative for the World Council of Churches, used the word "'terrified' to describe the atmosphere at a panel on refugees, where Palestinian women arrived to "find the room packed with anti-Palestinian Israel supporters." Even conference organizers had mixed assessments of the damage done by the Israeli/Palestinian issue: while most said it raised strong ill feelings, not all agreed that it had "derailed" the conference, as Zionist delegates like Pogrebin maintained.[29]

Many, however, recognized that the Zionist controversy distracted delegates from other crucial issues. Some Western delegates expressed "outrage" that delegates preferred to voice "global platitudes" that "obscure[d] the realistic examination of the plight of women."[30] Agreeing with Abzug, historian Judith Zinsser writes that the issue created a false binary between feminism and politics: "in playing out this controversy [over Zionism is racism], all of the delegates endorsed the realities of the patriarchal system of international relations...[and] unintentionally ratified the view that women's concerns were marginal, apolitical, and thus outside of the usual meanings of 'politics.'"[31]

Radical anti-imperialist activists in an integrated San Francisco group known as the Alliance Against Women's Oppression observed that "a strongly pro-Zionist position became the most clearly articulated and widely held position in both the liberal and radical sectors of the women's movement." Institutions of the movement were "consumed with questions of Jewish identity and anti-Semitism," and as a result women activists ignored pressing anti-imperialist causes, such as those in the Middle East.[32] Historically allied with labor, feminist, antiracist, revolutionary and antiwar groups, these activists wrote immediately after Israel's 1982 invasion of Lebanon, insisting on the obligation of the women's movement to represent women in Lebanon and in the Palestinian territories, areas occupied by Israel. Invoking an alliance only just beginning to earn visibility, they argued that Israel "upholds apartheid in South Africa and cooperates in the development of nuclear technology with what must surely be the world's most despised and despicable state." If Zionism's purpose were to "make the world safe for Jews," these women argued, then why were Israel's policies "holding back liberation struggles around the world"? In seeing these separate struggles as interconnected, these women felt that the stakes in these debates were too high to ignore: ultimately, for them, the question was "whether the U.S. women's movement can become an integral, active component of the international struggle against oppression."[33]

As this reproof demonstrates, controversies over Zionism and apartheid frustrated potential alliances between liberation movements across the world, including the women's movement. Many feminists—both Jewish and non-Jewish—were quick to point out that the imperialist and anti-imperialist debates at the UN conferences fell within the realm of international diplomacy, and did not necessarily reflect grassroots feminist ideas. These same women strongly criticized some Jewish feminists for the "disturbing political consequences" of their near-exclusive focus on identity politics and anti-Semitism. Rather, they urged all women to find common ground and focus on a "politics of issues."[34] When looking ahead to the next UN women's conference in Kenya five years later, feminists—and especially those supportive of Zionism—minced no words in expressing their dire predictions for what another controversy over Zionism might mean. Margaret Daley, a US Congressional Staff Advisor to the US Delegation to the Copenhagen and Nairobi conferences, observed that "the Kenyan hosts did not want Nairobi to be the graveyard of the women's movement."[35]

For Jewish women, the stakes had been raised by delegates to Mexico City, not only over Zionism and their roles and agendas in the women's movement, but also over the gender politics of the Jewish communal world. Certainly Jewish organizations planned comprehensive responses to the notion that "Zionism is racism," but would men or women shape the responses put forward at the future UN women's conferences? Affiliated Jewish women lacked power in mainstream American Jewish communal organizations commensurate with the sum total of all the work they did within these organizations.[36] They mobilized to craft their own responses to 3379 in groups such as the National Council of Jewish Women. They built their own alliances and ran their own workshops in Nairobi. The Leadership Conference of National Jewish Women's Organizations, active for a decade on the cause of Soviet Jewry, issued public statements supporting President Carter's decision to oppose "Zionism is Racism."[37]

Male leaders in mainstream Jewish organizations—and they were nearly all male leaders—tried to take over for women who had been working in the feminist movement for many years. One Jewish leader described it as nothing short of a "power struggle."[38] Zionist Jewish women were granted separatism in the UN women's conferences. Shattering conventional gendered expectations of traditional Jewish culture and religion, they used it as a strategy for finding their voice.[39] In statements of confidence or hesitation, they consistently drew on their own authority as long-standing feminist activists in insisting that critiques of Zionism not "derail" the conference away from women's issues. Of the UN Nairobi conference, for example, Evelyn Sommer of the Women's International Zionist Organization wrote: "I approach it with trepidation....We are going to support Israel and because we have been dedicated to women's rights for 60 years. We expect to have 120 women there from all parts of the world, and we are going to conduct a workshop on battered women."[40]

Other Zionist Jewish women exercised leadership in working to build alliances prior to the Nairobi conference. Convening meetings in New York and in cities across the United States, Israel, and Europe, they hoped they might prevent the attacks they had witnessed in Copenhagen.[41] Pogrebin joined with Marlene Provizer of the National Jewish Community Relations Advisory Council, New Jewish Agenda's (NJA's) Executive Director Reena Bernards and National Co-Chair Christie Balka, and together they organized a series of dialogues with Arab, Jewish, and African American women that ran for a year and a half in New York City prior to the conference. NJA was a newly formed progressive, grassroots Jewish organization, and its leaders stepped out into the fray of Zionism is racism with firm intentions to build bridges of understanding.[42]

These dialogues were to encourage all women to understand each other's convictions and to feel they would be seen and heard. The organizers felt they met with some success. Pogrebin wrote that the Black-Jewish women's groups, which included several dozen women, "helped soften the anti-Israel attacks that...resurface[d] in Nairobi," and also, importantly, "helped press for resolutions opposing South African apartheid as well."[43]

At a workshop on apartheid in Nairobi, Provizer sat among Third World and Western women listening to speakers of the ANC, some of whom "were critical of Israel." It was her turn to speak, and she recalls "just shaking the whole time." Fearful that anti-Zionism or anti-Semitism would disrupt the workshop—or shut it down altogether—she felt relieved that those in the room "applauded very politely."[44] The room's applause signaled to Provizer that Jewish women allied with Zionism could carve out a space in the anti-apartheid movement—and other liberation movements. Because, as Provizer explained, Jewish women, like all women there, wanted to find some way for the conference to focus broadly on "land rights, education, clean water, and child care." "We got to Nairobi," she explains, and "saw African women walking 60 miles a day to be a part of this life changing experience." "We cared about Israel," notes Provizer, "but it wasn't the only thing we cared about."[45]

Yet the tensions in the setup and execution of the pre-conference meetings and later the conference sessions reflected broader, unresolved tensions—both in the positioning of the Zionist Jewish women and of some segments of the women's movement more broadly. Carole Haddad, National Coordinator for the Feminist Arab Network, wrote to NJA's Bernards to complain that the New York City dialogues' leadership was exclusive—with no Arab or African American women involved in the planning—and "tightly controlled" so that all non-Jewish women wishing to speak about Israel's Occupation were asked to "bury our issues and our pain." Haddad also noted that Pogrebin's signature on the invitation letter "created doubt about the motives behind the proposed dialogue," as Pogrebin was the author of a "viciously anti-Arab article in *Ms.* Magazine" that "not only insulted Arabs...but also Jews who do not equate anti-Zionism with anti-Semitism."[46] At the sessions, too, women of all backgrounds and political perspectives had to walk a fine line, for there were women present who saw clear parallels between Zionism and apartheid, and who wanted to speak about issues of concern with Israel's Occupied Territories.

NJA attempted to walk this fine line, adding important qualifiers to its perspective on Zionism. Its leaders held workshops in Nairobi aimed at minimizing tensions so as to allow for coalition building, bringing together Arab and Jewish women from across the world. NJA members distributed 4,000 copies of a brochure that offered guidelines for dialogues, including one point that noted "Zionism is a multi-faceted movement for Jewish national liberation and it is therefore unconstructive to the process of dialogue to assert that it is equivalent with racism (this is not to deny that racist policies do exist within Israel)."[47] NJA's parenthetical acknowledgment distanced them from those who rejected any criticism of Israeli policies, yet left them within the conference's Zionist camp.

Western Zionist delegates joined Israeli delegates in defending Zionism, Israel's alliance with South Africa, and also its treatment of Palestinians in the Territories. Israeli delegation leader Sara Doron, a national legislator in the conservative Likud Party, relied on the tactic of denying that Israel alone should be "singled out" for criticism. She was quoted in the *Los Angeles Times* as saying that "the problems of Israel—particularly of Palestinian women living in Israeli-occupied Arab lands—should not be singled out at the conference when there are refugees all over the world." Israeli delegate Naomi Chazan, who later served as a legislator in the liberal Meretz Party, told a news conference: "It is imperative to separate Zionism from racism.... Israel and the Jewish people abhor apartheid. It is demeaning to the just cause of black people and an insult to the Jewish people, because it is intrinsically anti-Semitic."[48]

The moment of the Nairobi conference coincided with an unprecedented level of energy in the global antiapartheid movement, reaching across the world onto college campuses, legislative agendas, and UN conferences alike. While the *LA Times* article first documented an anti-Israel protest at the women's conference, it went on to observe another protest as well:

> A larger group protesting apartheid, South Africa's legalized racial segregation system, were led in song at the university by black nationalists from the African National Congress and the South-West Africa People's Organization. Women and scores of men sang "God Bless Africa" in Xhosa—a language of many South African blacks—and brandished their fists, shouting, "Victory to the people!" They listened to speakers from the two guerrilla movements fighting to overthrow the government in the last bastion of white rule on the African continent.[49]

Dramatic language matched the dramatic activism unfolding on the world stage. Competing for the attention of the delegates and the press, demonstrations against Israel and South African apartheid coincided. Delegates had to choose which to attend and respond to, just as they had to decide where to stand and vote on both issues.

They remained utterly divisive down to the final moments of the conference. The *New York Times* reported that negotiations over the final document's paragraphs "broke down" over the following issues: "a call for economic sanctions" against apartheid South Africa, "condemnation of Zionism as an obstacle to peace," a description of the "plight of the Palestinians and redistribution of the world's wealth between rich and poor."[50] On the final night of the conference, "by a variety of stratagems, including breaking for a recess of over five hours, Margaret Kenyatta, President of the Conference, former mayor of Nairobi, and Kenya's ambassador to the United Nations, gaveled through the most controversial paragraph, No. 95. This section had originally included a condemnation of Zionism," the issue that had occasioned so much controversy in Mexico City and in Copenhagen. In its amended form in the Nairobi Forward-Looking Strategies document, this provocative clause became the less specific condemnation of "all forms of racism and racial discrimination."[51]

NJA issued a press release applauding its members' important role in "shifting a deadlocked conversation toward dialogue." "I found a hunger for contact on all sides," noted Balka, so "NJA intends to persist in this dialogue."[52] Pogrebin wrote of Nairobi that "[t]his time, Jewish women came home battered but not broken."[53]

Maureen Reagan, daughter of President Ronald Reagan and head of the U.S. delegation to Nairobi, reported that "We came home with a document, and it doesn't say Zionism, so we think it's a first-class win for us and for women and the U.N. system as a whole." Although many of the American delegates disagreed with her father's policies—most notably his "constructive engagement" with apartheid South Africa—they could not unify around their sentiments toward what had transpired at the UN conference.[54] Scholars write of the "new international consensus women were slowly building about women's rights" at the Nairobi conference, which "produced a new feeling of solidarity among women from all over the world."⁵⁵ Apartheid and Zionism created and reinforced divides that detracted from this consensus.

Upon reflection, some delegates ranked apartheid and Zionism as the two "key anti-imperialist issue[s]" of the Nairobi conference. While Namibian and South African women differed over the issue of armed struggle, noted British Delegate Mandana Hendessi, they united over "the ending of apartheid and independence of Namibia." There was no unity, however, on the idea proposed by members of a Western "pro-Zionist" lobby, that "'Zionism is the national liberation movement of the Jews.'" The group "included black women from the US who drew parallels between the oppression of the Jews and that of the blacks," and they "frequently attached the 'anti-Semitic' label to any woman who opposed Zionism." Hendessi blamed "the state of Israel today," along with "Israel's importance to US imperialism" for preventing "real cooperation" between Israeli and Palestinian women.⁵⁶

Within the American women's movement, activist and academic Eleanor Roffman and others were often labeled "self-hating" when they gave voice to these ideas and to their own anti-Zionism. The accusations were "very intimidating to a lot of progressive Jewish women," Roffman says, "who might otherwise have taken a progressive stand on Israel and the Middle East."⁵⁷ Yet in some grassroots American feminist organizations, Jewish women carved out spaces to debate these new definitions of Zionism and apartheid and how to respond to them.

In Boston, Roffman joined Feminist Jews for Justice, which she described as "a place to be with other women who felt similar to you and lived in similar socio-cultural conditions." Many of the members had parents who had lived through pogroms or other anti-Semitic attacks, as Roffman's had. With a working-class background, Roffman considered herself a Zionist until her trip to Israel in 1976, when she saw first-hand the treatment of Palestinians in the Territories. In the women's movement, and specifically with other left Jewish women, she began working out what she came to see as the connections between imperialism and Zionism. For her and others in the group, it was the language of the antiapartheid movement, specifically, that lent itself to a deeper examination of what was happening in Israel. "Conversations about Israel and South Africa contributed to people's growing consciousness," she said. Later, Roffman joined the Boycott, Divestment, and Sanctions movement, which applied the language and tactics of the anti-South African apartheid movement to the Israeli/Palestinian conflict. She speaks of her role in global liberation struggles as that of a Jewish feminist.⁵⁸

Founded in 1988, the Jewish Women's Committee to End the Occupation (JWCEO) held weekly vigils in New York City outside of the offices of major Jewish organizations. Its cofounders were: peace and antiapartheid activist and author Grace Paley; author, academic, and gay rights activist Irene Klepfisz; and author Clare Kinberg. Klepfisz and Kinberg were leaders in NJA. The three women organized the group and the vigils to demonstrate "that there was not unanimous support in the American Jewish community for the Israeli government's policies in the West Bank and Gaza."⁵⁹

These brief portraits suggest how Zionism and apartheid were linked through painful controversies within the global women's movement that often left American (and other nations') Jewish, Zionist women, along with Palestinian women and their allies, feeling alienated, frustrated, and alone. At times, claims made by actors on all sides of these issues relied on fundamentally misleading distortions: that all Zionist ideology supported ridding the Middle East region of non-Jews; that all Palestinian ideology supported Jewish genocide. Bolstered by these falsehoods, and too by bruised feelings of invisibility and victimhood, women could not find common ground. For the purposes of this study, this meant that many Jewish women struggled to find space for themselves in the antiapartheid and women's movements.

American Jewish Women against Apartheid

Scholars have examined the immense successes of American Jewish feminist women within the Jewish world, as well as Jewish women's contributions to feminism and to the Civil Rights movement.[60] The narratives for some of these women end with a departure from the left over specifically Jewish issues: Israel, Zionism, and anti-Semitism.[61] Analyzing Jewish women's encounters with apartheid, however, reveals narratives that reflect back on the politics of mainstream American Jewish organizations, as well as the women's movement in the United States and around the world; to hear the voices of Jewish women is to hear feminist critiques of the American Jewish establishment's sexism, homophobia, intolerance for dissent, and Zionism, as well as their critiques of the limits of coalition building over apartheid.

Within the narratives presented here are the worldviews of antiapartheid Jewish women who stayed in the movement when others departed, largely because of the movement's critiques of Israel and Zionism. These brief biographical snapshots belong in studies of white American contributions to the antiapartheid movement, studies that reflect back on white privilege and racial hierarchies. These snapshots belong too in studies of Jewish women's contributions to the movement, reflecting back on American Jewish political commitments in the age of the antiapartheid movement's growing power and visibility.

Sharon Kleinbaum

Rabbi Sharon Kleinbaum's family's activist history goes back to her suffragist mother and socialist father. Her father grew up in a Yiddish-speaking, secular, immigrant, socialist family in the Bronx. Kleinbaum recalls his sobbing at the death of Dr Martin Luther King. The defining experience she cites first, though, was his experience as a socialist and pacifist during World War II. As a social worker, he agreed to work in psychiatric hospitals for his alternative wartime service. He found that career army men were sympathetic to his not wanting to fight, while the Jewish chaplains, she explains, would not forgive him for his refusal to bear arms.[62]

Kleinbaum rejected the Jewishness that she saw outside of her childhood world of family and friends, where, she says, the Holocaust and Israel served as the foundations of Jewishness. She joined her older brother's work for Cesar Chavez and the United Farm Workers, canvassed for Eugene McCarthy at age nine, and in eighth grade announced at a school debate that "Nixon should be impeached for war crimes."[63] When asked about her Jewish family history, she consistently refers to the fact that they saw Jewish historical legacies as liberal and left political commitments. But as her story of her father's World War II pacifism suggests, she often felt alienated from the Jewish world: she attended a new Orthodox high school in her town, traveling with them to the huge protests over "Zionism is Racism" at the United Nations in 1975. But by her senior year she felt wholly "uncomfortable with the position of women" in that movement. In hindsight, she attributes that discomfort in part to her coming out: "I didn't see any place for me as a lesbian in the Jewish world," she said.[64]

In college at Barnard, she remained alienated from any Jewish religious identity, unaffiliated with a synagogue community and disconnected from Israel and Zionism as well. Organized, affiliated Judaism meant political conservatism to her, best represented by the Columbia students who wrote "Reagan" on their yarmulkes in support of his 1980 presidential bid.[65] Racism, sexism, homophobia, conservative Zionism, and Reaganite conservatism marked the mainstream Jewish world that she encountered.

Kleinbaum tells of how she came to understand the possibilities for sustaining the divergent brand of Jewishness her family modeled once she began studying Jewish history. She took a course called "Jews and Revolution" with one of the pioneers of Jewish feminism and Jewish feminist scholarship, Dr Paula Hyman. "Everyone in the class was interested in the 'Jews' part of the course title," she recalled, "I was the only one interested in the Revolution part."[66] The course transformed her. In learning about legacies of Jewish radicalism, Kleinbaum began to "integrate" her identity as a radical, political, secular, Jew.

Following the global-minded protests of her family, Kleinbaum joined the Committee Against Investment in South Africa in 1978, as a first-year student at Barnard.[67] She took part in teach-ins and demonstrations, and in May 1978, she led a sit-in at the Columbia Graduate School of Business. So fresh was the memory of the Columbia Student Strike and protests ten years before, the University kept the building open until midnight so they would not have to arrest the students; they "got them to sell out," Kleinbaum says, by promising that President McGill would meet with six of them the following day.[68] Kleinbaum was one of the six, and their efforts led to Columbia's divestment.[69]

Kleinbaum's religious journey took her back to the Jewish world. In rabbinical school, she became what she terms a "progressive Zionist," which she considers herself still today. "I am passionately Zionist and passionately critical [of Israeli policies]," she says, drawing attention to the growth of Jewish settlements on the West Bank and also the treatment of African refugees in Israel.[70]

Kleinbaum is now the rabbi of the largest gay, lesbian, bisexual, transgender, and queer/questioning synagogue in the world, Congregation Beit Simhat Torah in New York City, where she sees faith motivating her political work. In that regard, she calls herself a member of a "dying breed," because she says that those who see their Jewish faith as motivating their activism seem today to be on the conservative end of the political spectrum. That conservatism, what she terms the "old boys' network" that dominates the Jewish world, finds her still "on its margins."[71] They often receive her harshly: Orthodox rabbis have compared her to Hitler for "killing the Jewish soul" with her political activism, especially over gay rights and the Israeli/Palestinian conflict.[72] But she is happy there on the margins, she says, as that's where "healthy things happen."[73] Only on those margins does she feel comfortable engaging the broader issues of the world as a Jew.

Criticisms of Kleinbaum draw attention to patriarchal and homophobic norms and intolerance for progressive positions that still characterize parts of the mainstream Jewish community. Her voyage to her own version of Jewishness is instructive for other reasons as well. At her greatest distance from Zionism, as a student in the years of the UN women's conferences, she was most involved in the antiapartheid movement, and thus she remained unaffected by the storms of protest rippling outward from diplomatic language linking Israel, Zionism, and apartheid. When she reentered the organized Jewish world as an adult, it was on her own terms, and therefore, in her words, on its margins.

Ruth Messinger

A historical glance at Ruth Messinger finds her, in contrast to Kleinbaum, right in the center of New York City politics acting on a strong antiapartheid agenda. Like Kleinbaum, Messinger speaks of her political advocacy work as having its origins in her Jewish family history. "The version of Judaism with which I was raised was not focused on what rituals you observed, what denomination you belonged to," she said, "It focused on living as a Jew, which meant working toward justice."[74]

Messinger's mother, Marjorie Wyler, worked in Public Relations for the Jewish Theological Seminary in Manhattan, and "interpreted Judaism to the interfaith community." Her mother was responsible for the first public relations advertisements that spoke about the environment and domestic violence as Jewish issues. Although her family took Jewish prayer and ritual seriously, and though they were leaders in the Jewish world, Messinger chose a story apart from those facts to explain her antiapartheid activism.

She chose instead a court case in which her mother played a key role: *Wilder v. Sugarman*, which began in 1974. Shirley Wilder was a young African American girl in need of foster care but rejected from both private and public agencies because of her race. Noting the racism of these state-subsidized agencies, Judge Justine Wise Polier helped to initiate the class action suit. All New York foster care agencies were listed as defendants, including Jewish agencies. Even with a position on the board of a Jewish childcare association that got city funding, Messinger's mother agreed that a Jewish agency that received city funds should give care to all people. Her position did not earn her friends. Jewish agencies largely protested the suit, arguing that any proposal that diminished the racist policies that led to Wilder's situation would impinge on their religious freedom.[75]

Given the growing conservatism she observed in American Jewish organizations in the 1970s, especially on Civil Rights issues, Messinger worked for justice largely outside of the organized Jewish world. She was a part of the founding of the progressive NJA, offering a workshop presentation at its founding conference in December of 1980.[76] She also celebrated Nelson Mandela's visit to the United States in 1990 with another new, progressive Jewish organization discussed in chapter 7, Jews for Racial and Economic Justice.

But importantly, Messinger participated in the feminist, antiwar, and Civil Rights movements mainly through her work in secular organizations. She learned about South African apartheid through her Civil Rights activism. A member of the New York City Council from 1978 to 1989, Messinger began her public antiapartheid activism as one of the leaders of the move to divest New York City's municipal funds from South African investments in 1984.[77] These were strident actions in an era when most mainstream Jewish organizations were just beginning to appear at antiapartheid protests. This move also prompted the City to stop doing business with all companies that sold goods or services to the apartheid regime. She worked too with New York City labor unions, which together formed the Labor Committee Against Apartheid, to protect the rights of South African workers during the divestment campaigns.[78]

In May 1987, Messinger ran for the Harvard Board of Overseers as a candidate representing Harvard and Radcliffe Alumni/ae Against Apartheid, a group that worked tirelessly to convince Harvard to divest from South Africa.[79] Eventually, Messinger and the group succeeded in electing Archbishop Desmond Tutu to the Board as a write-in candidate in 1989.

Messinger "knew nothing about what the Jewish world was doing with regard to apartheid" at that time. "I already had plenty of differences with the organized Jewish community," she reports. As an elected civic leader, 12 years on the New York City Council and 8 as Manhattan borough president, she wanted to see "rabbis take more vibrant stands, federations and synagogues get more involved" in world issues, instead of focusing so exclusively on American Jewish assimilation and Israel.[80]

After decades of frustration with mainstream Jewish priorities, Messinger joined the mainstream, organized Jewish world in 1998 as CEO of the American Jewish World Service, a faith-based human rights organization.

There she continues to work at the intersection of Jewishness and social justice activism. She talks to the Jewish world about what Jews should do about poverty, which, she admits, is "easier than dealing with Israel."[81]

The Jewish world continues to bristle at her work. The editor of the *New Jersey Jewish News* accused her of putting too much emphasis on "engagement with the wider world." "I don't think we can go as far as Messinger," he writes, "who perceives ethnic loyalties as an obstacle to a general philanthropic and altruistic impulse."[82]

For Messinger, the particular leads to the universal, as she cites her Jewish identity motivating her impulse to fight apartheid and now global inequality. By her lights, many who profess to balance the two allow internal Jewish priorities to outweigh the pressing global issues—like apartheid—that demand a Jewish response. She speaks of finding a "faith heroine" in Helen Suzman, a South African Jewish human rights activist and for 36 years a member of the liberal Progressive Party in Parliament. Suzman spoke out against apartheid in a pro-apartheid, male-dominated society. Suzman "was not a religious Jew," writes Messinger, who also describes herself with these words, "but her values, actions, and life-long struggle for justice expressed a deeply Jewish sensibility."[83]

In a 2009 essay, Messinger spoke back to anti–United Nations sentiment and also to criticisms about prioritizing Jewish communal issues over global crises. In a book about a group of NGOs dedicated to preventing and ending genocide and war crimes, Messinger drew on the idea of these loyalties as promoting altruism and justice. She cowrote the contribution titled "Toward a Jewish Argument for the Responsibility to Protect." Even while she asserted that this responsibility "does not produce a consensus position from the entire Jewish community," she argued that it is grounded in Jewish text and "supported by the particular arc of Jewish historical experience."[84] Certainly Zionists—Jewish feminists and others—offered no consensus on the United Nations and the work of NGOs from the 1970s through today.

Messinger voyages through Jewish texts to demonstrate what she designates as a Jewish imperative: to act when life is at risk. "In its original form," she writes, "the phrase ['Never again'] functioned as a particular rallying cry for Holocaust survivors. It still holds this narrow meaning when used in response to anti-Semitic incidents....Over time, however, the words have come to include a broader commitment among both Jews and non-Jews to respond to atrocity crimes committed against any people."[85]

Messinger's points intersect with the debates over American Jewish antiapartheid work that ran through the twentieth century: urgent debates over Jewish loyalty (to South African, American, and Israeli Jews, to Zionism in its many forms) and Jewish universalism are debates about the very nature of Jewishness itself. Messinger locates her antiapartheid work within the realm of her Jewish work toward justice, and she sees it as imperative that Jewishness is aligned with this work throughout history and throughout the world.

Jewish Women and Apartheid in South Africa and the United States

Scholars of white, South African, Jewish, antiapartheid, activist women define their Jewishness as encompassing universalist work and include them in the canon of Jewish history in postapartheid South Africa—but not without controversy. There are high-stakes debates over who belongs in this canon, and how their belonging might alter the truth about how the organized Jewish world responded to apartheid in South Africa. These historical debates shed light on American Jewish women's activism and the way it challenges conventional narratives of Jewishness and gender. Because, as with American Jewish women in this era, the work of South African radicals such as Ruth First and Ray Alexander shattered conventional gendered expectations in their decisions to join the protests of Black Africans against apartheid.[86] Their histories reveal the complexities of re-canonizing radical antiapartheid activists; they also raise the difficult issue of how to assess the role Jewishness played in their work.[87]

Journalist Glenn Frankel writes that radical South African antiapartheid activist Ruth First was "a minority within a minority within a minority: a left-wing radical in a right-wing country, a white person in a Black liberation movement, and a woman in a male-dominated world."[88] She was also a radical *Jewish* woman amidst an organized Jewish community that refused to tackle the injustice of apartheid. Born in 1925 South Africa to Lithuanian-born communist parents, First was a communist, a tireless political activist, journalist, and researcher exposing the savage inequalities of apartheid. She worked alongside Nelson Mandela and Oliver Tambo, leaders in the ANC, among many others. In 1982, the South African police assassinated her while she was in exile in Mozambique.[89]

Frankel notes that "Jewishness ceased to be part of [the] self-identity" of First and her husband, Joe Slovo, and indeed many of the Jewish radical activists. They had "little but scorn" for Jewish culture and for "the timidity of South African Jews who did not actively oppose apartheid even when they found it distasteful"; they also were "unceasingly critical" of Israel "and its dependence on the imperialist west."[90] Their anti-Zionism found them in the company of Third World activists across the world. It is particularly important from a South African Jewish vantage point, as South African Jewry historically gave the largest donations to Israel of any Jewish community in the world.[91]

Ray Alexander was born in Latvia to Jewish parents actively engaged in underground radical politics. She moved to South Africa as a teenager, rejecting Zionism for socialism.[92] She was a radical, antiapartheid, trade union activist. In 1954, she co-founded the Federation of South African Women, a nonracial women's rights organization, with activists Helen Joseph, Lilian Ngoyi (later the first woman elected to the executive committee of the ANC), and Florence Mkhize (later one of the founding members of the United Democratic Front). Alexander spoke openly in interviews of how she connected her Jewish family history to her lifelong dedication to struggles for racial and economic justice. "My early experiences of anti-Semitism prepared me well for my later struggles against apartheid," she writes, "I cannot understand how Jews can fail to see the link." Her father's religious tutorials "persuaded" her "of the need to be sensitive to the fate of the least powerful; as a Jew I was obliged to love and respect the stranger."[93] An interviewer once suggested that "the values that have governed her life are those of the Jewish and biblical tradition," and asked her whether "religion played a part in her life." Her answer was "No... I am simply motivated by a moral vision which I like to think is part of the universal quest to be human."[94] "I don't think of myself as Jewish," she once said, "Because I just felt that I belonged to the world. I'm internationalist."[95]

Members of a vibrant, radical movement, First and Alexander occupy two points on a spectrum of Jewish-inflected activism: First's story makes clear how the politics of organized Judaism appeared antithetical to her work, and thus led her to reject it; Alexander's story shows how she sought to integrate, or perhaps supplant, historical Jewish belonging and memory with her own, universalist activism. Rejecting white supremacy, capitalism, patriarchy, Zionism, and Jewish affiliation, they, like Kleinbaum and Messinger, model two approaches on the wide spectrum of Jewish identity and belonging.

As with Kleinbaum and Messinger, locating First and Alexander in Jewish history—as other scholars have done and will continue to do with great rigor—offers a compelling lesson in intracommunal debates and legacies, in the balancing of universal and particular priorities. But it also means engaging in painful contests over memory, Jewish interests, and definitions of Jewishness. South African Jewish historian Gideon Shimoni writes, for example, that First's "double sense of alienation from white South African and Jewish communal norms was undoubtedly engendered in her by her parents...both of whom were communists."[96] Shimoni sees this "radicalism rooted in the home environment" as "a formative factor in the making of many Jewish radicals."[97] Indeed, for First, Alexander, and others, he finds an "almost regular pattern" in the influence of the "parental home" creating "ready-made radical[s] so to speak."[98] He marshals this evidence in support of a specific agenda: to push First, Alexander, and their comrades to the margins of South African Jewish history. Jewish radicalism is passively (perhaps pathologically) acquired through inheritance; mainstream Jewish belonging is, in contrast, the normative choice. Central to Shimoni's history, then, are the mainstream, affiliated Jews who did not speak out against apartheid for fear of drawing the hostility of the apartheid regime.[99]

In recent years, scholars and laypeople alike have attempted to integrate liberal and radical Jewish antiapartheid activists into the canon of South African Jewish history. They are "counted" as Jewish in the postapartheid world in order to counter the memory of an otherwise acquiescent leadership. But scholars Claudia Braude and Rhoda Rosen navigate a far more complicated path to integrating radical Jews, in particular, into that history. They conclude that alienation—from an authoritarian government, from white supremacy, and importantly, from mainstream Jewish identity—can be an expression of Jewishness itself.[100] Apart from mainstream Jewry, radical Jews thus arrived at their activist commitments by claiming the memory of Jewish alienation, while organized South African Jewry disavowed those memories and stood silent in the face of racist oppression. Fierce debates over the "canon" of Jewish history, and over the means and politics of its revision, then, reflect the internal divisions and complicated history of this community.[101]

Jewish women antiapartheid activists in the United States and South Africa often placed themselves at a distance from the Zionist mainstream Jewish world. Analyzing American Jewish women's roles in the global women's movement and South African Jewish women's roles in the radical union and antiapartheid movements lays bare strong critiques of Jewish life, emerging from their worldviews as activists and as women. With no consensus to speak of, Jewish leaders drew from the memories and legacies of anti-Semitism and the Holocaust in divergent ways across the second half of the twentieth century. Some said that taking a stand against apartheid endangered Jewish unity, and would make Jews vulnerable to anti-Semitism in South Africa, the United States, and Israel; others proposed taking a stand against apartheid as the only way to be true to the universalist lessons embedded in Jewish history and religious teachings.[102]

Analyzing Jewish women's multidimensional roles in the global antiapartheid movement forces us to reckon with global controversies over Zionism and racism, as well as internal controversies over ideology and practices in Jewish life. These currents prevented broad-based coalition building on apartheid and other vital colonialist issues. The same painful debates over communal priorities played out on college campuses and in the founding (and dismantling) of new Jewish organizations in the same era, and then lived on in real and virtual spaces into the twenty-first century. The final chapters of this study will chart the course of Jewish encounters with apartheid, with particularism and universalism, into our own times, assessing their impact and cost.

6

New Agendas: The Organizational Jewish Response to Apartheid

In the early 1980s, as the global antiapartheid movement grew stronger, American Jewish men and women navigated the currents of protest over Zionism, Israel, South Africa, and apartheid, forging their own paths to the antiapartheid movement. American Jews joined these efforts as individuals, in secular organizations, and in Jewish organizations such as the Jewish Labor Committee and New Jewish Agenda.

Adding to the complexity of these efforts was the fact that the word apartheid was increasingly heard in conversations about Israel: because of Israel's relationship with South Africa, but also because of the frequent critiques by African and Asian nations and their allies that likened Israeli policies to those of apartheid. The Jewish left began to utilize the word to talk about Israel, especially after the election of Prime Minister Menachem Begin in 1977, which ended three decades of Labor Party rule in Israel. In a 1981 issue of *Jewish Frontier*, Labor Zionist activist and kibbutz member David Twersky wrote that he had just returned from South Africa, and that "South Africa has a warning, a model of what Israel could become."[1]

As historian Adam Mendelsohn points out, many Jewish organizations positioned themselves in the antiapartheid movement in the 1980s in order to gain or regain credibility in the eyes of Civil Rights and other African American organizations. South African Jewish historian Gideon Shimoni concurs, writing that mainstream American Jewish organizations' support for sanctions was motivated by "domestic concerns with relations between blacks and Jews."[2] According to this narrative, American Jews saw their work against apartheid, in a sense, as currency, theirs to trade for support for Israel and Zionism (and later for the cause of Soviet Jewry).

This chapter examines the shifting positions of Jewish organizations in the 1980s with regard to apartheid and Zionism. Progressive Jews saw their antiapartheid activism as growing out of their Civil Rights and anticolonialist commitments. Some spoke of the imperative of Jewish Holocaust memory to their work. Other Jewish leaders held fast to their reservations about the antiapartheid movement. They spoke of prioritizing Jewish unity and consensus and their wariness of the movement's criticisms of Israel. In the 1970s, as the movement grew, many American Jewish groups thought the price of involvement in the antiapartheid movement was too high. Israel and Soviet Jewry were top priorities, and these issues often prevented Jewish leaders from taking firm, public stands against apartheid. As the antiapartheid movement rose in its power and visibility, so too did the price of not taking a firm public stand on state sanctioned oppression in South Africa.

Even with debates raging internally, then, Jewish organizations on all sides of this issue came together to protest apartheid in the mid-1980s. These moments of unity belied their divergent motivations and agendas, as well as their intense hostility to each other. Those would come into even sharper relief as the century closed.

* * *

The evidence was abundantly clear that apartheid, Zionism, and Israel created profound divides between African Americans and American Jews. With these dynamics in mind, leaders of the WJC and World Zionist Organization (WZO) commissioned a survey of 16 members of the Congressional Black Caucus in 1984. Their goal was "to assess the perceptions of the Representatives on social and political issues involving relations between the Black and Jewish communities [including] issues such as the Jewish bond to Israel, Israel's relations with Black Africa and Israel's relations with South Africa."[3] Clearly the WJC and WZO sensed a crisis, and indeed, nearly all the Representatives who were surveyed felt that the relationship between Blacks and Jews had "deteriorated in the last year."[4] Although the study is largely impressionistic, the findings recorded under the heading "Jews and Apartheid" offer compelling evidence of African American leaders' doubts about Jewish opposition to apartheid. Only three Representatives said that the "American Jewish community is opposed to apartheid." Eight replied that "they were unaware of American Jewish opposition to apartheid." Ten "said they were unaware of South African Jewish opposition to apartheid." The surveyors concluded "that this is one of the areas in which more communication and information between the two communities is needed."[5]

Far more visible than American Jews' work against apartheid in the 1980s were their efforts for Soviet Jewry, Jews in the Soviet Union who were denied legal protection for religious expression. Along with devotion to Israel, Soviet Jewry increasingly unified American Jews during this period. According to the most recent history of this campaign, the cause helped to offset the fact that, with rapid social mobility and the decline of anti-Semitism, there was "increasingly very little Jewish about being a Jew" in the United States.[6] Activists for Soviet Jewry used language and imagery from the Holocaust in conveying the urgency of their cause: "The six million are no more. Now three million face spiritual extinction."[7]

As early as 1967, Civil Rights leaders Martin Luther King, Jr, A. Philip Randolph, Bayard Rustin, Roy Wilkins, and Whitney Young signed a letter of support for the "protest against the widespread anti-Jewish practices, both official and unofficial, of the Soviet Union."[8] Now, strategic exchanges over apartheid and Soviet Jewry laid the groundwork for renewed communication between African Americans and American Jews—a conversation that could steer clear of the complexities of Israel's treatment of Palestinians and South African treatment of Blacks under apartheid. Two decades after King's statement, Jewish leaders attempted to carry that sentiment forward, at times proposing "a black/Jewish trade-off, to wit: a black leadership statement on Soviet Jewry in exchange for a Jewish statement on South Africa."[9]

By the mid-1980s, progressive students on some campuses conducted joint human rights programming for Soviet Jews and Black South Africans. In 1985 and 1986, for example, Boston University student groups organized "Freedom Music: A Tribute to Black South Africans and Soviet Jews." Co-sponsored by Alpha Kappa Alpha Sorority and B'nai B'rith Hillel, among others, the concert featured jazz, Black South African and Jewish music, and the performance of the Black Drama Collective of an Athol Fugard play. During a 15-minute intermission, audience members were encouraged to sign letters of protest to President Reagan (for apartheid) and to a Russian refusenik (for Soviet Jewry).[10] The Reform Movement in American Judaism began a "Prisoner of Apartheid" program modeled on its "Prisoner of Conscience" program for Soviet Jews, where synagogues "adopt" political prisoners of the apartheid regime, writing letters to them and also lobbying for their release.[11]

But Soviet Jewry was also a cause of the neoconservative right, as it drew attention to the "evils" of communism.[12] This made for deep Cold War conflicts over apartheid, Jewishness, Israel, and Palestine, especially in sites of antiapartheid activism such as college campuses.

Many campuses were active sites of antiapartheid and South African divestment campaigns, beginning with Hampshire College, the first to divest after a student takeover of a campus building in 1977.[13] As a trustee of Hampshire College, Cora Weiss, long an anticolonial, women's rights, and Civil Rights activist and wife of Peter Weiss of the ACOA, played a key role in bringing the students' demands to the Board. This was the same year as the torture and murder of Stephen Biko, a student antiapartheid activist and leader in South Africa's Black Consciousness movement. At historically Black colleges and universities as well as all others in the United States, apartheid protests grew out of Black Civil Rights activism and global Black solidarity.[14]

These events grew in number as segments of the antiapartheid movement within South Africa joined to form the United Democratic Front in 1983, an umbrella organization for students, workers, and women, as well as leaders and members of cultural, religious, sport, and trade union organizations. They also multiplied as townships erupted in violence in response to the South African elections of 1983–1984. The United Nations condemned these elections as void, and there was a consensus among those in the Movement that the elections simply attempted to validate minority rule. A new constitution drafted by the government was a means to the same ends, granting legislatures to Indian and "colored" citizens while denying power to the Black majority.

Finally, all American antiapartheid protests after 1984 grew also from the incredible force of the Free South Africa Movement (FSAM), a coalition of church, student, Civil Rights, and women's groups coordinated by TransAfrica and the Congressional Black Caucus. It began on November 21, 1984, when four African American leaders entered the Washington, DC South African embassy and refused to leave until the South African government ended apartheid and released Nelson Mandela: Randall Robinson, president of TransAfrica; Congressman Walter Fauntroy; US Civil Rights Commissioner Mary Frances Berry; and law professor and Carter administration official Eleanor Holmes Norton. Sit-ins spread throughout the nation, with celebrities and political leaders taking part and at times getting arrested. African American activists founded FSAM after the United States again abstained from a United Nations condemnation of white South Africa's repressive tactics. Its leaders sought to use grassroots organizing in order to force President Reagan to abandon his policy of "constructive engagement" with South Africa, and to oblige American leaders to stop protecting South Africa in global forums.[15] Trade unionists, college students, and other activists and leaders caught the note of urgency and made use of the strategies as protests exploded across the United States.

For college students, especially, antiapartheid messages traveling through cultural currents reinforced stories in the news, presenting models of political activism and solidarity. South African singer Miriam Makeba's 1963 testimony against apartheid at the United Nations gave her great notoriety as an activist artist. Beginning with her exile in 1961 in the United States, first as a protégée of Harry Belafonte and then as a celebrated artist in her own right, Makeba made music that introduced millions of Americans to Africa and to the apartheid struggle for decades.[16] Released in 1985 by Artists United Against Apartheid, "Sun City" was a "visual and aural montage" with a radical challenge embedded within it: the song's lyrics linked cultural performances at South Africa's Sun City resort in the "Black homeland" of Bophuthatswana with endorsements of apartheid. The lyrics urged all artists to follow the United Nations boycott and refuse to "play Sun City." As music scholar Neal Ullstead notes, "Sun City's" music video had artists—including Bruce Springsteen, Darlene Love, Lou Reed, Miles Davis, Stanley Jordan, Gil Scott-Heron, Peter Gabriel, and many others—challenging the Reagan administration and other artists to actively oppose apartheid. It also educated listeners and viewers to apartheid's brutalities. Along with the massive Mandela Tributes in England in 1988 and 1990 (at which Makeba, Amampondo, the Mahotella Queens, Whitney Houston, Dire Straits, and many others performed), "Sun City" reached millions of people around the world, contributing to the democratization of protests on American college campuses and beyond.[17] These protests made the antiapartheid movement a global force to be reckoned with.

Tapping into these currents, students at Johns Hopkins University built a shantytown to raise awareness of the conditions of Blacks living under apartheid, and worked for the university's divestment in 1986, as South African Black citizens were living under martial law.[18] Debates raged over South Africa and Israel in the student newspaper. Drawing attention to Soviet support for the ANC, the College Republicans erected a "Gulag" on campus to demonstrate "what they perceived majority rule would bring to South Africa."[19] One member of the Hopkins Jewish League took issue with a graduate school publication that linked South African apartheid with Israel, calling accusations of trade between the two nations the new "Blood Libel" that threatened the safety and security of all Jews.[20] Conservative students countered the publication's conclusions with the defensive stance adopted by many Jewish organizations: they drew attention to South Africa's dependence on Arab States, arguing that Israel should not be singled out for condemnation. Tensions reached a fevered pitch soon after, when three fraternity brothers burned down the campus activists' shantytown.[21]

Like Hopkins and other campuses across the country, Brandeis University, a Jewish-sponsored, nonsectarian university founded in 1948, was the site of an active campaign for South African divestment beginning in the late 1970s, when Brandeis students and faculty began protesting their University's investments in South Africa.[22] Its Board of Trustees signed on to the Sullivan Principles in 1977. Named for African American minister Rev. Leon Sullivan, this code meant that any company with which Brandeis did business had to treat its employees equally regardless of race in and outside of the workplace, a practice that clearly contradicted the treatment of all workers under apartheid. Activists at Brandeis, like many around the world, felt the Principles did not go far enough. In 1978, a group of students "who support full divestment from South Africa" presented their case to the administration, citing divestment as "the only acceptable moral course of action for Brandeis" in contributing to the end of apartheid.[23] Faculty, staff, and students organized events, demonstrations, and leafleting; students boycotted classes to raise support and awareness of the issue.[24]

Although many American colleges engaged in such actions, Brandeis's Jewish origins, its large undergraduate Jewish population, and its myriad other ties to the American Jewish community made it, in many ways, appear as a microcosm of the larger American Jewish world. Jewish newspapers throughout the United States covered the tensions that flared throughout Brandeis's long antiapartheid movement. The Brandeis campaign was especially riveting for its uses of memory, and especially of Holocaust consciousness. Students accused administrators of holding a "wait and see attitude" toward divestment and apartheid, when that attitude was "historically implicated in the murder of six million Jews in World War II."[25] The Student Senate in particular noted that Brandeis, "with its heritage built on the legacy of the Holocaust," should be especially sensitive to the urgency of [apartheid]."[26] Rabbi Albert Axelrad, Brandeis's progressive Chaplain and

B'nai B'rith Hillel director, made this linkage explicit, calling apartheid "the single most heinous, nefarious outrage to have been perpetrated on members of the human family since the horrors of Nazism." "It is both morally and educationally inappropriate," he wrote, "for a university, especially ours, rooted as it is in the history and values of the Jewish people, to accept funding which accrues from such an atrocious system, thereby participating in propping it up and perpetuating it." Active in politically progressive campaigns such as Breira, Rabbi Axelrad had long advocated for full divestment, submitting a resolution to the Massachusetts Board of Rabbis in April 1978 for all Jewish individuals and institutions to boycott South African products.[27]

Liberal and conservative college activists clashed sharply in contests over Jewishness and apartheid. In 1985, as on many campuses, Brandeis students built a shantytown to draw attention to the plight of South African Blacks and to force Brandeis University to divest.[28] Meanwhile, conservative Jewish student activists sought to turn attention to what they saw as the competing cause of Soviet Jewry. In November 1985, leaders of the College Republicans lobbied Brandeis President Evelyn Handler, urging her to lead the university to divest from companies that do business with the Soviet Union because of its discriminatory treatment of Jews. Clearly modeling their activism on the South African divestment campaign, the six students marched on the quad carrying signs that read "STOP: Save the Oppressed People," and handed out leaflets of the Young Conservative Foundation, which sponsored the national movement.[29]

More petitions, protests, sit-ins, die-ins, arrests, and hearings over South African divestment followed at Brandeis.[30] Soviet Jewry activists now questioned the Jewish loyalty of those who worked for divestment. Guessing that "most…of those involved in the shantytown are Jews," one student wrote that "if morality is the issue" in fighting apartheid, would the "shantytowners encourage divestment from any oppressive regime" including the "Soviet Union, Cuba, Syria and Iran"? "My basic concern" he concluded, "is that Jews fight for Jews and people fight for *all* people, not just black South Africans." "The first obligation of the Jew," he told the Brandeis *Justice*, "is to fight for their own cause….Surely the cause of Soviet Jewry is as worthy as the cause of South Africa."[31] The internal contradictions to these statements speak to the strong tensions within debates over balancing particular and universal commitments.

The tension between the two groups, too, was both strong and palpable. When shantytown protesters received a threatening note, the College Republicans quickly issued a statement denying that their members authored it.[32] The same students pledged to build a Soviet style Gulag alongside the South African shantytown to highlight the Soviet influence on the ANC in South Africa and to draw attention to what they saw as a rival cause.[33]

Rabbi Albert Axelrad expressed deep satisfaction and pride with the shantytown, noting that "Judaism's teachings on the matter [of divestment] are lucidly clear." He also expressed his fear that the antiapartheid and divestment movements "not fall prey to the insidious, propagandistic slants of the anti-Israel and anti-Jewish elements within certain leftist circles." He decried the hypocrisy of singling out Israel for its trade with South Africa. While asserting that "I do lament and deplore Israeli trade with oppressive regimes"—from South Africa to Nicaragua—he noted that Israel had few options for survival. Citing a statement from the Union of American Hebrew Congregations, the organization of the US Reform Movement, Axelrad enumerated South African, Israeli, and American Jewish contributions to fighting apartheid, and warned of those who would "co-opt" the movement "seeking the delegitimization and diplomatic isolation of Israel." He praised the "integrity and decency" of Brandeis's means of protest for not devolving into "unjustifiable and unnecessarily divisive sidetracking and recrimination." Axelrad concluded by expressing his hope that Brandeis's contributions to the global movement would have a "salutary influence," and that all could be "collaborators in creative and dogged struggle" in seeking to "rid the world of the unspeakable evil" of apartheid.[34]

Radical students did find outlets for their criticisms of Israel, using Holocaust imagery to illuminate the connections they saw to apartheid. In the radical campus magazine *The Watch*, with a series of photos titled "Dachau: Then and Now," student photographers analogized the Holocaust with Israel's Occupation and with apartheid South Africa.[35] When students then claimed the magazine's editors permitted anti-Semitic contributions, one student wrote that accusations of anti-Semitism were being used "as a justification for ignoring criticism of Israel's controversial policies."[36] Criticisms of state oppression in South Africa marked a moment open for conversations about other forms of state oppression, these students asserted. They lamented the missed opportunity to talk about Israel's policies at Brandeis. Over two decades later, with Israel's Occupation continuing, Jewish students at Brandeis continued to feel this same tension.[37]

Leaders of the B'nai B'rith Hillel Foundation, the sponsor of Jewish programming and ritual leadership on many college campuses, subscribed to the same deep reservations as Rabbi Axelrad. They too feared that the moment might be captured by anti-Zionist strains within the antiapartheid movement. They grew especially troubled over the "distortion of truth being promoted by anti-Israel forces," which "may bring harm to the pro-Israel consensus in America." Most troubling was that "the Zionism-racism equation has become a common-place slogan heard at antiapartheid organizing events on campus. Well-intentioned student activists, for lack of understanding the true character and purpose of Zionism, internalize the lie. They accept the insidious propaganda about Zionism and condemn the alleged South African-Israel alliance as a conspiracy of two racist states."[38]

In 1985, on the tenth anniversary of the Zionism is racism resolution 3379, the Foundation commissioned a booklet authored by Yosef Abramowitz, a student antiapartheid activist from Boston University. Abramowitz detailed the ways in which Zionist Jewish college students were forced to choose between their Jewish and their activist commitments. "Anti-Zionists have introduced their own agenda into [these] protest activities," he said, calling this dynamic "the exploitation of the anti-apartheid movement."[39] At University of California Berkeley, he noted, an Ad Hoc Committee Against Apartheid in South Africa and Israel distributed anti-Zionist material at a rally focused on divestment from South African apartheid. According to Abramowitz, at University of California Davis, leaders in the antiapartheid movement insisted Jewish students agree to three demands before they could join the coalition: (1) denounce Israel and South Africa; (2) denounce Zionism; (3) support UN Resolution 3379. Faced with what they considered anti-Semitic attacks on Israel, college students across the United States felt "betrayed....isolated and intimidated." They ultimately formed their own groups, including "Jews Against Apartheid" at the University of Pennsylvania.[40]

Key to Abramowitz's arguments in distancing Israel from South Africa and apartheid were his careful claims to the "historical Jewish commitment to civil and human rights." In South Africa, he pointed to antiapartheid politicians such as Dr Helen Suzman along with South African Communist Party and ANC leader Joe Slovo, husband of activist journalist Ruth First. Abramowitz concluded that "the South African/Jewish community is more progressive than the society around them, and its positions put the lie to the claim that Zionism like apartheid is a racist philosophy."[41]

Abramowitz's book rested on several myths, common currencies for those defending both Israel's policies and Jewish responses to apartheid. First, in presenting a unified Jewish opposition to apartheid, Abramowitz revised the history of both South African and American Jewish positions. He also ignored the anti-Zionism of Joe Slovo and many of Slovo's radical Jewish colleagues in the antiapartheid movement. Finally, Abramowitz vastly underestimated how intimate were the commercial ties between Israel and South Africa.[42]

Abramowitz captured many of the tensions that had challenged a straightforward opposition to apartheid for both South African and American mainstream Jewish organizational leaders: tensions between universalism and particularism, Jewish unity and belonging, criticism of Israeli policies and American Jewish unity and consensus. Indeed, the Jewish unity argument—that the safety of South African Jews stood between all Jews and antiapartheid—lived on. In 1985, Prime Minister Yitzhak Shamir insisted that Israel was obliged to retain ties to South Africa because of the large Jewish population there. "We are not going to change the character of our relations with South Africa. There is a large Jewish community in South Africa and that has to be taken into account."[43]

Belying the "pro-Israel consensus in America," organizations and individuals continued to stake positions in these debates by framing critiques of Israel's policies and South African apartheid as extensions of their own sense of Jewishness. NJA stands as the best example. NJA was founded by American Jewish progressives in December 1980, after Breira collapsed under the weight of intense, vitriolic, internal and intracommunal tensions and right-wing attacks.[44] NJA's national platform, adopted in 1982, highlighted the organization's commitment to "progressive human values." Supporting movements for civil liberties, the environment, feminism, disability and gay rights, condemning anti-Semitism, discrimination, and militarism, the platform spelled out NJA's support for democratic movements in Israel and the United States. Its members denounced the "spiraling arms race" of the Cold War, which led Israel to compromise "Jewish ethics" by building alliances with South Africa.[45]

Importantly, NJA achieved significant recognition by mainstream Jewish communal groups, such as the Jewish Federation Council of Los Angeles, and at times collaborated with those groups in their activism.[46] They also sought to counter the conservative Jewish presence on college campuses—those who competed with, or destroyed, antiapartheid shantytowns in Cold War battles over Jewish visibility and loyalty—organizing progressive Jewish students to build coalitions for social justice with other student groups.[47] Like the National Jewish Community Relations Advisory Council (NJCRAC) and other Jewish organizations, NJA took note of the decreasing trends of mainstream Jewish affiliation in younger Jews. NJA presented itself as an alternative organization in which college students and adults could address pressing global issues as Jews.

NJA's grassroots organizing meant that the national organization as well as individual chapters signed on to their own causes, including antiapartheid. In 1984, the national organization of NJA joined other progressive groups in Mobilization for Peace and Justice, a campaign that worked to keep South Africa out of the Olympic Games. The Northampton, Massachusetts, chapter worked to support exiled South African poet-activist Dennis Brutus after the Reagan administration attempted to deport him.[48]

Leaders of the NJA walked a fine line in their programming, often meeting criticism from mainstream Jewish leaders along predictable lines. Detroit's Jewish Community Council, among others, expressed deep anxiety when NJA brought Reverend Zacharia Mokgoeboto and Rabbi Ben Isaacson to the United States from South Africa. Mokgoeboto was a Soweto minister in the Black Dutch Reformed Church and a leader of the Belydendekring, a dissident group of nonwhite ministers within that church. Isaacson first spoke out against apartheid in the 1960s, challenging the organized South African Jewish community's silence. Leaders feared that Isaacson's "previous attacks on the South African Jewish community" could be "detrimental to black-Jewish relations locally and even be used by those who try to link the antiapartheid campaign with anti-Israel efforts." NJA garnered support from other Jewish organizations only with assurances that Rabbi Isaacson would avoid "anti-Israel or anti-Jewish fallout."[49] For the six-week, 23-city national tour of Mokgoeboto and Isaacson, NJA worked with the Washington Office on Africa in a rare Black/Jewish partnership in those years.

Indeed, NJA continued to build multiracial coalitions at conferences, meetings, and programs on antiracist organizing. Its members dedicated great energy to making their work reach as many constituencies as possible. This meant that NJA created spaces for often painful conversations about race and religion (among many other overlapping categories) with apartheid and Zionism inevitably invoked when members talked about how to remain visible as Jews in struggles against oppression.[50]

Although the JLC worked to decouple their South African work from critiques of Israel, and though they were mired in conflict with African American leaders on domestic issues, it, too, continued antiapartheid work in the 1980s. In 1984, the JLC joined with the A. Philip Randolph Institute and the Negro Trade Union Leadership Council to support Congressman William Gray III's amendment to the Export Administration Act that prohibited new corporate investment in apartheid South Africa. Their statement of support carefully presented their arguments: historically, their coalition had supported "black and non-racial trade unions in South Africa" through the AFL–CIO, because "the rise of the black trade union movement represents an institutional vehicle for reform." Gray's amendment "can bring about real change in South Africa without undermining the growing democratic forces within that country."[51]

The measure died in the Senate, but these efforts contributed greatly to building support for the Anti-Apartheid Act passed by Congress in 1986 following the mass protests around the world and those tied to the Free South Africa Movement in the United States. The JLC then joined "Jewish, Black, Hispanic, and Italian trade unionists" to establish the Ethnic Labor Coalition, which supported antiapartheid bills and attempted to add language to them to "guarantee freedom of association to the emerging black trade unions" in South Africa.[52]

As pressure mounted to take a position on apartheid, some mainstream Jewish groups relied on the progressive organizations that had taken early antiapartheid stands. In 1985, NJCRAC called on the president of the JLC, Herbert Magidson, to serve as a resource on apartheid South Africa. Magidson, who was also vice-president of the American Federation of Teachers, credited the "fundamental values" of the Jewish community for what he saw as it consistent opposition to apartheid. His own political awakening grew out of the internationalism of the labor movement, whose leaders "saw the battle for human and civil rights in a world-wide context—well before the advent of globalization made obvious nations' interdependency." Magidson asserted that these commitments allowed the JLC to transcend domestic and global controversies, to engage in antiapartheid work despite disagreements over school autonomy in New York, or Zionism on the world stage.[53]

Magidson spoke to NJCRAC leaders about his 1981 tour of South Africa. He had been accompanied by an "integrated group of six trade union activists from the AFT and the ILGWU who spent four weeks in South Africa developing relationships with and understanding the plight of young Black workers who were trying—against incredible odds—to form trade unions." Magidson spoke of the brutality of apartheid, about the successes of the Black Freedom movement in South Africa, and about the failure of President Reagan's policy of constructive engagement, which Black South Africans and many others interpreted as support for apartheid. To the NJCRAC board, he concluded by asserting a Jewish imperative in fighting against apartheid:

> For Jews to fight for the rights of other Jews—or for Blacks to fight for the rights of other Blacks is not too unusual or too unexpected. It is understood as fighting for a member of one's family. But for Jews in the U.S. to stand up and be counted for Blacks in South Africa is truly ennobling, because it signifies that there is a larger family—the family of humankind....Our commitment to fight for abolition of apartheid in South Africa and its replacement with a government committed to freedom and human rights for all is an essential responsibility we have for ourselves as well as for Black South Africans.[54]

Just a few months before Magidson's presentation, mainstream Jewish organizations had joined with NJA and the JLC in taking public stands against apartheid. On Christmas Day, 1984, 300 members of NJA, along with members of the JLC and the American Jewish Committee, gave a "day off" to "Christian demonstrators" by continuing their picketing outside the South African Embassy in Washington, DC. These were the first days of protests of the Free South Africa Movement.

A few members of the American Jewish Congress had already been arrested in early December. Acknowledging the long gap in mainstream Jewish groups' involvement with apartheid, Rabbi David Saperstein, director of the Religious Action Center of the Reform Movement, announced that "This protest and demonstration today is the start of what we see as increased Jewish involvement against apartheid in South Africa."[55]

Christmas that year overlapped with the eighth and final day of Chanukah, the Jewish holiday commemorating the rededication of the Second Temple in Jerusalem with the victory of the Maccabean revolt against the Greek/Syrian armies of Antiochus. Jewish organizations spoke of their contributions to the TransAfrica protest as part of the "festival marking the victory of the few over the many." "If we can make another contribution to black-Jewish cooperation," said Hyman Bookbinder, the Committee's Washington representative and a longtime Civil Rights ally, "it is a day well spent. Our central message today is for the people of South Africa—a message of determination that freedom-loving people around the world will continue to voice our condemnation of apartheid."[56] They lit menorahs, and spoke of how the Chanukah holiday recalls "a distant time...when freedom and independence were victorious over oppression." Above all, the Jewish organizational leaders wanted to remind African Americans that Jews "are indeed close allies in the struggle for human freedom and social justice everywhere."[57]

Motivated by this commitment, American Jewish organizational leaders lobbied for the Comprehensive Anti-Apartheid Act of 1986. This act called for economic sanctions against South Africa, the release of Nelson Mandela, and the banning of all new investments in South Africa. Direct air links, including those of South African Airways, were also banned in this legislation. First proposed by Congressman Ron Dellums of California in 1972, the act was passed over the veto of President Reagan—the first twentieth-century override of a presidential veto on a matter of foreign policy.

Jewish organizational leaders traveled a long road to reach support for this act. In some cases, it took an outsider to bring new energy for an antiapartheid position. Arnold Aronson accomplished this at NJCRAC. Aronson had brought his Civil Rights credentials to NJCRAC in 1945; while working there, he was a cofounder of the Leadership Conference on Civil Rights (LCCR). After retiring from NJCRAC, Aronson continued to be an activist, serving as secretary of the LCCR. Seeking to revive Jewish communal attention to Civil Rights and social policy issues, in 1982 he recruited Marlene Provizer to join the staff.[58] Provizer had worked in social welfare policy advocacy, in Civil Rights and women's organizations, and would soon attend the UN Women's conference in Nairobi; once at NJCRAC, she was "shocked" at the state of intergroup relations between Jews and African Americans, and also at the lack of women in upper level staff and lay positions. Provizer used her position at NJCRAC to convince the many Jewish organizations it represented "to take up the anti-apartheid issue and eventually to evolve a Jewish communal response [supporting] sanctions, which culminated in pretty active Jewish communal Jewish participation in the Anti-Apartheid Act."[59]

Nearly every major Jewish organization issued statements in support of the 1986 Act, including the JLC, the National Council of Jewish Women, the American Jewish Committee, the Union of American Hebrew Congregations (UAHC), the NJCRAC, and scores of smaller Jewish organizations in cities across the United States.[60] For use in community synagogues, the UAHC published a guide titled *Ending Apartheid: A Manual for Individual and Congregational Use*.[61] Clearly, these groups sidelined any reservations—those that had prevented them from taking earlier public, organizational stands against apartheid—in the wake of tremendous global support for the movement.

But internal documents of Jewish organizations demonstrate that questions of Jewish loyalty and unity—among American, South African, and Israeli Jews—remained connected to long-simmering feelings of anxiety over anti-Israel, anti-Zionist, and anti-Semitic ideologies that had historically been part of Third World and antiapartheid movements. For some, blaming Resolution 3379 on Third World nations amounted to sounding an alarm for a second Holocaust: "By denigrating Zionism," noted Gerald Kraft, President of B'nai B'rith International, in 1985, "the Jewish state was ultimately to be dehumanized, a process which the world ought to have learned from the Nazis." Israel was "progressive, a true parliamentary democracy, universalist in outlook, having a culture with a fiercely held belief in moral principles of the biblical prophets." Now, Kraft wrote, the nation was pitted against the "totalitarian communists and repressive regimes of those Arab countries who were among the sponsors of the...resolution."[62]

Some Jewish leaders took their points still further, assailing Third World nations for the resolution and taking them to task for not supporting Israel, despite world Jewry's repeated condemnation of apartheid. Iconoclast Rabbi Arthur Hertzberg was a longtime advocate for American Civil Rights, former president of the American Jewish Congress, and current vice-president of the WJC, which had long wrestled over whether or not to publicly oppose apartheid. He asserted that the Third World received "billions and billions" in support "without even a thank you." Hertzberg concluded that leaders of Third World nations viewed the resolution as an equal exchange for "all of the generations of colonialism and exploitation." These nations relied on "the famous code words, 'You owe us something....'" he explained. Hertzberg was particularly incensed at the Third World for its sponsorship of Resolution 3379—even using the "undiplomatic word...swinish"—given "that in the forefront of the battle against apartheid there has been the world Jewish community."[63] Erasing the ambivalence of much of organized Western Jewry toward apartheid, he cited the WJC's 1975 passage of an antiracist, antidiscriminatory resolution as evidence of a long-standing, steadfast Jewish opposition to apartheid.

After "fact finding tours" of South Africa, other American rabbis also relied on this oversimplified past, concluding that "the general consensus among Jews is and always has been out-rage over Apartheid" and that "the South African Board of Deputies has consistently condemned Apartheid." One observer reported that "Jews in South Africa are indeed duplicating the performance of Jews in the civil rights movement in America."[64]

American Jewish leaders often failed to note that South African Jewish leaders had only just moved on the issue of apartheid. In 1985, the SAJBD "explicitly stated that the Board rejected apartheid." Editors of the liberal *Israel Horizons*, who had awaited the Board's antiapartheid stand for decades, took note. "Until recently," wrote one journalist in 1986, "there have been no groups which have identified themselves as Jewish *and* against apartheid." There too, these same pressing questions of visibility, security, and loyalty were of the utmost importance: South African Jews shied away from the ANC and the United Democratic Front because of their "anti-Israel rhetoric."

Never before had the Board mentioned apartheid by name. But in material distributed at the WJC meeting in Jerusalem in 1986, Aleck Goldberg, director of the Board, sounded "apologetic" for its antiapartheid statement, referring back to the Board's long ago pledge to remain uninvolved in politics. He explained, however, that "'apartheid' no longer has the same political connotations," so that even if the "Board came closer to the fine dividing line between politics and morality, it is very doubtful it was crossed."[65]

The editors of *Israel Horizons* noted that the SAJBD's actions did not suggest that its members were "becoming flaming radicals." But they applauded the Board's "recognition of its responsibility to take a moral stand as tension deepens in South Africa." Within the same issue of the journal, other writers came close to dismissing the claim that South African Jews were in precarious positions, given the fact that, in short, they could leave. They "have the right—and perhaps an obligation—to choose between living with apartheid, working against apartheid or leaving both South Africa and apartheid." Such arguments went hand in hand with calls for Israel to "divorce herself" from South Africa politically and economically—without concern if the motivation was "particularist or universal."[66]

These articles proved important vehicles for the struggles of left Jews. The left-Zionist organization Americans for Progressive Israel mailed them to African American and union allies in their coalition as evidence of their true commitment to the antiapartheid cause—and doubtless too to testify to the difficult position they were in with regard to Israel.[67] South African and American Jewish opposition to apartheid mirrored the by-now quite mainstream antiapartheid stand of social groups across the world. But for some members of these two groups, South Africa's ties to Israel *and* increasingly heard parallels between apartheid and Israel's Occupation continued to present obstacles to full participation in the antiapartheid movement.

The same new realities that mandated antiapartheid positions for American Jewish organizations imperiled the friendship of South African and American Jews. There was no love lost between members of South Africa's Jewish community and American Jewish leaders who supported sanctions and divestment. The 1985–1987 report to South African Jewry of the SAJBD indicated that members of the Board were "somewhat hostile" to NJCRAC's antiapartheid stand. NJCRAC consistently strove to "represent the majority opinion of our member agencies," and it became clear to NJCRAC leaders that the American Jewish Committee's "cautious" approach to apartheid, its TransAfrica Chanukah protest notwithstanding, was due to its very close relationship with the SAJBD.[68]

Even within the global movement of Reform Judaism, South African religious leaders expressed distress when American Jews spoke out in favor of "boycotts and divestment." At the 1985 Assembly of the National Federation of Temple Sisterhoods (NFTS), which represented the women of Reform Judaism, delegates passed a Resolution on Apartheid that supported both boycotts and divestment as means to end apartheid. Here was a clear sign of Jewish women exercising their power to engage in global issues. South African delegates raised immediate concerns about whether or not sanctions would be "productive." Delores Wilkenfeld, president of NFTS, indicated that these women did not take issue with the cause. "Our South African constituents," she says, referring to Reform women in that nation, "had long been activists against apartheid.... Not only antiapartheid but also social activists—working for needs of Black communities."[69] But they did not support boycotts or divestment.

(Male) leaders in the SAUPJ—South Africa's Reform movement— echoed these concerns, writing to the NFTS that such tactics would "cause grave hardships to all the inhabitants of South Africa." Certainly these leaders joined a chorus of South Africans—including Helen Suzman and other liberals—who rejected global boycotts.[70] Indeed, the following year, Suzman spoke to the graduating class of Reform rabbis at New York's Hebrew Union College–Jewish Institute of Religion. She had received the

College's prize for "work that enhances values and ideals derived from Jewish teachings." In her address, she said she "understood the moral abhorrence and the pleasure it gives you to demonstrate." But she warned against divestment, asserting that she could not "see how wrecking the economy of the country will ensure a more stable and just society."[71]

In making their case against boycotts and divestment, South African Reform leaders compromised their argument for Jewish unity to persuade American Jews not to endorse divestment. They did this by indicating their dissent from the positions of the SAJBD. In their resolution, sisterhood leaders had praised the SAJBD's statement opposing apartheid; SAUPJ leaders now reminded them that "the Reform Movement in South Africa has been the only Jewish organization to constantly oppose racial injustice in this country." Drawing attention to the Board's silence, they bucked Jewish unity within South Africa. But they also asked pointedly for unity among Reform Jews when they requested that American Reform leaders consult with them before "debating resolutions of this nature."[72]

The tensions continued through the International Reform Movement's debates over South African sanctions. Soon after, South African Reform leaders openly and stridently urged American Reform leaders not to support sanctions. Leslie Bergman, vice chairman of the SAUPJ, reiterated his organization's rejection of apartheid. But he testified that "sanctions would drive his country into Third World status and lead to the creation of a class of Jewish economic refugees." When he urged American Jews not to support sanctions but instead to work with his group to "create reforms" in South Africa, American activist Rabbi Balfour Brickner protested. "I think they're trying to cover their own behinds," he said. "They want us to keep quiet and get out." Brickner drew an analogy with the American Civil Rights movement, when "the Jews in the South told us in the North to do the same thing." Brickner weighed the particularist implications, the cracks in Jewish unity, the "cost" of sanctions to South African Jews. "These sanctions are going to hurt everyone in South Africa," he agreed. But, he concluded, "we were right to stake a stand. It was better than sitting back and doing nothing at all."[73]

In late summer, 1988, American Jewish communal leaders in NJCRAC planned a mission to South Africa in order to "acquire firsthand knowledge" of conditions there. They felt strongly that such knowledge was necessary because "the [American] Jewish community relations field has had a long-standing position opposing apartheid."[74] In South Africa, NJCRAC representatives reported having a tense and difficult meeting with the SAJBD. "Questions were raised," observed one traveler, "with respect to our political motivation in taking up the anti apartheid axe.... Some objection was voiced to our assuming the position of the moral high ground. It was argued that both in the U.S. and in many parts of the world, racial prejudice exists—and yet we have picked up the cause with such fervor only in South Africa." This was despite the fact that the SAJBD and the South African Jewish community had been "loyal friends of Israel."[75]

Diana Aviv, associate executive vice-chair of NJCRAC, had emigrated from South Africa to the United States in 1975. She led the 1988 mission during which South African leaders argued the illogic of singling out South Africa's racist repression over that of other nations. The SAJBD were "icy cold, and very angry," she notes, in their meetings with the NJCRAC delegation. They opposed sanctions in a "vigorous and vehement way," remaining firm that apartheid was "not the American Jewish community's business." Relying on fears first invoked in the 1950s, South African Jewish leaders expressed their anxieties that American Jewish antiapartheid positioning "would make them a target of [Prime Minister] Botha's anti-Semitism," and threatened that it would "jeopardize the relationship between American and South African Jews."[76]

The experiences of Rabbi Brian Walt, an antiapartheid activist, like Aviv born in South Africa, speak to the complex expectations each community had of the other. Walt joined NJA in its early years, working on South Africa and Israeli/Palestinian campaigns. Soon after his rabbinical ordination, Walt spoke to the American Jewish Committee about the antiapartheid activism that had gotten him blacklisted and arrested in South Africa. Committee leaders were thrilled with Walt's talk, and had great plans to use him as a resource: a Jewish South African antiapartheid activist surely could build bridges toward African American communal groups, healing a growing rift over domestic and global affairs. Soon after, in December 1987, the first Intifada (translated as a "shaking off") began, the Palestinian uprising in protest of Israel's Occupation. Walt joined the protest outside of the Israeli consulate in Philadelphia. "Three days later," he says, "I was blacklisted from the Jewish community." Jewish leaders "had been given a directive," and his critique of Zionism prevented him from talking to American Jewish audiences about South African apartheid or Israel.[77]

For American Jews, the sweeping success of the global antiapartheid movement meant the sidelining of their reservations about the movement and the public embrace of its goals by Jewish organizations. Although many—perhaps most—opposed apartheid as individuals, deep anxieties about Israel and anti-Semitism had long prevented this embrace. Now, some went so far as to revise history, to position Jews in South Africa, Israel, and the United States as longtime, firm, public opponents of apartheid. These revisions erased the intense complexities of Jewish positions on South African and Israeli policies. They also erased the divisiveness that had characterized the intracommunal politics of American and South African Jews.

To Be A Zionist and Fighting Apartheid: "A Lonely Movement Indeed"

Members of the Zionist left such as Walt took pains to discuss the difficult position they were in when vehemently protesting apartheid amidst Israel's isolation and anti-Zionist, anti-Israel, and anti-Semitic sentiment around the world. These were steep challenges, for even the means of antiapartheid protests themselves were gradually becoming visible as vehicles of protest against Israeli policies. At the University of Michigan in 1988, for example, during the first Intifada, a Palestinian rights group built a shantytown on campus to represent Israeli oppression of Palestinians. A few months later, when terrorists attacked an Israeli school bus, members of a Zionist student group responded by erecting a school bus on campus to draw attention to the impact of Arab terrorism on Israeli Jews.[78]

First and foremost, left Zionists felt obligated to talk about the mistakes Israel had made, specifically faulting Israel for its ties to South Africa. Yet as the editors of *Israel Horizons* expressed, "we should always make it known that we are criticizing as socialist Zionists, and that for us support for the continued existence of Israel is central." Importantly, though, the same tensions carried forward from the debates immediately following World War II. Socialist Zionists spoke of the need to be "mindful" of the "precarious situation" of South African Jews, specifically of not making "it appear that the anti-apartheid movement in the United States is a 'Jewish affair,'" as this would lead to "anti-Jewish reprisals by other South African [w]hites."

On college campuses, in the women's movement, in progressive Jewish organizations, the pressing question emerged: should progressive Zionists make allies with anti-Israel groups in the "urgent" battle against apartheid? Such a compromise seemed necessary to some left Zionists in 1985, given what they saw as the "mistakes on the part of successive Israeli governments, as well as the political cunning of Israeli enemies." For, as the editors of *Israel Horizons* suggested, "if we advocated cooperation with only those groups and individuals that share our entire worldview, we would be a lonely movement indeed." Left Zionists advocated "critical dialogue with other activists," "a continuing effort to build ties of understanding and cooperation between our movement and other progressive movements throughout the world."[79]

Rejecting a more narrow identity politics, the Jewish left worked carefully and tentatively to build coalitions with other "progressive movements." Making such friends, they hoped, would yield the payoff of more momentum toward their agendas. Given the Cold War, with-us-or-against-us mentality of Jewish conservatives, as Peter Weiss described, this work left activists in positions of tremendous vulnerability. Conservatives graded their work as tests of Jewish unity—and found them failing. Writer Rael Jean Isaac, whose strong criticisms of Breira contributed to that organization's demise, joined others in issuing equally strong attacks against NJA.[80] She assailed the organization, for example, for "cooperating closely with some of the most viciously anti-Israel organizations in the United States."[81] Attacking its work in Nicaragua and for Palestinian rights alongside its criticisms of American foreign policy, Isaac also spoke with tremendous disparagement of the struggle for NJA members to balance universal and particular commitments, to be a part of liberation campaigns as Jews. She saw them as tainted by communism, and as traitors to Jewish peoplehood: as "progressives," NJA members "came under constant pressure to take stands in conformity with the anti-Israel positions of the radical left." Its members "truly hate Israel" because Israel "bars Jews as a group from joining ranks with political revolutionaries," and because it "interferes with their espousing a universalism they feel is the hallmark of 'prophetic Judaism.'" They suffer from "the all-too-familiar pathological Jewish self-hatred."[82] NJA "becomes far more impassioned about 'racism' than anti-Semitism....and indicates no concern over the way the concept of racism has been perverted by the Arabs so as to define Zionism as racism."[83] And when Isaacs aimed to discredit NJA, she targeted Civil Rights and antiapartheid activists Rabbis Balfour Brickner and Arthur Waskow.[84]

Commentators moved swiftly whenever they heard Jewish activists analogizing Israel's treatment of Palestinians with South African apartheid. These fears were especially acute in Jewish antiapartheid activism. "Even in its South African campaign," Isaac accused NJA of promoting "a group whose leadership has made its hostility to Israel clear and uses Israel's trade relations with South Africa as an excuse for more intemperate attacks upon Israel." Indeed, she found a deeper agenda in the antiapartheid speaking tour of Rabbi Isaacson and Rev. Zacharaiah Mokgoebo, sponsored by NJA and the Washington Office on Africa. Because Mokgoebo's Church was led by Dr Allan Boesak, and Boesak had once spoken on "Israeli apartheid and Palestinian Resistance," the Isaacson/Mokgoebo antiapartheid tour clearly had as one of its goals to label Israel's policies as "apartheid."[85]

* * *

Not all assessments of the state of American Jewish attitudes toward Israel were as damning. In a thoughtful article about the changing relationship between American Jews and Israel in 1987, Mimi Alperin, chair of the American Jewish Committee's Executive Committee, emphasized the central role of South Africa's ties to Israel in those changes:

> What *has* happened to make Israelis more insecure is the increasing willingness of American Jews to criticize Israel publicly. From the war in Lebanon to more recent issues—ranging from Israel's relations to South Africa, to its policy towards Soviet emigration, to its recent attempts to define who is a Jew...American Jewry is becoming more assertive in expressing its point of view.[86]

American Jews are removing the "rose colored glasses" they wore when their "unquestioning adulation" accompanied Israel's "long and difficult struggle for existence," she noted, referencing the wars of Israel's first (nearly) four decades. Alperin saw American Jews' emerging critiques of Israel as in line with their universalist work in the United States: "American Jewry has long been in the forefront of efforts to perfect American democracy," she wrote; now, American Jews were ready to "roll up our sleeves and, for better or worse, to pitch in and help Israel strengthen her democratic ideals."[87]

To gauge the accuracy of Alperin's observations, one needed to look no further than at American Jewish responses to the US tour of Nobel laureate, South African Anglican Archbishop Desmond Tutu, which had just concluded as she sat down to write. At an interfaith breakfast sponsored by the American Jewish Congress, to an audience of 150 religious leaders, the Archbishop expressed his surprise with reports that Israel "collaborates with the government of his country." The Jewish press reported his stating that "We really cannot see how that could ever be consistent with who you are, your history," he said. Drawing out these historical parallels, he likened the apartheid government to the Nazis. Tutu stated that opposition to apartheid was found in religious universalism, that it was "not a political issue, it is our faith and it has very deep roots in your history, your tradition."[88] Echoing the phrasing of David Hammerstein, a student activist in the 1970s, Tutu nodded toward Israel's political situation, likening it to that of his home nation. "One does understand Israel of course," he said, "because she too has suffered a measure of isolation and must try to find friends where she can." But he regretted the toll this took on Black/Jewish ties, saying it "is costing [Israel] dear in terms of black perceptions. You know what is happening to black and Jewish relationships in this country and part of that is due to this South African-Israel connection." The Jewish press reported that Tutu concluded by paying homage to the many radical Jewish antiapartheid activists in South Africa, noting that "we have so many tremendous Jewish people in the struggle for justice and peace at home."[89]

Jewish leaders bristled at Tutu's observations and analogies, subjecting him to criticism that remained strong and sharp. They called Tutu's ideas anti-Semitic, and defended Israel's trade with South Africa by comparing it with other nations.[90] The Stephen Wise Free Synagogue in Manhattan, headed by Rabbi Balfour Brickner, a former member of Breira and supporter of NJA, was later forced to defend its choice of Archbishop Tutu to receive an award for his contributions to the battle against apartheid.[91] To accusations of anti-Semitism, Tutu responded only that "these charges are without foundation and part of an orchestrated campaign of vilification against me by the proponents of apartheid."[92] In 1989, he expressed his faith that he and Holocaust survivor, author, academic, activist, and Nobel Peace Prize winner Elie Wiesel could mediate peace in the Middle East. A decade and a half later, he and Wiesel would take opposing sides on a boycott of Israel, and American Jews again revived charges of "Jew hatred" for Tutu stretching back to his visits in the 1980s.[93]

As these struggles illustrate, the quest for friends turned perilous in the mid-1980s. Anxieties and accusations muddied what Rabbi Albert Axelrad had thought should be "lucidly clear": the mainstream Jewish position on apartheid. Because activists and laypeople across the world now utilized an expansive definition of apartheid, many mainstream Jewish leaders felt that they had to police the boundaries of Zionism and Israel even more carefully. New, global realities in the antiapartheid movement and in attitudes toward Israel/Palestine meant that Jewish leaders had to carve out public antiapartheid positions that left little room for conversations about Israel's friendship with South Africa and about Israel's Occupation. Progressive Jews sometimes managed to hold these commitments in a difficult balance, as evidenced by their embracing Archbishop Desmond Tutu on his 1987 tour. Other Jewish leaders largely demonized Tutu on this and future occasions.

One year before the fall of apartheid, in the book *With Friends like These: The Jewish Critics of Israel*, scholar Edward Alexander wrote a scathing criticism of Israel's "enemies." His arguments tied those "enemies" to the antiapartheid struggle. Archbishop Desmond Tutu's visit to Israel, his words linking apartheid to the Holocaust and to Israel's treatment of Palestinians, appeared alongside of Nelson Mandela's and Yasser Arafat's linkages of "Tel Aviv and Pretoria regimes" on the first page of the book.[94] His conclusions continued to suggest that Jewishness and Jewish loyalty were commitments that precluded affiliation or sympathy with anticolonialist movements, with antiapartheid or Palestinian rights. It remained an either/or proposition, because from his perspective, the stakes were too high.

In Jewish organizations across the United States, Jewish men and women of all ages weighed their priorities and their options. Often those options narrowed, as when NJA fell apart in the 1990s.[95] Still, Progressive Jews sought out alternative sites of belonging, continuing to protest what they saw as a lack of democracy in American Jewish organizations alongside their global protests against apartheid in South Africa and Israel's Occupation.[96]

7

"Our South Africa Moment": American Jews' Struggles with Apartheid, Zionism, and Divestment

In the 1980s and the 1990s, though Israel remained the single largest recipient of American foreign aid, many American Jews continued to feel under siege by anti-Zionist rhetoric that they saw sliding into anti-Semitism.[1] Mainstream Jewish organizations had by then added their voices to the powerful antiapartheid movement, but they did so with an eye on the movement leaders' rhetoric and actions with regard to Israel and Israeli policies. This had been their practice since the painful breakup of the New Left, the rise of Cold War alliances, and the Third World/Global South's mobilization around Palestinian rights.

To understand the flashpoints encountered in this study is to engage three interconnected narratives: growing resistance to South African apartheid, rising global attentiveness to the Israeli/Palestinian conflict, and increasingly tense disputes within American Jewish life over apartheid, Zionism, and Israeli policy. Within international diplomatic and global activist circles, the use of the word apartheid was on the rise as a descriptor of Israel's Occupation. This study, then, ends as it began: with American Jews struggling to answer questions about Jewish unity, about how to utilize Jewish power and influence, about tolerance for dissent in American and Western Jewish communities, and about the significance of a global liberation movement for them as Jews. Modeled on the successes of the twentieth-century antiapartheid movement, Palestinians' twenty-first-century liberation movement was framed increasingly as a struggle against Israeli apartheid.[2]

Mandela in New York, 1990

Nations Divided began with the story of Nelson Mandela's 1990 release from prison and the beginning of apartheid's end in South Africa. As Mandela prepared for a visit to the United States, Jews around the world expressed shock and dismay over his embrace of Yasser Arafat, labeled a terrorist and an enemy of the Jewish people. Mainstream Jewish leaders rejected Arafat as the leader of the Palestinian liberation movement. Other Jews, however, saw in the Palestine Liberation Organization the possibility for negotiation and diplomacy. Although vigorously rejecting terrorist responses to Israeli aggression, they granted Arafat the political legitimacy and visibility they felt was necessary to begin peacemaking. Several members of NJA and other American Israeli/Palestinian peace groups formed a delegation that met with Arafat in Tunis in 1987, for example. They aimed to understand each other's "concerns and fears." At a news conference, one of the delegates noted that their meeting went "beyond questions of dialogue" between Jews and Palestinians. "There's a history of denial of their existence," he said, referring to Palestinians.[3] Afif Safieh, an aide to Arafat in the PLO, spoke at NJA's 1987 biennial Convention at the University of California Los Angeles. "With enemies like you," Safieh joked with his audience, "who needs friends?"[4]

To assuage the fears of those who rejected Arafat as a terrorist and an enemy to Israel and to Jews, Nelson Mandela agreed to meet with the SAJBD before he departed for his tour of Europe and the United States. Members of the SAJBD told American Jewish leaders that Mandela remained committed "to the wellbeing of the South African Jewish community" and pledged "his unswerving opposition to racism and anti-Semitism" and to Israel's right to exist in "secure borders." Mandela also "expressed appreciation for the role Jews had played in the struggle against apartheid."[5]

As Mandela departed for his tour, the mainstream, organized Jewish South African population had reached a moment of transformation. Thousands of Jews had left South Africa, with the population declining from about 120,000 to 100,000 through the 1980s and early 1990s.[6] There was movement, too, in the way the community was reorienting its history with regard to radical (and liberal) Jews' contributions to the end of apartheid. Up until these years, Jewish leaders had treated radical activists, especially, with tremendous hostility. According to one scholar of South African Jewish activism, they were "long written out of histories celebrating the achievements of the South African Jewish community."[7] With Mandela's release and the end of apartheid, there were movements to "recanonise" radical Jews in the eyes of South Africa and the world.[8] Laying claim to a collective Jewish heritage that included this successful struggle for human rights gave meaning and ethnic distinction to Jews beyond whiteness in the emerging new "Rainbow Nation" of postapartheid South Africa—a term coined by Archbishop Desmond Tutu.[9] But these claims tapped into long-standing controversies among South African Jews, just as Mandela's visit prompted debates among American Jews.[10]

After their meeting with Mandela, members of the SAJBD directly reassured leaders of the NJCRAC, the umbrella organization of American Jewish institutions. They then worked with African American leaders and members of Congress to plan a meeting with Mandela prior to his stop in the United States. On June 10, 1990, Mandela met with six American Jewish organizational leaders for two hours in Geneva. At the meeting, Jewish leaders and Mandela spoke about their positions with regard to Israel and the PLO. The leaders felt that both sides had clarified their attitudes, and that subsequently "the American Jewish community could fully and actively participate in the welcome of Mr. Mandela to the United States."[11] Leaders such as Abraham Foxman of the Anti-Defamation League had previously "denounced the ANC as totalitarian and a threat to Israel"; he left the meeting praising Mandela as a "great hero of freedom" in *The New York Times*.[12]

Hundreds of thousands of people thronged the venues to see and hear Nelson Mandela and his wife Winnie Mandela, herself a towering figure in the antiapartheid movement and later head of the Women's League of the ANC. One columnist wrote that "America has begun a great love affair with the Mandelas," calling them heroes not only in their own land "but also in the United States where people are starved for leaders with character, commitment and integrity."[13] The African American response to Mandela's visit proved overwhelming, a poignant and celebratory moment in diaspora activism and connection. As historian James Meriwether writes:

> Mandela's triumphal visit in 1990 marked an especially moving moment in black America's embrace of contemporary Africa. For black America, Mandela transcended being an African leader and became an African American leader as well. Receiving Mandela as one of their own, African Americans saw him presenting to white America a symbol not only of what an African could be but of what an African American could be.[14]

American Jewish antiapartheid activists, those who had stayed with the movement through its difficult debates over Zionism, greeted him in diverse venues. Herb Magidson, president of the JLC, saw Mandela at an AFL–CIO convention. Mandela "thanked the delegates for steadfast support of him during his many years of captivity." Magidson wrote that he "was privileged to be a delegate to that convention and I remember vividly Mandela explaining how such support gave him sustenance....[This] help[s] to explain why serious domestic battles between Blacks and Jews did not cause a fundamental change in Jewish attitudes toward apartheid. If anything, it strengthened Jewish resolve because it provided an activity that helped to ameliorate the difficult position that both Blacks and Jews were in...in the 1960s."[15]

Although Magidson's recollection of consistent Jewish opposition to apartheid among Jews might reflect individual Jewish positions, it does not square with the historical record of mainstream Jewish organizations until the mid-1980s. Yet in his antiapartheid activism, he worked with both Jews and non-Jews, in the JLC and in secular labor unions. Outside of Jewish organizations, Magidson tells us, African Americans, self-identified American Jews, and others united against apartheid. Magidson populates the antiapartheid movement and American Jewish history with Jews who approached apartheid through the issues of labor and the right to organize.

Like Fritz Flesch in the 1950s, they did this work in labor unions even when mainstream Jewish groups largely disappeared from the antiapartheid movement. And so Magidson's presence at Mandela's speech meant much to him as a union leader and as a Jew.

When Mandela arrived in Boston, activist and academic Eleanor Roffman walked from her home in Jamaica Plain to Roxbury. Holding a photograph of Mandela and Arafat glued to a stick, she and a friend stood cheering on Warren Street as Mandela opened his car door to wave in person to the huge crowds of people who had gathered to greet him. Roffman had heard Winnie Mandela speak the night before, and she was thrilled to be in the presence of both leaders on their American tour. She recalls happily the cries of approval she received—especially the cheers of those who had gathered at a Mosque on Blue Hill Avenue when they saw her sign. This moment marked for her the full integration of her views on Israel, South Africa, and apartheid, and she claimed her membership in the liberation movements of Black South Africans and Palestinians.

Surely Roffman's sign would have earned the enmity of American Jewish Zionists. Mandela's visit presented them with a difficult moment—even with the reassurances of Jewish leaders. Once again, many felt forced to walk a careful line between their commitments to Jewish loyalty (to Israel and Zionism) and to global liberation struggles. Tensions over Mandela showcased the role of apartheid in heated debates over Zionism and Jewishness that had spanned the Cold War; it also spotlighted the role of apartheid in the damage done to Black/Jewish relations.

Although American Jewish organizational leaders reassured the world that the Jewish antiapartheid fight "Has No Strings"—that they remained committed to the cause of antiapartheid with no qualifications—many American Jews met Mandela's visit with ambivalence, and even protests.[16] This response stood in stark contrast to the unqualified celebrations among union members and African Americans, to cite just two examples. In Miami, Nelson Mandela received a hero's welcome from the American Federation of State, County, and Municipal Employees. Outside, Jewish groups joined Cuban groups in protesting Mandela's support for Arafat and Fidel Castro.[17]

For many American Jewish Zionists, the PLO was an extremist terrorist organization that sought to destroy Israel and wrought destruction on Israel's population. Because their ties to Israel were a central component of their Jewish identity and visibility, and because Mandela expressed support for Arafat's aim of Palestinian liberation, some Zionist American Jews struggled to place Mandela in the pantheon of heroes. Albert Vorspan, director of the Reform movement's Commission on Social Action, wrote to Mandela in advance of his visit, congratulating him but also testifying to the "deep hurt and perplexity" over his relationship to the PLO. Vorspan offered Mandela a corrective to his definition of Zionism, stating that it would be "more appropriate to equate the dream of your people to Zionism, the liberation movement of the Jewish people, which resulted in the establishment of the democratic state of Israel nearly 42 years ago."[18]

Rabbi Myer Kripke, a columnist for the Omaha *Jewish Press*, articulated the terms of this struggle as well:

> Mandela's vaunted morality has disappeared entirely, totally vanished. His view of other countries is based not on morality at all, but on pragmatic considerations alone. He would embrace the devil if the devil would vote against apartheid. He shows no concern for the men, women, and children, Jews, Muslims, Christians and others—people!—murdered by Arafat, Castro and Ghadaffi. This is the politician-opportunist at his worst, no moralist at all... I do not hesitate to call Mandela a hero of our times. But he is a hero with a blind spot. He is blind to every evil except the evil of apartheid. His blind spot is as morally crippling as his determination is bold.[19]

In an "open letter" to Mandela in the pages of *Reform Judaism*, Cecil Epril, a former South African journalist living in the United States, expressed his dismay with what he saw as Mandela's compromised principles. Mandela had compared Arafat's struggle against colonialism with the antiapartheid struggle in South Africa, and asserted that if this truth "alienated the powerful Jewish community in South Africa, that's too bad." Epril noted the historic Jewish contributions to the antiapartheid struggle in South Africa, including Helen Suzman's important role in Parliament. He cited Israel's aid to Black Africa. He earnestly asked Mandela to weigh the "heavy charges against the PLO" and come to understand why Jews, so long persecuted, wished for Mandela to reassure them of his dedication to "mutual goodwill."[20]

Conservative American Jews used Mandela's visit to remark on the fate of American Cold War allies. In the American Jewish Committee's *Commentary* magazine, anticommunist scholar Joshua Muravchik parsed Mandela's statements to determine whether he had expressed "apologies" or "regret" for his past support of the PLO or for past critiques of the South African Jewish community. Muravchik bemoaned the fact that Mandela's "rhetoric bears the earmarks of years spent in a Communist milieu." He noted that Jewish opposition to Mandela's positions informed a broader discussion about South Africa and the United States in global politics. That opposition tempered what he saw as otherwise unreserved enthusiasm for Mandela; it forced the United States to think harder about where the South African economy might be headed, and how South Africa might—or might not—continue to serve as a post-Cold War ally.[21]

Many allies of Mandela read these sentiments with anger and dismay, with dashed hopes that a Jewish communal embrace of Mandela would contribute to a healing of the rift between African Americans and Jews. Writing in the pages of *Tikkun*, progressive activist and academic Cornel West wrote that he "understood why some Jews might be upset with Mandela," and that "every prophet deserves criticism." But he also called it "imperative that that Black and Jewish progressives reflect seriously on the Mandela example... in order to keep alive the precious values of individuality and democracy while strengthening the possibilities of a principled coalition across racial lines in the US." West wrote of his admiration for "progressive nationalists such as

Michael Lerner [editor of *Tikkun*], Nelson Mandela, and Edward Said," who balanced "universal moral outlooks and international perspectives" and drew from the "prophetic elements in our respective religious traditions."[22] West hoped that balancing particularist interests with universal commitments to justice would lead to unity in American struggles for equality.

There were American Jews who wished to celebrate Mandela's life as Jews. In *The New York Times*, activist, scholar, and journalist Alisa Solomon urged Jewish leaders not to "test Mandela on Israel," citing a poll that indicated that a majority of American Jews supported Israel's territorial concessions for peace with Palestinians. Indeed, the ANC, along with "countless American Jews...and Israelis" (including members of the Knesset and military officers) supported Palestinian rights. Solomon noted that in Israel and around the world, these issues were debated, while "only in America's mainstream Jewish leadership is discussion denied." Because "supporting Palestinian rights and supporting Israel are not mutually exclusive," she wrote, "the mainstream Jewish leaders misrepresent the people for whom they claim to speak."[23] "The Jewish community's decision to stand up for a cause of such clear moral rectitude as the fight to end apartheid should not be held hostage" to Mandela's position on Israel, his use of the word colonialism to describe the Occupation, or his dedication to Palestinian self-determination. Solomon saw it as a missed opportunity for American Jews.

For just as Israeli/Palestinian controversies pulled apart any united communal Jewish welcome of Mandela, so too were these controversies causing tremendous strife internal to that Jewish community. Donna Nevel, Marilyn Kleinberg Neimark, Alisa Solomon, and other progressive Jews in New York City felt that mainstream Jewish leadership no longer embraced the same values of community members whom they were to represent. Active in campaigns for justice in Latin America and South Africa, they decided to form a Jewish organization dedicated to local struggles for justice—where mainstream Jewish organizations were far too underrepresented. "When just at that moment the 'official' Jewish organizations announced that they would not participate in the city's welcome of Mandela,"[24] Solomon recalled:

> that seemed to crystallize all too well the direction the "official" community was going—and it was also a sign of the way Israel politics was skewing the local agenda. In discussing some kind of inaugural event at the meeting...someone suggested that we welcome Mandela and there was unanimous enthusiasm for the idea.[25]

A small committee organized the evening (including Solomon, Rabbi Marshall Meyer and Rabbi Rolando Matalon, both of Manhattan's Temple B'nai Jeshurun) on June 15, 1990. The Welcome Service for Nelson Mandela was the first ever event of the organization then named Jews for Racial and Economic Justice (JFREJ).[26]

Led by activist Rabbi Balfour Brickner, Rabbi Meyer, and Rabbi Matalon at Temple B'nai Jeshurun, the service aimed at "rededicating ourselves to the struggle for racial and economic justice." There were greetings from Mayor David Dinkins, from performer and activist Harry Belafonte (who was co-chair of the Nelson Mandela New York Welcome Committee), and Manhattan Borough President Ruth Messinger. On the list of supporters were many whose names also appear in these pages: Rabbi Arthur Hertzberg, Letty Cottin Pogrebin, Messinger, Morris Schappes, Arthur Waskow, and Peter Weiss. NJA's Manhattan chapter appears in the list as well.

A JFREJ founder who had planned the event with Alisa Solomon and others, Henry Schwarzchild offered the evening's concluding remarks. Schwarzchild had fled Nazi Germany after Kristallnacht in 1938, arriving in the United States one year later. He worked for Civil Rights and civil liberties and mobilized against the death penalty. As a witness to the growth of Nazism, he pledged that "Whatever the cost, I would not live in a period of major social, moral events and be a bystander." Taking a clear position on decades of debates over the legacy and meaning of the Holocaust for American Jews, Schwarzchild stood at the Center of JFREJ's Welcome Service for Mandela. He spoke of JFREJ members as "a group of disparate people, including believers and unbelievers, moderates and radicals," who have come together "around the intuition that the Jewish task of justice is being neglected in our own society."

> We here no longer suffer much from the handicaps of ethnicity or poverty, but we thrive in the presence of, even partly as a consequence of, the social sins of the racial distress and economic pain of others. Jews for Racial and Economic Justice came together to find a way not to stand silently by at the blood (literal and metaphoric) of our brothers and sisters, or at their joy. We expect that the African American community of this city and this country will receive Nelson Mandela much the way East European Jewry is said to have received Theodor Herzl, as an emblem and harbinger of liberation. We rejoice with them at this visit.[27]

Reaching back into Jewish history, Schwarzchild found his analogy for Black liberation in the earliest moments of the modern political Zionist movement. That analogy, that definition of Zionism as a liberation theology in itself, had long sustained a kinship among African Americans, Africans, Israelis, and American and other nations' Jews. Schwarzchild's use of the analogy signaled unqualified allegiance to the cause of antiapartheid, in a moment when mainstream American Jewish organization distanced themselves from that cause with qualifications about Mandela's "loyalty" to Israel, Zionism, and Jews.[28]

JFREJ's first event was an unqualified success. A thousand people attended, and they raised $30,000 to present to the ANC.[29] This organization continues to work on campaigns for the rights of immigrants, workers, and the poor in New York City. JFREJ members hold a diverse array of political positions with regard to the Israeli/Palestinian conflict. First convening on common ground with regard to a global issue—honoring Mandela's visit, his defiance, strength, and grace as a leader in the antiapartheid movement—JFREJ members have since that moment devoted all of their resources to local issues.[30]

The final chapter of this study follows the arc of American Jewish struggles with apartheid after the fall of South African apartheid—from local receptions of Mandela's United States visit in 1990 to American coverage of the complicated eulogizing of Mandela by Jews and Palestinians in late 2013. In those years, a series of new crises emerged: in global diplomatic gatherings, such as those of the United Nations; and in local, heated debates over Israeli apartheid and the Boycott, Divestment, and Sanctions movement, which targets Israel. In each, the complex legacies of apartheid and the contentiousness of its global application prevented crucial conversations.

Global: Durban I and II

The year after Mandela's visit and the founding of JFREJ, Zionists and Israel supporters around the world celebrated the repeal of the Zionism is racism resolution by the United Nations. Introduced by President George H. W. Bush in December 1991, United Nations Resolution 46/86 repealed the 1975 Resolution 3379 whose passage had been so utterly traumatic to Zionists the world over. The passage of 46/86 was Israel's condition of participation in the Madrid Peace Conference, and its redemptive qualities must not be understated. But the repeal of 3379 ultimately did not mark the victory of one "definition" of Zionism over the other, according to the painful analysis offered by Anson Laytner in 1976. As leaders of antiapartheid and other Third World liberation movements began issuing strong—and at times anti-Israel or anti-Semitic—critiques, Laytner had asked why the Third World hated Zionism. Rejecting the idea that Zionism was a form of Jewish liberation, they defined it instead as a form of racism, colonialism, and imperialism. Apartheid became deeply entangled in these debates over Zionism and Israel's policies toward Palestinians and other non-Jews. Despite the appeal of 3379, those who continued to view Zionism as a liberation movement could not ignore the increasing visibility of a global movement that likened Israeli policies toward Palestinians to apartheid.

Journalist and author Samuel Freedman recalled the first stirrings of the movement to divest from Israel in the 1990s, modeled on the successful antiapartheid divestment from South Africa in the 1970s and 1980s. For him, Jewish antiapartheid activism left Jews vulnerable to accusations of discrimination and oppression in Israel. "A growing and sophisticated population of Muslim Americans supplied the passionate rank-and-file for the campaign against Israel," Freedman wrote. "And the passive or active involvement of many American Jews in the antiapartheid movement left them tongue-tied and embarrassed when it came to asserting why Israel shouldn't taste the same harsh medicine."[31] Meanwhile, activists of all backgrounds, from Israel, Europe, and the United States, issued calls to boycott products made in Israel or in Jewish settlements of the Occupied Territories from the late 1980s through the early 2000s.

Apartheid again became a crucial part of conversations about Zionism in international diplomatic and human rights organizations leading up to 2001, as the world prepared for a United Nations conference to address racism and colonialism in Durban, South Africa. In 1978 and 1983, when Resolution 3379 was still on the books, the United States and Israel boycotted the United Nations conferences on Racism and Racial Discrimination in Geneva. Most saw these conferences as successful because they rallied world opinion against the apartheid regime in South Africa. But American and Israeli leaders feared attacks on Zionism and Israel.[32]

The repeal of the Zionism is racism resolution might have led to both nations' presence at the next conference on race in Durban, a site chosen to celebrate the success of the global antiapartheid movement. While it was officially called the 2001 United Nations World Conference against Racism, Racial Discrimination, Xenophobia, and Related Intolerance (or WCAR), for many Jewish leaders and community members, "Durban" became synonymous with vigorous efforts to discredit Israel, Zionism, and Jewish people worldwide. Although the Zionism is racism resolution had been repealed, historian Gil Troy wrote, "Durban essentially repealed the repeal by casting Israel as 'today's ultimate villain.'" He observed that the revived "Zionism is racism charge helped anti-Israel sentiment degenerate into Jew hatred masked by high-minded human rights rhetoric."[33]

Activists had hailed the UN-sponsored event as an unprecedented opportunity for the world community to discuss legacies of colonialism and other long-standing problems, such as xenophobia and racism. But fear of the United Nations delegates' bashing Israel—dating back to the 1975 resolution, with anxiety deepening over each incident seen as emerging from that same set of ideas—created a tense lead-up to the conference. A few weeks before Durban began, the White House announced that General Colin Powell, the first African American to be Secretary of State, would not attend. Jesse Jackson and other Civil Rights leaders strongly criticized the decision, while David Harris of the American Jewish Committee said that "If the United States does not go, nobody in the Jewish community will shed a tear."[34]

Some Jewish leaders, however, worked to pave the way for American and American Jewish attendance and support at Durban—and that meant brokering understanding between African Americans and American Jews. Recalling past moments when issues had been used as currency, the Jewish press recorded that "In exchange for their support for the Jewish cause—and to maintain harmony in occasionally bumpy relations—some blacks want Jews to stand with them on slavery, which in Durban may include a demand for reparations." Rabbi Marc Schneier of the Foundation for Ethnic Understanding worked with the World Jewish Congress and the Congressional Black Caucus, for example, to author a letter that condemned the United Nations' anti-Israel language and also supported "the efforts of African American leaders to raise and address important issues surrounding the historic tragedy of slavery and the resulting efforts to seek reparations."[35]

Ultimately, such efforts could not prepare anyone for what actually transpired at Durban, nor could they preclude or dampen the intense and overwhelming response. Not at the conference itself, but at the parallel NGO conference, representatives of several nations issued a declaration equating Israel's policies in the Occupied Territories with apartheid. Mary Robinson, the UN High Commissioner for Human Rights, refused to endorse it or bring it to the main forum. Yet Israelis and Americans walked out of the conference in protest, and the two forums merged in many people's minds into one pernicious, anti-Semitic gathering.

Like the UN women's conferences, and in line with the historic tension between the United Nations and Israel, what followed was a "battle over perceptions," with both sides in the battle claiming their statements as the "truth" of what actually happened.[36] Hillel Neuer, head of UN Watch, a group that monitors the world body for perceived bias against Jews and anti-Semitism, called Durban "a festival of hate and anti-Semitism."[37]

Other observers and participants rejected this perception of Durban, arguing instead that the conference was really about a call for reparations from nations that had lived under various kinds of colonialism. By their lights, the savage inequalities of the new, postapartheid South Africa, given voice in the antipoverty protests outside of the Durban conference, provided a fitting setting. In this demand for a new accounting, there were apologies to be made, historical artifacts to be returned, histories to be written. Activists also aimed for development programs in Africa. Activist, journalist, and author Naomi Klein termed these "a demand for a radical New Deal for the global South."[38] When a few Islamic countries began again to insert language into drafts of the Durban Declaration equating Zionism with racism and downplaying the impact of the Holocaust, the United States delegation had the "perfect excuse to flee the scene," wrote Klein. Once they departed (and still before the Durban conference began), delegates removed the offensive language. Ironically, as Klein points out, the final declaration was in fact praised by Israeli leaders. But the damage had been done.

According to Klein, for Zionist delegates there were two traumatic pieces to Durban. First there was the anti-Semitism that was "real and frightening." Second there was the "international consensus building" around the idea that "Israel's citizenship and security laws" were a "version of apartheid, deserving of the same kind of economic sanctions that ultimately put an end to the practice in South Africa."[39]

Many decried the use of the word apartheid to describe Israel, just as they had decried the use of the word racism to describe Zionism, calling it nothing short of anti-Semitism. International law expert Ruth Wedgwood traced its origin to the "fatal bargain" made by the ANC in its fight against apartheid: in exchange for help from Islamic nations, the ANC pledged "reciprocal help against Israel," and in that exchange lay the origin of the Israel apartheid "trope."[40] For Wedgwood and many other Zionists, Durban marked yet another failure on the part of the United Nations to treat Israel fairly, to check the influence of anti-Zionist forces that imperiled Israel and

Jews throughout the world, to weigh Israel's use of force equally to Arab terrorism. For these activists, "the once, future, always resolution" from the UN, though officially repealed, lived on.[41]

Rabbi Abraham Cooper, Associate Dean of the Simon Wiesenthal Center, a global Jewish human rights organization and NGO, joined others in attacking human rights groups for their role in the conference. He challenged human rights leaders over their silence on anti-Semitic incidents and on the attempt to insert anti-Zionist language into the forum's final declaration. Cooper dismissed the idea that this language represented the "voice of the victims" in the Israeli/Palestinian conflict. "Well," he concluded, "the concerns of one group of victims—the Jewish people—were left off that document, with the silent acquiescence of Amnesty International and Human Rights Watch."[42]

These perceptions of Durban continued to distance Zionist Jews from human rights organizations, as Jewish loyalty and human rights activism in this realm remained an "either/or" choice. It also divided African Americans and Jews, and kept the United States wary of future UN conferences that might invoke criticisms of Israel. This interpretation of Durban also motivated the channeling of many resources into presenting competing "truths" about Israel and Zionism.

Civil Rights organizations, meanwhile, pressed another interpretation: that the United States used accusations of anti-Zionism to excuse itself from difficult and pressing conversations about reparations for the Transatlantic slave trade. With the goal of bringing the United States to world court for the crime of slavery, the December 12th movement brought 400 delegates to the Durban conference in 2001.[43] Movement leaders claimed that the United States falsely cited the Israeli/Palestinian conflict as the cause of its walkout, when really the United States sought to avoid conflict on reparations.

Choices appeared stark: one could side with the United States and Israel or participate in conversations about global racism and colonialism. Durban pushed the wedge still deeper between these issues, leaving little space for antiracist Jews with allegiance to Israel, or for American Jews invested in seeing a United States presence at Durban. Klein and others chart the historic and far reaching impact of this battle over perceptions of the Durban conference. For the purposes of this study, what remains significant is the role that apartheid played in preventing major world powers from engaging in conversations about the cost of colonialism or envisioning new social and economic arrangements.[44] Once again, the tensions over apartheid and Zionism created chasms between Zionists and anti-Zionists, and between mainstream Jewish organizations and those with anticolonialist agendas. As Klein writes, the "minority death match" over Durban only served to widen the fissures between Jews and African Americans.[45]

Academic and mainstream journals from around the world registered the fallout from the Durban protests. Radical economist Samir Amin noted that "voices from Asia and Africa" were most clear in their condemnation of Israel's treatment of Palestinians, Israel's "planned 'bantustanisation' of

Palestine (Israel here applying down to the last details the methods of South Africa's former apartheid)...[These]make up the final chapter in a long history of imperialism which is racist, by definition." The Americans, in allying with Israel, "openly declared their intention to sabotage the proceedings."[46] "The spirit of Bandung breathes again," Amin concluded, referring to the 1955 conference of "Afro-Asian solidarity." Bandung "set in motion a first round of national liberation movements which primed the world for coming changes." Bandung planners excluded Israel in 1955 because of its colonialist alliances, and Israel's boycott of Durban nearly half a century later again left that nation outside of these conversations once again.[47]

Durban ended on September 7, 2001. Four days later, its program faded into the background for many across the world. Samuel Freedman wrote about how the attacks on 9/11 and the ensuing war in Iraq proved to be "distractions" for the growing movement to boycott Israel, which increasingly likened Israel's policies to apartheid. "Even on campuses, redoubts of pacifism, the prevailing mood turned chilly toward anything resembling advocacy for the Islamic world."[48]

Israel's political leaders, however, at times explicitly used the language of apartheid in discussion of their policies. In 2003, Prime Minister Ariel Sharon revealed that he relied on South Africa's Bantustan model in constructing a possible "map of a Palestinian state." The so-called independent Black regimes of the Bantustans in South Africa were a device to prop up the apartheid regime, and Israel was one of the only nations to establish commercial and diplomatic ties to the Bantustans.[49] Sharon's language as well as these ties provided still more fuel to the fire of the anti-Zionists' crusade against Israel.[50]

At the April 2009 follow-up conference to Durban's WCAR, called the Durban Review Conference or "Durban II" held in Geneva, Switzerland, delegates were charged with measuring the progress toward the goals set at Durban. The United Nations took steps to appease the United States and other nations disappointed with WCAR. They agreed on the final declaration's text before the conference even began, with no references to Israel, Zionism, or reparations for the TransAtlantic slave trade. For months, American Jewish groups and Israel pressured President Barack Obama to boycott the conference.[51] They did boycott, again citing concerns that it could be used as a forum for anti-Semitism, especially as Jewish groups had expressed their disappointment that Iran and Libya had been appointed to the conference planning committee.

Once again, opposing sides took their positions. "The U.N. conference seems to be exactly the right place for our new president to show the world that his administration's commitment to 'change we can believe in' means rejecting our country's tarnished legacy of violating international law, undermining the United Nations and using American exceptionalism to justify walking away from the leadership responsibility many in the world expect of the United States," noted Danny Glover, actor and producer, and also board chair of TransAfrica, a Washington-based African American human rights and social justice advocacy organization founded on the issue of apartheid. Imani Countess, senior director of public affairs with TransAfrica Forum, echoed Glover's comments. "This decision is inconsistent with the values this administration has touted," she stated. "Boycotting this conference sends a mixed message about the US's intentions when it comes to racism and intolerance." President Obama said he would welcome the chance to be "involved in a useful conference that addressed continuing issues of racism and discrimination around the globe." But, he added, he wanted to avoid a repetition of the 2001 Durban conference during which "folks expressed antagonism toward Israel in ways that were oftentimes completely hypocritical and counterproductive."[52]

The WJC, meeting in Jerusalem four months before the conference, issued a resolution that indicated members' fears of "the high possibility that Durban II will constitute an unwarranted and illegitimate attack on democratic freedoms, international human rights law, and an attack on Israel, not only through a series of one-sided and inaccurate resolutions, but also by ignoring the worst forms of racism that continue in a number of parts of the world." They acknowledged that "some governments played a constructive, vital and courageous role at Durban," but lamented that they were "unable to prevent abuses of process." Switching entirely to the future tense, the group outlined their anxieties further: "[the WJC members] STRONGLY BELIEVE that the 'red lines'which: single out or demonise any one State; introduce the policy of opposing defamation of religion; delete condemnation of anti-Semitism; remove calls for Holocaust commemoration; or construct a hierarchy of racisms, will be crossed at the Durban II Conference." The Resolution concluded with the following statement: "[The World Jewish Congress] ACCORDINGLY NOW REQUESTS JEWISH COMMUNITIES WORLDWIDE TO FORTHWITH CALL UPON THEIR RESPECTIVE GOVERNMENTS TO IMMEDIATELY WITHDRAW FROM THE DURBAN REVIEW PROCESS AND NOT ATTEND THE REVIEW CONFERENCE IN APRIL 2009."[53]

Since 1950, WJC leaders struggled to maintain Jewish unity, a particularist priority, in the face of broad, universalist struggles for liberation. Immediately after World War II, when this study began, the WJC cooperated with the United Nations, consistently referring to the need for human rights laws in the wake of Jewish genocide. In the new century, measuring Jewish loyalty and history against commitments to other sites of modern injustice continued to prove difficult. As Durban I and II made clear, the WJC felt the cost of engaging with these global campaigns proved too high; to engage critiques that encompassed anti-Semitic arguments would have been too much of a threat to its particularist priorities.

Many world leaders expressed regret that this conference, like its predecessor (and like many of the proceedings of the UN women's conferences of the twentieth century), would be a missed opportunity to talk about central human rights issues. "I am shocked and deeply disappointed by the United States decision not to attend a conference that aims to combat racism, xenophobia, racial discrimination and other forms of intolerance worldwide," said Navi Pillay, then the new UN high commissioner for human rights and a native of South Africa. "A handful of states have permitted one or two issues to dominate their approach to this (antiracism) issue, allowing them to outweigh the concerns of numerous groups of people that suffer racism and similar forms of intolerance to a pernicious and life-damaging degree on a daily basis all across the world."[54]

American Civil Rights activists and their allies across the globe saw America's refusal to attend as in line with a long history of failing to take seriously the issues of racism, colonialism, and human rights.[55] Kali Akuno, an activist with the Malcolm X Grassroots Movement, also expressed his deep disappointment that the Obama administration continued the political trajectory of the Bush administration in boycotting Durban II. "Answering for the crimes of the Bush regime," however, "is not the only reason the Obama administration doesn't want to engage the DRC [Durban Review Conference] however. It also doesn't want its weak civil and human commitments to be exposed and scrutinised before the world." Akuno wrote that the boycott's broad implications should mobilize individuals on the left: "Anti-racist, anticolonial, and anti-imperialist activists throughout the world must take decisive action to stop this political charade and reclaim the space that is rightfully ours."[56]

The boycott, which was joined by Australia, the Netherlands, Israel, and Canada, pleased mainstream Jewish groups. They showed their presence at the Geneva conference, ready to "fight the good fight," according to one NGO monitor leader.[57] Indeed, the WJC hosted a parallel meeting of the International Jewish Caucus, including representatives from scores of Jewish groups.[58] These groups gathered to make their presence known, and to encourage the world community to reflect on what they perceived as an unfair portrait of Zionism and Israel.

Ultimately, the president of the Islamic Republic of Iran, Mahmoud Ahmadinejad, spoke at the conference. Zionist Jewish groups seized on his anti-Israel, anti-Semitic rhetoric, insisting that the traffic of such ideas justified the boycott and their competing gathering. Many who had supported American attendance at the conference, including members of the Congressional Black Caucus, expressed their regret that Ahmadinejad's "inappropriate and out-of-line remarks would obscure the only international forum to address racism, racial discrimination, and xenophobia."[59]

Durban II also drew energy from a new movement that cemented the language of apartheid to Israel—and utilized the strategies of the successful antiapartheid movement to fight Israel's policies toward non-Jews. In 2005, 170 Palestinian organizations issued a call for a Global BDS Movement—boycott, divestment, and sanctions—for Israel.[60]

With the activist model of the antiapartheid movement as a template, the BDS movement lists as its mission: "[t]o strengthen and spread the culture of Boycott as a central form of civil resistance to Israeli occupation and apartheid."[61] Also in 2005, activists programmed the first Israel Apartheid

Week (IAW) with speakers who focused on Palestinian political prisoners, Israel's policies toward Palestinians, and the BDS movement. Beginning in Toronto, IAW spread to nearly 100 cities across the world by 2013. Activist and academic Eleanor Roffman says that her work against South African apartheid in the 1980s gave her the language and theory to protest Israeli apartheid; the BDS movement "gave her the practice." She supports the goals of the BDS movement and IAW "to economically disable the occupation." Like others in the movement, she argues that "it worked before."[62]

In his 2009 article titled "Back with a Vengeance—Divestment," Samuel Freedman writes that "when it comes to the rhetoric about a unitary state in Palestine, American Zionists (and perhaps Israelis, as well) do not fully grasp the potency of the South African analogy. They spend a lot of energy and verbiage making the case that Israel does not practice apartheid, but they haven't come up with nearly as effective an answer for why the South African model of peaceful transformation, full enfranchisement and majority rule shouldn't be applied to Israel and the Palestinian territories as well."

For Freedman and his supporters, the application of South Africa's postapartheid model to Israel evoked terrifying visions. A one-state solution, they contend, would erase the Jewish character of Israel. Maintaining their commitment to a definition of Zionism as a liberation movement for Jews means advocating for a two-state solution, so that both groups can pursue liberation by realizing their own nationalism.[63]

With readers of the *Washington Jewish Week*, Freedman shared his deep concern that "rock stars" like Naomi Klein, who support BDS, would win over younger Jews. And he ended ominously: "don't assume, this time, that our side is destined to win."[64] Freedman's framing of "our" and (implicitly) "their" sides paints a stark portrait of how the BDS movement has divided American Jews.

The Jewish Federations of North American (JFNA) and the Jewish Council for Public Affairs (JCPA)—formerly the NJCRAC—see the BDS movement as a threat so serious that in October 2010 they dedicated $6 million dollars over the next three years to the Israel Action Network. The network is defined as a "rapid-response team charged with countering the growing campaign to isolate Israel as a rogue state akin to apartheid-era South Africa—a campaign that the Israeli government and Jewish groups see as an existential threat to the Jewish state." According to the JFNA's president and CEO, Jerry Silverman, Israeli leaders identify the "delegitimization of Israel"—by the BDS movement and others—"as the second most dangerous threat to Israel, after Iran's pursuit of nuclear weapons."[65] The group's website touts the organization's defeating or "neutralizing" BDS and similar movements across the United States in order to "counter the assault on Israel's legitimacy."

Of special concern are BDS events held on college campuses. The fears of IAN members here echo those expressed by NJCRAC leaders in 1969, when they met to strategize about how to counter anti-Israel propaganda on the left—and how best to keep Israel an integral part of the lives of young

American Jews. The IAN traces the source of BDS propaganda back through struggles for Palestinian rights, through the Zionism is Racism resolution, Durban I and II, and the Goldstone report (mentioned below). It offers multiple counternarratives to invoke during potential campus encounters with BDS rhetoric. Resources include a "cookbook" that guides college students through preparing and responding to a BDS campaign, including "recipes" and "tools," such as statements by two Nobel Laureates and many Jewish communal leaders on why BDS threatens peacemaking and the values of academic freedom.[66]

This is only one of hundreds of online resources for opposing BDS and IAW, recipes for battles over Israeli policies, American Jewish unity, and Zionism's connection to apartheid. At University of California Berkeley in 2010, the Student Senate voted on whether to divest from companies that, according to BDS supporters, sold weapons to Israel's military to be used against Palestinian civilians. Letters of support for the divestment bill arrived from many Berkeley faculty members, and from Naomi Klein, Archbishop Desmond Tutu, Alice Walker, a group of Women Nobel Peace Laureates, and scores of other famous academic, political, and cultural figures.[67] Opponents of the bill met with the American Israel Public Affairs Committee, the Anti-Defamation League, and the Jewish Council for Public Affairs (formerly NJCRAC). Opponents had a teach-in, and met one-on-one with student senators. Nobel Laureate Elie Wiesel wrote to oppose it.

Discussion of the vote spanned the country. When the voting meeting finally arrived, debate ran through the night, and the bill narrowly met defeat. BDS called the close vote a "moral victory," a sign of a changing tide on the divisive issue.[68]

BDS activists came to similar conclusions about their loss in the Food Cooperative in Park Slope, Brooklyn, in March 2012 after a prolonged, heated debate over a referendum on a boycott of Israeli-made products. A store founder testified to the fact that the store carried only a handful of Israeli-made products, so the boycott would not have drastically altered the items sold by the 39-year-old co-op. But others mentioned the heavy ideological battle. Mayor Michael Bloomberg spoke in opposition to the ban, encouraging New Yorkers to "do more business with Israel, not less."[69] At the vote, boycott opponents linked BDS to the Ku Klux Klan. They spoke of how the antiapartheid movement did not destroy South Africa, as they felt the BDS movement would destroy Israel—or Israel as a Jewish state.

The close vote—1,005 against and 653 in favor—felt like a sort of victory to some activists. "It doesn't actually matter if the Coop boycotts Israel or not," wrote Kiera Feldman, journalist and Coop member, in *The Nation*. "Just having the debate is a symbolic victory for the pro-boycott camp. It might once have been safe to assume that in Park Slope, Brooklyn, progressive Jews would side with their more conservative coreligionists on matters pertaining to Israel. No longer."[70]

Others agreed that the vote testified to a definitive lack of consensus among American Jews about apartheid and Israel. From East Jerusalem,

Omar Barghouti, a Palestinian human rights activist and cofounder of the BDS movement, said that "regardless of the outcome, the fact that the debate had reached Park Slope reflected the momentum the cause had gained." He concluded with words that evidenced his hope that the movement was indeed reaching the power and momentum of the antiapartheid movement in the 1980s and 1990. "We are fast reaching our South Africa moment."[71] Barghouti predicts that smaller, local, commercial, and cultural boycotts of Israel will grow more widespread, becoming as visible and effective as anti-South African apartheid protests were in the 1980s.

In this moment, some Jewish activists and commentators want to alter the terms of the debate. Indeed, liberal Jewish groups like Americans for Peace Now (APN)—who dissent from many statements of mainstream Jewish groups regarding Israel—take pains to point out the faulty logic of those who press the label apartheid onto Israel's treatment of Palestinians, standing firm on the viability of a two-state solution as a means to end the Occupation and the violence. Journalist and author Peter Beinart writes that "by targeting all of Israeli society—and frequently comparing their effort to the global antiapartheid struggle—the BDS movement sends the message that just as the apartheid state was dismantled in South Africa, so must the Jewish state be dismantled today." Beinhart calls for a "Zionist BDS" where only products of the Jewish settlements are boycotted.[72] Rabbi Sharon Kleinbaum, APN leaders, and others agree.

But there appears little room for nuance in these passionate debates. When the director of the IAN, for example, suggested that an organization committed to Israel as a secure Jewish state might also support targeted boycotts of settlement-made products, he drew the ire of *Commentary* editors. They accused him of "legitimizing the delegitimizers" and said that his action "doesn't seem to be serving the best interests of American Jewry."[73]

BDS and—as President Jimmy Carter's book, discussed below, demonstrate—the word "apartheid" evoke the shrill responses historically associated with other sharp criticisms of Israel or Zionism. In such an intensely polarized environment, constructive conversations prove nearly impossible. Instead of an exchange of ideas, both sides dig in their heels and reassert their positions with stronger rhetoric and more anger and frustration. What remains feels to many like an "either/or" choice of particularist loyalty or universalist commitments to justice.

Local: Brandeis and Carter's *Palestine: Peace Not Apartheid*

The furious controversy over the publication of former President Jimmy Carter's 2006 book *Palestine: Peace Not Apartheid* testifies to the deep emotions evoked in these debates. Many American Jews loudly and publicly criticized Carter's analogy of Israel's policies toward Palestinians in the Territories with apartheid South Africa—and even accused him of being anti-Semitic. Scholar Sasha Polakow-Suransky writes that "the knee-jerk reaction to Carter's book...resembled Jewish organizations' reflexive denial of the Israeli-South African alliance during the 1970s and 1980s." He notes that Israelis were far more capable of engaging in nuanced and sophisticated discussions of Carter's book, and that some "were openly supportive of Carter."[74]

Such support was almost impossible to hear among those American Jews who were deeply invested in a particularist brand of Jewish unity, visibility, and difference. Scores of Jewish organizations blasted Carter for his criticism of Israel. Leaders of the Anti-Defamation League penned an open letter to Carter in which they wrote that "[t]rue sensitivity to Israel and American Jews would be demonstrated by ceasing these one-sided attacks and apologizing for damaging the good name of the State of Israel and the Jewish people."[75] Carter encountered protests throughout the nation on his book tour, which began "with a few faint complaints and has escalated to a full scale furor."[76] Jonathan Demme's documentary, *Jimmy Carter: Man from Plains*, captures Carter's book tour. Woven throughout the film is the debate over whether or not Carter would speak at Brandeis University. Indeed, Carter's Brandeis moment comprises the film's finale, capturing in one locality a microcosm of American Jewish internal discord.

Brandeis University's reception of President Carter offers a revealing window onto the Zionism/apartheid controversy within the mainstream American Jewish community. The University invited him, but his path there was far from straightforward. The idea of his visit sparked vociferous debate, and for a time Brandeis considered revoking the invitation.[77] Critics of Carter's book wanted to invite him to a debate with Alan Dershowitz, Harvard law professor and vocal supporter of Israel. Ultimately, Dershowitz received a separate invitation to speak immediately after Carter at the same lectern, in the same auditorium.

To an auditorium packed with 1,700 people, Carter explained his use of the term "apartheid," citing the fact that Israel had set aside highways for Israelis only, and noting too that liberal Israelis, "from newspaper journalists to professors to peace activists, also refer to Israeli policy on the West Bank as apartheid."[78] He advocated for full Israeli withdrawal from the Territories. He encouraged students and faculty to form a Brandeis delegation to tour the West Bank for three days, and return to share their findings with the Brandeis community, the nation, and Congress.

President Carter acknowledged that his use of the term apartheid to describe Israel's policies exclusively in the Territories "caused great pain in the Jewish community." He said that he chose the title to be "provocative" and to draw attention to the unjust treatment of Palestinians. He praised Israel, and said that its policies in the Territories run counter to its values and to the goals of peacemaking in the region. Nodding toward the Jewish character of the school, he said that Brandeis's was "the most exciting invitation I've ever received," save for Congress's invitation to deliver his inaugural address.[79] "I've been through political campaigns," he said, where he was "stigmatized and condemned by political opponents." But response to his book marked the "first time" he had ever been called "a liar, bigot, anti-Semite, coward, and plagiarist. This has hurt me and members of my family." "I can take it," he said, but he refused to respond to those who had engaged in these attacks.[80]

Immediately following Carter's talk, Alan Dershowitz took the stage. He indicated that, like Carter, he favored a two-state solution, an end to the Occupation, an end to the settlements. But he blasted Carter for presenting "the maximalist Palestinian view" which ran counter to peacemaking.[81] Dershowitz referred to the "two Jimmy Carters": "the Brandeis Jimmy Carter," who was "terrific," and the "Al Jazeera Jimmy Carter," who presents "a very different perspective."[82]

Outside of Carter and Dershowitz's talks, protesters gathered: some to attack Carter's ideas, and others—including members of a local chapter of Jewish Voice for Peace (JVP)—to support him. The controversies surrounding his book and his appearance on campus wore on. Alumni and other donors expressed their disappointment as the University took a wider assessment of the full cost of Carter's visit. Because, as the University's head fundraiser said, most of the donors "come through the Jewish door," officials feared a loss of funds. In Boston's *Jewish Advocate*, Morton Klein, President of the Zionist Organization of America, warned that the danger lay in Brandeis's "bringing and affiliating with people who are anti-Israel... because they have credibility as a Jewish-oriented institution."[83] All eyes fixed on Brandeis, and though the drop in donations never materialized, faculty began discussions in which they expressed their feelings that they "could not speak freely about the Middle East" on campus.[84] Emboldened by Carter's visit, critics of Israeli policy began conversations about other controversial speakers, testing the limits of the campus's ability to tolerate dissenting positions on Israel. In 2011, Brandeis students again ran up against those boundaries in another argument over Zionism and apartheid. The *Boston Globe* reported that Brandeis was "renewing a roiling debate over the limits of dissent within the American Jewish community." The student board of Brandeis Hillel, the leading Jewish organization on campus, refused to affiliate with JVP, which supported Carter and also supported the BDS movement. Hillel's international policies, which guide its chapters on hundreds of campuses around the world, prohibited any affiliation with BDS supporters. Brandeis Hillel student leaders said that JVP and Hillel had "very different" definitions of what it meant to be pro-Israel.[85] JVP supporters insisted that Hillel's refusal contradicted its "admissions statement," which "affirms the necessity of a pluralistic Jewish life on campus with partisanship to none."[86]

In an article in the New York *Jewish Week*, Brandeis's Jonathan Sarna, a professor of American Jewish history and a respected global expert on American Jewry, considered the significance of JVP's struggles with Brandeis Hillel:

> One of the last times the issue of who is in and who is out in the American Jewish community was debated came after the Yom Kippur War in 1973 when an organization called Breira [alternative] was formed. It advocated making

territorial concessions to the Palestinians and said the national aspirations of the Palestinian people should be recognized in order to achieve lasting peace. We look back and are surprised that a position that is today [widely accepted] was so controversial in its day...Will we look back in 50 years and say the same thing about JVP? I can't tell you.[87]

Despite a petition with 1,000 signatures, including students, 50 rabbis, 100 faculty members, parents, and alumni, Hillel formally rejected JVP's bid for membership. One of the students called the vote "the latest failure of the American Jewish establishment."[88] In these controversies, Brandeis is not alone: campus Hillel chapters and Jewish Student Unions across the United States are increasingly on the defensive when students invite individuals they consider "anti-Zionist" to speak on campus.

Brandeis continues to be a site for clashing definitions of American Jewish identity. In 2010, "Occupation Awareness Week" competed with "Israel Peace Week" on the campus calendar.[89] In 2012, students hosted Ali Abunimah, a pro-Palestinian activist and founder of the website Electronic Intifada, as the official speaker of IAW. "I think it is important that these questions are being asked at Brandeis, of all college campuses," Abunimah said, also referencing the university's Jewish ties and character. "I think that college students and universities in general ought to be and at best are the consciences of our societies."[90] IAW student organizer Noam Lekach told the Brandeis student newspaper: "We were worried before that people would be too alienated from this and not want to listen...and we would not be able to deliver our message because of the word [apartheid]." His fears were assuaged by the "hundreds" of comments about IAW on Facebook. "So I think the use of this term [Israel Apartheid Week] really provoked important debate," he concluded, "and I am happy about that."[91]

Brandeis's Zionist groups did not protest, instead holding a "pro-Israel party" the same evening. They regretted what had happened in previous years, such as when they staged a walk out of a talk given by Noam Chomsky; they had "lost their cool," according to one student, and "looked like we were not open to dialogue." At Brandeis's second IAW, they opted for a more subdued response.[92]

American Jews who support the BDS movement and those who support the IAN are engaged in a fierce war of words, especially over the word apartheid. IAN members have accused Jewish BDS supporters of being anti-Semitic, self-hating, and threatening Israel's very existence. "Naive, misinformed and possibly ill-intentioned faculty departments" have been criticized across the country for cosponsoring events for IAW.[93] Likewise, a Brandeis alum who was active in the campus antiapartheid movement in the late 1970s assailed IAW activists for their use of "false, perverted terms" that "provokes hatred and violence—not debate."[94] As this book goes to press, Brandeis and the BDS movement once again appear together in national headlines, as Brandeis dropped its membership in the American Studies Association (ASA) after

ASA members voted to boycott Israel. Academic and Jewish organizational leaders invoke this event in heated discussions of the politics of academic freedom and the politics of Israel/Palestine.[95]

College campuses such as Brandeis served as centers of radical dissent and activism in the Civil Rights, antiwar, women's, and gay rights movements; they were crucial sites for the antiapartheid movement in the 1980s. Even granting allowances for what many see as a lack of room for diverse voices regarding Israeli policy in the American Jewish community, Brandeis carries on this tradition of serving as a place for vigorous discussions and vibrant disagreements over local and global issues. Importantly, at Brandeis and on other campuses, Jewish college students founded an expressly *Jewish* organizational home for their BDS activism. Although subjected to attacks, and often denied formal recognition by mainstream Jewish communal organizations, these progressive groups do not appear to be breaking apart, as Breira and NJA did. This fact alerts us to the growing momentum, even growing American Jewish momentum, behind progressive critiques of Israeli policy toward Palestinians.

Israel and Apartheid in International Diplomacy

By the early twenty-first century, apartheid language had become intricately bound up in global criticisms of Israeli policies. In December 2008 and January 2009, Israel went to war in Gaza; 13 Israelis and 1,400 Palestinians died. American Jews and other activists protested throughout the world.[96] When the UN Human Rights Council sponsored a fact-finding mission headed by Judge Richard Goldstone, a prominent Jewish South African human rights judge, controversy ensued. In addition to his credentials as a global human rights expert, a liberal antiapartheid judge and a crucial figure in South Africa's transition to democracy, Goldstone is a self-identified Zionist, active in Jewish communal work in Israel and in international Jewish education.

Israel refused to cooperate with the UN mission. On the basis of the testimony gathered in the report, Goldstone and the other mission leaders found both Israel and Hamas guilty of war crimes. Throughout the debates that followed, as commentators raised questions about the accuracy of the report's data, Israeli political leaders and American Jewish communal leaders blasted Goldstone with ad hominem attacks. Israeli Prime Minister Benjamin Netanyahu labeled him "an evil, evil man," his report "a defamation" of the Jewish people.[97] American Jewish groups followed suit, labeling Goldstone a "self-hating Jew," and threatening his family. He was nearly banned from his grandson's bar mitzvah in South Africa.

American critics also saw Goldstone as part of a larger conspiracy originating in the human rights community. "The publication of an abbreviated version of the Goldstone report, accompanied by a number of essays, and edited by some of the most publicly identified anti-Israel activists involved in BDS and IAW," wrote one critic, "reflects the cynical abuse of human rights for the purposes of political warfare. These abuses include anti-democratic and decidedly anti-Israel strains, exploiting the Holocaust to advance the idea that Zionism denies justice to Palestinians."[98]

A small group of progressive American Jews supported Goldstone. Feminist, journalist, activist, and past president of APN, Letty Cottin Pogrebin called it an "un-Jewish assault on Richard Goldstone."[99] *Tikkun* editor Rabbi Michael Lerner presented the Tikkun award to Justice Goldstone in spring 2011, demonstrating support and admiration. In response, vandals attacked Lerner's home three times, leaving behind posters that depicted Lerner and "Islamic extremists" as "Nazis" intent on destroying Israel.[100]

A few months later, a London-based NGO called the Russell Tribunal on Palestine held its third annual meeting to investigate "violations of international law committed by Israel against the Palestinian people."[101] Named for the 1966 organization founded by Bertrand Russell to investigate crimes against International Law in the Vietnam War, the Russell Tribunal on Palestine held what they called a "hearing" to judge whether or not Israel was guilty of the crimes of apartheid. The "Tribunal of Conscience" met in Cape Town and attracted attention throughout the world for its strong criticisms of Israeli policies, of American "complicity," and of the United Nations' "failure to fulfill its obligation" to encourage respect for international law. When the Tribunal concluded that Israel's policies were "akin to apartheid," Jewish leaders registered their vehement protests. Perhaps most notable in this group was Richard Goldstone: in an editorial in *The New York Times*, he termed the charge of apartheid "false and malicious," concluding that it "precludes, rather than promotes, peace and harmony."[102] Even with his disputation of the apartheid label, many American Jews continued to vilify Goldstone.

In the United States after a trip to Gaza, author and activist Alice Walker garnered press coverage for the statements she authored in support of the Russell Tribunal's work. Archbishop Desmond Tutu joined her in issuing supportive statements. Walker signed on to the BDS movement in 2012. When she later refused a publisher's offer to distribute her novel, *The Color Purple*, in Israel, she cited her experiences with the Israeli/Palestinian conflict alongside those of Tutu's: "I grew up under American apartheid," she wrote to the publishers at Yediot Books, "and this was far worse. Indeed, many South Africans...including Desmond Tutu, felt the Israeli version of these crimes is worse even than what they suffered under the white supremacist regimes that dominated South Africa for so long."[103] For this action, and as testament to the high degree of polarization in these debates, she was branded an anti-Semite by Jewish communal leader and author Daniel Gordis, among others.[104]

Use of the word apartheid to describe the Israeli/Palestinian conflict continues to grow in acceptance. Pogrebin, who took her first trip to the West Bank in 2011, wrote in "The A-Word in Hebron" that two separate sets of laws applied to Palestinians and Jews there, and that Palestinians lacked freedom of movement. She wrote:

> If one opens one's eyes to the truth, the unmentionable becomes unavoidable—"A" for arrogance, and yes, for apartheid. It hurts me just to write that word. As a life-long, Israel-loving, peace-seeking Zionist, I disdained the hyperbolic label and the facile, incendiary parallels to pre-Mandela South Africa that, for years, have been propagated by Jimmy Carter and some pundits on the left. I've made at least two dozen trips to Israel since 1976 and, though strongly critical of its government's policies toward Palestinians within and outside the Green Line—whether under Labor, Likud or Kadima leadership—I never felt that extreme indictment was warranted by the facts on the ground. Then again, until last month, I had never been to Hebron. Justice-loving Jews cannot keep denying what is happening under Israeli auspices in Hebron; we can never say we didn't know.[105]

Most recently, journalist and progressive Jewish leader Leonard Fein wrote a heartfelt and despairing note to commemorate the forty-sixth anniversary of the Israeli Occupation. In 1971, Fein wrote that Zionism was "revolutionary," that Israel's "promise" lay in that nation's "rejection of the assumptions of universalism" (in that it is a nation created for Jews) but also its "useful precedent and helpful insight" into how the "typically reactionary consequences of particularist nationalism may be avoided."[106] The "idea of Israel," Fein asserted, is "a society parochial in structure but universal in ideology."[107] In 2014, Fein sits on the board of APN with Pogrebin and Peter Weiss. He contributes often to its website, where he recently quoted the Israeli organization Peace Now in saying "the Occupation corrupts":

> Forty-six years and counting. A resolution of the conflict becomes more remote with the passage of time. Earlier hopes come to seem naïve. The status quo governs, and few ask whether it is sustainable. That is the heart of the corruption. And that is the heart of the ongoing threat, the threat not merely to the Israel of our dreams and sometimes fantasies, but to the quotidian Israel, the everyday Israel to which we are so resolutely attached.[108]

Fein does not invoke the word apartheid. Yet his essay owes a debt, first to his own vast exposure to Israel through study and travel, and then to the exposure to Israeli policies that emerges out of anticolonialist, human rights protests of Israel. Champions of Israel, seen by many as model figures who have balanced American universalist strivings for justice alongside Jewish commitments, Pogrebin and Fein testify to an emerging trend among Zionist Jews in the United States. They write of their painful realizations about contemporary Israel and its Occupation.

These realizations have led to encounters with apartheid of the most profound character. At the 2012 International Solidarity Conference of the ANC, delegates from nine countries demonstrated their support for the BDS movement. When one delegate objected, "The ANC chairman Baleka Mbete strongly responded, saying that she has been to Palestine herself and that the Israeli regime is not only comparable but 'far worse than apartheid South Africa.'"[109]

Zev Krengel, president of the SAJBD, accused Mbete of trying "as usual, to bash and demonise Israel." In a statement reminiscent of the language of SAJBD's stand through the mid-1980s on South African apartheid, he told the press of his deep disappointment with the vote, and expressed his fear that the ANC's support for BDS might "incite a level of anti-Israel feeling." He also warned of repercussions in South Africa's global alliances, as "Israel was starting to see the South African government as being as hostile as the Iranian regime."[110]

Krengel's arguments set him apart from more liberal Jews in South Africa. As Peter Beinart, South-African born journalist and author of *The Crisis of Zionism* writes, in South Africa, "Zionism has become a dirty word." Only the most conservative South African Jews defend Israel: because of Israel's longtime alliance with apartheid South Africa; because the antiapartheid movement downplayed ethnic and racial identities; because of the anti-imperialist commitments of the ANC; because young Jews equate Zionism with Israel's policies. "As passionate universalists," writes Beinart, "the ANC Jews generally lacked the commitment to Jewish peoplehood that underlies Zionism."[111]

Unlike the 1950s, however, these debates over the universal and the particular expand far beyond South African and other Western Jewish communities. They stretch across the globe and reach into communities, both Jewish and not. Israeli apartheid debates draw from many global diasporas—Jewish, Palestinian, African—and gain momentum from the long-standing mobilization of human rights groups. Now the questions about apartheid are refracted through lenses of global capitalism, human rights, and group belonging. Social media also serve as sites of debate and contest. Recently, the *Boston Globe* reported that Israel has begun to hire college students to post "pro-Israel messages on social media networks—without needing to identify themselves as government-linked." The prime minister's office announced that students would receive "full or partial scholarships to combat anti-Semitism and calls to boycott Israel online." Conflating anti-Semitism and the BDS movement, Israel's government seeks to repair its increasingly tarnished reputation.[112]

The ANC vote in fact corresponded to the release of a documentary that explicitly compares South African apartheid with Israeli Occupation. In contrast to Carter's book, it also compares the treatment of non-Jews within Israel's 1948 borders to apartheid South Africa. (White, South-African-born) Ana Nogueira and (Jewish, Israeli-born) Eron Davidson together directed and produced *Roadmap to Apartheid*. The documentary reaches back into history—and to the counternarrative offered by Israel's ambassador to South Africa, Yitzhak Unna, in 1976—to portray apartheid South Africa as the outgrowth of Boer/Afrikaaners' strong desire for redemption, self-determination, and historical preservation and visibility in the face of oppression, much as

Zionism and Israel are for many Jews. The film examines mobility, access to land and water, civil liberties, marriage and citizenship rights for Jews and non-Jews in Israel and the Territories. It builds on the "rhetorical" use of the term to document analogous unjust policies in South Africa and Israel/Palestine. The film tackles such issues as bantustans and political prisoners, along with road building and other infrastructural needs whose distribution reflects the great injustices faced by Palestinians in their daily lives. Leaders in B'Tselem, the Israeli Information Center for Human Rights in the Occupied Territories, present testimony, as do other prominent leaders and laypeople in Israel and South Africa. Narrated by Alice Walker, the film juxtaposes chilling footage of apartheid South Africa and Palestine.

Roadmap to Apartheid captures the voices of several individuals studied in these pages. Sasha Polakow-Suransky (among many others) appears on camera to talk about the Cold War ties between Israel and South Africa beginning in the 1970s, with both nations struggling to find allies on the world stage, sharing common sentiments about feeling at war with an indigenous population. Ali Abunimah, IAW speaker at Brandeis and founder of the Electronic Intifada, provides historical narrative and analogies. The documentary spotlights the BDS movement and how it modeled itself on the antiapartheid campaign. It concludes with a vision of what the end of apartheid might mean for Israel. South African activists—Black and white—testify to how liberating was the end of that nation's apartheid, its release from a "corrosive" set of laws that led to a more inclusive future.

Outside of the scope of this documentary is a consideration of the intense emotions of American Jewish encounters with the apartheid label for Israel. Since World War II, American Jews have wrestled with their commitments to particularist Jewish unity and to universalist causes. Those who fear the decline of Jewish particularism fear Jewish invisibility—in Israel and in the diaspora. They have at times responded to the challenges of universalist campaigns by refusing to thoughtfully engage the "outsiders" who oppose them—grouping together left/liberal Jews, human rights groups, and representatives of the Global South. In the name of Jewish unity, they have created divisiveness. That divisiveness manifested itself again in the observance of an occasion of tremendous sadness as this book goes to press.

Mourning Nelson Mandela, 2013

In December 2013, the world grieved over the loss of Nelson Mandela: they mourned his death and celebrated his heroic life of defiance and humility. This moment once again drew back the curtain on intracommunal debates among Jews. As world leaders descended on South Africa for Mandela's funeral, Israel announced that Prime Minister Netanyahu would not attend due to the high cost of travel. Furor erupted from all parts of the globe. "If 'the whole world is coming to South Africa'...and Israel is not among them," asked a reporter for the English-language version of the Israeli newspaper *Haaretz*, "what message would its absence send? Would it be an admission that because of the apartheid label, Israeli leaders fear being embarrassed by expected protests from anti-Israel groups?" According to South African Jewish leaders, Netanyahu's refusal to attend marked a surrender to this threat, and also, importantly, flew in the face of longtime South African Jewish contributions to Israel.[113]

In the *Forward*, Richard Goldstone wrote an article headlined by Mandela's tribal name, "Recalling Madiba's Long Walk with Jews." Goldstone recounted Mandela's "complex relationship with Israel and the Jews of South Africa." The PLO and ANC, Helen Suzman and Joe Slovo: all appeared in his narrative to honor Mandela's many commitments, and to do justice to the fine line Mandela walked in endorsing the self-determination of both Jews and Palestinians. Other warm and emotional outpourings followed this same model.[114]

In other venues, leaders struggled to make sense of the disparate claims on Mandela's legacy. Jews and Palestinians "take away different lessons from his struggle," noted one reporter.[115] Hatem Abudayyeh, a Palestinian-American and the executive director of the Arab American Action Network in Chicago, asserted that "We do consider Nelson Mandela to be our leader....There's a sort of replication of that antiapartheid movement in Palestine and across the world for those that are doing Palestine advocacy and Palestine support work."[116] Palestinian activists invoke the language and symbolism of Mandela's struggle in the BDS movement and also, for example, in staging protests on Robben Island, where Mandela spent 18 of his 27 years in prison.[117]

Many Jews applauded the fact that Mandela supported "Zionism as the national liberation movement of the Jewish people."[118] Indeed, while countless mainstream English-language articles parsed out Mandela's relationship to communism and to the strategy of violence, far more Jewish periodicals published pieces on what they considered to be the "real story," correcting the "widespread misapprehension that Mandela was an opponent of Zionism and Israel."[119] In The New York *Jewish Week*, Rabbi Irving Greenberg wrote that:

> Jews should not be thrown off by the tension between Mandela's universal stature and his flaws on Jewish issues. Jews should proclaim his greatness and urge—nay, challenge—the Arab nations to walk in his footsteps. The main hope for a true Arab Spring is that they come up with a Mandela of their own who can lead them beyond tribalism and sectarianism, beyond the politics of resentment and revenge, to a society that offers democracy and peace to all.[120]

In testimony to the enormity of Mandela's universal lessons for the world, nearly all of these essays claim Mandela's legacy for particular positions on all sides of the debate over Israel and Palestine.

It is always tempting to conclude that the urgency of any historical question—this one focused on the challenges of confronting Jewish positions on South African apartheid and Israel's Occupation—has never been so pressing as it is at this moment. As this study makes clear, the stakes have long been, and remain, quite high. By looking carefully at the history of this highly polarized debate, however, we find models of individuals and organizations who, at times, effectively rejected the "either/or" equation and found ways to meet their commitments to the universal and the particular. While tolerance for dissenting Jewish voices dwindled, they remained connected to—indeed drew upon—their sense of Jewishness, without compromising on broader questions of global and local justice. They opened themselves to friendships and alliances, and with varying degrees of grace and tenacity, struggled to create a path that allowed American Jews to fuse their identities and responsibilities as Jews and as global citizens. Perhaps it is in their stories—and too, in the sum total of the stories we will hear about Mandela in years to come—that we can find a roadmap for coming to terms with apartheid and Jewishness, and with universalism and particularism more broadly, in the twenty-first century.

Notes

Introduction: Apartheid and American Jews

1. Dr Martin Luther King stated these ideas in his acceptance speech for the Nobel Peace Prize in 1964. "Martin Luther King, Jr.'s Acceptance Speech," The official website of the Nobel Prize, accessed August 26, 2009, http://nobelprize.org/nobel_prizes/peace/laureates/1964/king-acceptance.html. David Hostetter takes note of this speech, in which King mentions American ideals and South African apartheid before an international audience. [Hostetter, *Movement Matters: American Antiapartheid Activism and the Rise of Multicultural Politics* (New York: Routledge, 2006), 1.]
2. On July 31, 1990, leaders of the National Jewish Community Relations Advisory Council (NJCRAC), an umbrella organization for mainstream Jewish organizations, issued a memo to all of its member agencies which summarized the response of these organizations to Mandela's relationship to Yasser Arafat and his sentiments toward Israel and American Jews. [from Herbert Wander, Co-Chair, Ad Hoc Committee on Apartheid, and Diana Aviv, Assistant Director, NJCRAC, to NJCRAC and CJF Member Agencies, July 21, 1990, Reform Action Committee Papers, American Jewish Archive (AJA), Cincinnati, OH.]
3. See, for example, The 'Bashing' of Israel," advertisement of FLAME, "Facts and Logic about the Middle East," *New York Times*, June 12, 1990.
4. Murray Friedman, *The Neoconservative Revolution: Jewish Intellectuals and the Shaping of Public Policy* (New York: Cambridge University Press, 2005). Friedman devotes a small amount of space to conservative leadership within Jewish organizations. Several prominent American Jewish historians have challenged some of the points of Friedman's posthumously published book. See, for example, Gerald Sorin, review of *The Neoconservative Revolution*, by Murray Friedman, *The American Historical Review* 111, no. 4 (October 2006): 1219–1220. Michael Staub concludes his book, *Torn at the Roots*, with an analysis of the intense criticism of Breira, a left-leaning American organization founded in the 1970s as an "alternative" (the translation of the Hebrew word) to mainstream positions on Israel. Staub's remains the most important study of these debates in American Jewish organizations. Michael Staub, *Torn at the Roots: The Crisis of Jewish Liberalism in Postwar America* (New York: Columbia, 2002). See also Stuart Svonkin, *Jews against Prejudice: American Jews and the Fight for Civil Liberties* (New York: Columbia University Press, 1997).
5. See, for example, Rafael Medoff, *Jewish Americans and Political Participation* (Santa Barbara, CA: ABC/CLIO, 2002); Gal Beckerman, *When They Come for*

Us We'll Be Gone: The Epic Struggle to Save Soviet Jewry (New York: Houghton Mifflin, 2010).
6. Hasia Diner, *In the Almost Promised Land: American Jews and Blacks, 1915–1935* (Westport, CT: Greenwood Press, 1977); Cheryl Lynn Greenberg, *Troubling the Waters: Black-Jewish Relations in the American Century* (Princeton, NJ: Princeton University Press, 2006); Eric L. Goldstein, *The Price of Whiteness: Jews, Race, and American Identity* (Princeton, NJ: Princeton University Press, 2006).
7. Svonkin, *Jews against Prejudice*.
8. Michael Staub, *The Jewish 1960s: An American Sourcebook* (Waltham, MA: Brandeis University Press, 2004).
9. Michael Galchinsky, *Jews and Human Rights: Dancing at Three Weddings* (Lanham, MD: Rowan and Littlefield, 2008); Sasha Polakow-Suransky, *The Unspoken Alliance: Israel's Secret Relationship with Apartheid South Africa* (New York: Pantheon Books, 2010).
10. Interestingly, a call for transnational Jewish history appeared in a comparative journal of South African and American Studies, in the midst of a contentious debate over the response of South African Jews to apartheid. See Jennifer Glaser, "Beyond the Farribel: Towards a Transnational Reassessment of Jewish Studies," *Safundi: The Journal of South African and American Studies* 10, no. 1 (2009): 99–104.
11. David Hollinger defines "communalist" approaches to American Jewish history as those "with an emphasis on communal Jewry, including the organizations and institutions" that emphasize Jewish peoplehood. "Dispersionist" Jewish history "takes fuller account of the lives in any and all domains of persons with an ancestry in the Jewish diaspora." While this study travels infrequently beyond the Jewish world, it does count and examine the contributions of Jewish anti-apartheid work done outside of the communal Jewish world. Importantly, it also examines the contests over what was to be the response of the "Jewish people" to apartheid, and how that response contributed to the "alienated, indifferent, or ambivalent" attitude toward Jewish belonging. Hollinger, "Communalist and Dispersionist Approaches to American Jewish History in an Increasingly Post-Jewish Era," *American Jewish History* 95, no. 1 (March 2009): 4; Tony Michels, "Communalist History and Beyond: What is the Potential of American Jewish History" *AJH* 95, no. 1 (March 2009): 64. Edited by Eric Goldstein, this issue of *AJH* includes a thoughtful exchange on Hollinger's ideas by Hasia Diner, Paula Hyman, Tony Michels, and Alan Kraut. My thinking here was also strongly influenced by Hasia Diner and Tony Michels's essay "Considering American Jewish History," *OAH Newsletter* 35 (November 2007): 9, 18.
12. See, for example, Penny M. Von Eschen, *Race against Empire: Black Americans and Anticolonialism, 1937–1957* (Ithaca, NY: Cornell University Press, 1997); Francis Njubi Nesbitt, *Race for Sanctions: African Americans against Apartheid, 1946–1994* (Bloomington, IN: Indiana University Press, 2004); James H. Meriwether, *Proudly We Can Be Africans: Black Americans and Africa, 1935–1961* (Chapel Hill, NC: University of North Carolina Press, 2001).
13. Temma Kaplan, *Crazy for Democracy: Women in Grassroots Movements* (New York: Routledge, 1996); Pamela E. Brooks, *Boycotts, Buses, and Passes: Black Women's Resistance in the U.S. South and South Africa* (Amherst, MA: University of Massachusetts Press, 2008). The most recent volume to examine Jewish

women in postwar America takes on the daunting task of making Jewishness visible in the Cold War era, when assimilation, migration, and upward mobility challenged the cohesiveness of Jewish communities. This collection looks at Jewish religious life, efforts for world Jewry, and representations of Jews in American popular culture. Hasia Diner, Shira Kohn, and Rachel Kranson, eds, *A Jewish Feminine Mystique: Jewish Women in Postwar America* (New Brunswick: Rutgers University Press, 2010).

14. Mary Dudziak, *Cold War, Civil Rights: Race and the Image of American Democracy* (Princeton, NJ: Princeton University Press, 2000); Odd Arne Westad, *The Global Cold War* (Cambridge, MA: Cambridge University Press, 2007); Thomas Borstelmann, *The Cold War and the Color Line: American Race Relations in the Global Arena* (Cambridge, MA: Harvard University Press, 2003).

15. Franklin Hugh Adler, "South African Jews and Apartheid," *Patterns of Prejudice* 34, no. 4 (2000): 24; Shula Marks, "Apartheid and the Jewish Question," *Journal of Southern African Studies* 30, no. 4 (December 2004): 889–900; Milton Shain and Richard Mendelsohn, eds., *Memories, Realities, and Dreams: Aspects of the South African Jewish Experience* (Cape Town: Jonathan Ball Publishers, 2002); Immanuel Suttner, "Introduction," in *Cutting Through the Mountain: Interviews with South African Jewish Activists* (London: Viking, 1997); Shirli Gilbert, "Jews and the Racial State: Legacies of the Holocaust in Apartheid South Africa, 1945–60," *Jewish Social Studies: History, Culture, Society* 16, no. 3 (Spring/Summer 2010): 55; Gideon Shimoni, *Community and Conscience: The Jews in Apartheid South Africa* (Hanover, NH: University Press of New England, 2003).

16. See, for example, Christopher Coker, *The United States and South Africa, 1968–1985: Constructive Engagement and Its Critics* (Durham, NC: Duke University Press, 1986); Kevin Danaher, *In Whose Interest? A Guide to U.S.-South Africa Relations* (Washington, DC: Institute for Policy Studies, 1984); Princeton N. Lyman, *Partner to History: The U.S. Role in South Africa's Transition to Democracy* (Washington, DC: United States Institute of Peace Press, 2002); Brian J. Hesse, *The United States, South Africa and Africa: Of Grand Foreign Policy Aims and Modest Means* (Burlington: Ashgate, 2001); Thomas Borstelmann, *Apartheid's Reluctant Uncle: The United States and Southern Africa in the Early Cold War* (New York: Oxford University Press, 1993). Borstelmann's analysis employs the methods of social history to document attitudes toward southern Africa in the United States.

17. To cite just one example: of college student divestment activists, Bradford Martin writes that in addition to anti-racism, "what fueled the movement was students' realization of U.S. economic ties to the apartheid regime." Martin, *The Other Eighties: A Secret History of America in the Age of Reagan* (New York: Hill and Wang, 2011), 52. Other social histories of the movement include Brooks, *Boycotts, Buses, and Passes,* and Kaplan, *Crazy for Democracy.*

18. Michael Galchinsky writes that "Diapora Jewish activists enthusiastically embraced international human rights in the 1950s and 1960s, but since the mid-1960s and especially after Israel's Six-Day War in 1967, their enthusiasm has declined due to the conflicts among their commitments to international Human Rights, Jewish nationalism, and domestic pluralism." This study of Jewish struggles over apartheid demonstrates that the tension among these three commitments began immediately after World War II (Galchinsky, *Jews*

and Human Rights, 3). James Loeffler's recent article supports this argument. It shows that debates among Jewish leaders over human rights at the 1945 United Nations Conference in San Francisco represented an intracommunal struggle for political power and influence in which Zionism played an important role. Loeffler, "'The Conscience of America': Human Rights, Jewish Politics, and American Foreign Policy at the 1945 United Nations San Francisco Conference," *Journal of American History* 100, no. 2 (September 2013), 401–428.

19. I use the term Third World as it was used during the Cold War, to refer to nations who were not aligned with the United States/NATO or with the Soviet Union/Communist Bloc. Many of these developing nations had colonial pasts, from which they were emerging as this study begins. I also use the more contemporary terms of Global North and Global South.

20. Michael Melchior, "Zionism, Racism, and the Distortions of the Durban conference," *Midstream Magazine* (September 1, 2001): 4–7. Journalist Naomi Klein writes that the anti-Israel language had "no chance of making it into the final draft" of the conference resolution and that the clauses "gave the U.S. government the perfect excuse to flee the scene," to avoid the contentious issues of reparations raised by the conference. Klein, "Minority Death Match: Jews, Blacks, and the 'Post-racial' Presidency," *Harper's Magazine* (September 2009): 59. For analysis of these developments, see chapter 7.

21. Ruth Wedgwood, "Zionism and Racism Again: Durban II," *World Affairs* 171, no. 4 (Spring 2009): 84–88.

22. Quote from Benjamin Pogrund, "Durban II: Another Opportunity Missed," *The Guardian*, April 24, 2009, http://www.guardian.co.uk/commentis free/2009/apr/24/durban-racism-conference-ahmadinejad. Pogrund was a journalist for the anti-apartheid *Rand Daily Mail* before leaving for London in 1986; he now lives in Israel. Pogrund used this 2009 article to dispute the label of apartheid for Israel's treatment of Palestinians.

23. Website of the Palestinian BDS National Committee (BNC), accessed August 25, 2009, http://www.bdsmovement.net.

24. Website of the Jewish Federation of North America Israel Action Network, accessed July 16, 2013, http://israelactionnetwork.org/aboutus/.

25. Here I refer to crises of all types: of nations and peoples at war, but also crises of perceived invisibility through integration and assimilation.

26. The efforts of the Council on African Affairs, founded in 1937, deserve particular mention, as their fundraising and lobbying (of American presidential administrations, as well as the United Nations) drew international attention to South African apartheid long before other groups engaged the issue. See Hollis R. Lynch *Black American Radicals and the Liberation of Africa: The Council on African Affairs, 1937–1955* (Ithaca, NY: Cornell University Africana Studies and Research Center, 1978); Penny M. Von Eschen, *Race against Empire*; Francis Njubi Nesbitt, *Race for Sanctions: African Americans Against Apartheid, 1946–1994* (Bloomington. IN: Indiana University Press, 2004); George M. Fredrickson, *Black Liberation: A Comparative History of Black Ideologies in the United States and South Africa* (New York: Oxford University Press, 1995).

27. Staub, *Torn at the Roots*, 18. Here I rely on Michael Staub's formulation about the crucial importance of intracommunal debates:

> It is not possible to understand how American Jewish political commitments splintered, shifted, and intensified without attending closely to

the manner in which people made their arguments. The postwar history of American Jews' running conflicts with each other is a deeply emotional one, and only by taking emotions seriously can we make sense of it. This also means retraining our ears to hear fully what exactly was being said and reentering the imaginative universe of past decades. It means becoming attuned to rhetorical strategies as well as overt claims, noting the unexpected echoes and overlaps between conflicting positions and letting go of our contemporary presumptions about what many key concepts—among them faith, loyalty, and survival, assimilation and adherence to tradition, self-hatred and self-affirmation—were once thought to mean.

28. In *The Color of Jews*, Melanie Kaye/Kantrowitz includes a section titled "Apartheid/American Style," in which she writes about Mandela's 1990 visit to New York along with a historical analysis of the systems of racial categorization and hierarchy in the United States. Kaye/Kantrowitz's important work documenting American systems of privilege and power explodes the myth that all Jews are white, encouraging contemporary cross-class and cross-race anti-racist activism. The American Jews whom I write about in these pages all hold the privileges of whiteness, and, for the most part, were and are middle-class. Their positions in these systems are crucial to the level of risk they encountered in their activism. Kaye/Kantrowitz was among the first American scholars to refer to the Israeli-built "security wall" in Palestine as an "Apartheid Wall." Kaye/Kantrowitz, *The Color of Jews: Racial Politics and Radical Diasporism* (Bloomington, IN: Indiana University Press, 2007), 16, 18, 211.

1   Postwar Conflicts over Racial Justice

1. James H. Meriwether, *Proudly We Can Be Africans: Black Americans and Africa, 1935–1961* (Chapel Hill, NC: University of North Carolina Press, 2001); Carol Anderson, *Eyes off the Prize: The United Nations and the African American Struggle for Human Rights, 1944–1955* (Cambridge, UK; New York: Cambridge University Press, 2003).
2. Mark Mazower's provocative study of the United Nations, *No Enchanted Palace*, argues that the original founders of the United Nations—including Jan Smuts, South African prime minister, and white supremacist—envisioned its purpose as protecting the sovereignty and dominance of imperial nations. The United Nations came to focus more on minority rights, according to Mazower, largely because of India's challenge to colonialism—in their own nation, and in the racist treatment of Indian citizens of South Africa. The struggle over race in South Africa became part of the larger struggle for "the soul of the UN." Mark Mazower, *No Enchanted Palace: The End of Empire and the Ideological Origins of the United Nations* (Princeton, NJ: Princeton University Press, 2009), 171. Michael Galchinsky examines the struggles of Jewish human rights advocates to maintain their commitments in the 1960s, in light of the work of the "new UN majority…to turn Israel into an international pariah." He designates this as a set of "continuing failures of the international human rights system with regard to Israel." Michael Galchinsky, *Jews and Human Rights: Dancing at Three Weddings* (Lanham, MD: Rowan and Littlefield, 2008), 3, 23.

3. Mazower discusses this shift in the General Assembly (GA) in the late 1940s; by 1960, when 16 new, independent states won independence and joined the GA, the "Afro-Asian bloc was worth 46 out of 99 votes. The continent that had enjoyed the smallest representation in 1946 had the most numerous grouping of states two decades later." Mark Mazower, *No Enchanted Palace*, 186. The focus of the GA shifted from the defense of empire to the breakup of empire. Still, as Mazower notes, the attention to South African apartheid in the UN's General Assembly affected little change, as the Security Council (especially the United States and England) extended "toleration" toward apartheid (186). Rob Skinner writes about the important campaigns launched by the Council on African Affairs (CAA) and the divides between the CAA and the National Organization for the Advancement of Colored People over faith in the Soviet Union. Rob Skinner, *The Foundations of Anti-Apartheid Liberal Humanitarians and Transnational Activists in Britain and the United States, c. 1919–1964* (New York: Palgrave Macmillan, 2010), 72–76. On the CAA, see the website of the African Activist Archive, accessed March 23, 2012, http://africanactivist.msu.edu/organization.php?name=Council+on+African+Affairs and Hollis R. Lynch, *Black American Radicals and The Liberation of Africa: The Council on African Affairs, 1937–1955* (Ithaca, NY: Cornell University Africana Studies and Research Center, 1978).
4. Peter Jackson and Mathieu Faupin, "The Long Road to Durban: The United Nations Role in Fighting Racism and Racial Discrimination," *UN Chronicle*, September 2007, http://www.un.org/Pubs/chronicle/2007/issue3/0307p07.html.
5. United Nations Commission on the Racial Situation in the Union of South Africa, Resolution IV, February 25, 1954, in World Jewish Congress Papers, American Jewish Archives, Cincinnati, OH. See also Enuga S. Reddy, "The United Nations and the Struggle for Liberation in South Africa," 47–49, located on the website of the African National Congress, http://www.anc.org.za/docs/misc/1992/roadtodemocracyl.pdf.
6. Michael Galchinsky analyzes the rise of Jewish nongovernmental organizations in "Building Human Rights," chap. 1 of *Jewish Human Rights*.
7. Gerhart M. Riegner, *Never Despair: Sixty Years in the Service of the Jewish People and the Cause of Human Rights* (Chicago, IL: Ivan R. Dee, 2006), 183. Galchinsky writes about Jewish contributions to the UN Declaration of Human Rights as motivated by "their religious tradition, the negative example of the Holocaust, and by self-interest" [Galchinsky, *Jewish Human Rights*, 33]. James Loeffler writes that the American Jewish Committee's commitment to human rights emerged out of an internal struggle for power within the American Jewish community and in the American political landscape more broadly—specifically its struggle with Zionist leaders and organizations like the American Jewish Congress. AJC leaders continued to prioritize integration, to position Jews as politically influential without drawing attention to "ethnic parochialism" in the form of Zionism or more narrow Jewish interests so as to avoid anti-Semitism:

> Though the enormity of the Holocaust had become clear by war's end, American Jewish leaders still interpreted its meaning through lenses of prewar political ideologies. For the AJC, for example, human rights addressed Jewish concerns to the extent that it offered a solution to the broad ongoing dangers of nationalism and fascism, rather than providing moral redress for the recent past of Jewish mass death. Human rights

were less a moral imperative in the context of Nazi anti-Semitism and the European Jewish catastrophe than a response to the crisis of Western liberalism....Hence, human rights could be framed as a Jewish religious contribution to American internationalist values but not a plea for Jewish rights per se (Loeffler, "'The Conscience of America': Human Rights, Jewish Politics, and American Foreign Policy at the 1945 United Nations San Francisco Conference," *Journal of American History* 100, no.2 (September 2013), 409, 425.
8. See Skinner, *Foundations of Anti-Apartheid*, 80.
9. Anderson, *Eyes off the Prize*, quoted on 87–88.
10. Many secular, white South African Jews joined radical political organizations that became vital to the vigorous antiapartheid movement. These Jews fervently rejected the positions of the SAJBD. On Jewish contributions to the movement, see Immanuel Suttner, *Cutting through the Mountain: Interviews with South African Jewish Activists* (New York: Penguin Group, 1997).
11. For this analysis, I am deeply indebted to Adam Mendelsohn, who shared with me his prodigiously researched Master's thesis, "Two Far South: The Responses of Southern and South African Jews to Apartheid and Racial Segregation in the 1950s and 1960s" (Unpublished MA Thesis, University of Cape Town, 2003). See especially Chapter nine, "A House Divided: A Case Study in Contrasting Approaches to South African Jewry." Some of Mendelsohn's thesis research appears in his article "Two Far South: Rabbinical Responses to Apartheid and Segregation in South Africa and the American South," *Southern Jewish History* 6 (2003): 63–132.
12. Perlzweig Memorandum, March 17, 1954, World Jewish Congress Papers, American Jewish Archives, Cincinnati, OH.
13. Maurice Perlzweig to Dr Goldman, March 19, 1954, World Jewish Congress Papers, American Jewish Archives, Cincinnati, OH.
14. Petegorsky to Perlzweig, March 17, 1954, World Jewish Congress Papers, American Jewish Archives, Cincinnati, OH.
15. Stuart Svonkin, *Jews against Prejudice: American Jews and the Fight for Civil Liberties* (New York: Columbia University Press, 1997), 18. In his masterful *American Judaism*, Jonathan Sarna writes about the postwar period as a time of "renewal" and "revival" in American Judaism, signaled by massive synagogue-building and growing interest in Jewish education, religious thought, and theology. He too notes that in this era, "universal causes like world peace, civil rights, interfaith relations, and opposition to the war in Vietnam dominated the American Jewish agenda." Jonathan Sarna, *American Judaism: A History* (New Haven, CT: Yale University Press, 2004), 274–282, 307.
16. Svonkin, *Jews against Prejudice*, 82. Svonkin quotes Petegorsky himself in his assertion of this point: in a speech made at the Biennial Convention of the AJCongress in 1948, Petegorsky asserted: "We are profoundly convinced that Jewish survival will depend on Jewish statehood in Palestine, on the one hand, and on the existence of a creative, conscious and well-adjusted Jewish community in this country on the other. Such a creative community can exist only within the framework of a progressive and expanding democratic society, which through its institutions and public policies gives full expression to the concept of cultural pluralism" (quoted in Svonkin, 81–82).
17. Petegorsky to Perlzweig, March 23, 1954, World Jewish Congress Papers, American Jewish Archives, Cincinnati, OH.

18. For the impact of the Sharpeville massacre on the Federation of South African Women (FSAW), see Cherryl Walker, "'Freedom Does Not Come Walking to You—It Must Be Won': Sharpeville and the Decline of the FSAW," in Cherryl Walker, *Women and Resistance in South Africa* (London: Onyx Publishers, 1982), 267–278.
19. Although no nation came to the defense of South Africa's apartheid regime about the Sharpeville massacre, both Britain and France abstained from a Security Council vote calling on the government to abandon apartheid (Mazower, *No Enchanted Palace*, 186). The text of this Security Council Resolution (Resolution 134, April 1, 1960) can be found in the United Nations collection, *The United Nations and Apartheid, 1948–1994* (New York: Department of Public Information, 1994), Document 15, pages 244–245.
20. Hakan Thorn writes that although Sharpeville is seen "as a turning point in modern South African history as well as a starting point for anti-apartheid mobilization," the international media inaccurately used Sharpeville as a "dominant way of framing apartheid." For the media reports, Sharpeville made "apartheid repression appear...as outbursts of violence, irrational, disorganized..."; apartheid repression was instead an "everyday terror, highly organized and systematic." Hakan Thorn, *Anti-Apartheid and the Emergence of a Global Civil Society* (New York: Palgrave Macmillan, 2006), xiii, xiv.
21. See James H. Meriwether, *Proudly We Can Be Africans: Black Americans and Africa, 1935–1961* (Chapel Hill, NC: University of North Carolina Press, 2001), 113.
22. Perlzweig to Maslow, May 13, 1960, World Jewish Congress Papers, American Jewish Archives, Cincinnati, OH.
23. My thinking here has been influenced by Kip Kosek's *Acts of Conscience: Christian Nonviolence and Modern American Democracy* (New York: Columbia University Press, 2009).
24. Perlzweig to Saron, South African Jewish Board of Deputies, May 16, 1960, World Jewish Congress Papers, American Jewish Archives, Cincinnati, OH.
25. Shimoni writes that the Board's shrill insistence on its "scrupulous noninvolvement in politics...reflected the public pressures to which it was relentlessly subjected and the intense moral strains inherent in its stance." *Jewish Affairs* 13, no. 1 (January 1958), quoted in Gideon Shimoni, *Community and Conscience: The Jews in Apartheid South Africa* (Hanover, NH: University Press of New England), 31. Shirli Gilbert studies the brief moment when mainstream South African Jewry—the SAJBD—linked Holocaust memory to antiracism. After the founding of Israel in 1948, these leaders mainly invoked Nazi anti-Semitism as "an impetus for motivating Jewish cultural, religious, and national existence." See Shirli Gilbert, "Jews and the Racial State: Legacies of the Holocaust in Apartheid South Africa, 1945–60," *Jewish Social Studies: History, Culture, Society* 16, no. 3 (Spring/Summer 2010): 55.
26. Perlzweig to Saron, South African Jewish Board of Deputies, May 16, 1960, World Jewish Congress Papers, American Jewish Archives, Cincinnati, OH.
27. "Notes of Private Conversations in Paris between Representatives of Various Leading Jewish Organizations," Folder 4, Box 5, Shad Polier Papers, Center for Jewish History (CJH), New York. This material is dated as "WJC expansion, 1955–1957," and the meeting likely took place in 1956.
28. Perlzweig to Turkow, May 10, 1960, World Jewish Congress Papers, American Jewish Archives, Cincinnati, OH.

NOTES

29. Shimoni, *Community and Conscience*, 149–50.
30. Perlzweig to Easterman, May 16, 1960, World Jewish Congress Papers, American Jewish Archives, Cincinnati, OH; Perlzweig to Easterman, May 26, 1960, World Jewish Congress Papers, American Jewish Archives, Cincinnati, OH.
31. Prinz to Perlzweig, May 20, 1960, World Jewish Congress Papers, American Jewish Archives, Cincinnati, OH. See Michael Meyer, ed., *Joachim Prinz, Rebellious Rabbi: An Autobiography—the German and Early American Years* (Bloomington, IN: Indiana University Press, 2007).
32. Perlzweig to Marchieness of Reading and Mr A.L. Easterman, copies to G. Riegner and N. Goldmann, June 7, 1960, World Jewish Congress Papers, American Jewish Archives, Cincinnati, OH. The *New York Times* noted resolutions about Jewish organizational representatives and about continued anti-Semitism in Germany. "Voters Using 'Religious Tests' Assailed by Jewish Congress," *New York Times*, May 3, 1960.
33. Perlzweig to Saron, May 16, 1960, World Jewish Congress Papers, American Jewish Archives, Cincinnati, OH.
34. Shimoni concludes his study by saying that despite "the heavy price paid in terms of moral values," the Board's decision not to protest apartheid was "in essence responsible and sagacious," given the Board's function as "defender of the Jewish community's safety, welfare, and interest." Shimoni, *Community and Conscience*, 275.
35. Adam Mendelsohn's 2003 thesis, "Two Far South," stands as the exception to this.
36. See, for example, Riegner, *Never Despair*, 428–429; Shimoni, *Community and Conscience*, 115.
37. Rob Skinner writes that "[i]n the wider world, the debate around segregation as an abuse of human rights was caught within the web of Cold War diplomacy," and in both the United States and South Africa "the reality and rhetoric of Cold War anticommunism was a potent barrier to official condemnation of apartheid." Skinner, *Foundations of Anti-Apartheid*, 80.
38. "Dear Sir" from Flesch, Fall 1966, Records of the American Committee on Africa (ACOA), Part 2, Reel 6. ACOA archive on deposit at the Amistad Research Center, Tulane University.
39. Flesch to Jacob Javits, US Senator, February 4, 1958, Records of the American Committee on Africa (ACOA), Part 2, Reel 6.
40. Flesch to Rabbi Israel Goldstein, February 8, 1958, World Jewish Congress Papers, American Jewish Archives, Cincinnati, OH.
41. "Remarks by Fritz Flesch," May 1961, in Records of the American Committee on Africa (ACOA), Part 2, Reel 6.
42. See for example, Shimoni, *Community and Conscience*, 114.
43. Israel Goldstein to Mr. Fritz Flesch, January 16, 1958, World Jewish Congress Papers, American Jewish Archives, Cincinnati, OH.
44. Declaration of Conscience, n.d. (December 1957), Records of the American Committee on Africa (ACOA), Part 2, Reel 5. On the Declaration of Conscience, see George M. Houser, *No One Can Stop the Rain: Glimpses of Africa's Liberation Struggle* (New York: Pilgrim Press, 1989), 123–124; Declaration quoted on 124. See also Skinner, *Foundations of Anti-Apartheid*, 151–153. On the American Committee on Africa (ACOA), see chapter 2.
45. Rabbi Eugene Lipman to Fritz Flesch, July 1, 1958, World Jewish Congress Papers, American Jewish Archives, Cincinnati, OH.

2 AMERICAN ZIONISM AND AFRICAN LIBERATION

1. Nancy Green writes of the American Black/Jewish alliance: "The history of interethnic relations is thus played out not only between individuals and institutional protagonists but also within the context of each of their relations with a more global society." Nancy Green, "Blacks, Jews, and the 'Natural Alliance': Labor Cohabitation and the ILGWU," *Jewish Social Studies* 4, no. 1 (Autumn 1997): 96.
2. Hasia Diner writes that "the Holocaust functioned as background, context, and justification" for the "liberal agenda" of American Jews in the postwar period. Hasia Diner, *We Remember With Reverence and Love: American Jews and the Myth of Silence after the Holocaust, 1945–1962* (New York: New York University Press, 2009), 293, 295.
3. Michael Staub, *Torn at the Roots: The Crisis of Jewish Liberalism in Postwar America* (New York: Columbia, 2002), 60.
4. Cheryl Lynn Greenberg, *Troubling the Waters: Black-Jewish Relations in the American Century* (Princeton, NJ: Princeton University Press, 2006), 195.
5. Stuart Svonkin writes of this transformation as a result of "the organized Jewish community's adoption of cold war liberalism." Placing more emphasis on the questions of what was "good or bad for the Jews" meant that the mainstream Jewish communal organizations lessened their commitment to liberal activism. Stuart Svonkin, *Jews against Prejudice: American Jews and the Fight for Civil Liberties* (New York: Columbia University Press, 1997), 177, 178); Staub, *Torn at the Roots*, 22.
6. See, for example, Carol Anderson, *Eyes Off the Prize: The United Nations and the African American Struggle for Human Rights, 1944–1955* (Cambridge, UK; New York: Cambridge University Press, 2003); Robert W. Cherny, William Issel, and Kieran Walsh Taylor, eds., *American Labor and the Cold War: Grassroots Politics and Postwar Political Culture* (New Brunswick, NJ: Rutgers University Press, 2004).
7. See, for a recent example, Riv-Ellen Prell, "Triumph, Accommodation, and Resistance: American Jewish Life From the End of World War II to the Six-Day War," in Marc Lee Raphael, ed., *The Columbia History of Jews and Judaism in America* (New York: Columbia University Press, 2008), esp. 132–133.
8. Rob Skinner, *The Foundations of Anti-Apartheid Liberal Humanitarians and Transnational Activists in Britain and the United States, c. 1919–1964* (New York: Palgrave Macmillan, 2010),162–163; "Report of the National Executive Committee of the PAC, Submitted to the Annual Conference, December 19–20, 1959," in Thomas Karis and Gail M. Gerhart, *From Protest to Challenge: A Documentary History of African Politics in South Africa, 1882–1964, Volume III* (Stanford, CA: Stanford University Press, 1977), 552.
9. In 1952, Americans for South African Resistance (AFSAR) was founded to support the Campaign for Defiance against Unjust Laws of South Africa's African National Congress. Founding members included Bayard Rustin, Rev. George Houser, Rev. Donald Harrington, Rev. Charles Trigg, and A. Philip Randolph. One year later, this group formed the American Committee on Africa (ACOA), in order to support the liberation struggle in Africa broadly. Based in New York, its members were religious, civil rights, student, labor, and community leaders and laypeople. See website of the African Activist Archive, accessed March 23, 2012, http://africanactivist.msu.edu/organization.php

?name=American+Committee+on+Africa. James Meriwether writes that the ACOA "included Black Americans but found it difficult to mobilize the people and resources of the African American community." He concludes that "the extent to which it could be a vehicle for African American concerns, then, remained problematic." James Meriwether, *Proudly We Can Be Africans: Black Americans and Africa, 1935–1961* (Chapel Hill, NC: University of North Carolina Press, 2001), 171.

10. Hakan Thorn, *Anti-Apartheid and the Emergence of a Global Civil Society* (New York: Palgrave Macmillan, 2006).
11. Tom Mboya, interview by George M. Houser in Houser, "Mboya Visits the United States," *Africa Today* 6, no. 3 (May/June 1959): 14.
12. "Africa Speaks at Carnegie Hall," *Africa Today* 6, no. 3 (May/June 1959): 18.
13. Mboya interview with George Houser, in Houser, "Mboya Visits the United States," 15.
14. Tom Shachtman, *Airlift to America: How Barack Obama, Sr., John F. Kennedy, Tom Mboya, and 800 East African Students Changed Their World and Ours* (New York: St. Martin's Press, 2009), 71.
15. Shachtman, *Airlift to America*. George Houser writes about the founding of the AASF in *No One Can Stop the Rain: Glimpses of Africa's Liberation Struggle* (New York: Pilgrim Press, 1989), 88, 89.
16. American Committee on Africa, *Who Speaks for Africa? A Report on the Activities of the American Committee on Africa* (New York, 1950), website of the African Activist Archive, Michigan State University, accessed February 16, 2011, http://africanactivist.msu.edu/document_metadata.php?objectid=32-130-D86. Harry Belafonte writes about appearing with Jackie Robinson and praises Cora Weiss for convincing Jack Kennedy to have his family foundation underwrite the AASF in his autobiography *My Song: A Memoir* (New York: Alfred A. Knopf, 2011), 195.
17. George M. Houser, *No One Can Stop the Rain: Glimpses of African's Liberation Struggle* (New York: Pilgrim Press, 1989), 86–89; Yevette Richards, *Maida Springer: Pan-Africanist and International Labor Leader* (Pittsburgh, PA: University of Pittsburgh Press, 2000), 199.
18. Avi Shlaim writes that Israel's aggressive Sinai Campaign (which resulted in the achievement of immediate military objectives, mainly access to the Straits of Tiran) represented a victory for "the Israeli defense establishment," for "military force" over diplomacy and for retaliation over negotiation. Israel's "own actions could henceforth be used as proof of the long-standing claim that it was a bridgehead of Western imperialism in the midst of the Arab world." Avi Shlaim, *The Iron Wall: Israel and the Arab World* (New York: W.W. Norton and Company, 2001), 185, 184. Shlaim's chapters three and four detail how this campaign contributed to Israel's deteriorating relationship with Africa. Michael Oren writes about this relationship in the context of the 1967 war. Oren, Chapter one, *Six Days of War: June 1967 and the Making of the Modern Middle East* (New York: Ballantine Books, 2003).
19. On Nasser's revolution, see Joel Gordon, *Nasser's Blessed Movement: Egypt's Free Officers and the July Revolution* (New York: Oxford University Press, 1992).
20. In 1955, Israel received an invitation to a conference of independent Asian and African states in Bandung, Indonesia. But "no sooner had the invitation

been issued than Indian premier Jawaharlal Nehru withdrew it" under pressure from Egypt, other Arab states, and Pakistan. Sasha Polakow-Suransky, *The Unspoken Alliance: Israel's Secret Relationship with Apartheid South Africa* (New York: Pantheon Books, 2010), 2. This exclusion was a "serious diplomatic defeat" for Israel, as it meant that "Asia viewed Israel neither as an Asian state nor as one rightly belonging to the nonaligned group of new nations then in the process of developing." The conference proved a platform for Egypt's President Nasser and other Arab Middle East delegates' "verbal onslaughts" against Israel and Zionism. Ran Kochan, "Israel in Third World Forums," in Michael Curtis and Susan Aurelia Gitelson, eds., *Israel in the Third World*, New Brunswick, NJ: Transaction Books, 1976), 253, 201, 252. Arye Oded emphasizes the importance of the Bandung incident on Israel's subsequent aid and outreach to Africa. Arye Oded, "Africa in Israeli Foreign Policy, Expectations and Disenchantments: Historical and Diplomatic Aspects," *Israel Studies* 15, no. 3 (Fall 2010): 122–124. On the broader historical importance of the Bandung Conference for anticolonialism, see Penny M. Von Eschen, *Race against Empire: Black Americans and Anticolonialism, 1937–1957* (Ithaca, NY: Cornell University Press, 1997), 168–173. Some scholars referenced Israel's exclusion from Bandung when Israel boycotted the United Nations World Conference against Racism in 2001, seeing both as missed opportunities to align and dialogue with African and Asian nations. See the final Chapter 7.
21. Meriwether, *Proudly We Can Be Africans*, 167.
22. Editorial, "Suez Blockade is Intolerable," *Israel Horizons* 7, no. 5 (May 1959): 6–7; "Cairo Report on Possible Surrender of Israel Cargo at Suez is Denied," *Jewish Telegraphic Agency* 6 (July 1959), http://archive.jta.org/article/1959/07/06/3059428/cairo-report-on-possible-surrender-of-israel-cargo-at-suez-is-denied.
23. Westad writes that Khrushchev's obsession with "China's threat to Soviet security," "a slow but positive reevaluation of...the potential for socialist revolution in the Third World," and awe at "Cuban and Vietnamese willingness to confront the United States": all of these were key ingredients to Soviet support to Third World movements in the late 1950s and throughout the 1960s. Odd Arne Westad, *The Global Cold War* (Cambridge, MA: Cambridge University Press, 2007), 159.
24. Ronald M. Segal and Dan Jacobson, "Apartheid and South African Jewry: An Exchange," *Commentary* 24 (November 1957): 424–431. The exchange followed the publication of Dan Jacobson's review of a book on South African Jewry, *The Jews in South Africa*, edited by Gustav Saron and Louis Hotz: "The Jews of South Africa: Portrait of a Flourishing Community," *Commentary* 23 (January 1957): 39–45. See also Jitendra Mohan, "South Africa and the Suez Crisis," *International Journal* 16, no. 4 (Autumn 1961): 327–357.
25. Paul Buhle and Robin D. G. Kelley, "Allies of a Different Sort: Jews and Blacks in the American Left," in *Struggles in the Promised Land: Toward a History of Black-Jewish Relations in the United States* (New York: Oxford University Press, 1997), 215.
26. Tom Shachtman recounts this story in *Airlift to America*, 75.
27. Golda Meir, *My Life* (New York: Putnam's Sons, 1975), 326–327; Jacob Abadi, "Algeria's Policy toward Israel: Pragmatism and Rhetoric," *The Middle East Journal* 56, no. 4 (Autumn 2002): 616–642; Seymour M. Hersh, *The Samson*

Option: Israel's Nuclear Arsenal and American Foreign Policy (New York: Random House, 1991), 36–37.
28. Westad, *The Global Cold War*, 105, 135–136. Like Mazower, Westad notes that the addition of independent, African nations to the United Nations in the 1950s altered its agenda and its role in world affairs: when the United States attempted to maintain its alliance with France at the United Nations, the Algerian War for Independence made this alliance a source of American "embarrassment." While the United States attempted to keep the global focus on the Cold War, and the United Nations its tool for intervention, United Nation's members gradually shifted this focus to the anti-colonialist movements. In this same spirit, African Americans drew strong parallels between domestic white supremacy and America's support for colonialism abroad.
29. Houser, *No One Can Stop the Rain*, 92.
30. Cora Weiss, email to the author, January 3, 2011.
31. There is very little material on the history of the Jewish Labor Committee (JLC). For an overview, see Arieh Lebowitz and Gail Malmgreen, "Introduction," *Archives of the Holocaust: An International Collection of Selected Documents, Volume 14, Robert F. Wagner Labor Archives, New York University, Records of the Jewish Labor Committee* (New York: Garland, 1993). For a critique of the effectiveness of the JLC's Civil Rights Work, see Herbert Hill, "Black-Jewish Conflict in the Labor Context: Race, Jobs, and Institutional Power," in V.P. Franklin, Nancy L. Grant, Harold M. Kletnick, and Genna Rae McNeil, eds., *African Americans and Jews: The Twentieth Century, Studies in Convergence and Conflict* (Columbia, MO: University of Missouri Press, 1998), 264–292.
32. "Israel and the Celebration of African Independence Day," n.d. (1959), Jewish Labor Committee, Series Three, Box 119, Tamiment Library, New York University.
33. A history of Hashomer Hatzair in the United States and its "effort to synthesize Zionism and revolutionary socialism" can be found in Ariel Hurwitz, ed., *Against the Stream: Seven Decades of Hashomer Hatzair in North America* (Tel Aviv: The Association of North American Shomrim, 1994), quote on 71.
34. Editorial, "The African Day Snub of Israel," *Israel Horizons* 7, no. 5 (May 1959): 4–5.
35. Editorial, "The Black Man's Burden," *Labor Israel* 38 (24 March 1950): 2. *Labor Israel* became *Israel Horizons* in 1952.
36. See especially C. C. Aronsfeld, "The New Challenge to the Jew in South Africa and Argentina," *Labor Israel* 43–44 (June 1950): 4. A scholar of the Holocaust, Aronsfeld wrote about the oppressive regimes of South Africa's D. F. Malan and Argentina's Juan Peron, warning that Jews in both nations "must fear not for the security of their bodies, but for the integrity of their souls." Offered assimilation and prosperity, Jews must "keep clear of that creeping corruption which offers the world but leaves the conscience desolate." It's important to note that this journal's editors also kept close watch on Abdul Nasser's hostility to Israel, the growing Cold War alliance of Arab nations against Israel, and Israel's ties to Black African nations.
37. "Africa Freedom Day," editorial, *The New York Times*, April 16, 1959.
38. Rev. Donald Harrington, "Israel's Participation Cited," letter to the *New York Times*, April 21, 1959.
39. Editorial, "The African Day Snub of Israel," 4–5.

40. Dan Georgakas details cooperation between Arab Americans and African Americans in labor protest, including a 1973 wildcat strike over the UAW's purchase of Israel bonds. Dan Georgakas, "Workers in Detroit," *Middle East Report and Information Project Reports* 35 (January 1975): 13–17.
41. Westad, *The Global Cold War*, 128.
42. On American Zionism through World War II, see Melvin Urofsky's *American Zionism from Herzl to the Holocaust* (Garden City, NY: Anchor Press/Double Day, 1975).
43. Meriwether, *Proudly We Can Be Africans*, 189. On SNCC, see, for example, Clayborne Carson, *In Struggle: SNCC and the Black Awakening of 1960* (Cambridge, MA: Harvard University Press, 1981); Cheryl Lynn Greenberg, *A Circle of Trust: Remembering SNCC* (New Brunswick: Rutgers University Press, 1998).
44. Meriwether, *Proudly We Can Be Africans*, 189–190.
45. In a section about Sharpeville, South African Jewish historian Gideon Shimoni writes that "...a balanced evaluation of the record of the rabbinate on the question of apartheid in South Africa ought to take into account the fact that, unlike the major Christian churches, Judaism had no adherents outside the white population of South Africa.... On the other hand, rabbis had very much to contend with the vulnerable minority-group status of Jews within the white racial group." Gideon Shimoni, *Community and Conscience: The Jews in Apartheid South Africa* (Hanover, NH: University of New England Press, 2003), 36.
46. Francis Njubi Nesbitt discusses this delay in *Race for Sanctions: African Americans against Apartheid, 1946–1994* (Bloomington, IN: Indiana University Press, 2004), 38–39.
47. "Emergency Action Conference on South Africa," Papers of the Jewish Labor Committee, Series 3, Box 332, Folder 54, Tamiment Library, New York University; *Annual Report of the American Committee on Africa* (New York, 1960), website of the African Activist Archive, Michigan State University, accessed February 16, 2011, http://africanactivist.msu.edu/document_metadata.php?objectid=32-130-D8C. Emphasis in the original.
48. "Emergency Action Conference on South Africa, Tuesday, May 31, 1960," Papers of the Jewish Labor Committee, Series 3, Box 332, Folder 54, Tamiment Library, New York University; on the actions of the Histadrut, see *Israel Horizons* 8, no. 5 (May/June 1960): 32.
49. Adam Mendelsohn's thesis details the exchanges between leaders of the American Jewish Congress and the World Jewish Congress regarding the Sharpeville massacre and apartheid policies overall; see "A House Divided: A Case Study in Contrasting Approaches to South African Jewry" Chapter nine in Mendelsohn, "Two Far South: The Responses of Southern and South African Jews to Apartheid and Racial Segregation in the 1950s and 1960s" (Unpublished MA Thesis, University of Cape Town, 2003).
50. Meriwether, *Proudly We Can Be Africans*, 191.
51. "24 Recommendations to Help End Apartheid in South Africa, A Summary of Resolutions Adopted by the Emergency Action Conference on South Africa-New York City-May 31 and June 1, 1960," Papers of the Jewish Labor Committee, Series 3, Box 165, Folder 36, Tamiment Library, New York University.

52. "ICFTU Sets May First as Date of Free Labor's Boycott of South Africa," in *News From International Confederation of Free Trade Unions,* New York, New York, April 14, 1960, Papers of the Jewish Labor Council, Series 3, Box 165, Folder 36, Tamiment Library, New York University. Tom Shachtman writes that though African unions, like the Kenyan labor federation led by Tom Mboya, were affiliated with the ICFTU, most ICFTU leaders "tried to keep African unions out of politics" Shachtman, *Airlift to America: How Barack Obama, Sr., John F. Kennedy, Tom Mboya, and 800 East African Students Changed Their World and Ours* (New York: St. Martin's Press, 2009), 40.

53. Greenberg, *Troubling the Waters*, 216. On this conflict, see also Hill, "Black-Jewish Conflict in the Labor Context," 80–81.

54. Hill writes about three events in this period: the strong series of articles that appeared in 1959–1960 in the *Pittsburgh Courier*, an African American newspaper with editions in Chicago, Detroit, and New York, which criticized the JLC's work in the AFL–CIO as a barrier to antiracist efforts in local affiliated unions; the JLC leadership's attack of the 1961 report of the NAACP that documented continued racism in AFL–CIO affiliates; the NAACP's response to a JLC resolution that accused the NAACP of anti-Semitism. See Hill, "Black-Jewish Conflict in the Labor Context," 268–280. See also Gilbert Jonas's narrative of these events in "Head to Head with the Garment Workers Union," chapter ten of Jonas, *Freedom's Sword: The NAACP and the Struggle against Racism in America* (New York: Routledge, 2005), 266–301. Jonas headed the NAACP's National Development Program from 1965–1995. Both Hill and Jonas are very critical of the Jewish Labor Committee's defense of the ILGWU's practices and its "attempt to discredit the NAACP's efforts and Hill's leadership" (Quote at 275).

55. Tony Michels, *A Fire in Their Hearts: Yiddish Socialists in New York* (Cambridge, MA: Harvard University Press, 2005), 253.

56. See Eric L. Goldstein, *The Price of Whiteness: Jews, Race, and American Identity* (Princeton, NJ: Princeton University Press, 2006), especially "Epilogue: Jews, Whiteness, and 'Tribalism' in Multicultural America."

57. See, for example, Jack Raymond, "15 African Nations Laud Israeli Aid," *New York Times*, October 9, 1960; "Israel: A Surplus of Brains," *Newsweek* (August 20, 1962): 43–44, 49. See also coverage in the progressive *Jewish Currents*. In 1960, the press noted the many technical exchanges arranged by Israel: African farmers and other agricultural experts traveled to Israel from 16 nations for training, and Israeli experts also worked in new African nations. "It Happened in Israel" column, *Jewish Currents* 14, no. 10 (November 1960): 31.

58. Jack Raymond, "15 African Nations Laud Israeli Aid," *New York Times*, October 9, 1960.

59. Hope Yomekpe, "The Challenge of Africa in the 20th Century," A speech to the New York Women's Council, reprinted in *Israel Horizons* 9, no. 4 (October 1961): 28.

60. Mordechai E. Kreinin, *Israel and Africa: A Study in Technical Cooperation* (New York: Praeger, 1964), 6.

61. See, for this viewpoint, Balfour Brickner, "Jewish Youth, Israel, and the Third World," *Reconstructionist* 36, no. 3 (March 27, 1970).

62. Editorial, "Apartheid Isolates South Africa," *Israel Horizons* 9, no. 5 (November 1961): 6. The editors noted the "position of the Jewish community" in South

Africa as one of the "extremely important questions involved whenever Israel takes some action against South Africa." In these years, the editors also began to report on an upsurge of anti-Semitism in South Africa, especially after the Rivonia trial of 1963–1964, when Jews were prominently on trial for their leadership in the banned African National Congress. See, for example, *Israel Horizons* 10, no. 1 (January 1962): 31; the second quote can be found in the editorial "Israel is Counted on South Africa Issue," *Israel Horizons* 11, no. 7 (August/September 1963): 8.
63. Shimoni, *Community and Conscience*, 52–54. The South African Government allowed funds to be transferred to Israel again after the 1967 war, which Shimoni calls "the turning point in restoring normalcy for South African Jewry" (54).
64. Helen Suzman, *In No Uncertain Terms: A South African Memoir* (New York: Alfred A. Knopf, 1993), 114.
65. Joel Peters, *Israel and Africa: The Problematic Friendship* (London: British Academic Press, 1992), 14.
66. Tawfik Zayyad, "Israel's Setbacks in Africa," *Political Affairs* 52, no. 7 (July 1973): 58.
67. Important studies of Bayard Rustin's life and work include: Jervis Anderson, *Bayard Rustin: Troubles I've Seen* (New York: HarperCollins, 1997); John D'Emilio, *Lost Prophet: The Life and Times of Bayard Rustin* (New York: Free Press, 2003); Richard D. Kahlenberg, *Tough Liberal: Albert Shanker and the Battles over Schools, Unions, Race, and Democracy* (New York: Columbia University Press, 2007). Anderson writes of Rustin's friendship with Golda Meir (340–341). For more on Rustin's support of Israel, see chapter 6.
68. William Patterson, "Black View of Israel," *Sun Reporter* (San Francisco, CA) 24, no. 26 (June 24, 1972): 6.
69. Polakow-Suransky, *The Unspoken Alliance*, 28.
70. Peters, *Israel and Africa*, 12.
71. On Ungar, see Adam Mendelsohn, "Two Far South: Rabbinical Responses to Apartheid and Segregation in South Africa and the American South," *Southern Jewish History* 6 (2003): 63–132.
72. "Israel Gives Added Hope to Africans," *New Pittsburgh Courier*, 1 no. 46 (February 18, 1961): 7.
73. "Conference on Africa and the Jews," The Editor's Diary, *Jewish Currents* 15, no. 4 (April 1961), 23.
74. Ibid.
75. Polakow-Suransky, *The Unspoken Alliance*, 33.
76. Gideon Shimoni, *Community and Conscience*, 46–54. Gus Saron, head of the SAJBD, wrote to a friend in the United States that "the Government made it clear that it did not desire that Israel's policy should react unfavourably upon the position of Jews in this country" (Gus Saron to Dean Nathan Cohen, March 15, 1962, Papers of the National Jewish Community Relations Council, Center for Jewish History, New York).
77. On American Negro Leadership Conference on Africa (ANLCA), see David Hostetter, *Movement Matters: American Antiapartheid Activism and the Rise of Multicultural Politics* (New York: Routledge, 2006), 70.
78. Gus Saron to Mr. Sam Spiegler, November 27, 1962, Papers of the National Jewish Community Relations Council, Center for Jewish History, New York; Gus Saron to Sam Spiegler, November 28, 1962, National Jewish Community

Relations Advisory Council papers, Box 119, Folder 9, Records, 1940–1994, Center for Jewish History, New York.
79. Sam Spiegler to Gus Saron, December 5, 1962, Papers of the National Jewish Community Relations Council, Center for Jewish History, New York.
80. The article itself is not extant in the files.
81. Gus Saron to Mr Saul E. Joftes, March 8, 1962, Papers of the National Jewish Community Relations Council, Center for Jewish History, New York.
82. Ibid.
83. For more on this divide within South African Jewry, see chapter 5. My thinking here has been influenced by, among other texts, Peter Beinart, "The Israel Debate in South Africa," *Open Zion* (blog), January 29, 2013, http://www.thedailybeast.com/articles/2013/01/29/the-israel-debate-in-south-africa.html.
84. On South African Jews and the Rivonia trial, see Glenn Frankel, *Rivonia's Children: Three Families and the Cost of Conscience in White South Africa* (New York: Farrar, Straus, and Giroux, 1999).
85. Gus Saron to Sam Spiegler, November 15, 1963, National Jewish Community Relations Advisory Council papers, Center for Jewish History, New York.
86. Gus Saron to Sam Spiegler, May 8, 1964, National Jewish Community Relations Advisory Council papers, Center for Jewish History, New York. Adam Mendelsohn studies the connections between Jewish responses to segregation in the Southern United States and to apartheid in South Africa in "Two Far South," *Southern Jewish History* 6 (2003).
87. Quoted Skinner, *Foundations of Anti-Apartheid*, 199.
88. Westad, *The Global Cold War*, 106.

3 Jews or Radicals?

1. Adam Mendelsohn documents the antiapartheid activity of the American Jewish Congress in this period, most notably its National Conference on the South African Crisis in 1965. See "After Sharpeville," Chapter ten in Mendelsohn, "Two Far South: The Responses of Southern and South African Jews to Apartheid and Racial Segregation in the 1950s and 1960s" (Unpublished MA Thesis, University of Cape Town, 2003), 125. The Congress called for "full economic sanctions" and also adopted an anti-apartheid educational program in 1966. The "Brief Review" offered by the program noted that (1) If the United States denounces apartheid, it risks drawing attention to its "own failings in the area of civil rights and segregation"; (2) South African Jewish leaders, "rightly or wrongly...maintain that to adopt a collective Jewish policy [on apartheid] would be to embroil the Jewish community in fierce party politics and endanger its safety"; (3) Israel has condemned apartheid at the United Nations, despite the "risk that the Israeli position at the U.N. might somehow wrongly be imputed to South African Jews by their government." With these and other facts, participants were asked to consider if apartheid is "a threat to world peace" and other questions. "Program on Apartheid," American Jewish Congress, National Women's Division, July 1966, American Jewish Congress Papers, Box 123, Folder 22, Center For Jewish History, New York City.
2. "African Jews Defy Bias," *Tri-State Defender* (Memphis, TN) 9 no. 22 (April 11, 1964): 6.

3. See, most recently, Stephen Whitfield's essay, "Influence and Affluence, 1967–2000," in *The Columbia History of Jews and Judaism in America* (New York: Columbia University Press, 2008). In writing about the response of the African American community to the forced resignation of United Nations Ambassador Andrew Young after his meeting with a representative of the Palestine Liberation Organization in 1979 (see chapter 7), American Jewish Committee historian Marianne Sanua writes that a discussion of Young's resignation turned into a "forum for black grievances against Jews...These included the Jewish stand on affirmative action, relations between Israel and South Africa, and Jewish intellectuals, who allegedly had become 'apologists for the status quo.'" Sanua, *Let us Prove Strong: The American Jewish Committee, 1945–2006* (Waltham, MA: Brandeis University Press, 2007), 214. Quote from Roger Wilkins, "Black Leaders' Meeting: 'Watershed' Effort for Unanimity," *New York Times*, September 24, 1979, cited in Sanua, 428n50.
4. Paul Buhle and Robin D. G. Kelley, "Allies of a Different Sort: Jews and Blacks in the American Left," in Jack Salzman and Cornel West, eds. *Struggles in the Promised Land: Toward a History of Black/Jewish Relations in the United States* (New York: Oxford University Press, 1997), 214.
5. Stuart Svonkin, *Jews against Prejudice: American Jews and the Fight for Civil Liberties* (New York: Columbia University Press, 1997), 191.
6. Chapter 5 discusses the responses of Jewish women to patriarchy in Jewish religious and communal life.
7. Bill Novak, "The Making of a Jewish Counter Culture," in Jacob Neusner, ed., *Contemporary Judaic Fellowship in Theory and Practice* (New York: Ktav Publishing, 1972). Novak later helped to found Breira: A Project of Concern in Diaspora-Israel Relations, which advocated for a two-state solution after the Yom Kippur War in 1973. Michael Staub writes of the rich history of Breira as an American Jewish dissenting organization with regard to Israel in Chapter eight of Staub, *Torn at the Roots: The Crisis of Jewish Liberalism in Postwar America* (New York: Columbia, 2002). On Breira in this study, see chapter 4.
8. Riv-Ellen Prell, *Prayer and Community: The Havurah in American Judaism* (Detroit, MI: Wayne State University Press, 1989).
9. Prell, *Prayer and Community*, 89–92.
10. On the Jewish ethnic revival of these years, see "I Take Back My Name," Chapter five of Matthew Frye Jacobson, *Roots Too: White Ethnic Revival in Post-Civil Rights America* (Cambridge, MA: Harvard University Press, 2008).
11. For the rise of a distinctly Jewish feminism linked to Zionism, see chapter 5.
12. Jonathan Sarna, *American Judaism: A History* (New Haven, CT: Yale University Press, 2004), 315.
13. Sarna, *American Judaism*, 315. Nathan Abrams writes of the transformation of Norman Podhoretz, Jewish intellectual and editor of the American Jewish Committee's *Commentary Magazine*, after the 1967 war. From its founding in 1945, the magazine had stressed "universalism, but now the magazine embraced particularism with a new zeal and fervor," an "inward-looking Jewish particularism." This new worldview linked Holocaust consciousness with a new, brand of Zionism in seeing all threats to Israel and Jews as possibly giving "posthumous victories to Hitler." Emil L. Fackenheim, "Jewish Faith and the Holocaust," *Commentary* 46:2 (August 1968), quoted in Nathan Abrams, *Norman Podhoretz and Commentary Magazine: The Rise*

and *Fall of the Neocons* (New York: Continuum International Publishing Group, 2010), 73, 74.
14. See Deborah Dash Moore, "From David to Goliath: American Representations of Jews around the Six-Day War," in Eli Lederhendler, ed., *The Six-Day War and World Jewry* (Bethesda, MD: University Press of Maryland, 2000).
15. Staub, *Torn at the Roots*, 149. Staub offers a portrait of the sharp and painful debates within the American Jewish community in this period.
16. Michael Galchinsky, *Jews and Human Rights: Dancing at Three Weddings* (Lanham, MD: Rowan and Littlefield, 2008), 49.
17. Prell, *Prayer and Community*, 86.
18. Michael Oren, *Six Days of War: June 1967 and the Making of the Modern Middle East* (New York: Ballantine Books, 2003), 8.
19. Oren, *Six Days of War*, 27–28.
20. Prell describes the Havurah movement in American Judaism as emerging from members who felt a "shared indictment of Jews, America, and the American New Left." Prell, *Prayer and Community*, 87, 91.
21. Odd Arne Westad, *The Global Cold War* (Cambridge, MA: Cambridge University Press, 2007), 106.
22. Francis Njubi Nesbitt notes the presence of the antiapartheid struggle on the agendas of all Civil Rights organizations—from Black Power to the National Association for the Advancement of Colored People to the Student Nonviolent Coordinating Committee—in the 1960s. Taking a break from the Alabama Civil Rights drive, Dr Martin Luther King joined the American Committee on Africa at a Human Rights Day rally on December 10, 1965, in New York City. He urged Western and Eastern nations to join in the international sanctions movement against South Africa. Nesbitt, *Race for Sanctions: African Americans against Apartheid* (Bloomington, IN: Indiana University Press), 63.
23. Mendelsohn, "After Sharpeville," Chapter ten of "Two Far South," 127.
24. For this perspective among Jewish youth, see Balfour Brickner, "Jewish Youth, Israel, and the Third World," *Reconstructionist* 36, no. 3 (March 27, 1970): 7–13.
25. Leonard J. Fein, "The New Left and Israel," in Mordecai S. Chertoff, ed., *The New Left and the Jews* (New York: Pitman Publishing Company, 1971), 148.
26. Fein, "The New Left," 143.
27. Fein, "The New Left," 147, 146.
28. Editorial, "The Vote against Apartheid," *Israel Horizons* 15, no. 9–10 (November/December 1967): 5.
29. Joel Sokolsky, "South Africa Jewry, Apartheid, and American Attitudes," *Judaism* (American Jewish Congress) 29, no. 4 (1980): 407.
30. Editorial, "The Vote against Apartheid," *Israel Horizons* 15, no. 9–10 (November/December 1967): 5.
31. Quoted in Marc Schneier, *Shared Dreams: Martin Luther King, Jr. and the Jewish Community* (Woodstock, VT: Jewish Lights Publishing, 1999), 161. Thomas Borstelmann notes that internationally, the Suez crisis "played out along racial lines." Quoting *Time Magazine*, he writes that "the 'nonwhite' nations of the world lined up against Britain and France in a virtually solid front." "Suez," *Time*, August 20, 1956, p. 17, quoted in Borstelmann, *The Cold War and the Color Line: American Race Relations in the Global Arena* (Cambridge, MA: Harvard University Press, 2001), 102. This stood true in

South Africa as well, with Black South Africans supporting Egypt, and South African white Jews—those affiliated with Jewish institutions—supporting Israel. See Jitendra Mohan, "South Africa and the Suez Crisis," *International Journal* 16, no. 4 (Autumn 1961): 327–357.
32. "The Moral Responsibility in the Middle East," letter published in *The New York Times*, June 4, 1967.
33. Andrew D. Weinberger to Roy Wilkins, June 7, 1967, Papers of the NAACP, Special Subject Files, 1966–1970, Series A: "Africa" through "Poor People's Campaign," Reel 14, Group IV, frame 837. Microfilm collection edited by John H. Bracey, Jr, and Sharon Harley, Black Studies Research Sources (Bethesda, MD: University Publications of America, 2002), original records housed at the Library of Congress.
34. Roy Wilkins Straight Wire (Telegram), June 6, 1967, Papers of the NAACP, Special Subject Files, 1966–1970, Series A: "Africa" through "Poor People's Campaign," Reel 14, Group IV, Frame 850.
35. "Replies Received Re Poll of Entire Board of Directors on Israeli-Arab Situation and Whether NAACP Should Issue Statement," Polled June 6 [1967], Papers of the NAACP, Special Subject Files, 1966–1970, Series A: "Africa" through "Poor People's Campaign," Reel 14, Group IV, Frame 854.
36. Memorandum from Henry Lee moon to Mr Wilkins, June 7, 1967, Papers of the NAACP, Special Subject Files, 1966–1970, Series A: "Africa" through "Poor People's Campaign," Reel 14, Group IV, Frame 868.
37. Schneier, *Shared Dreams*, 164–166. Shortly before his death, when faced with a hostile question about Zionism at a Harvard University gathering, Dr King responded: "When people criticize Zionists they mean Jews, you are talking anti-Semitism." John Lewis, "King's Special Bond with Israel," *San Francisco Chronicle*, January 21, 2002. Branch also cites a letter King wrote in September 1967 after the passage of anti-Israel resolutions at the National Conference for New Politics: "Israel's right to exist as a state in security is incontestable," he wrote to Morris Abram, president of the American Jewish Committee. "At the same time the great powers have the obligation to recognize that the Arab world is in a state of imposed poverty and backwardness that must threaten peace and harmony." Taylor Branch, *At Canaan's Edge, America in the King Years, 1965–1968* (New York: Simon and Schuster, 2006), 639.
38. Branch, *At Canaan's Edge*, 620.
39. Sol Stern, "My Jewish Problem—and Ours: Israel, the Left, and the Jewish Establishment," *Ramparts* 10 (August 1971): 32, quoted in Staub, *Torn at the Roots*, 289.
40. Ariel Hurwitz, ed., *Against the Stream: Seven Decades of Hashomer Hatzair in North America* (Tel Aviv: The Association of North American Shomrim, 1994), 136–138.
41. Chaim Shur, *Shomrim in the Land of Apartheid: The Story of Hashomer Hatzair in South Africa, 1935–1970* (Israel: Ma'arechet Publishing House, 1998), 117.
42. Ibid., 121.
43. Ibid., 317.
44. *Israel Horizons* 12, no. 1 (January 1964): 28. The editors noted that this was especially prominent among "Jews engaged in commerce and industry."
45. Seymour M. Hersh, *The Samson Option: Israel's Nuclear Arsenal and American Foreign Policy* (New York: Random House, 1991), 263.

46. Sasha Polakow-Suransky, *The Unspoken Alliance: Israel's Secret Relationship with Apartheid South Africa* (New York: Pantheon Books, 2010), 46.
47. Cyrus Leo Sulzberger, "Strange Nonalliance," *New York Times* April 30, 1971.
48. Gideon Shimoni, *Community and Conscience: The Jews in Apartheid South Africa* (Hanover, NH: University of New England Press, 2003), 149.
49. National Jewish Community Relations Advisory Council, Reassessment Conference on Combating Anti-Semitism Today, September 14–16, 1968, Jewish Labor Committee Series 3, Box 120, Folder 29, Tamiment Library, New York University. In his study of Israel and South Africa's *Unspoken Alliance*, Sasha Polakow-Suransky titles the chapter on the late 1960s "Losing the Left: Israel, Apartheid, and the Splintering of the Civil Rights Coalition" (New York: Pantheon Books, 2011), 171.
50. National Jewish Community Relations Advisory Council, Reassessment Conference on Combating Anti-Semitism Today, September 14–16, 1968, Jewish Labor Committee Series 3, Box 120, Folder 29, Tamiment Library, New York University.
51. See, for example, Rabbi Albert S. Axelrad's response to criticisms of college Hillel organizations for not addressing the concerns of young Jews who feel alienated from the Jewish establishment. In an essay, Axelrad, Jewish Chaplain and Adviser to Students at Brandeis University, enumerated the "tensions which tug at radical Jewish students," and offers suggestions for how Jewish campus communities might respond. Under the heading "Empathy for Israel versus the radical Third World critique," he writes:

    Many Jewish radicals do empathize with Israel, but their loyalty is not blind. They are not convinced that Israel is completely blameless for the Middle East Impasse. They are fearful of the possibilities of Jewish chauvinism and militarism. Sometimes they are susceptible to propaganda which simplistically links Israel with American imperialism, and disregards the progressive, socialistic tendencies manifested in Israel's internal life and in her aid programs to Africa and South America.

    Rabbi Albert S. Axelrad, "Encountering the Jewish Radical: The Challenge for Campus Rabbis and Student Groups," in James A. Sleeper and Alan Mintz, eds, *The New Jews* (New York: Vintage Books, 1971), 115.
52. Svonkin, *Jews against Prejudice*, 193.
53. Button, "Chase Manhattan–Partner in Apartheid, SDS," Students for a Democratic Society, 1965, Andrew Norman Collection, digital image in the website of the African Activist Archive, http://africanactivist.msu.edu/image.php?objectid=32-131-C0.
54. Waskow's first arrest was at an antisegregation protest in his hometown of Baltimore.
55. Among his tasks on the ACOA board was to work on grassroots organizing, to hire a "field staff...both in middle-class white areas and in black communities" in select cities based on access to resources and/or connections to South African politics ("city with a congressman on the African sub-committee plus a South African consulate" or with an industry tied to southern Africa). Arthur Waskow to Executive Board, American Committee on Africa, January 15, 1969, American Committee on Africa Papers, Part I, Reel 5.
56. Channing Phillips was a minister and Civil Rights activist, the head of Robert Kennedy's presidential campaign in 1968. When Kennedy was killed,

delegates—including Waskow—pledged their votes to Phillips, making him the first African American to receive votes for the presidential nomination at a Democratic National Convention. Staub also discusses the Freedom Seder and the birth of Jews for Urban Justice (JUJ) in *Torn at the Roots*, 163–193. JUJ existed from 1967 to 1971 (see Chapter five of Staub, *Torn at the Roots*).

57. Waskow talks about this event in "Interview of Rabbi Waskow, February 22, 2012," Jews and Leftist Politics in Philadelphia Project, Feinstein Center for American Jewish History, Temple University, Philadelphia, PA.
58. On Jewish renewal see the website of Tikkun, accessed February 1, 2013, http://www.tikkun.org/nextgen/what-is-jewish-renewal. A full biography of Waskow can be found at the website of the Shalom Center, accessed February 1, 2013, http://theshalomcenter.org/node/1145. Waskow, interview with the author, February 21, 2013.
59. Rabbi Arthur Waskow, interview with the author, February 21, 2013. Waskow talks about the hostile reactions to his activism among other Jewish leaders in "Interview of Rabbi Waskow, February 22, 2012."
60. Peter Weiss, "We Should Listen; We Should Talk Back," (American Jewish) *Congress Bi-Weekly* 34, no. 13 (October 16, 1967), copy in Papers of the National Association for the Advancement of Colored People, Special Subject Files, 1966–1970, Series A: "Africa" through "Poor People's Campaign," Reel 31, Frames 781–784.
61. A brief biography of Peter Weiss can be found with the catalog of the small collection of his papers at the website of the Swarthmore College Peace Collection, last modified, June 27, 2012, http://www.swarthmore.edu/Library/peace/CDGA.S-Z/WeissPeter.htm.
62. Weiss had articulated this position publically for at least a decade. In May of 1959, he testified before the United States Senate's Committee on Foreign Relations on amendments to the Mutual Security Act of 1954, urging policies that would "cement ties of friendship" with independent African nations seeking economic development. "Great political harm can come from our failure to be prepared for such contingencies," he noted. Weiss cited the example of Guinea, newly independent with a "void" left behind from the withdrawal of "French arms, personnel, and equipment." When the United States failed to respond to Guinea's request for aid, Czechoslovakia stepped in, giving the world "the erroneous impression that Guinea was turning away from the West." Peter Weiss, Vice Chairman of the Executive Board, American Committee on Africa, *Hearings before the Committee on Foreign Relations, United States Senate*, May 1959, http://kora.matrix.msu.edu/files/50/304/32-130-D88-84-al.sff.document.acoa001024.pdf.
63. Peter Weiss, "We Should Listen; We Should Talk Back," (American Jewish) *Congress Bi-Weekly* 34, no. 13 (October 16, 1967), copy in Papers of the National Association for the Advancement of Colored People, Special Subject Files, 1966–1970, Series A: "Africa" through "Poor People's Campaign," Reel 31, Frames 781–784. One year later, Leonard Fein also published an essay about Jews and African Americans, in which he examined what Jews and African Americans might gain by working together for racial justice. Published in the pages of *Israel Horizons*, Fein's eloquent essay captures well the era of "wrenching confusion," the "not subtle times" when "freedom and fire are not subtle." Fein concludes that Jews are not white, and that ultimately, Jews and African Americans "ought indeed to be a special relationship based not

upon a common enemy" nor a "common history but based instead upon a common purpose, the purpose of teaching America at long last what pluralism is all about." Leonard J. Fein, "Negro and Jew: A 'Special Relationship,'" *Israel Horizons* 16, no. 9 (November 1968): 6, 9.
64. With his wife, actress and activist Ruby Dee, Ossie Davis wrote a memoir, *With Ossie and Ruby: In This Life Together* (New York: William and Morrow Company, 1998). Davis and Dee write about their favorable encounters with American Jews in the movements for racial and economic justice, but do not mention Israel or Zionism in their book. "Anti-Semitism and racism were one and the same," they write. "In *The Daily Worker*...[I read that] the struggles of the Jewish people in Germany, the colonization of the people in Africa, and the persecution of Negroes all over America overlapped" (111).
65. Ossie Davis, "The Hard Road to a Black 'Jerusalem,'" *Israel Horizons* 17, no. 3 (March 1969): 16, 19.
66. Peter Weiss, email to the author, July 27, 2009.
67. Milton Himmelfarb, "American Jewish Congress," *Commentary* (August 1960): 160.
68. Peter Weiss, interview with the author, November 17, 2010.
69. This organization was founded in 1983. See William Minter and Sylvia Hill, "Anti-Apartheid Solidarity in United States–South Africa Relations: From the Margins to the Mainstream," in South Africa Democracy Education Trust, *The Road to Democracy in South Africa Volume 3: International Solidarity* (Pretoria: Unisa Press, 2008), located on the website of "RFK in the Land of Apartheid," http://www.rfksafilm.org/html/doc_pdfs/MintnerHill.pdf.
70. "Censorship, Liberal Style," Editorial, *The Liberator* 9, no. 2 (February 1969): 3.
71. "Negro Leaders Ask U.S. Jets for Israel," *New York Times*, June 28, 1970. John D'Emilio writes that Bayard Rustin "never wavered in his support for Israel even as he acknowledged that it 'created a tension' with his personal pacifism." He rejected some other African American leaders' sympathy with the Palestine Liberation Organization, arguing that hatred of Israel emerged from " 'proto-fascist dictatorships' in the region, and that their 'prolonged and inflammatory calls for the destruction of Israel can only divert precious attention, energy, and resources away from an attack on the pressing social and economic problems of the Arab people." Quoted in *Lost Prophet: The Life and Times of Bayard Rustin* (New York: Free Press, 2003), 482–483.
72. On Black Nationalism in the United States, see Darren W. Davis and Ronald E. Brown, "The Antipathy of Black Nationalism: Behavioral and Attitudinal Implications of an African American Ideology," *American Journal of Political Science*, 46, no. 2 (April 2002): 239–252.
73. "Call It Treason," Letter to the Editor, *Liberator* 10, no. 8 (August 1970): 22.
74. Copy of a letter, July 28, 1970, from Charles Hightower to Congressman Charles Diggs, Papers of the American Committee on Africa, Part 1, Reel 3.
75. Peter Weiss to Charles Hightower, August 7, 1970, Papers of the American Committee on Africa, Part 1, Reel 3.
76. Peter Weiss, interview with the author, January 23, 2013.
77. "Peter Weiss told Bayard [Rustin], subject to subsequent action that the Steering Committee..." Memo from Janet Hooper to the Executive Board of ACOA, August 17, 1970, Papers of the American Committee on Africa, Part 1, Reel 3.

78. "I was interested in your reference to Meir Yaari, since I know him and consider myself considerably to the left of him in the spectrum of Israeli politics," Peter Weiss to Charles Hightower, August 7, 1970, Papers of the American Committee on Africa, Part 1, Reel 3.
79. Charles Hightower to Representative Diggs, August 10, 1970, Papers of the American Committee on Africa, Part 1, Reel 3.
80. Richard P. Stevens to the Staff and Board of the American Committee on Africa, September 27, 1970, Papers of the American Committee on Africa, Part 1, Reel 3.
81. Ibid.
82. "SOUTH AFRICAN AIRWAYS: TELL IT LIKE IT IS!" editorial, *Sun Reporter* (San Francisco, CA) August 9, 1969.
83. "An Air Link with South Africa Urged" and "Jewish Group Protests," *New York Times* April 3, 1969. George Houser narrates the protests of African Americans and the American Committee on Africa to this air link between South Africa and the United States in *No One Can Stop the Rain* (New York: Pilgrim Press, 1989), 276–277. President Johnson authorized South African Airways to begin flights in 1968, and despite protests the flights began to travel in and out of John F. Kennedy Airport in 1969.
84. Samuel H. Wang, "An Open Letter to the American Jewish Congress," *New York Times*, April 25, 1969.
85. Wang, "An Open Letter."
86. "After Sharpeville," Chapter 10 of Mendelsohn, "Two Far South," 126.
87. Maurice L. Perlzweig to Gerald Mr Riegner, October 9, 1969, World Jewish Congress Papers, American Jewish Archives, Cincinatti, OH. Perlzweig's assessment of others' perceptions of global Jewish influence—his measuring Jewish contributions to global democracy and justice alongside or against work specifically for Jewish communities—resonates with the findings of James Loeffer, "'The Conscience of America': Human Rights, Jewish Politics, and American Foreign Policy at the 1945 United Nations San Francisco Conference," *Journal of American History* 100: 2 (September 2013): 401–428.

4 "South Africa Needs Friends": Cold War Narratives and Counternarratives

1. For Farber, this miscalculation in American foreign policy was revealed most clearly in the tragedies of September 11, 2001. David Farber, *The Iran Hostage Crisis and America's First Encounter with Radical Islam* (Princeton, NJ: Princeton University Press, 2005), 5, 167.
2. One scholar of American Jewish Israel advocacy sees the domestic disagreements between African Americans and Jews in the 1970s as having a "Middle East spillover effect." This study, in contrast, argues for the central role of apartheid in those disagreements. Martin Raffel, "History of Israel Advocacy," in Alan Mittleman, Jonathan D. Sarna, and Robert Licht, eds, *Jewish Polity and American Civil Society: Communal Agencies and Religious Movements in the American Public Sphere* (Lanham, MD: Rowan and Littlefield Publishers Inc., 2002), 143.
3. "An Appeal by Black Americans against United States Support of the Zionist Government of Israel," Advertisement, *The New York Times* November 1, 1970.

4. Sasha Polakow-Suransky, *The Unspoken Alliance: Israel's Secret Relationship with Apartheid South Africa* (New York: Pantheon Books, 2011), 53.
5. Cyrus L. Sulzberger, quoted in Polakow-Suransky, *The Unspoken Alliance*, 65.
6. Polakow-Suransky, *The Unspoken Alliance*, 73. It is interesting to note that through the 1960s, members of the Zionist left praised Israel's refusal to sell arms to South Africa as a measure of its opposition to apartheid. See *Israel Horizons* 11, no. 9 (November 1963): 30.
7. Gideon Shimoni, *Community and Conscience: The Jews in Apartheid South Africa* (Hanover, NH: University of New England Press, 2003), 160.
8. Polakow-Suransky, *The Unspoken Alliance*, 63.
9. *Jewish Currents*, 27, no. 3 (March 1973): 47; Rabbi Brian Walt was one of the Jewish day school graduates who authored *Strike* (Walt, Interview with the author, May 30, 2013). American Jews responded in predictable ways to the 1973 antiapartheid protests of South African Jewish students. Those on the left praised the students, and also claimed the antiapartheid heroism of unaffiliated, mostly Communist South African Jews, noting that "although the Board has refused to act as a Jewish spokesman, the proportion of Jews in prison for combatting the apartheid policy is extremely high" *Jewish Currents*, 27, no. 6 (June 1973): 47. In contrast, more mainstream American Jews highlighted the "small group" of students' "attacks on Israel" first, calling their articles about Israel of the "'New Left' variety." The report then notes that the Jewish students also criticized local Jewish leaders for not taking a "stand against apartheid" ("South African Student Journal Hit for New Left Stance," *Jewish Telegraphic Agency* May 16, 1973, http://archive.jta.org/article/1973/05/16/2965103/south-african-jewish-student-journal-hit-for-new-left-stance.)
10. In 1962, the South African Jewish Board of Deputies General Secretary Gus Saron noted that the Board "has been unable to sift out the moral from the political aspects of racial policies" in South Africa, and the Board had a strict nonpolitical position. Gus Saron to Mr Saul E. Joftes, March 8, 1962, Papers of the National Jewish Community Relations Council, Center for Jewish History, New York.
11. Joel Sokolsky, "South Africa Jewry, Apartheid, and American Attitudes," *Judaism* (American Jewish Congress) 29, no. 4 (1980): 414, 413.
12. Ibid., 407.
13. Polakow-Suransky, *The Unspoken Alliance*, 64.
14. Ibid., 67.
15. Gideon Shimoni, *Community and Conscience*, 156. Shimoni notes the Jewish individuals in Israel and South Africa who voiced opposition to Israel's cooperation with South Africa.
16. Vorster's quote is recorded in C.L. Sulzberger, "Strange Nonalliance" *The New York Times*, April 30, 1971; in Thomas Borstelmann, *The Cold War and the Color Line* (Cambridge, MA: Harvard University Press, 2001), 240; in Paul Gordon Lauren, *Power and Prejudice. The Politics and Diplomacy of Racial Discrimination* (Boulder, CO: Westview Press), 238.
17. Abraham Ben-Zvi, *The United States and Israel: The Limits of a Special Relationship* (New York: Columbia University Press, 1993), 83.
18. Staub, *Torn at the Roots*, 281.
19. Leonard Fein, ally of Breira, on the 1975 Conference "Should Israel Talk to the PLO?" in Alex Klein, "J Street's Forerunner" *Tablet Magazine*, March

23, 2012, http://www.tabletmag.com/jewish-news-and-politics/94906/j-streets-forerunner.
20. William Novak, "The Breira Story," and "Breira's Finances," *Genesis 2* (March 16, 1977): 6. In response to criticisms such as those of Rael Isaacs, discussed in chapter 6, Novak is quick to point out that Rubin also gave "several million dollars" to United Jewish Appeal, the mainstream, communal Jewish organization. Goldmann advocated for negotiation with the Palestine Liberation Organization. He appears in chapter 1, as concerned about the continuity of Jewish diaspora life. He was also a fervent critic of Israel's diplomacy and militarism and of American Jewish leaders' attitudes toward Israel.
21. Klein, "J Street's Forerunner"; Staub, *Torn at the Roots*, 287. The "Mission Statement" of Breira also appears in Marla Brettschneider, *Cornerstones of Peace: Jewish Identity Politics and Democratic Theory* (New Brunswick, NJ: Rutgers University Press, 1996), 109.
22. Brickner wrote that American Jews "call for free speech in every other facet of American life" except in discussions of the Middle East. "My Zionist Dilemmas," *Sh'ma: A Journal of Jewish Responsibility* 1 (November 9, 1970): 4.
23. "African Jews Defy Bias," *Tri-State Defender* (Memphis, TN), 9, no. 22 (April 11, 1964): 6.
24. "Says Time Running out for Peace in S. Africa," *Tri-State Defender* (Memphis, TN) 10, no. 32 (June 11, 1960): 4. On Ungar, see Adam Mendelsohn, "Two Far South: The Responses of Southern and South African Jews to Apartheid and Racial Segregation in the 1950s and 1960s" (Unpublished MA Thesis, University of Cape Town, 2003).
25. "An Appeal from Black Trade Unionists: Support Israel," *New York Times*, October 23, 1973.
26. Black Americans to Support Israel Committee, *New York Times* 23 November 1975. See Jervis Anderson, *Bayard Rustin: Troubles I've Seen* (New York: Harper Collins, 1997), 339–341. On Rustin's earlier pro-Israel stands, see chapter 3.
27. William Patterson, "Black View of Israel," *Sun Reporter* (San Francisco, CA) 29, no. 26 (June 24, 1972): 6.
28. Nations also unsuccessfully called for Israel's ouster from the United Nations in 1985. Jake C. Miller, "Black Viewpoints on the Mid-East Conflict," *The Journal of Palestine Studies*, 10, no. 2 (Winter 1981): 39–40.
29. "Israel Expulsion Blasted by Two Black Newspapers," *Oakland Post*, August 13, 1975.
30. Richard Yaffe, "Foes ponder unseating of Israel in UN," The New York *Jewish Week* 184, no. 50 (May 31, 1975): 1. Some observers assert that UN Resolution 3379 resulted from these foiled attempts to oust Israel from the UN. On Resolution 3379, see below.
31. "South Africa the Problem," The New York *Jewish Week*, 185, no. 3 (June 21, 1975): 16. See also chapter 4, "Moynihan on the Move, October 1975," in Gil Troy, *Moynihan's Moment: America's Fight against Zionism as Racism* (New York: Oxford University Press, 2013).
32. See Abraham A. Ben-Zvi, *The United States and Israel: The Limits of a Special Relationship* (New York: Columbia University Press, 1993), 77–102.
33. Polakow-Suransky, *The Unspoken Alliance*, 88.

34. *The United Nations and Apartheid, 1948–1994* (New York: Department of Public Information, 1994), 48.
35. My thinking here has been influenced by Peter Beinart, *The Crisis of Zionism* (New York: Times Books, 2012); Robert Meister, *After Evil: A Politics of Human Rights* (New York: Columbia University Press, 2012).
36. Ofra Friesel details how the Soviets and their allies attempted to replace (or add to) a UN condemnation of anti-Semitism with one of Zionism. While 1965 marked "the first time in the United Nations that Zionism was compared to racially biased movements," these comparisons were increasingly common in human rights and activist circles by the late 1960s. This study focuses on Jewish responses to both the diplomatic and grassroots discourses. Ofra Friesel, "Equating Zionism with Racism: The 1965 Precedent," *American Jewish History* 97, no. 3 (July 2013): 303.
37. Judy Froman, *An Examination of the United Nations General Assembly Resolution 3379, 10 November 1975, Which Determines that Zionism is Racism and Racial Discrimination* (Thesis, Harvard Law School, Professor Henry Steiner's seminar on Human Rights, May 1991), 7–8.
38. "Situation in South Africa Resulting from the Policies of Apartheid," Section G of United Nations Resolution 3151, "Policies of *apartheid* of the government of South Africa," 2201st Plenary meeting, December 14, 1973, http://www.un.org/ga/search/view_doc.asp?symbol=A/RES/3151(XXVIII)&Lang=E&Area=RESOLUTION.
39. These statements can be read at United Nations Resolution 3379, "Elimination of all forms of racial discrimination," 2400th Plenary Meeting, November 10, 1975, http://unispal.un.org/UNISPAL.NSF/0/761C1063530766A7052566A2005B74D1.
40. Quote from Borstelmann, *Cold War*, 240.
41. Middle East scholar Joel Peters also notes that "Israel's critics have pointed to this relationship as confirmation of the illegitimacy and the racist nature of Zionism." These critics "set out to portray Israel and South Africa as fellow pariah states, which, drawn together by a shared ideology, have created an alliance which poses a threat to international peace and security, and have capitalized on this issue in their efforts to ostracize Israel from the international community." Joel Peters, *Israel and Africa: The Problematic Friendship* (London: British Academic Press, 1992), 147. Scholar Jane S. Jaquette writes that evidence of the "deepening of U.S. isolation" at the United Nations lay in its number of dissenting votes in the General Assembly: in 1960, the United States cast 2 negative votes; in 1970, 17; in 1980, 45. "Between 1975 and 1980," she writes, "the United States accounted for one-fourth of all the single negative votes cast." Jane S. Jaquette, "Losing the Battle/Winning the War: International Politics, Women's Issues, and the 1980 Mid-Decade Conference," in *Women, Politics, and the United Nations*, ed. Anne Winslow (Greenwood, CT: Greenwood Press, 1995), 47.
42. Quote from Thomas Borstelmann, *The Cold War and the Color Line: American Race Relations in the Global Arena* (Cambridge, MA: Harvard University Press, 2003), 240.
43. Friesel, "Equating Zionism with Racism," 286.
44. Judy Froman, *An Examination of the United Nations General Assembly Resolution 3379, 10 November 1975, Which Determines that Zionism is Racism*

and Racial Discrimination (Thesis, Harvard Law School, Professor Henry Steiner's seminar on Human Rights, May 1991), 77–83.
45. Quoted in "Black Scholars Urge Draft's Defeat," *Jewish Telegraphic Agency*, November 10, 1975, http://archive.jta.org/article/1975/11/10/2973572/antizionist-draft-denounced-by-jewish-nonjewish-black-leaders.
46. Troy, *Moynihan's Moment*, 4.
47. Ibid., 77.
48. I quote here only the sections of each author's work dealing directly with Resolution 3379. Noam Chomsky wrote: "The notorious UN Resolution identifying Zionism as a form of racism can properly be condemned for profound hypocrisy, given the nature of the states that backed it (including the Arab states) and (arguably) for referring to Zionism as such rather than the policies of the State of Israel." Importantly, though, he adds that "restricted to these policies, the resolution cannot be criticized as inaccurate." *Fateful Triangle: The United States, Israel, and the Palestinians* (Cambridge, MA: South End Press, 1983, 1999), 158. Edward Said wrote that "it is right that they [Israel's achievements for Jews] not sloppily be tarnished with the sweeping rhetorical denunciation associated with 'racism.'" Edward Said, "Zionism from the Standpoint of its Victims," 1979, reprinted in Moustafa Bayoumi and Andrew Rubin, eds, *The Edward Said Reader* (New York: Random House, 2007), 166.
49. "Arabs lose many allies in drive to condemn Zionism as 'racism,'" The New York *Jewish Week*, November 1, 1975. Upon the passage of the United Nations Resolution, Israel Ambassador to the UN Chaim Herzog addressed the General Assembly. He began by noting that the date coincided with the anniversary of Kristallnacht, the German attacks against Jewish homes, synagogues, and businesses that began the Holocaust. Herzog rued the fact that the United Nations had begun as an "anti-Nazi alliance," but that the current anti-Semitism embedded in the discussion and passage of this resolution meant that "Hitler would have felt at home." Israeli Ambassador Herzog's Response to Zionism Is Racism Resolution, November 10, 1975, website of the Jewish Virtual Library, American-Israeli Cooperative Enterprise, http://www.jewishvirtuallibrary.org/jsource/UN/herzogsp.html. Scholar Robert Meister asserts that the link "between Israel and the Holocaust was not inevitable," and instead marked a conscious choice: Israel "could...appear as either the last gasp of settler colonialism in the Middle East—or as something else, a homeland to the Seventh Million, those who had survived the Holocaust." Meister notes that Israeli leadership then worked to build the "Nazi-Arab equation," in which threats to Israel's existence from Arab nations were seen as equal to the ultimate destruction of Nazi anti-Semitism, and thus Israel's actions were to be insulated from critique because all of their actions were necessary to realize "Never Again." Israel's was "an exceptional form of victimhood." Robert Meister, *After Evil: A Politics of Human Rights* (New York: Columbia University Press, 2011), 194, 195.
50. Troy, *Moynihan's Moment*.
51. Moshe Decter, Director of Research, American Jewish Congress, *"To Serve, To Teach, to Leave," The Story of Israel's Development Program in Black Africa* (New York: American Jewish Congress, 1977), 10.
52. "Called Apartheid's Ally, Israeli Jibes Russians with So. African Trade," The New York *Jewish Week*, November 13, 1976, 4.

53. Polakow-Suransky, *The Unspoken Alliance*, 3,159; Naomi Chazan, "The Fallacies of Pragmatism: Israeli Foreign Policy towards South Africa," *African Affairs* 82, no. 327 (1983): 171, 173. In 1983, Hebrew University professor (and later a member of the Knesset for the left-wing Meretz Party) Naomi Chazan wrote that "The Vorster visit [of 1976] in effect drew Israel and South Africa into a complex network of mutual collaboration." Chazan wrote before the release of the classified information that comprised the basis of much of Polakow-Suransky's study.
54. Moshe Decter, "South Africa and Black Africa: A Report on Growing Trade Relations," *Jewish Frontier* 43 (October 1976): 18. This study does not seek to answer these crucial questions. In his recent book, Peter Beinart addresses why "one might focus on Israel's misdeeds" more than those of other nations: because of a sincere attachment to Israel, and because Israel is seen as a "Western outpost in the Middle East" and Western critics of imperialism find its human rights abuses worthy of their critical lens. Peter Beinart, *The Crisis of Zionism* 56–57.
55. Polakow-Suransky, *The Unspoken Alliance*, 92.
56. Robert G. Weisbord and Richard Kazarian, Jr, *Israel in the Black American Perspective* (Westport, CT: Greenwood Press, 1985), 102.
57. On this point, see Polakow-Suransky, *The Unspoken Alliance*, 233–234.
58. Terence Smith, "Vorster Visit to Israel Arouses Criticism," *The New York Times*, April 18, 1976.
59. "Vorster Visit Marks New Israel-South Africa Ties," MERIP Reports 47 (May 1976): 21–22.
60. *Africa Research Bulletin*, April 1976, p. 4009, quoted in Joel Peters, *Israel and Africa: The Problematic Friendship* (London: British Academic Press, 1992), 163.
61. See Polakow-Suransky, *Unspoken Alliance*, 164–170.
62. "Friendship between Israel and So. Africa Blossoming," *Oakland Post* May 5, 1976.
63. "From Where I Sit: Women Prisoners in South Africa," *Tri-State Defender* (Memphis, TN), December 4, 1976.
64. "From Where I Sit: Dr. Kissinger's African Odyssey," *Tri- State Defender* (Memphis, TN) May 1, 1976.
65. "Both Wrong and Stupid," Editorial, *The New Outlook* (September/October 1976), 3–4.
66. Sheldon Ranz, "Skeleton in the Closet," *Jewish Currents* 31, no. 1 (January 1977): 8–9.
67. "Rustin Replies," *Near East Report* 20 (November 3, 1976): 185.
68. "Israel-South Africa Issue," Editorial, *Jewish Currents* 31, no. 1 (January 1977): 26–27.
69. "Africa Offered $ Billion Bribe to Shun Israel," The New York *Jewish Week*, March 13, 1977, 7.
70. Quoted in Weisbord and Kazarian, *Israel in the Black American Perspective*, 142, 143.
71. Ishmael Flory, "What I Think," *New Pittsburg Courier*, May 1, 1976.
72. Anson Laytner, "Why Does the Third World Oppose Zionism?" *Modern Outlook* (November 1976), 18–22.
73. Philip Slomovitz, "Historic Editorial Mission Views Hope for Justice," *The Jewish News* (New York), June 11, 1976.

74. Philip Hochstein, "South African Jews Seen Vital Link in Evolving New Policies," The New York *Jewish Week*, May 30–June 6, 1976, 24–25.
75. Irwin J. Stein, "An Interview with Israel's Ambassador to South Africa," *Sentinel* (Chicago), July 8, 1976.
76. Stein, "An Interview," 12.
77. "Pan Am Offers Israel Tour Via Brazil, So. Africa," The New York *Jewish Week*, 186, no. 46 (May 8, 1977): 14.
78. Nelson Mandela, *Long Walk to Freedom: The Autobiography of Nelson Mandela* (Boston, MA: Little, Brown, and Company, 1994), 483–484.
79. Francis Njubi Nesbitt, *Race for Sanctions: African Americans against Apartheid, 1946–1994* (Bloomington, IN: Indiana University Press, 2004), 103.
80. Quoted in Dan Goldberg, "In Australia, Some South African Jews Still Stained by Apartheid," *Haaretz*, January 29, 2013, http://www.haaretz.com/jewish-world/jewish-world-features/in-australia-some-south-african-jews-still-stained-by-apartheid.premium-1.500017.
81. Denis Diamond, "Letter from Johannesburg," *Hadassah*, 58, no. 2 (October 1976): 19, 33–34.
82. "Junket for U.S. Jewish Editors to South Africa," editorial, *Jewish Currents* 30 (October 1976): 29.
83. Polakow-Suransky, *The Unspoken Alliance*, 110.
84. See Ibid., 3.
85. David Hammerstein, "Marching to Pretoria," *The Jewish Radical* 9, no. 3 (August 1978), 12, Tamiment Library, New York University.
86. Ibid.
87. See, for example, "Fair Play for Israel," in *Jewish Currents* 31, no. 3 (1977): 34–35. This piece was an editorial in the Black weekly *Oklahoma Eagle*, defending Israel's right to not be "singled out" for its trade with South Africa; *Currents* editors reprinted it because they saw it as a "straight-from-the-shoulder" editorial from a "highly regarded" weekly.
88. Borstelmann, *The Cold War and the Color Line*, 252.
89. Cheryl Lynn Greenberg, *Troubling the Waters: Black-Jewish Relations in the American Century* (Princeton, NJ: Princeton University Press, 2010), 242.
90. "Nation: With Sorrow and Anger," *Time Magazine*, September 3, 1979, http://www.time.com/time/magazine/article/0,9171,948578-3,00.html. Israel's relationship to South Africa continued to play a pivotal role in Black/Jewish relations in the United States. Yosef Lifsh was the Hasidic driver of a car in the Lubavitcher Rebbe's motorcade in Crown Heights on August 19, 1991; he ran a light, hit a car, and struck two children, Gavin and Angela Cato, on the sidewalk, killing Gavin and injuring Angela. The incident touched off days of rioting and violence, including the murder of an Orthodox Jewish student, Yankel Rosenbaum, a few hours later. African Americans vented their frustration and anger when a grand jury failed to indict Lifsh. Al Sharpton and other activists decided to sue him in a wrongful death civil lawsuit. According to New York law, the summons for such a lawsuit had to be delivered personally. Lifsh had returned home immediately after the jury announced its decision. So Sharpton flew to Israel the day before Yom Kippur, September 17, 1991, to give him notice. Sharpton told an Israeli audience that, in view of the imminence of the Jewish Day of Atonement, Israel should hand over Lifsh: "This would help Israel repent for her sins, particularly the sin of having military and

commercial relations with the government of South Africa." Quoted in Edward S. Shapiro, *Crown Heights: Blacks, Jews, and the 1991 Brooklyn Riot* (Waltham, MA: Brandeis University Press, 2006), 21.
91. "Black American Lobby Backs Palestinian State," *New York Times*, August 28, 1979.

5 Jewish Women, Zionism, and Apartheid

1. Marlene Provizer, interview with the author, June 7, 2013.
2. The idea of the International Women's Year and the conference was originally to commemorate the twenty-fifth anniversary of the Women's International Democratic Federation, founded in Paris in late 1945. It also marked a watershed for the Commission on the Status of Women, founded in 1946 as a commission of the United Nations Economic and Social Council (ECOSOC), the principal global policy-making body focused on gender equality and women's social progress. See Devaki Jain, *Women, Development, and the UN: A Sixty-Year Quest for Equality and Justice* (Bloomington, IN: Indiana University Press, 2005), 65–72. South Africa was not represented at these women's conferences.
3. Jain, *Women, Development, and the UN*, 69.
4. Niamh Reilly, *Women's Human Rights: Seeking Gender Justice in a Global Age* (Malden, MA: Polity Press, 2009), 53.
5. Margaret Snyder, "Walking My Own Road: How a Sabbatical Year Led to a Career at the UN," in *Developing Power: How Women Transformed International Development*, ed. Arvonne S. Fraser and Irene Tinker (New York: Feminist Press, 2004), 42.
6. Virginia R. Allan, Margaret Galey, and Mildred E. Persinger, "World Conference of International Women's Year," in *Women, Politics, and the United Nations*, ed. Anne Winslow (Greenwood, CT: Greenwood Press, 1995), 35–36.
7. Allan, Galey, and Persinger, "World Conference," 41.
8. Here I refer to my findings in the many archival collections I visited. Kathleen A. Laughlin's article "'Our Defense against Despair'" analyzes the post World War II activism of the National Council of Jewish Women [NCJW], working with the federal government in social welfare activism on issues such as Jewish welfare, civil rights and liberties, religious tolerance, and Israel. Laughlin explains that NCJW first "eschewed Zionism, preferring to emphasize the acculturation of immigrants in the United States. The Holocaust changed the group's position, and the NCJW used its relationship with the state department and alliances with women's organizations to advocate for the creation of a Jewish state" (Laughlin, "'Our Defense against Despair': The Progressive Politics of the National Council of Jewish Women after World War II," in Hasia Diner, Shira Kohn, and Rachel Kranson, eds, *A Jewish Feminine Mystique: Jewish Women in Postwar America* (New Brunswick, NJ: Rutgers University Press, 2010), 50).
9. Melissa Klapper carefully documents Jewish women's involvement in "gendered activism" in *Ballots, Babies, and Banners of Peace: American Jewish Women's Activism, 1890–1940* (New York: New York University Press, 2013).
10. This chapter utilizes both communalist and dispersionist approaches to US Jewish history. On these approaches, see David Hollinger's important essay, "Communalist and Dispersionist Approaches to American Jewish History in

an Increasingly Post-Jewish Era, *American Jewish History* 95 no. 1 (March 2009): 1–32.
11. In 1972, a well-educated group of Jewish women calling themselves *Ezrat Nashim* (the term used for the women's section of a traditional synagogue, translated as "help for women" or "Jewish enclave") petitioned the Conservative movement's rabbis with the first agenda of Jewish feminism. In that same year, Sally Priesand was ordained as the first female rabbi of the Reform movement. In 1973, over 400 Jewish women attended the first National Jewish Women's Conference in New York City. As Paula Hyman, historian of Jewish feminism and a member of *Ezrat Nashim*, has written, "it took secularized Jews, influenced by the rise of feminism in America in the 1960s, to establish a Jewish feminist movement that provided a radically different modern form to strivings for gender equality." A brief statement by Paula Hyman on the activism of *Ezrat Nashim* can be found in The New York *Jewish Week*, July 27, 1974, 12: "The women of Ezrat Nashim…along with other Jewish women, are beginning to redress the ceremonial imbalance and age-old sexism within Judaism by developing meaningful rituals celebrating the birth and maturation of girls, and by drawing up nonsexist curricula for all levels of Jewish education." Hyman writes about the birth of Jewish feminism in "Jewish Feminism Faces the American Women's Movement," in Pamela Nadell, ed., *American Jewish Women's History: A Reader* (New York: New York University Press, 2003), 297–309. Matthew Frye Jacobson includes a discussion of the impact of the ethnic revival—and ethnic identity—to second-wave white feminism and antiracism in *Roots Too: White Ethnic Revival in Post-Civil Rights America* (Cambridge, MA: Harvard University Press, 2006).
12. Melissa Klapper's history of Jewish women's activism in the suffrage, birth control, and peace movements from 1890 to 1940 also engages these themes. Klapper writes that for these women "there was no conflict between communalist and dispersionist activism," that these causes "offered Jewish women exciting opportunities to be swept up in gendered activism without abandoning Jewish meaning." Events of the 1930s, with "particular threats to Jewish survival and the apparent silence of their activist colleagues," sparked a "reevaluation of what it meant to be Americans, Jews, and women" and "forced them to renegotiate their activism in light of their personal identities." Klapper concludes that Jewish women "did not so much abandon their internationalist ideals as gradually and painfully redirect them to Jewish identity rather than universal peace" (Klapper, *Ballots, Babies, and Banners of Peace*, 14, 4, 204).
13. Margaret E. Galey, "The Nairobi Conference: The Powerless Majority," *PS* (Political Science) 19, no. 2 (Spring 1986): 257.
14. On the Jewish ethnic revival, see chapter 3. See also "I Take Back My Name," Chapter 5 of Jacobson, *Roots Too*; on the ethnic revival and feminism, see Jacobson's Chapter 6, "Our Heritage is Our Power." The New York Jewish Feminist Organization released a statement after Mexico City, protesting the "slur on Zionism" as anti-Semitic. "Feminists view slur on Zionism as anti-Semitic, The New York *Jewish Week*, September 6, 1975, 39.
15. Letty Cottin Pogrebin, *Deborah, Golda, and Me: Being Female and Jewish in America* (New York: Crown Publishers, Inc., 1991), 154. Gil Troy writes of the transformation of feminist Betty Friedan after Mexico City in Troy,

Moynihan's Moment: America's Fight against Zionism as Racism (New York: Oxford University Press, 2013), 83–86, 178–179.
16. Ellen Cantarow, "Zionism, Anti-Semitism, and Jewish Identity in the Women's Movement," *Middle East Report* 154 (September–October 1988): 39.
17. Pogrebin, *Deborah, Golda, and Me*, 155.
18. "Women's Year parley distorted by UN males, says Bella," The New York *Jewish Week*, July 19, 1975, 20.
19. Pogrebin, *Deborah, Golda and Me*, 157. On African American women and the United Nations, see Hanes Walton, Jr, *Black Women at the United Nations* (San Bernadino, CA: Borgo Press, 1995).
20. Letty Cottin Pogrebin, "Anti-Semitism in the Women's Movement," *Ms. Magazine*, June 1982, 45. Website of the Jewish Women's Archive, accessed June 16, 2013, http://jwa.org/feminism/_html/_pdf/JWA102e.pdf. Matthew Frye Jacobson discusses this moment in *Roots Too*, 364–384.
21. Pogrebin, "Anti-Semitism in the Women's Movement," 65.
22. Statement of Letty Cottin Pogrebin, adapted from *Deborah, Golda, and Me*, website of the Jewish Women's Archive, accessed June 16, 2013, http://jwa.org/feminism/_html/JWA102.htm.
23. Miriam Goodman, "PLO Hijacks Conference on Women," *The Jewish Press* (Omaha, NE), 59, no. 48 (August 15, 1980): 1.
24. Regina Schreiber, "Copenhagen: One Year Later," *Lilith* (New York), 8 (January 31, 1981): 30.
25. Charlotte G. Patton, "Women and Power: The Nairobi Conference, 1985," in *Women, Politics, and the United Nations*, ed. Anne Winslow (Greenwood, CT: Greenwood Press, 1995), 62.
26. Jane S. Jaquette, "Losing the Battle/Winning the War: International Politics, Women's Issues, and the 1980 Mid-Decade Conference," in *Women, Politics, and the United Nations*, ed. Anne Winslow (Greenwood, CT: Greenwood Press, 1995), 57.
27. Jain, *Women, Development and the UN*, 70.
28. Robin Morgan, quoted in *Bella Abzug: How One Tough Broad from the Bronx Fought Jim Crow and Joe McCarthy, Pissed Off Jimmy Carter, Battled for the Rights of Women and Workers, Rallied Against War and for the Planet, and Shook up Politics Along the Way*, ed. Suzanne Braun Levine and Mary Thom (New York: Farrar, Straus, and Giroux, 2007), 239. Another story of bridge-building happened in Israel itself, at a conference on women sponsored by Haifa University in response to the anti-Zionism in Copenhagen. Lyndee Myeza, a Methodist and Zulu Sowetan activist, protested when the conference tour included a stop at a nearby diamond merchant. The tour company apologized, Myeza's speech was "the hit of the conference," and she was invited back for six months by Histadrut, Israel's labor federation, for an International Training Center program. David Twersky, "A South African Epilogue," *Jewish Frontier* 49 (February 1982): 9.
29. Cantarow, "Zionism, Anti-Semitism, and Jewish Identity," 38.
30. This perspective made invisible the ways in which Palestinian women felt that Zionism affected their realities. UN World Conference of the UN Decade for Women, Copenhagen, Denmark, July 14–30, 1980, *Report of the Congressional Staff Advisers to the U.S. Delegation Submitted to the Committee on Foreign Affairs, U.S. House of Representatives* (Washington, DC: U.S. Printing Office,

December 1980), 10, University of Florida Digital Collections, http://ufdc.ufl.edu/UF00088999/00001/19j.
31. Judith P. Zinsser, "From Mexico to Copenhagen to Nairobi: The United Nations Decade for Women, 1975–1985," *Journal of World History* 13, no. 1 (Spring 2002): 152–153.
32. "Zionism in the Women's Movement: Anti-imperialist Politics Derailed," Alliance Against Women's Oppression, *AAWO Discussion Paper Number 4* (San Francisco), October 1983, 2.
33. Alliance Against Women's Oppression, 12. For contemplative essays from this period on relationships between African American and white Jewish women on the left, see Elly Bulkin, Minnie Bruce Pratt, and Barbara Smith, *Yours in Struggle: Three Feminist Perspectives on Anti-Semitism and Racism* (Ithaca, NY: Firebrand Books, 1984).
34. "Letters Forum: Anti-Semitism," *Ms. Magazine* 11, no. 8 (February 1983): 13.
35. Galey, "The Nairobi Conference," 257.
36. "Fair Play for the Majority of American Jews—Women," *Jewish Journal* (FL) November 3, 1993, 26A; "Cracking the Glass Ceiling: New Philanthropy Trust Tackles Women's Role in Jewish Communal Life," The New York *Jewish Week*, October 6, 2000, 15.
37. "Women's Groups Laud Carter for UN Vote against Resolution," The New York *Jewish Week*, November 23, 1980, 17.
38. Marlene Provizer, interview with the author, June 7, 2013.
39. "Women Map UN Conference Strategy," The New York *Jewish Week*, June 14, 1985, 4.
40. Elenore Lester, "Seek to Counter Bias at Kenya Conference: Earlier Anti-Israel Attacks Are Deplored," The New York *Jewish Week*, June 14, 1985, 4.
41. "Preparation's Payoff: Anti-Zionism Muted, Feminism Advanced at Nairobi," The New York *Jewish Week*, August 2, 1985, 11.
42. For more on the New Jewish Agenda, see chapter 6.
43. Pogrebin, *Deborah, Golda, and Me*, 161.
44. Marlene Provizer, Oral History Library, American Jewish Committee: Irving M. Engel Collection on Civil Rights, New York Public Library, Dorot Jewish Division 18–19.
45. Provizer, interview with the author, June 7, 2013.
46. Carole Haddad to Reena Bernards, July 1, 1985, website of the New Jewish Agenda, http://newjewishagenda.net/?attachment_id=174. Emphasis in the original.
47. Quoted in Ezra Berkley Nepon, *Justice, Justice, Shall You Pursue: A History of New Jewish Agenda* (Oakland, CA: Thread Makes Blanket Press, 2012), 46.
48. "Israeli Delegates at U.N. Conference Call Apartheid Abhorrent," *Los Angeles Times*, July 20, 1985, http://articles.latimes.com/1985-07-20/news/mn-5876_1_news-conference. The following year, Naomi Chazan authored an article in *African Affairs* warning Israel of the widespread criticism of its ties to South Africa. She highlights the role of Vorster's visit to Israel in drawing "Israel and South Africa into a complex network of mutual collaboration." Chazan, "The Fallacies of Pragmatism," *African Affairs* 82, no. 327 (April 1983): 173. Sasha Polakow-Suransky writes about this article in *The Unspoken Alliance: Israel's Secret Relationship with Apartheid South Africa* (New York: Pantheon Books, 2010), 159–161.

49. "Israeli Delegates at U.N. Conference Call Apartheid Abhorrent," *Los Angeles Times*, July 20, 1985, http://articles.latimes.com/1985-07-20/news/mn-5876_1_news-conference.
50. Elaine Sciolino, "Disputes on Key Issues Stall Kenya Parley," *The New York Times*, July 26, 1985.
51. Zinsser, "From Mexico to Copenhagen to Nairobi," 164. On this moment, see also Galey, "The Nairobi Conference," 257.
52. New Jewish Agenda, press release, July 23, 1985, quoted in Nepon, *Justice, Justice*, 47.
53. Pogrebin, *Deborah, Golda, and Me*, 161.
54. Nadine Brozan, "Maureen Reagan Assesses Nairobi," *New York Times*, August 1, 1985.
55. Jain, *Women*, 87; Reilly, *Women's Human Rights*, 58.
56. British Delegate Mandana Hendessi reported that "right-wing Zionists" among the delegates "refused to recognize the existence of Palestinians," and their efforts "profoundly shaped the conference." For example: their agenda thwarted the attempts of "some socialist Jews," who tried to start a dialogue with Palestinian women. Mandana Hendessi, "Fourteen Thousand Women Meet: Report from Nairobi, July 1985,"*Feminist Review* 23 (Summer 1986): 149–150.
57. Quoted in Cantarow, "Zionism, Anti-Semitism, and Jewish Identity," 43.
58. Eleanor Roffman, interview with the author, May 31, 2013.
59. Quoted in "Historical Background," in the Jewish Women's Committee to End the Occupation of the West Bank and Gaza Records (CDG-A), Swarthmore College Peace Collection, http://www.swarthmore.edu/library/peace/CDGA.A-L/JewishWomensCommittee.htm.
60. See, for example, Pamela Nadell, "A Bright New Constellation: Feminism and American Judaism," in Marc Lee Raphael, ed., *The Columbia History of Jews and Judaism in America* (New York: Columbia University Press, 2008). Melissa Klapper analyzes Jewish women's contributions to the suffrage, peace, and birth control movements in *Ballots, Babies, and Banners of Peace*.
61. On Jewish women and radical feminism, see Joyce Antler, "'We Were Ready to Turn the World Upside Down': Radical Feminism and Jewish Women," in Hasia Diner, Shira Kohn, and Rachel Kranson, eds, *A Jewish Feminine Mystique: Jewish Women in Postwar America* (New Brunswick: Rutgers University Press, 2010). See also the women interviewed in Dina Pinsky, *Jewish Feminists: Complex Identities and Activist Lives* (Urbana, IL: University of Illinois Press, 2010), especially Chapter 3, "Encountering Difference: The Search for Belonging in the Women's Movement."
62. Sharon Kleinbaum, interview with the author, January 26, 2011.
63. Sharon Kleinbaum," in Philip Gambone, *Travels in a Gay Nation: Portraits of LGBTQ Americans* (Madison, WI: University of Wisconsin Press), 187, and interview with the author, January 26, 2011.
64. Rebecca Steinitz, "Liberation through Religion: A Conversation with Rabbi Sharon Kleinbaum," *Stories of Impact* (blog), Arcus Foundation, October 15, 2010, http://www.arcusfoundation.org/socialjustice/impact/stories_of_impact/liberation_through_religion_a_conversation_with_rabbi_sharon_kleinbaum/.
65. Kleinbaum, interview with the author, January 26, 2011.
66. Ibid.

67. Columbia and Barnard students founded the Committee after trying to block the appointment of former Secretary of State Henry Kissinger to an endowed chair at the University in 1977.
68. This sit-in led to Columbia's divestment from Stocks and Bonds directly associated with South Africa; Columbia did not fully divest until 1991. See "Student Sit-In At Columbia," *New York Post* May 2, 1978; "Demonstration at Columbia," *New York Daily News* May 2, 1978; Kleinbaum, email to the author, May 18, 2011; "275 Occupy Business School; 700 Rally for CU Divestiture; McGill to meet sit-in Leaders," *Columbia Daily Spectator* May 2, 1978. That issue of the *Spectator* was devoted almost entirely to the protest and its aftermath. Kleinbaum also led a meeting the following January at which about a hundred students discussed several pressing issues, including divestment. Ann Koshel, "Campus, Community Issues Aired at Informal Gripe Session in BHR," *Columbia Daily Spectator* January 31, 1979.
69. Although she was living personally as a lesbian, Kleinbaum felt that she could not come out in the antiapartheid movement, as it was "not very feminist," dominated by "lefty macho types." After college, her focus turned to feminist antimilitarism. For her Women's Pentagon Action protest in 1981, shortly after college, she spent a month in Alderson Federal Prison. Kleinbaum, email to the author, May 13, 2011.
70. Kleinbaum, interview with the author, June 5, 2013.
71. Kleinbaum, interview with the author, January 26, 2011.
72. "Sharon Kleinbaum," in Gambone, *Travels in a Gay Nation*, 192.
73. Kleinbaum, interview with the author, January 26, 2011.
74. Ruth W. Messinger Oral History, May 20, 2008, Indiana University-Purdue University Indianapolis, website of the IUPUI University Library Special Collections and Archives, http://hdl.handle.net/2450/5053; Ruth Messinger, interview with the author, January 6, 2011.
75. Messinger, interview with the author.
76. Nepon, *Justice, Justice*, 15.
77. American Committee on Africa, "Public Investment and South Africa Newsletter," Number 5 (May 1984), 4–5, website of the African Activist Archive, http://kora.matrix.msu.edu/files/50/304/32-130-CCA-84-al.sff.document.acoa000608.pdf.
78. "New York Labor Committee Against Apartheid: The Right to Notice and Negotiation, Supporting Labor in South Africa Through Sanctions Legislation," n.d. (1988), website of the African Activist Archive, http://kora.matrix.msu.edu/files/50/304/32-130-D-84-african_activist_archive-a0a0c2-a_12419.pdf.
79. The Board of Overseers is a 30-member governing body for Harvard second only to the seven-member Harvard Corporation in decision making powers for the University. Sara Frankel, "Alumni Urge Harvard to Divest," *Mother Jones*, May 1987, 12; Messinger, interview with the author.
80. Messinger, interview with the author.
81. Ibid.
82. Andrew Silow-Carroll, "Ruth Messinger: We're Okay; They're Not," *New Jersey Jewish News*, posted May 28, 2009, http://njjewishnews.com/justASC/2009/05/28/ruth-messinger-were-okay-theyre-not/.
83. Ruth Messinger, "My Faith Heroine: Helen Suzman," posted September 30, 2011, Tony Blair Faith Foundation, http://www.tonyblairfaithfoundation

.org/blogpost/my-faith-heroine-helen-suzman-ruth-messinger-0. See Helen Suzman, *In No Uncertain Terms: A South African Memoir* (New York: Knopf, 1993).
84. Ruth Messinger and Aaron Dorfman, "Toward a Jewish Argument for the Responsibility to Protect," in Richard H. Cooper and Juliette Voinov Kohler, *Responsibility to Protect: The Global Moral Compact for the 21st Century* (New York: Palgrave Macmillan, 2009), 61.
85. Messinger and Dorfman, "Toward a Jewish Argument," 67.
86. South African affiliated Jewish women, those whose organizational work fell under the umbrella of the SAJBD, demonstrated their critiques of apartheid through work that grew out of, and reinforced, conventional gender expectations, through social work in the Black community. The South African Reform Jewish Movement—known as the South African Union for Progressive Judaism (SAUPJ)—took the strongest stand of any of the Jewish movements against apartheid but remained vehemently anti-divestment through the end of apartheid; women in that movement embraced social work as a means of protest. The Moses Weiler School in Alexandra Township serves as a prime example of this activism. Funded and for generations led by Reform Jewish Sisterhood women, teachers there have educated thousands of Black South African children in the townships, even battling against the Bantu Education Acts of the early 1950s to retain control of the school's teachers' contracts and facilities. Interview with Delores Wilkenfeld, former president of National Federation of Temple Sisterhoods, March 28, 2011. On the SAUPJ, see chapter 6.
87. Scholars who placed women in the center of liberation movements for social change offer particularly instructive models for studying these women. See Cherryl Walker, *Women and Resistance in South Africa* (London: Onyx Press, 1982); Pamela E. Brooks, *Boycotts, Buses, and Passes: Black Women's Resistance in the U.S. South and South Africa* (Amherst, MA: University of Massachusetts Press, 2008); Temma Kaplan, *Crazy for Democracy: Women in Grassroots Movements* (New York: Routledge, 1996); Temma Kaplan, *Taking Back the Streets: Women, Youth, and Direct Democracy* (Berkeley, CA: University of California Press, 2004).
88. Glenn Frankel, *Rivonia's Children: Three Families and the Cost of Conscience in White South Africa* (New York: Continuum, 1999), 47. On the history of gender in early South Africa, see Cheryl Walker, ed., *Women and Gender in Southern Africa to 1945* (Cape Town: David Philip Publishers, 1990).
89. Ruth First wrote about her solitary confinement in *117 Days: An Account of Confinement and Interrogation Under the South African 90-Day Detention Law* (New York: Penguin, 2009) (first edition, 1965). For eloquent testimonies to First's activism, research, and writing, see Shula Marks, "Ruth First: A Tribute," *Journal of African Studies* 10, no. 1 (October 1983): 123–127; AnnMarie Wolpe, "Tribute to Ruth First," *Feminist Review* 13 (Spring 1983): 3–4.
90. Frankel, *Rivonia's Children*, 54.
91. Gideon Shimoni, *Community and Conscience: The Jews in Apartheid South Africa* (Hanover, NH: University Press of New England, 2003), 46–54.
92. In her autobiography, Alexander writes that she rejected the Balfour Declaration of 1917, which established the British commitment to creating a Jewish homeland in Palestine. Ray Alexander Simons, *All My Life and All My Strength*, ed. Immanuel Suttner (Johannesburg: STE publishers, 2004), 40.

93. Charles Villa-Vicencio, *The Spirit of Freedom: South African Leaders on Religion and Politics* (Berkeley, CA: University of California Press, 1996), 23, 26; Suttner, *Cutting through the Mountain*, 23–47. Ray Alexander later took her husband's last name of Simons. In her autobiography, written under her married name, Simons recounted how she wrote to a former love in Latvia that she was staying in South Africa: "although I was not in love with any other man, I was indeed 'in love' with the people here, the country and the struggle against race discrimination, which, I explained, is the same as anti-Semitism," (*All My Life*, 81).
94. Villa-Vicencio, *The Spirit of Freedom*, 31.
95. Suttner, *Cutting through the Mountain*, 44. In the introduction to Alexander's autobiography (edited by Suttner), Iris Berger writes that "Simons's commitment to the Communist Party of South Africa was intrinsically tied to her Eastern European Jewish heritage" ("Introduction" to Simons, *All My Life*, 7).
96. Shimoni, *Community and Conscience*, 86.
97. Ibid., 89, 86.
98. Ibid., 82, 83.
99. In a review of Shimoni's book, *Community and Conscience*, Claudia Braude writes that Shimoni "has made no historiographical break from, perpetuating instead, the defensive discourse of the apartheid years." Further, she asserts that "defending the SAJBD against criticism from Jews involved in liberalism, Shimoni underwrites the Jewishness of the leadership's political quiescence" [Claudia Braude, "Commissioning, Community, and Conscience," *Safundi* 10, no. 1 (January 2009): 83, 84].
100. Braude, "Commissioning"; Rhoda Rosen, "The Making of an East European Jewish Legacy in Contemporary South Africa," *Shofar* 25, no. 1 (Fall 2006): 83.
101. Sally Frankenthal writes that South Africa's cohesive, organized Jewish community had little tolerance for dissent: now, it is "undergoing a diaspora version of 'normalization,'" wrestling with its internal divisions. Sally Frankethal, "South African Jewish Women," *Jewish Women 2000: Conference Papers from the Hadassah Research Institute on Jewish Women*, Helen Epstein, ed., Working Paper 6 (November 1999): 74. It should be noted that Claudia Braude's scholarly conclusions have occasioned controversy, most recently in the case of the essay cited above in the journal *Safundi*. Braude called it a "*farribel*," the Yiddish word for a family quarrel, and the other articles in that issue of the journal speak to the political, ideological, and generational differences that ground the debates over/in South African Jewish history. See *Safundi* 10, no. 1 (January 2009): 77–98.
102. Scholar Gil Troy analyzes Jewish women's strong and painful responses to the "Zionism is racism" resolution at the UN Women's Conferences. He addresses the Jewish "reawakenings" of women like Pogrebin, and presents Jewish loyalty as the clear (and clearly urgent) choice over global women's activism in the United Nations. "Like Pogrebin, and Theodor Herzl, many discovered that anti-Semitism can make the Jew, but it is more satisfying for the Jew to make the Jew. Yet many feminists, Jewish and not, felt that solidarity with international women's conferences was more important to the movement than the fate of the Jews" (Gil Troy, "When Feminists Were Zionists," *Tablet Magazine*, March 8, 2013, http://www.tabletmag.com/jewish-arts-and-culture/books

/126348/when-feminists-were-zionists. Troy drew this material from his book, *Moynihan's Moment*).

6 NEW AGENDAS: THE ORGANIZATIONAL JEWISH RESPONSE TO APARTHEID

1. David Twersky, "The Soweto Wimpy," *The Jewish Frontier* 48 (August /September 1981): 35.
2. Gideon Shimoni, *Community and Conscience: The Jews in Apartheid South Africa* (Hanover, NH: University Press of New England, 2003), 152.
3. Kitty O. Cohen, "Black-Jewish Relations in 1984: A Survey of Black Congressmen," in *Strangers and Neighbors: Relations between Blacks and Jews in the United States*, ed. Maurianne Adams and John Bracey (Amherst, MA: University of Massachusetts Press, 1999), 689.
4. Cohen, "Black-Jewish Relations in 1984," 690.
5. Ibid., 698, 699.
6. Gal Beckerman, *When They Come for Us, We'll be Gone: The Epic Struggle to Save Soviet Jewry* (New York: Houghton Mifflin, 2010), 45.
7. Abraham Joshua Heschel, *Insecurity of Freedom: Essays on Human Existence* (New York: Farrar, Straus, and Giroux, 1966), 272. Hasia Diner writes of the use of images of the Holocaust to analogize Soviet Jewish experience. Hasia Diner, *We Remember with Reverence and Love: American Jews and the Myth of Silence after the Holocaust, 1945–1962* (New York: New York University Press, 2009), 278–286.
8. Martin Luther King, A. Philip Randolph, Bayard Rustin, and Whitney Young to Dr Morsell, March 29, 1967, Papers of the NAACP, Special Subject Files, 1966–1970, Series A: "Africa" through "Poor People's Campaign," Reel 15, Frame 391.
9. "MP to CVB," National Jewish Community Relations Advisory Council, 27 November 1984, National Jewish Community Relations Advisory Council Papers, Jewish Council for Public Affairs, New York City.
10. See Roberta Shiffman to Abe Schuchman, March 13, 1986 (with attached programs and documents of "Freedom Music"), Papers of the North American Jewish Students Appeal, Center for Jewish History, New York.
11. "UAHC Steps up Anti-apartheid Campaign," *Jewish Telegraphic Agency*, October 15, 1986, http://www.jta.org/1986/10/15/archive/uahc-steps-up-anti-apartheid-campaign#ixzz2ZsqW7uSZ. Rabbi David Saperstein, Director of the Reform Movement's Religious Action Center, was instrumental in this and other antiapartheid campaigns.
12. Michael Galchinsky writes that neoconservative activism on behalf of Soviet Jews did not grow out of United Nations human rights commitments because these activists thought the United Nations "had been degraded and made repulsive by its anti-Zionism." Michael Galchinsky, *Jews and Human Rights: Dancing at Three Weddings* (Lanham, MD: Rowan and Littlefield, 2008), 23. For more on the United Nations and Israel, see chapter 5.
13. President Adele Simmons to Mrs. Cora Weiss, March 20, 1979, Hampshire College Archives, Hampshire College Library Center, Amherst, MA.
14. Nicole M. Jackson offers a compelling analysis of the antiapartheid activism on the campuses of integrated as well as historically Black colleges and universities in the 1980s. Her chapter on Mills College, a women's HBCU,

offers evidence of the ways in which African American women students challenged the male-dominated nature of the antiapartheid movement with feminist analyses of apartheid, and with spotlights on Black and female South African leaders and cultural figures. [Remembering Soweto: American College Students and International Social Justice, 1976–1988, Masters' Thesis, Ohio State University, 2009].
15. Francis Njubi Nesbitt tells this story in "The Free South Africa Movement," Chapter 6 of *Race for Sanctions: African Americans against Apartheid, 1946–1994* (Bloomington, IN: Indiana University Press, 2004).
16. The 1959 film "Come Back, Africa," filmed secretly in South Africa by (American Jewish) filmmaker Lionel Rogosin, also contributed to Makeba's success. Her marriage to Black Panther and Student Nonviolent Coordinating Committee leader Stokely Carmichael caused great controversy, and they moved to Guinea in the late 1960s, not returning to tour the United States until 1987. See April Sizemore-Barber's fascinating discussion in "The Voice of (Which?) Africa: Miriam Makeba in America," *Safundi* 13, no. 3–4 (July–October 2012): 251–276; Miriam Makeba with James Hall, *Makeba: My Story* (New York: New American Library, 1987); Harry Belafonte writes about his relationship with Makeba and his own antiapartheid work in Belafonte with Michael Schnayerson, *Harry Belafonte: My Song, A Memoir* (New York: Alfred A. Knopf, 2011). On Afrikaans antiapartheid music, see Albert Grundlingh, "'Rocking the Boat' in South Africa? Voelvry Music and Afrikaans Anti-Apartheid Social Protest in the 1980s," *The International Journal of African Historical Studies* 37, no. 3 (2004): 483–514.
17. Neal Ullestad, "Diverse Rock Rebellions Subvert Mass Media Hegemony," in Reebee Garofalo, ed., *Rockin' the Boat: Mass Music and Mass Movements* (Cambridge, MA: South End Press, 1992), 48–52. On the Mandela tribute concerts, see Garofalo, "Nelson Mandela, The Concerts: Mass Culture as Contested Terrain," in Garofalo, ed., *Rockin' the Boat*; and Christopher Ballantine, "A Brief History of South African Popular Music," *Popular Music* 8, no. 3 (October 1989): 305. On the importance of South African music to the antiapartheid movement, see Shirli Gilbert, "Singing against Apartheid: ANC Cultural Groups and the International Anti-apartheid Struggle," *Journal of South African Studies* 33, no. 2 (June 2007): 421–441; Michael Drewett, "Music in the Struggle to End Apartheid: South Africa," in Martin Cloonan and Reebee Garofalo, *Policing Pop* (Philadelphia, PA: Temple University Press, 2003), 153–165; and Denis-Constant Martin, "Music beyond Apartheid?" translated by Val Morrison, in Garofalo, ed., *Rockin' the Boat*.
18. On the politics of Shantytowns, see "'Unsightly Huts': Shanties and the Divestment Movement," Chapter 3 in Bradford Martin, *The Other Eighties: A Secret History of America in the Age of Reagan* (New York: Hill and Wang, 2011).
19. Daniel Furman, "Hopkinsburg: Activism on Campus, the 80s vs. Now," *The Johns Hopkins News-Letter*, February 18, 2009, http://www.jhunewsletter.com/2009/02/18/hopkinsburg-activism-on-campus-the-80s-vs-now-53861/.
20. "Letters," *The Johns Hopkins News-Letter*, May 2, 1986, 11–12. Blood Libels were false claims that Jews used the blood of Christian children for religious rituals; these Libels were the basis of historic anti-Semitic persecution.

21. Chris Spolar, "3 Indicted in Hopkins Shanty Fire; Fraternity Members Accused of Arson," *Washington Post*, May 30, 1986.
22. See Jon Wiener, "Students, Stocks, and Shanties," *The Nation* 11 (October 1986): 337–340.
23. "Statement to the Press" (authored by Brandeis University students), April 12, 1978, Gordon Fellman Papers, 1949–2006, Brandeis University Archives, Waltham, MA.
24. See Anne Exter, "Senate Votes to Support April 5 Strike," *The Justice* (Brandeis University), March 27, 1979, Gordon Fellman Papers, 1949–2006, Brandeis University Archives, Waltham, MA.
25. "Brandeis University's Involvement in Corporations Doing Business in South Africa: The Students' Perspective," Report by the Brandeis University Student Senate, March 26, 1979, Gordon Fellman Papers, 1949–2006.
26. Keith W. Jenkins, Brandeis University Student Senate President to "Professors, Student leaders, the Brandeis Community," March 22, 1979, Gordon Fellman Papers, 1949–2006, Brandeis University Archive, Waltham, MA. Brandeis's radical student magazine, *The Watch*, often invoked Holocaust analogies with apartheid. See Danny Weinstraub, "Will We Never Forget?" *The Watch* 7, no. 1 (October 31, 1986): 3, Brandeis University Archives, Waltham, MA.
27. "Resolution," April 3, 1978, submitted by Rabbi Albert S. Axelrad. In his accompanying letter, Rabbi Axelrad asked the Executive Director of the Board of Rabbis to consider "the particular appropriateness of the history and ideals of Pesach [Jewish holiday of Passover] as they related to the plight of Blacks in South Africa." Rabbi Albert Axelrad to Rabbi Arnold Fine, April 6, 1978, Gordon Fellman Papers, 1949–2006, Brandeis University Archives, Waltham, MA.
28. Albert Vorspan and David Saperstein, *Tough Choices: Jewish Perspectives on Social Justice* (New York: UAHC Press, 1992), 149.
29. Rick Hess, "Republicans Protest Brandeis Investments," *The Justice* (Brandeis University), November 26, 1985, Brandeis University Archives, Waltham, MA.
30. Jeff Greenbaum, J. B. Kraz, and Carol Gerwin, "20 Arrested in Divestment Protest, Students Occupy Library, Trustees Delay Decision," *The Justice* (Brandeis University), December 9, 1986, 1.
31. Brandeis had a high percentage of Jewish students, estimated in those years at well above 50 percent. There are no estimates for the percentage of Jewish students in Brandeis's antiapartheid movement, but likely it mirrored the College at large. Gabi Aizenberg, "Jews First—Care For Your Own," letter, *The Justice* (Brandeis University), February 19, 1986.
32. Mark Altman, "Shantytown on Brandeis Campus Sharpens Call for Divestment," *The Jewish Advocate*, February 13, 1986.
33. Steve Kipnis, "Soviet Investment Protested," *The Justice* (Brandeis University) April 1, 1986, Brandeis University Archives, Waltham, MA.
34. Rabbi Albert S. Axelrad, "Israel and South African Apartheid: Toward a Proper Perspective," *The Watch* (Brandeis University), May 7 1986, 14–15. While awaiting a decision from the Board of Trustees about full divestment in February 1987, Rabbi Axelrad joined with Brandeis's two other chaplains in fasting as a sign of protest "Chaplains Speak on Fast," *The Justice* (Brandeis University), February 17, 1987.
35. "Dachau, Then and Now," *The Watch* (Brandeis University) 7, no. 3 (February 10, 1987), 18–19.

36. Marion S. Berman, "Anti-Semitism?" *The Watch* 7, no. 4 (March 1987): 3.
37. See chapter 7.
38. Rabbi Stanley A. Ringler, introduction to Yosef I. Abramowitz, *Jews, Zionism and South Africa* (Washington, DC: The Campus Program of B'nai B'rith International, 1985), 1, 2.
39. Abramowitz, *Jews, Zionism and South Africa*, 30.
40. Ibid., 33.
41. Ibid., 42.
42. Sasha Polakow-Suransky, *The Unspoken Alliance: Israel's Secret Relationship with Apartheid South Africa* (New York: Pantheon Books, 2010), 168.
43. "Shamir has 'No Plans for Move against South Africa,'" *Jerusalem Post*, September 29, 1985, quoted in Joel Peters, *Israel and Africa: The Problematic Friendship* (London: I.B. Tauris, 1992), 169.
44. Michael Staub analyzes the rise and demise of Breira in "If We Really Care about Israel: Breira and the Limits of Dissent," in Tony Kushner and Alisa Solomon, *Wrestling with Zion: Progressive Jewish-American Responses to the Israeli-Palestinian Conflict* (New York: Grove Press, 2003), 89–104.
45. New Jewish Agenda National Platform, adopted November 28, 1982, New York, in Ezra Berkley Nepon, *Justice, Justice, Shall You Pursue: A History of New Jewish Agenda* (Oakland, CA: Thread Makes Blanket Press, 2012), 113.
46. Daniel Rozsa Lang/Levitsky, "Hidden Agenda: Lessons from NJA, Lost and Learned," in Nepon, *Justice, Justice*, 101.
47. See the panel "The Present Generation: Issues on College Campuses," in *Carrying It on: A National Conference Organizing against Anti-Semitism and Racism for Jewish Activists and College Students*, New Jewish Agenda, November 9–10, 1991, Philadelphia, published by *Bridges* magazine, Seattle, WA, 1992.
48. Nepon, *Justice, Justice*, 24; Cameron Duodu, "Dennis Brutus Obituary," *The Guardian*, February 23, 2010, http://www.guardian.co.uk/world/2010/feb/23/dennis-brutus-obituary.
49. Allan Gale, Assistant Director, Jewish Community Council, to Diana Aviv, NJCRAC, January 29, 1987, National Jewish Community Relations Advisory Council Papers, Jewish Council for Public Affairs, New York City. Kathleen Hendrix, "Minister, Rabbi Join Hands in Battle against Apartheid," *Los Angeles Times*, March 19, 1987, http://articles.latimes.com/1987-03-19/news/vw-13873_1_south-africa.
50. At New Jewish Agenda's final National Conference in 1991, speakers from all backgrounds engaged in dialogue about how best to organize against anti-Semitism and racism. Representatives from the Latino, Asian American, Native American, Arab American, and African American communities were active in these dialogues. In his talk "Growing up in South Africa: The Holocaust, Jewish Identity, and the Struggle against Oppression," Richard Weiner spoke of his encounters with South African Zionism and anti-Semitism, with American homophobia and Israeli oppression of Palestinians. His eloquent narrative concludes with homage to NJA, which he considered central to his work against oppression as a progressive Jew [*Carrying It on: A National Conference Organizing against Anti-Semitism and Racism for Jewish Activists and College Students*, New Jewish Agenda, November 9–10, 1991, Philadelphia (published by *Bridges* magazine, Seattle, WA, 1992)].

51. "Statement of the Jewish Labor Committee, the A. Philip Randolph Institute, and the Negro Trade Union Leadership Council on Amendments to the Expert Administration Act Introduced by Congressman William Gray, III," August 2, 1983, Jewish Labor Committee Papers, Series 3, Box 165, Folder 38, Tamiment Library, New York University.
52. Martin Lapan, Executive Director, Jewish Labor Committee, letter to Community Relations Councils, Jewish Federations and Welfare Funds, June 13, 1985, Jewish Labor Committee Papers, Series 3, Box 165, Folder 39, Tamiment Library, New York University.
53. Herb Magidson, email to the author, April 22, 2011.
54. "Presentation to the NJCRAC 1985 Plenum by Herb Magidson, President, Jewish Labor Committee, February 18, 1985, San Francisco, California, " in Jewish Labor Committee Papers, Series 3, Box 165 Folder 39, Tamiment Library, New York University; Herb Magidson, email to the author, April 22, 2011.
55. Gerald M. Boyd, "Jews Back Blacks in Racism Protest," *New York Times*, December 11, 1984, http://www.nytimes.com/1984/12/11/us/jews-back-blacks-in-racism-protest.html.
56. "Chanukah Rally Hits Apartheid," *Jewish Exponent* December 28, 1984, clipping in Jewish Labor Committee File, Series 3, Box 165, Folder 38, Tamiment Library, New York University; Nepon, *Justice, Justice*, 40.
57. Quoted in Peter Perl, "Jewish Groups Demonstrate at Embassy," December 26, 1984, *The Washington Post*, clipping in the New Jewish Agenda Papers, Southern California Library for Social Studies and Research, Los Angeles.
58. Marlene Provizer, interview with the author, June 7, 2013. Provizer later earned praise for her work building bridges between Jewish and African American communities as executive director of the Jewish Fund for Justice. "One Success Story: The Jewish Fund for Justice is a model for social action between blacks and Jews," *Baltimore Jewish Times* 208, no. 8 (December 25, 1992): 41.
59. Marlene R. Provizer, Oral History Library, American Jewish Committee: Irving M. Engel Collection on Civil Rights, New York Public Library, Dorot Jewish Division, 14.
60. These are documented in a memo of the National Jewish Community Relations Advisory Council entitled "NJCRAC Member Agency Activity on Apartheid," authored by Marlene Provizer, Assistant Director, and sent to their Member Agencies on October 31, 1985. Papers of the Religious Action Committee, American Jewish Archive, Cincinnati, Ohio.
61. Dr Rita Kaunitz and Rabbi David Saperstein published this guide on February 26, 1987, through the Commission on Social Action of the Central Conference of American Rabbis and the UAHC, Reform Action Committee of the Union of American Hebrew Congregations Files, American Jewish Archive, Cincinnati, OH.
62. Gerald Kraft, Presentation, and Gerald Uzi Narkis, Chairman, Information Department, World Zionist Organization, Presentation, in *Zionism is Racism: An Assault on Human Rights, a Report and Program Guide*, a conference sponsored by B'nai B'rith International, World Jewish Congress, World Zionist Organization, Hosted by the U.S. Department of State, December 10, 1985 (B'nai B'rith International: Washington, DC, 1985) n.p.
63. Professor Arthur Hertzberg, Vice President, World Jewish Congress, Presentation, in *Zionism is Racism: An Assault on Human Rights*.

64. Edwin Black, "The Cutting Edge," *The Jewish Press* (Omaha, NE), 63, no. 21 (February 7, 1986): 5.
65. Quoted in "Between Black and White: The Jews of South Africa," *Israel Horizons* 34 no. 5/6 (May/June 1986): 10–11.
66. Katya Gibel Azoulay, "Jews, Israel, and South Africa," *Israel Horizons* 34 no. 5/6 (May/June 1986): 12–14.
67. Arieh Lebowitz, Americans for Progressive Israel, to Cleveland Robinson, Chair, New York Anti-Apartheid Coordinating Council, c/o District 65 UAW-AFL-CIO, June 5, 1986, Cleveland Robinson Papers, Tamiment Library, New York University.
68. Diana Aviv to Al Chernin, NJCRAC, August 14, 1987, National Jewish Community Relations Advisory Council Papers, Jewish Council for Public Affairs, New York City.
69. Delores Wilkenfeld, interview with the author, March 28, 2011.
70. Lionel Conyer, Chairman, South African Union for Progressive Judaism, to Madam President, National Federation of Temple Sisterhoods, November 21, 1985, Special Collections, David Belin/Jewish Outreach Papers, Box 14, University of Michigan, Harlan Hatcher Graduate Library.
71. Jane Perlez, "Hebrew Union Issues Degrees," *The New York Times*, June 2, 1986. Helen Suzman writes about her opposition to sanctions in her Chapter 14, "Sanctions—Pressure from Without," *In No Uncertain Terms: A South African Memoir* (New York: Alfred A. Knopf, 1993).
72. Lionel Conyer, Chairman, South African Union for Progressive Judaism, to Madam President, National Federation of Temple Sisterhoods, November 21, 1985, Special Collections, David Belin/Jewish Outreach Papers, Box 14, University of Michigan, Harlan Hatcher Graduate Library.
73. R. Feinstein, "South African Jews Angered at Anti-apartheid position," *Jewish World*, January 20–26, 1989, in Reform Action Committee Papers, American Jewish Archives, Cincinatti, OH.
74. Diana Aviv to NJCRAC Ad Hoc Committee on Apartheid, "Report on Mission to South Africa, August 18–September 1, 1988," September 29, 1988, National Jewish Community Relations Advisory Council papers, Jewish Council for Public Affairs, New York City, 2.
75. Ibid., 12.
76. Diana Aviv, interview with the author, July 16, 2009.
77. Rabbi Brian Walt, interview with the author, May 30, 2013.
78. Albert Vorspan and David Saperstein, *Tough Choices: Jewish Perspectives on Social Justice* (New York: United American Hebrew Congregations Press, 1992), 149.
79. "Abolish Apartheid," Editorial, *Israel Horizons*, 33, no. 7/8 (September/October 1985): 4, 31.
80. Michael Staub writes that Isaac's goal in attacking Breira was "to destabilize the left-center, secular-religious, Zionist-non-Zionist coalition that Breira had sought to build. And the strategy worked." Staub also traces Isaac's conservative associations, including an affiliation with Gush Emmunim. Staub, *Torn at the Roots: The Crisis of Jewish Liberalism in Postwar America* (New York: Columbia, 2002), 303, 361 n66.
81. Rael Jean Isaac, *The Anti-New Jewish Agenda* (New York: Americans for a Safe Israel, 1987), 1–2; "New Jewish Agenda Can't Hide Its Extremism," *Jewish Advocate* (Boston) December 10, 1992.

82. Isaac, *Anti-New Jewish Agenda*, 4. Susan Glenn examines the "historicity" of Jewish "self- hatred" in "The Vogue of Jewish Self-Hatred in Post-World War II America," *Jewish Social Studies*. n.s. 12 (Spring/Summer 2006), 95–136.
83. Isaac, *Anti-New Jewish Agenda*, 17.
84. Ibid., 14, 3.
85. Ibid., 15.
86. Comment, Mimi Alperin, *American Jewish Committee Journal*, Autumn 1987, 12.
87. Ibid.
88. Howard Taylor, Jr and John Flinn, "Tutu Blasts Western Powers for Toleration of Apartheid," *San Francisco Examiner*, January 22, 1986, in "Apartheid" Files of Jewish Council for Public Affairs, New York City.
89. Black, "The Cutting Edge."
90. "Tutu Praises Contribution of Some South African Jews to Anti-apartheid Struggle but Condemns Israeli," *Jewish Telegraphic Agency*, March 11, 1987, http://www.jta.org/1987/03/11/archive/tutu-praises-contribution-of-some-south-african-jews-to-anti-apartheid-struggle-but-condemns-israeli.
91. Black, "The Cutting Edge"; "Don't Tout Tutu," Letter to the editor, *Reform Judaism* 18, no. 4 (Summer 1990): 5; "Tutu Says He and Elie Wiesel Can 'mediate' Mideast Peace," *Jewish Telegraphic Agency*, February 1, 1989, http://www.jta.org/1989/02/01/archive/tutu-says-he-and-elie-wiesel-can-mediate-mideast-peace.
92. "Tutu Praises Contribution of Some South African Jews to Anti-apartheid Struggle but Condemns Israeli," *Jewish Telegraphic Agency*, March 11, 1987.
93. "Tutu Says He and Elie Wiesel Can 'mediate' Mideast Peace," *Jewish Telegraphic Agency*, February 1, 1989. On the boycott debate, see chapter 7.
94. "Introduction" to Edward Alexander, *With Friends like These: The Jewish Critics of Israel* (Shapolsky Publishers: New York, 1993), 3.
95. See Nepon, *Justice, Justice*.
96. In 1992, several progressive Jewish groups protested the lack of tolerance for dissent in American Jewish mainstream organizations. See "Peace groups unite, say they'll be 'silenced no more,'" *Northern California Jewish Bulletin* (San Francisco), April 24, 1992; "Focus on Jews and Israel: Jewish Peace Groups Unite behind 'Project Speak Out,'" *The Washington Report on Middle East Affairs* 9 (May 31, 1992): 59.

7 "Our South Africa Moment": American Jews' Struggles with Apartheid, Zionism, and Divestment

1. In 2013, American aid to Israel was estimated at about $3 billion per year annually since 1948, with exceptions for years when Israel was at war. This estimate excludes loan guarantees and the transfer of surplus military equipment to Israel, but does include aid designed to help Israel buy military equipment from American companies. Ora Coren and Nadan Feldman, "U.S. Aid to Israel Totals $233.7b Over Six Decades," *Haaretz*, March 20, 2013, http://www.haaretz.com/business/u-s-aid-to-israel-totals-233-7b-over-six-decades.premium-1.510592.
2. In this chapter I formally end my usage of quotation marks around the word "apartheid" when it follows "Israeli." This study chronicles the adoption of the

word in describing Israel's policies, and my dropping this usage is indicative of this widespread adoption in Human Rights and other conversations.
3. Carolyn Skorneck, "American Jewish Delegation Meets with Arafat in Tunis," *Gainesville Sun*, June 14, 1987.
4. Robert Weiss, "Jewish Unit Hears Arafat Call for Joint Talks," *Los Angeles Times*, July 12, 1987, http://articles.latimes.com/1987-07-12/local/me-3625 _1_liberal-jewish.
5. Herbert Wander, Co-Chair, Ad Hoc Committee on Apartheid, and Diana Aviv, Assistant Director, Memorandum to NJCRAC and CJF Member Agencies, July 31, 1990, Religious Action Committee Papers, American Jewish Archives, Cincinnati, Ohio.
6. High levels of emigration cut across all racial groups in South Africa, especially among those with advanced degrees.
7. "Introduction" in Immanuel Suttner, *Cutting Through the Mountain: Interviews with South African Jewish Activists* (New York: Penguin Group, 1997), 3.
8. Suttner, "Introduction," *Cutting through the Mountain*, 3.
9. Significantly, it was precisely this desire to claim whiteness that led organized South African Jewry to remain silent on the issue of apartheid for so long.
10. One article published by the Jewish Telegraph Agency in the run up to the 1994 South African elections captures these controversies. Ronnie Kasrils was a South African antiapartheid activist who joined the ANC after being radicalized by the Sharpeville massacre in 1960. An ANC parliamentary candidate in the election, he berated South African Jews for "not moving with the times." "The Jews here are totally self-involved and narrow and don't appreciate the aspirations of all the people of South Africa," he said. Lester Fuchs, a Jewish candidate for the liberal Democratic Party, spoke instead of the South African Jewish community's role in "making South Africa a peaceful and democratic country." He referenced Jewish contributions to the antiapartheid movement: "Jews can, as in the past, play a role out of all proportion to their numbers," he said. "Behind the Headlines: South African Jews Are Nervous but Hopeful as Elections Approach," *Jewish Telegraphic Agency*, March 22, 1994, http://www.jta.org/1994/03/22/archive/behind-the-headlines-south-african-jews-are-nervous-but-hopeful-as-elections-approach.
11. Herbert Wander, Co-Chair, Ad Hoc Committee on Apartheid, and Diana Aviv, Assistant Director, Memorandum to NJCRAC and CJF Member Agencies, July 31, 1990, Religious Action Committee Papers, American Jewish Archives, Cincinnati, Ohio, 7.
12. Letter to the Editor, *New York Times*, June 24, 1990. Sasha Polakow-Suransky tells this story in Polakow-Suransky, *The Unspoken Alliance: Israel's Secret Relationship with Apartheid South Africa* (New York: Pantheon Books, 2010), 212–213; Harry Belafonte writes of his work in arranging Mandela's US itinerary and also this meeting in Belafonte with Michael Schnayerson, *Harry Belafonte: My Song, A Memoir* (New York: Alfred A. Knopf, 2011), 394–400.
13. Meseeu, "Seeing Eye: AMANDLA!" *Michigan Citizen*, July 12, 1990.
14. James H. Meriwether, *Proudly We Can Be Africans: Black Americans and Africa, 1935–1961* (Chapel Hill, NC: University of North Carolina Press, 2001), 244.
15. Herb Magidson, email to the author, February 19, 2011. Richard Kahlenberg writes of the meeting of Mandela with Albert Shanker and other members of

the AFL–CIO Executive Committee in 1990 in Kahlenberg, *Tough Liberal: Albert Shanker and the Battles Over Schools, Unions, Race, and Democracy* (New York: Columbia University Press, 2007), 261.
16. Andrea Barron, "Jews and Israel," *The Washington Report on Middle East Affairs* 4 (September 30, 1990): 60.
17. Edwin Ali, "A Storm in a Teapot," *Caribbean Today* (Miami) 1, no. 8 (July 31, 1990): 8.
18. Albert Vorspan, Director, Commission on Social Action of Reform Judaism, to Nelson Mandela, March 1, 1990, Reform Action Committee Papers, American Jewish Archives, Cincinnati, OH.
19. Myer Kripke, *The Jewish Press* (Omaha), 47, no. 41 (July 6, 1990): 6.
20. Cecil Epril, "An Open Letter to Nelson Mandela," letter to the editor, *Reform Judaism* 18, no. 4 (Summer 1990): 4–5.
21. Joshua Muravchik, "Mandela in America," *Commentary* 90, no. 4 (October 1990): 11–18.
22. Cornel West, "Why I Write for *Tikkun*," *Tikkun* 5 (September/October 1990): 59–60.
23. Alisa Solomon, "Don't Test Mandela on Israel," *New York Times*, June 8, 1990. With Tony Kushner, Alisa Solomon is the coeditor of *Wrestling with Zion: Progressive Jewish-American Responses to the Israeli-Palestinian Conflict* (New York: Grove Press, 2003).
24. This was prior to Mandela's meeting Jewish leaders in Geneva.
25. Alisa Solomon, email to the author, March 22, 2011.
26. In her important examination of the racial arrangements and politics of the twenty-first-century United States, *The Color of Jews*, Melanie Kaye/Kantrowitz, the first director of Jews for Racial and Economic Justice (JFREJ), writes of the organization's first meeting. See "Apartheid/American Style," in chapter 1, "Are Jews White?" in Kaye/Kantrowitz, *The Colors of Jews: Racial Politics and Radical Diasporism* (Bloomington, IN: University of Indiana Press, 2007), 19.
27. Henry Schwarzchild's Remarks at the Welcome Service held by JFREJ and Congregation B'nai Jeshrun, New York, June 15, 1990, in *Mensches in the Trenches*, Jews for Racial and Economic Justice, Tenth Anniversary Booklet, December 10, 2000, emailed to the author by Alisa Solomon.
28. Daniel Rozsa Lang/Levitsky notes the "clear, consistent politics of anti-racism and anti-colonialism of [JFREJ's] founding moment." Lang/Levitsky, "Hidden Agenda: Lessons from NJA, Lost and Learned," in Ezra Berkley Nepon, *Justice, Justice, Shall You Pursue: A History of New Jewish Agenda* (Oakland, CA: Thread Makes Blanket Press, 2012), 103.
29. Kaye/Kantrowitz, *The Colors of Jews*, 19.
30. It should be noted that JFREJ did once issue a statement against the Occupation. Alisa Solomon, email to the author, March 22, 2011.
31. Samuel Freedman, "Back with a vengeance—divestment," *Washington Jewish Week*, March 26, 2009, 16.
32. Peggy Maisel, "Lessons from the World Conference against Racism: South Africa as a Case Study," *Oregon Law Review* 81 (2002): 739–770.
33. Gil Troy, *Moynihan's Moment: America's Fight against Zionism as Racism* (New York: Oxford University Press, 2013), 257, 259, 260.
34. Jane Perlez, "Powell Will Not Attend Racism Conference in South Africa," *New York Times*, August 28, 2001.

35. "Jews, Blacks, Seek Common Agenda for Anti-racism Conference in Durban," *Jewish Telegraphic Agency*, August 15, 2001, http://www.jta.org/2001/08/15/archive/jews-blacks-seek-common-agenda-for-anti-racism-conference-in-durban. On the history of the reparations movement, see Michael T. Martin and Marilyn Yaquinto, "Reparations for America's 'Holocaust': Activism for Global Justice," *Race and Class* 45, no. 4 (2004): 1–25.
36. Naomi Klein, "Minority Death Match: Jews, Blacks, and the 'Post-Racial' Presidency," *Harper's Magazine* (September 2009):54.
37. "At Risk of Early Derailment; The UN, Israel and Racism," *The Economist* (November 29, 2008):60. See also Samir Amin, "World Conference on Racism: Asking the Real Questions," *Economic and Political Weekly*, 36, no. 49 (December 8–14, 2001): 4523–4524; Ian Williams, "South Africa's Apartheid Experience Informs Israel-Palestine Discussion at Durban Racism Conference," *The Washington Report on Middle Eastern Affairs* (November 2001):27–28; Jonny Sinaga, "Durban: Admission Unreserved," *UN Chronicle* 38, no.2 (June–August 2001): 56.
38. Klein, "Minority Death Match," 57.
39. Ibid., 60.
40. Ruth Wedgwood, "Zionism and Racism, Again: Durban II," *World Affairs* (Spring 2009):87.
41. Ibid., 88.
42. Rabbi Abraham Cooper, letter to the editor, *New York Times* June 3, 2002.
43. The December 12th Movement International Secretariat is an NGO with consultative status at the United Nations that has participated in the Commission on Human Rights since 1989. Its members are critical of the impact of colonialism and capitalism on African peoples, and have led the fight for reparations for US slavery. See Delores Cox, "Black Delegation Attends Geneva Conference to Fight for Reparations," *Workers World* (Harlem, New York City), April 23, 2009, http://www.workers.org/2009/world/geneva_0430/.
44. Activists and scholars have begun using the term "global apartheid," defined as "an international system of minority rule whose attributes include: differential access to basic human rights; wealth and power structured by race and place; structural racism, embedded in global economic processes, political institutions and cultural assumptions; and the international practice of double standards that assume inferior rights to be appropriate for certain 'others,' defined by location, origin, race or gender," Salih Booker and William Minter, "Global Apartheid," *The Nation*, July 9, 2001, 11. Booker was Executive Director and Minter is a Senior Research Fellow at Africa Action, the US-based Africa advocacy group that incorporated the American Committee on Africa, among other organizations. See also Leith Mullings, ed., *New Social Movements in the African Diaspora: Challenging Global Apartheid* (New York: Palgrave Macmillan, 2009).
45. Naomi Klein, "Minority Death Match," 54.
46. Amin, "World Conference on Racism," 4523–4524.
47. Ibid., 4524.
48. Samuel Freedman, "Back with a Vengeance–Divestment," *Washington Jewish Week*, March 26, 2009, 16.
49. On Israel's ties to the Bantustans, see Jane Hunter, "Israel and the Bantustans," *Journal of Palestine Studies*, 15 no. 3 (Spring 1986): 53–89.
50. Akiva Eldar, "People and Politics/Sharon's Bantustans Are Far from Copenhagen's Hope," *Haaretz*, May 13, 2003, http://www.haaretz.com

/print-edition/features/people-and-politics-sharon-s-bantustans-are-far-from-copenhagen-s-hope-1.10275, and quoted in Peter Beinart, *The Crisis of Zionism* (New York: Henry Holt and Company, 2012), 73.
51. See, for example, Natasha Mozgovaya, "Jewish Republicans Slam Obama for Unclear Durban II Stance," *Haaretz*, April 16, 2009, http://www.haaretz.com/news/jewish-republicans-slam-obama-for-unclear-durban-ii-stance-1.274190.
52. Imani Countess and President Obama quoted in Zenitha Prince, "U.S. Boycotts UN Racism Conference," *New Pittsburgh Courier*, 100, no. 17 (April 29–May 5, 2009): A8
53. Resolution on Durban II, 13th Plenary Assembly of the World Jewish Congress, Jerusalem, January 26–27, 2009, http://www.worldjewishcongress.org/Features/durban2.html#. Emphasis in the original.
54. "UN Rights Chief Shocked by U.S. Boycott of Anti-racism Conference," Xinhua News Agency, April 20, 2009, http://news.xinhuanet.com/english/2009-04/20/content_11217644.htm; Navi Pillay, "UN Must Act on Racism," *The Guardian*, April 20, 2009, http://www.theguardian.com/commentisfree/2009/apr/20/un-conference-racism-durban.
55. Vernellia R. Randall, "U.S. Fails to Fight against Global Racism," *Michigan Citizen*, 31, no. 15 (February 22–28, 2009): A6.
56. Kali Akuno, "Obama and the Durban Review Conference," *New York Beacon* 16, no. 14 (April 9–15, 2009): 22.
57. Abe Selig, "Jewish Groups Ready to 'Fight the Good Fight' in Geneva," *Jerusalem Post*, April 16, 2009, http://www.jpost.com/International/Jewish-groups-ready-to-fight-the-good-fight-in-Geneva.
58. The groups included: Anti-Defamation League; Australia/Israel and Jewish Affairs Council; B'nai B'rith International; CEJI: A Jewish Contribution to an Inclusive Europe; Conference of Presidents of Major American Jewish Organizations; European Jewish Congress; European Union of Jewish Students; Jewish Human Rights Coalition (UK); NGO Monitor; Simon Wiesenthal Center; South African Jewish Board of Deputies; Women's International Zionist Organization; World Jewish Congress; and World Union of Jewish Students. Associated Press, "UN Human Rights Chief: Jewish, Muslim Lobbying May Undermine 'Durban II,'" *Haaretz*, April 2, 2009, http://www.haaretz.com/news/un-human-rights-chief-jewish-muslim-lobbying-may-undermine-durban-ii-1.273400.
59. Representative Barbara Lee of California in a statement by the Congressional Black Caucus, quoted in Neil MacFarquhar, "Iranian Calls Israel Racist at Meeting in Geneva," *New York Times*, April 21, 2009.
60. Website of the Palestinian BDS National Committee (BNC), accessed June 16, 2013, http://www.bdsmovement.net/; Naomi Klein, "Israel: Boycott, Divest, Sanction," *The Nation*, January 26, 2009, posted online January 7, 2009, http://www.thenation.com/article/israel-boycott-divest-sanction#axzz2btLTqiAu.
61. Website of the Palestinian BDS National Committee (BNC), accessed August 10, 2013, http://www.bdsmovement.net/bnc.
62. Eleanor Roffman, interview with the author, May 31, 2013.
63. Importantly, some liberal and left Jews in the United States—among them Peter Weiss—support the two-state solution as "the only feasible way to end the Occupation and the indignities which it inflicts on the Palestinian people" (email to the author, August 17, 2013).
64. Freedman, "Back with a Vengeance—Divestment," 16.

65. Jacob Berkman, "Federations, JCPA Teaming to Fight Delegitimization of Israel," *Jewish Telegraphic Agency*, October 24, 2010, http://www.jta.org/news/article/2010/10/24/2741418/jfna-and-jcpa-create-6-million-network-to-fight-delegitimization-of-israel.
66. See website of the BDS Cookbook, http://www.stopbds.com/?page_id=1093. There are also pro-divestment materials online, though with far fewer resources behind their production. For a tracing of the history of threats to Israel leading to the BDS movement, see Aaron Jacob, "The Campaign against Israel's Legitimacy: Answers to Israel's Critics," American Jewish Committee Office of Government and International Affairs, October 2010, accessed at website of the Israel on Campus Coalition, http://israelcc.org/docs/countering-bds-documents/the-campaign-against-israel%27s-legitimacy_ajc.pdf.
67. Shirin Ebadi, Mairead Maguire, Rigoberta Menchu Tum, and Jody Williams. Dina Omar, "At Berkeley, Moral Victory despite Divestment Vote Loss," May 3, 2010, website of the Electronic Intifada, http://electronicintifada.net/content/berkeley-moral-victory-despite-divestment-vote-loss/8809.
68. Jonathan Nathan-Kazis, "How to Beat Back Israeli Divestment Bill: Get Organized," *Jewish Daily Forward*, April 21, 2010, http://forward.com/articles/127439/how-to-beat-back-israel-divestment-bill-get-organ/; Dina Omar, "At Berkeley, Moral Victory."
69. Kirk Semple and Gersh Kuntzman, "Food Co-Op Rejects Effort to Boycott Israeli-Made Products," *The New York Times*, March 27, 2012, http://www.nytimes.com/2012/03/28/nyregion/park-slope-food-co-op-to-decide-on-boycott-vote.html.
70. Kiera Feldman, "BDS and the Park Slope Food Coop: Why the Vote against Was a Win for the Boycott," *The Nation*, March 29, 2012, http://www.thenation.com/article/167118/bds-and-park-slope-food-coop-why-vote-against-was-win-boycott#ixzz2YqemMnc2.
71. Semple and Kuntzman, "Food Co-Op Rejects Effort."
72. Beinart, *The Crisis of Zionism*, 190–191, 194.
73. Alana Goodman, "With Friends like These: Jewish Federation's 'Anti-Boycott' Group Says Israel Boycotts Are Acceptable," *Commentary*, March 17, 2011, http://www.commentarymagazine.com/2011/03/17/with-friends-like-these-jewish-federation%E2%80%99s-%E2%80%98anti-boycott%E2%80%99-group-says-israel-boycotts-are-acceptable/.
74. Polakow-Suransky, *Unspoken Alliance*, 235. Polakow-Suransky's epilogue offers a thoughtful and comprehensive analysis of the analogy of South African apartheid in Israel/Palestine.
75. Glen Lewy (National Chairman) and Abraham Foxman (National Director) "An Open Letter to Jimmy Carter," Anti-Defamation League, December 20, 2006, http://www.adl.org/PresRele/IslME_62/4947_62.htm.
76. Julie Bosman, "Carter Book Stirs Furor with Its Views of Israelis' 'Apartheid,'" *New York Times*, December 14, 2006, http://www.nytimes.com/2006/12/14/books/14cart.html.
77. Paul Jankowski, "Jimmy Carter, Palestinian Art, and Brandeis," *Academe* 93, no. 5 (September–October 2007): 40–42, http://www.jstor.org/stable/40253553; Pam Belluck, "At Brandeis, Carter Responds to Critics," *New York Times*, January 24, 2007; Michael Powell, "Jimmy Carter's 'Peace' Mission to Brandeis," *The Washington Post*, January 24, 2007; Michael Grillo, "Carter to Speak," *The Justice* (Brandeis University), January 16, 2007.

78. Powell, "Jimmy Carter's 'Peace Mission.'"
79. Rachel Marder, "Carter Defends Book," *The Justice* (Brandeis University), January 20, 2007.
80. Jonathan Demme, dir., *Jimmy Carter: Man from Plains*, Sony Pictures Classic, 2007, DVD.
81. Transcript, Alan Dershowitz, "I am Pro-Palestine…I am Pro-Israel," *The Justice* (Brandeis University), January 30, 2007.
82. Belluck, "At Brandeis." Alan Dershowitz presents "The Case against Jimmy Carter" as an essay in *The Case against Israel's Enemies: Exposing Jimmy Carter and Others Who Stand in the Way of Peace*, Alan Dershowitz, ed.(Hoboken, NJ: John Wiley and Sons, 2008).
83. Lital Shair, "Donations Not Stalled Even with Carter Visit," *The Justice* (Brandeis University), March 13, 2007.
84. Rachel Marder and Lital Shair, "Carter Departs, Issues Remain," *The Justice* (Brandeis University), February 6, 2007.
85. Peter Schworm, "Brandeis Groups Clash on Israel Stance," *The Boston Globe*, March 11, 2011, http://www.boston.com/news/local/massachusetts/articles/2011/03/11/brandeis_groups_clash_over_stance_on_israel/.
86. Ain Stewart, "Consensus Seen Taking Shape on Boycotts," The New York *Jewish Week*,March 15, 2011, http://www.thejewishweek.com/news/new_york/consensus_seen_taking_shape_boycotts.
87. Stewart, "Consensus Seen Taking Shape."
88. Philip Weiss, Brandeis Hillel imposes pro-Israel litmus test, excluding 'Jewish Voice for Peace' chapter, March 9, 2011, http://mondoweiss.net/2011/03/brandeis-hillel-imposes-pro-israel-litmus-test-excluding-jewish-voice-for-peace-chapter.html.
89. Ariel Wittenberg, "Israel Advocates, Critics Duel at Brandeis," *Jewish Advocate* (Boston, MA) 201, no. 46 (November 12, 2010): 4.
90. Naomi Zeveloff, "Israel Apartheid Week Comes to Brandeis," *The Forward*, March 1, 2012, http://forward.com/articles/152248/israel-apartheid-week-comes-to-brandeis/.
91. Fiona Lockyer, "Abunimah Speaks at Israel Apartheid Week," *The Justice* (Brandeis University) March 5, 2012, http://www.thejustice.org/news/abunimah-speaks-at-israel-apartheid-week-1.2809407#.UgOkB9LVCSo.
92. Zeveloff, "Israel Apartheid Week Comes to Brandeis."
93. Stephen Kuperberg, "Engaging with Israel on Campus Starts with Relationships," *Jewish News of Greater Phoenix*, 62, no. 39 (June 18, 2010): 9.
94. Bernard Macy, Brandeis '78, letter to the editor, "Reexamine Israel Apartheid Week," *The Justice* (Brandeis University), March 26, 2012, http://www.thejustice.org/forum/reader-commentary-1.2828702#.UgOZX9LVCSo.
95. Yair Rosenberg, "Brandeis Withdraws from American Studies Association: Becomes Second University to Do So after ASA's Israel Boycott," *Tablet*, December 18, 2013, http://www.tabletmag.com/scroll/156687/brandeis-withdraws-from-american-studies-association.
96. In *The Nation*, Adam Horowitz and Philip Weiss write about American Jewish leaders' responses to the Gaza war. Horowitz and Weiss, "American Jews Rethink Israel," October 14, 2009, http://www.thenation.com/article/american-jews-rethink-israel#axzz2WrZ3SWaP.
97. "Dershowitz: Goldstone is a Traitor to the Jewish People," *Haaretz*, January 31, 2010, http://www.haaretz.com/news/dershowitz-goldstone-is-a-traitor-to-the-jewish-people-1.265833.

98. Gerald M. Steinberg, "The Goldstone Myth," book review of Adam Horowitz, Lizzy Ratner, Philip Weiss, eds, *The Goldstone Report* (New York: Nation Books, 2011), posted March 29, 2011, Scholars for Peace in the Middle East, http://spme.org/spme-research/book-reviews/book-review-by-gerald-m-steinberg-philip-weiss-adam-horowitz-and-lizzy-ratner-eds-the-goldstone-report/9622/.
99. Letty Cottin Pogrebin, "The Un-Jewish Assault on Richard Goldstone," Opinion, *The Jewish Daily Forward*, December 29, 2011, http://forward.com/articles/134322/the-un-jewish-assault-on-richard-goldstone/.
100. "Zionist Extremist Hate Crime against Rabbi Lerner: Third Attack on His Home and the Limits of "Freedom of the Press," *Tikkun Daily* (blog), March 16, 2011, http://www.tikkun.org/tikkundaily/2011/03/16/zionist-extremist-hate-crime-against-rabbi-lerner-3rd-attack-on-his-home-and-the-limits-of-freedom-of-the-press/.
101. Website of the Russell Tribunal on Palestine, http://www.russelltribunalonpalestine.com/en/sessions/final-session.
102. Richard Goldstone, "Israel and the Apartheid Slander," editorial, *New York Times*, October 31, 2011, http://www.nytimes.com/2011/11/01/opinion/israel-and-the-apartheid-slander.html.
103. Letter from Alice Walker to Publishers at Yediot Books, June 9, 2012, website of Palestinian Campaign for the Academic and Cultural Boycott of Israel, http://www.pacbi.org/etemplate.php?id=1917, and written about by Alison Flood, "Alice Walker Declines Request to Publish Israel Edition of *The Color Purple*," *The Guardian*, June 20, 2012, http://www.guardian.co.uk/books/2012/jun/20/alice-walker-declines-israeli-color-purple. On other artists' boycotting Israel, see Nathan Guttman, "Boycott Targets Stars from Elvis to Elton," *Forward*, 114, no. 3181 (May 28, 2010): 1, 5; n.a., "S. African Opera Won't Cancel Israel Tour," *The Jewish News Weekly of Northern California* (San Francisco, CA) 114, no. 44 (November 5, 2010): 13.
104. Daniel Gordis, "A Dose of Nuance: Walking Away from Alice Walker," *Jerusalem Post*, June 28, 2012, http://www.jpost.com/Opinion/Columnists/Article.aspx?id=275600.
105. Letty Cottin Pogrebin, "The A-Word in Hebron," *Forward*, March 23, 2011, http://forward.com/articles/136418/the-a-word-in-hebron/.
106. Leonard J. Fein, "The New Left and Israel," in Mordecai S. Chertoff, ed., *The New Left and the Jews* (New York: Pitman Publishing Company, 1971), 143.
107. Fein, "The New Left and Israel," 147, 146.
108. See Leonard Fein, "No Matter How You Slice It," website of Americans for Peace Now, accessed June 16, 2013, http://peacenow.org/no-matter-how-you-slice-it.html#.UfEvvNLVCSp.
109. Aarifah Nosarka, "Mbete's Support for Boycott of Israel Noted," *The Citizen* (South Africa) October 29, 2012.
110. Quoted in Ibid.
111. Peter Beinart, "The Israel Debate in South Africa," January 29, 2013, http://www.thedailybeast.com/articles/2013/01/29/the-israel-debate-in-south-africa.html.
112. Daniel Estrin, "Israel to Pay Students to Defend it Online," *Boston Globe*, August 15, 2013, http://www.bostonglobe.com/news/world/2013/08/14/israel-pay-students-defend-online/VsSiM0Ujs8xAwKXXd9uZyI/story.html.

113. Geoff Sifrin, "The Real Cost to Israel of Missing Mandela's Funeral," *Haaretz*, December 10, 2013, http://www.haaretz.com/news/nelson-mandela-1918–2013/.premium-1.562690.
114. Richard Goldstone, "Recalling Madiba's Long Walk with Jews," *Forward*, December 20, 2013, 1, 5.
115. Odette Yousef, "Palestinians and Jews Both Lay Claim to Mandela's Legacy," WBEZ 91.5, December 13, 2013, http://www.wbez.org/news/palestinians-and-jews-both-lay-claim-mandela%E2%80%99s-legacy-109375.
116. Ibid.
117. The protest on Robben Island was for the release of Marwan Barghouti from an Israeli prison. Barghouti is a Fatah leader (and a distant relation of Omar Barghouti, leader in the BDS movement). The *Forward* considered if Marwan Barghouti is "the Mandela of the Palestinians" (Nathan Jeffay, "Is Barghouti the Mandela of the Palestinians?" *Forward*, December 20, 2013, 1). Barghouti wrote a eulogy for Mandela from his jail cell.
118. Yousef, "Palestinians and Jews Both Lay Claim to Mandela's Legacy."
119. Ben Cohen, "Nelson Mandela and Zionism—the Real Story," *The Jewish Chronicle*, December 2013, http://thejewishchronicle.net/view/full_story/24204421/article-Nelson-Mandela-and-Zionism--the-real-story?instance=news_special_coverage_right_column
120. Rabbi Irving Greenberg, "Mandela, Apartheid, and the Jews," The New York *Jewish Week*, December 16, 2013, http://www.thejewishweek.com/editorial-opinion/opinion/mandela-apartheid-and-jews-0.

Bibliography

Books and Articles

Abadi, Jacob. "Algeria's Policy toward Israel: Pragmatism and Rhetoric." *The Middle East Journal* 56, no. 4 (Autumn 2002): 616–642.

Abramowitz, Yosef I. *Jews, Zionism and South Africa.* Washington, DC: The Campus Program of B'nai B'rith International, 1985.

Adler, Franklin Hugh. "South African Jews and Apartheid." *Patterns of Prejudice* 34, no. 4 (2000): 23–36.

Alexander Simons, Ray. *All My Life and All My Strength*, edited by Immanuel Suttner. Johannesburg: STE publishers, 2004.

Alexander, Edward. *With Friends like These: The Jewish Critics of Israel.* New York: Shapolsky Publishers, 1993.

Allan, Virginia R., Margaret Galey, and Mildred E. Persinger. "World Conference of International Women's Year." In *Women, Politics, and the United Nations*, edited by Anne Winslow, 29–44. Greenwood, CT:Greenwood Press, 1995.

Alliance Against Women's Oppression. "Zionism in the Women's Movement: Anti-imperialist Politics Derailed." AAWO Discussion Paper Number 4. San Francisco, October 1983.

Anderson, Carol. *Eyes off the Prize: The United Nations and the African American Struggle for Human Rights, 1944–1955.* Cambridge, UK: Cambridge University Press, 2003.

Anderson, Jervis. *Bayard Rustin: Troubles I've Seen.* New York: Harper Collins, 1997.

Antler, Joyce. "'We Were Ready to Turn the World Upside Down': Radical Feminism and Jewish Women." In *A Jewish Feminine Mystique: Jewish Women in Postwar America*, edited by Hasia Diner, Shira Kohn, and Rachel Kranson, 210–234. New Brunswick: Rutgers University Press, 2010.

Axelrad, Rabbi Albert S. "Encountering the Jewish Radical: The Challenge for Campus Rabbis and Student Groups." In *The New Jews*, edited by James A. Sleeper and Alan Mintz, 112–119. New York: Vintage Books, 1971.

Ballantine, Christopher. "A Brief History of South African Popular Music." *Popular Music* 8, no. 3 (October 1989): 305–310.

Barron, Andrea. "Jews and Israel." *The Washington Report on Middle East Affairs* 4 (September 30, 1990): 60.

Beckerman, Gal. *When They Come for Us We'll Be Gone: The Epic Struggle to Save Soviet Jewry.* New York: Houghton Mifflin, 2010.

Beinart, Peter. *The Crisis of Zionism.* New York: Henry Holt and Company, 2012.

Belafonte, Harry, with Michael Schnayerson. *Harry Belafonte: My Song, A Memoir.* New York:Alfred A. Knopf, 2011.

Ben-Zvi, Abraham A. *The United States and Israel: The Limits of a Special Relationship.* New York: Columbia University Press, 1993.
Borstelmann, Thomas. *Apartheid's Reluctant Uncle: The United States and Southern Africa in the Early Cold War.* New York: Oxford University Press, 1993.
———. *The Cold War and the Color Line.* Cambridge, MA: Harvard University Press, 2001.
Branch, Taylor. *At Canaan's Edge, America in the King Years, 1965–1968.* New York: Simon and Schuster, 2006.
Braude, Claudia. "Commissioning, Community, and Conscience." *Safundi* 10, no. 1 (January 2009): 77–90.
Brettschneider, Marla. *Cornerstones of Peace: Jewish Identity Politics and Democratic Theory.* New Brunswick, NJ: Rutgers University Press, 1996.
Brickner, Balfour. "Jewish Youth, Israel, and the Third World." *Reconstructionist* 36, no. 3 (March 27, 1970): 7–13.
———. "My Zionist Dilemmas." *Sh'ma: A Journal of Jewish Responsibility* 1 (November 9, 1970): 3–5.
Brooks, Pamela E. *Boycotts, Buses, and Passes: Black Women's Resistance in the U.S. South and South Africa.* Amherst, MA: University of Massachusetts Press, 2008.
Buhle, Paul and Robin D. G. Kelley. "Allies of a Different Sort: Jews and Blacks in the American Left." In *Struggles in the Promised Land: Toward a History of Black/Jewish Relations in the United States*, edited by Jack Salzman and Cornel West, 197–230. New York: Oxford University Press, 1997.
Bulkin, Elly, Minnie Bruce Pratt, and Barbara Smith. *Yours in Struggle: Three Feminist Perspectives on Anti-Semitism and Racism.* Ithaca, New York: Firebrand Books, 1984.
Cantarow, Ellen. "Zionism, Anti-Semitism, and Jewish Identity in the Women's Movement." *Middle East Report* 154 (September–October 1988): 38–43.
Carson, Clayborne. *In Struggle: SNCC and the Black Awakening of 1960.* Cambridge, MA: Harvard University Press, 1981.
Chazan, Naomi. "The Fallacies of Pragmatism: Israeli Foreign Policy towards South Africa." *African Affairs* 82, no. 327 (1983): 169–200.
Cherny, Robert W., William Issel, and Kieran Walsh Taylor, eds. *American Labor and the Cold War: Grassroots Politics and Postwar Political Culture.* New Brunswick, NJ: Rutgers University Press, 2004.
Chomsky, Noam. *Fateful Triangle: The United States, Israel, and the Palestinians.* Cambridge, MA: South End Press (orig. 1983) 1999.
Cohen, Kitty O. "Black-Jewish Relations in 1984: A Survey of Black Congressmen." In *Strangers and Neighbors: Relations Between Blacks and Jews in the United States*, edited by Maurianne Adams and John Bracey, 688–701. Amherst, MA: University of Massachusetts Press, 1999.
Coker, Christopher. *The United States and South Africa, 1968–1985: Constructive Engagement and Its Critics.* Durham, NC: Duke University Press, 1986.
Danaher, Kevin. *In Whose Interest? A Guide to U.S.-South Africa Relations.* Washington, DC: Institute for Policy Studies, 1984.
Davis, Darren W. and Ronald E. Brown. "The Antipathy of Black Nationalism: Behavioral and Attitudinal Implications of an African American Ideology." *American Journal of Political Science*, 46, no. 2 (April 2002): 239–252.
Davis, Ossie and Ruby Dee. *With Ossie and Ruby: In This Life Together.* New York: William and Morrow Company, 1998.
Decter, Moshe. *"To Serve, To Teach, to Leave,": The Story of Israel's Development Program in Black Africa.* New York: American Jewish Congress, 1977.

D'Emilio, John. *Lost Prophet: The Life and Times of Bayard Rustin*. New York: Free Press, 2003.

Dershowitz, Alan. "The Case against Jimmy Carter." In *The Case Against Israel's Enemies: Exposing Jimmy Carter and Others Who Stand in the Way of Peace*, 17–48. Hoboken, NJ: John Wiley and Sons, 2008.

Diner, Hasia. *In the Almost Promised Land: American Jews and Blacks, 1915–1935*. Westport, CT: Greenwood Press, 1977.

———. *We Remember with Reverence and Love: American Jews and the Myth of Silence after the Holocaust, 1945–1962*. New York: New York University Press, 2009.

Diner, Hasia, Shira Kohn, and Rachel Kranson, eds. *A Jewish Feminine Mystique: Jewish Women in Postwar America*. New Brunswick, NJ: Rutgers University Press, 2010.

Drewett, Michael. "Music in the Struggle to End Apartheid: South Africa." In *Policing Pop*, edited by Martin Cloonan and Reebee Garofalo, 153–165. Philadelphia, PA: Temple University Press, 2003.

Dudziak, Mary. *Cold War, Civil Rights: Race and the Image of American Democracy*. Princeton, NJ: Princeton University Press, 2000.

Farber, David. *The Iran Hostage Crisis and America's First Encounter with Radical Islam*. Princeton, NJ: Princeton University Press, 2005.

Fein, Leonard J. "No Matter How You Slice It," website of Americans for Peace Now, accessed June 16, 2013, http://peacenow.org/no-matter-how-you-slice-it.html#.UfEvvNLVCSp.

———. "The New Left and Israel." In *The New Left and the Jews*, edited by Mordecai S. Chertoff, 132–151. New York: Pitman Publishing Company, 1971.

First, Ruth. *117 Days: An Account of Confinement and Interrogation under the South African 90-Day Detention Law*. New York: Penguin (orig. 1965) 2009.

Frankel, Glenn. *Rivonia's Children: Three Families and the Cost of Conscience in White South Africa*. New York: Farrar, Straus, and Giroux, 1999.

Frankenthal, Sally. "South African Jewish Women." In *Jewish Women 2000: Conference Papers from the Hadassah Research Institute on Jewish Women*, edited by Helen Epstein. Working Paper 6 (November 1999): 71–78.

Frederickson, George M. *Black Liberation: A Comparative History of Black Ideologies in the United States and South Africa*. New York: Oxford University Press, 1995.

Friedman, Murray. *The Neoconservative Revolution: Jewish Intellectuals and the Shaping of Public Policy*. New York: Cambridge University Press, 2005.

Friesel, Ofra. "Equating Zionism with Racism: The 1965 Precedent." *American Jewish History* 97, no. 3 (July 2013): 283–313.

Galchinsky, Michael. *Jews and Human Rights: Dancing at Three Weddings*. Lanham, MD: Rowan and Littlefield, 2008.

Galey, Margaret E. "The Nairobi Conference: The Powerless Majority." *PS (Political Science)* 19, no. 2 (Spring 1986): 255–265.

Gambone, Philip. *Travels in a Gay Nation: Portraits of LGBTQ Americans*. Madison, WI: University of Wisconsin Press, 2010.

Garofalo, Reebee. "Nelson Mandela, The Concerts: Mass Culture as Contested Terrain." In *Rockin' the Boat: Mass Music and Mass Movements*, edited by Garofalo, 55–66. Cambridge, MA: South End Press, 1992.

Georgakas, Dan. "Workers in Detroit." *Middle East Report and Information Project Reports* 35 (January 1975): 13–17.

Gilbert, Shirli. "Singing against Apartheid: ANC Cultural Groups and the International Anti-apartheid Struggle." *Journal of South African Studies* 33, no. 2 (June 2007): 421–441.

———. "Jews and the Racial State: Legacies of the Holocaust in Apartheid South Africa, 1945–60." *Jewish Social Studies: History, Culture, Society* 16, no. 3 (Spring/Summer 2010): 32–64.

Glaser, Jennifer. "Beyond the Farribel: Towards a Transnational Reassessment of Jewish Studies." *Safundi: The Journal of South African and American Studies* 10, no. 1 (2009): 99–104.

Glenn, Susan. "The Vogue of Jewish Self-Hatred in Post-World War II America." *Jewish Social Studies* 12, no. 3 (Spring/Summer 2006): 95–136.

Goldstein, Eric L. *The Price of Whiteness: Jews, Race, and American Identity.* Princeton, NJ: Princeton University Press, 2006.

Gordon, Joel. *Nasser's Blessed Movement: Egypt's Free Officers and the July Revolution.* New York: Oxford University Press, 1992.

Green, Nancy. "Blacks, Jews, and the 'Natural Alliance': Labor Cohabitation and the ILGWU." *Jewish Social Studies* 4, no. 1 (Autumn 1997): 79–104.

Greenberg, Cheryl Lynn. *A Circle of Trust: Remembering SNCC.* New Brunswick, NJ: Rutgers University Press, 1998.

———. *Troubling the Waters: Black-Jewish Relations in the American Century.* Princeton, NJ: Princeton University Press, 2006.

Grundlingh, Albert. "'Rocking the Boat' in South Africa? Voelvry Music and Afrikaans Anti-apartheid Social Protest in the 1980s." *The International Journal of African Historical Studies* 37, no. 3 (2004): 483–514.

Hammerstein, David. "Marching to Pretoria." *The Jewish Radical* 9, no. 3 (August 1978): 12.

Hendessi, Mandana. "Fourteen Thousand Women Meet: Report from Nairobi, July 1985."*Feminist Review* 23 (Summer 1986): 147–156.

Hersh, Seymour M. *The Samson Option: Israel's Nuclear Arsenal and American Foreign Policy.* New York: Random House, 1991.

Heschel, Abraham Joshua. *The Insecurity of Freedom: Essays on Human Existence.* New York: Farrar, Straus, and Giroux, 1966.

Hesse, Brian J. *The United States, South Africa and Africa: Of Grand Foreign Policy Aims and Modest Means.* Burlington, VT: Ashgate, 2001.

Hill, Herbert. "Black-Jewish Conflict in the Labor Context: Race, Jobs, and Institutional Power." In *African Americans and Jews: The Twentieth Century, Studies in Convergence and Conflict*, edited by V.P. Franklin, Nancy L. Grant, Harold M. Kletnick, and Genna Rae McNeil, 264–292. Columbia, MO: University of Missouri Press, 1998.

Hostetter, David. *Movement Matters: American Antiapartheid Activism and the Rise of Multicultural Politics.* New York: Routledge, 2006.

Houser, George M. *No One Can Stop the Rain: Glimpses of Africa's Liberation Struggle.* New York: Pilgrim Press, 1989.

Hunter, Jane. "Israel and the Bantustans." *Journal of Palestine Studies* 15 no. 3 (Spring 1986): 53–89.

Hurwitz, Ariel, ed. *Against the Stream: Seven Decades of Hashomer Hatzair in North America.* Tel Aviv: Association of North American Shomrim, 1994.

Hyman, Paula. "Jewish Feminism Faces the American Women's Movement," In *American Jewish Women's History: A Reader*, edited by Pamela Nadell, 297–312. New York: New York University Press, 2003.

Isaac, Rael Jean. *The anti-New Jewish Agenda*. New York: Americans for a Safe Israel, 1987.
Jacobson, Dan. "The Jews of South Africa: Portrait of a Flourishing Community." Review of *The Jews in South Africa*, edited by Gustav Saron and Louis Hotz. *Commentary* 23 (January 1957): 39–45.
Jacobson, Matthew Frye. *Roots Too: White Ethnic Revival in Post-Civil Rights America*. Cambridge, MA: Harvard University Press, 2008.
Jain, Devaki. *Women, Development, and the UN: A Sixty-Year Quest for Equality and Justice*. Bloomington, IN: Indiana University Press, 2005.
Jaquette, Jane S. "Losing the Battle/Winning the War: International Politics, Women's Issues, and the 1980 Mid-Decade Conference." In *Women, Politics, and the United Nations*, edited by Anne Winslow, 45–60. Greenwood, CT: Greenwood Press, 1995.
Kahlenberg, Richard. *Tough Liberal: Albert Shanker and the Battles Over Schools, Unions, Race, and Democracy*. New York: Columbia University Press, 2007.
Kaplan, Temma. *Crazy for Democracy: Women in Grassroots Movements*. New York: Routledge, 1996.
———. *Taking Back the Streets: Women, Youth, and Direct Democracy*. Berkeley, CA: University of California Press, 2004.
Karis, Thomas and Gail M. Gerhart. *From Protest to Challenge: A Documentary History of African Politics in South Africa, 1882–1964*. Volume III. Stanford, CA: Stanford University Press, 1977.
Kaye/Kantrowitz, Melanie. *The Colors of Jews: Racial Politics and Radical Diasporism*. Bloomington, IN: University of Indiana Press, 2007.
Klapper, Melissa. *Ballots, Babies, and Banners of Peace: American Jewish Women's Activism, 1890–1940*. New York: New York University Press, 2013.
Klein, Naomi. "Minority Death Match: Jews, Blacks, and the 'Post-Racial' Presidency." *Harper's Magazine* (September 2009): 53–67.
Kochan, Ran. "Israel in Third World Forums." In *Israel in the Third World*, edited by Michael Curtis and Susan Aurelia Gitelson, 247–269. New Brunswick, NJ: Transaction Books, 1976.
Kosek, Kip. *Acts of Conscience: Christian Nonviolence and Modern American Democracy*. New York: Columbia University Press, 2009.
Kraft, Gerald and Uzi Narkis. Presentations. In *Zionism is Racism: An Assault on Human Rights. A Report and Program Guide*, a conference sponsored by B'nai B'rith International, World Jewish Congress, World Zionist Organization, Hosted by the U.S. Department of State, December 10, 1985. B'nai B'rith International: Washington, DC, 1985, n.p.
Kreinin, Mordechai E. *Israel and Africa: A Study in Technical Cooperation*. New York: Praeger, 1964.
Kushner, Tony and Alisa Solomon, eds. *Wrestling with Zion: Progressive Jewish-American Responses to the Israeli-Palestinian Conflict*. New York: Grove Press, 2003.
Lang/Levitsky, Daniel Rozsa. "Hidden Agenda: Lessons from NJA, Lost and Learned." In *Justice, Justice, Shall You Pursue: A History of New Jewish Agenda*, edited by Ezra Berkley Nepon, 93–107. Oakland, CA: Thread Makes Blanket Press, 2012.
Laughlin, Kathleen A. "'Our Defense against Despair': The Progressive Politics of the National Council of Jewish Women after World War II." In *A Jewish Feminine Mystique: Jewish Women in Postwar America*, edited by Hasia Diner, Shira Kohn,

and Rachel Kranson, 48–64. New Brunswick, NJ: Rutgers University Press, 2010.
Lauren, Paul Gordon. *Power and Prejudice: the Politics and Diplomacy of Racial Discrimination.* Boulder, CO: Westview Press, 1988.
Lebowitz, Arieh and Gail Malmgreen. Introduction to Volume 14. *Archives of the Holocaust: An International Collection of Selected Documents.* New York: Garland, 1993.
Levine, Suzanne Braun and Mary Thom, eds. *Bella Abzug: How One Tough Broad from the Bronx Fought Jim Crow and Joe McCarthy, Pissed off Jimmy Carter, Battled for the Rights of Women and Workers, Rallied against War and for the Planet, and Shook up Politics along the Way.* New York: Farrar, Straus, and Giroux, 2007.
Loeffler, James. "'The Conscience of America': Human Rights, Jewish Politics, and American Foreign Policy at the 1945 United Nations San Francisco Conference." *Journal of American History* 100, no. 2 (September 2013): 401–428.
Lyman, Princeton N. *Partner to History: The U.S. Role in South Africa's Transition to Democracy.* Washington, DC: United States Institute of Peace Press, 2002.
Maisel, Peggy. "Lessons from the World Conference against Racism: South Africa as a Case Study." *Oregon Law Review* 81 (2002): 739–770.
Makeba, Miriam with James Hall. *Makeba: My Story.* New York: New American Library, 1987.
Mandela, Nelson. *Long Walk to Freedom: The Autobiography of Nelson Mandela.* Boston, MA: Little, Brown, and Company, 1994.
Marks, Shula. "Ruth First: A Tribute." *Journal of African Studies* 10, no. 1 (October 1983): 123–128.
———. "Apartheid and the Jewish Question." *Journal of Southern African Studies* 30, no. 4 (December 2004): 889–907.
Martin, Bradford. *The Other Eighties: A Secret History of America in the Age of Reagan.* New York: Hill and Wang, 2011.
Martin, Denis-Constant. "Music beyond Apartheid?" translated by Val Morrison. In *Rockin' the Boat: Mass Music and Mass Movements,* edited by Reebee Garofalo, 195–208. Cambridge, MA: South End Press, 1992.
Martin, Michael T. and Marilyn Yaquinto. "Reparations for America's 'Holocaust': Activism for Global Justice." *Race and Class* 45, no. 4 (2004): 1–25.
Mazower, Mark. *No Enchanted Palace: The End of Empire and the Ideological Origins of the United Nations.* Princeton, NJ: Princeton University Press, 2009.
Medoff, Rafael. *Jewish Americans and Political Participation.* Santa Barbara, CA: ABC/CLIO, 2002.
Meir, Golda. *My Life.* New York: Putnam's Sons, 1975.
Meister, Robert. *After Evil: A Politics of Human Rights.* New York: Columbia University Press, 2012.
Mendelsohn, Adam. "Two Far South: Rabbinical Responses to Apartheid and Segregation in South Africa and the American South." *Southern Jewish History* 6 (2003): 63–132.
Meriwether, James H. *Proudly We Can Be Africans: Black Americans and Africa, 1935–1961.* Chapel Hill, NC: University of North Carolina Press, 2001.
Messinger, Ruth and Aaron Dorfman. "Toward a Jewish Argument for the Responsibility to Protect." In *Responsibility to Protect: The Global Moral Compact for the 21st Century,* edited by Richard H. Cooper and Juliette Voinov Kohler, 61–76. New York: Palgrave Macmillan, 2009.

Meyer, Michael, ed. *Joachim Prinz, Rebellious Rabbi: An Autobiography—the German and Early American Years*. Bloomington, IN: Indiana University Press, 2007.

Michels, Tony. *A Fire in Their Hearts: Yiddish Socialists in New York*. Cambridge, MA: Harvard University Press, 2005.

Miller, Jake C. "Black Viewpoints on the Mid-East Conflict." *The Journal of Palestine Studies*, 10, no. 2 (Winter 1981): 37–49.

Minter, William and Sylvia Hill. "Anti-Apartheid Solidarity in United States-South Africa Relations: From the Margins to the Mainstream." In South Africa Democracy Education Trust, *The Road to Democracy in South Africa. Volume 3: International Solidarity*.Pretoria: Unisa Press, 2008, 745–822. Located on the website of "RFK in the Land of Apartheid," http://www.rfksafilm.org/html/doc_pdfs/MintnerHill.pdf.

Mohan, Jitendra. "South Africa and the Suez Crisis." *International Journal* 16, no. 4 (Autumn 1961): 327–357.

Moore, Deborah Dash. "From David to Goliath: American Representations of Jews around the Six-Day War." In *The Six-Day War and World Jewry*, edited by Eli Lederhendler, 69–80. Bethesda, MD: University Press of Maryland, 2000.

Mullings, Leith, ed. *New Social Movements in the African Diaspora: Challenging Global Apartheid*. New York: Palgrave Macmillan, 2009.

Nadell, Pamela. "A Bright New Constellation: Feminism and American Judaism." In *The Columbia History of Jews and Judaism in America*, edited by Marc Lee Raphael, 385–405. New York: Columbia University Press, 2008.

Nepon, Ezra Berkley. *Justice, Justice, Shall You Pursue: A History of New Jewish Agenda*. Oakland, CA: Thread Makes Blanket Press, 2012.

Nesbitt, Francis Njubi. *Race for Sanctions: African Americans against Apartheid, 1946–1994*. Bloomington, IN: Indiana University Press, 2004.

New Jewish Agenda, *Carrying It on: A National Conference Organizing against Anti-Semitism and Racism for Jewish Activists and College Students*. Philadelphia, November 9–10, 1991. Published by *Bridges*. Seattle, WA, 1992.

Novak, Bill. "The Making of a Jewish Counter Culture." In *Contemporary Judaic Fellowship in Theory and Practice*, edited by Jacob Neusner, 139–148. New York: Ktav Publishing, 1972.

Oded, Arye. "Africa in Israeli Foreign Policy, Expectations and Disenchantments: Historical and Diplomatic Aspects." *Israel Studies* 15, no. 3 (Fall 2010): 121–142.

Oren, Michael. *Six Days of War: June 1967 and the Making of the Modern Middle East*. New York: Ballantine Books, 2003.

Patton, Charlotte G. "Women and Power: The Nairobi Conference, 1985." In *Women, Politics, and the United Nations*, edited by Anne Winslow, 61–76. Greenwood, CT: Greenwood Press, 1995.

Peters, Joel. *Israel and Africa: The Problematic Friendship*. London: British Academic Press, 1992.

Pinsky, Dina. *Jewish Feminists: Complex Identities and Activist Lives*. Urbana, IL: University of Illinois Press, 2010.

Pogrebin, Letty Cottin. *Deborah, Golda, and Me: Being Female and Jewish in America*. New York: Crown Publishers, Inc., 1991.

Polakow-Suransky, Sasha. *The Unspoken Alliance: Israel's Secret Relationship with Apartheid South Africa*. New York: Pantheon Books, 2010.

Prell, Riv-Ellen. "Triumph, Accommodation, and Resistance: American Jewish Life from the End of World War II to the Six-Day War." In *The Columbia History of Jews and Judaism in America*, edited by Marc Lee Raphael, 114–141. New York: Columbia University Press, 2008.

———. *Prayer and Community: The Havurah in American Judaism*. Detroit, MI: Wayne State University Press, 1989.

Raffel, Martin. "History of Israel Advocacy." In *Jewish Polity and American Civil Society: Communal Agencies and Religious Movements in the American Public Sphere*, edited by Alan Mittleman, Jonathan D. Sarna, and Robert Licht, 103–180. Lanham, MD: Rowan and Littlefield Publishers Inc., 2002.

Reddy, Enuga S. "The United Nations and the Struggle for Liberation in South Africa." On the website of the African National Congress, 47–49. http://www.anc.org.za/docs/misc/1992/roadtodemocracyl.pdf.

Reilly, Niamh. *Women's Human Rights: Seeking Gender Justice in a Global Age*. Malden, MA: Polity Press, 2009.

Richards, Yevette. *Maida Springer: Pan-Africanist and International Labor Leader*. Pittsburgh, PA: University of Pittsburgh Press, 2000.

Riegner, Gerhart M. *Never Despair: Sixty Years in the Service of the Jewish People and the Cause of Human Rights*. Chicago, IL: Ivan R. Dee, 2006.

Rosen, Rhoda. "The Making of an East European Jewish Legacy in Contemporary South Africa." *Shofar* 25, no. 1 (Fall 2006): 78–89.

Said, Edward. "Zionism from the Standpoint of Its Victims." In *The Edward Said Reader*, edited by Moustafa Bayoumi and Andrew Rubin. New York: Random House (orig. 1979), reprinted 2007, 114–168.

Sanua, Marianne. *Let us Prove Strong: The American Jewish Committee, 1945–2006*. Waltham, MA: Brandeis University Press, 2007.

Sarna, Jonathan. *American Judaism: A History*. New Haven, CT: Yale University Press, 2004.

Schneier, Marc. *Shared Dreams: Martin Luther King, Jr. and the Jewish Community*. Woodstock, VT: Jewish Lights Publishing, 1999.

Shachtman, Tom. *Airlift to America: How Barack Obama, Sr., John F. Kennedy, Tom Mboya, and 800 East African Students Changed Their World and Ours*. New York: St. Martin's Press, 2009.

Shain, Milton and Richard Mendelsohn, eds. *Memories, Realities, and Dreams: Aspects of the South African Jewish Experience*. Cape Town: Jonathan Ball Publishers, 2002.

Shapiro, Edward S. *Crown Heights: Blacks, Jews, and the 1991 Brooklyn Riot*. Waltham, MA: Brandeis University Press, 2006.

Shimoni, Gideon. *Community and Conscience: The Jews in Apartheid South Africa*. Hanover, NH: University Press of New England, 2003.

Shlaim, Avi. *The Iron Wall: Israel and the Arab World*. New York: W.W. Norton and Company, 2001.

Shur, Chaim. *Shomrim in the Land of Apartheid: The Story of Hashomer Hatzair in South Africa, 1935–1970*. Israel: Ma'arechet Publishing House, 1998.

Sizemore-Barber, April. "The Voice of (Which?) Africa: Miriam Makeba in America." *Safundi* 13, no. 3–4 (July–October 2012): 251–276.

Skinner, Rob. *The Foundations of Anti-Apartheid: Liberal Humanitarians and Transnational Activists in Britain and the United States, c. 1919–1964*. New York: Palgrave Macmillan, 2010.

Snyder, Margaret. "Walking My Own Road: How a Sabbatical Year led to a Career at the UN." In *Developing Power: How Women Transformed International Development*, edited by Arvonne S. Fraser, and Irene Tinker, 37–49. New York: The Feminist Press, 2004.

Sokolsky, Joel. "South African Jewry, Apartheid, and American Attitudes." *Judaism* (American Jewish Congress) 29, no. 4 (1980): 404–417.

Sorin, Gerald. Review of *The Neoconservative Revolution*, by Murray Friedman. *American Historical Review* 111, no. 4 (October 2006): 1219–1220.

Staub, Michael. *Torn at the Roots: The Crisis of Jewish Liberalism in Postwar America*. New York: Columbia University Press, 2002.

———. *The Jewish 1960s: An American Sourcebook*. Waltham, MA: Brandeis University Press, 2004.

Suttner, Immanuel. *Cutting through the Mountain: Interviews with South African Jewish Activists*. New York: Penguin Group, 1997.

Suzman, Helen. *In No Uncertain Terms: A South African Memoir*. New York: Alfred A. Knopf, 1993.

Svonkin, Stuart. *Jews against Prejudice: American Jews and the Fight for Civil Liberties*. New York: Columbia University Press, 1997.

Thorn, Hakan. *Anti-Apartheid and the Emergence of a Global Civil Society*. New York: Palgrave Macmillan, 2006.

Troy, Gil. *Moynihan's Moment: America's Fight against Zionism as Racism*. New York: Oxford University Press, 2013.

Ullestad, Neal. "Diverse Rock Rebellions Subvert Mass Media Hegemony." In *Rockin' the Boat: Mass Music and Mass Movements*, edited by Reebee Garofalo, 37–54. Cambridge, MA: South End Press, 1992.

United Nations. *World Conference of the U.N. Decade for Women, Copenhagen, Denmark, July 14–30, 1980. Report of the Congressional Staff Advisers to the U.S. Delegation*. Washington, DC: U.S. Printing Office, December 1980.

———. *The United Nations and Apartheid, 1948–1994*. New York: Department of Public Information, 1994.

Urofsky, Melvin. *American Zionism from Herzl to the Holocaust*.Garden City, NY: Anchor Press/Double Day, 1975.

Villa-Vicencio, Charles. *The Spirit of Freedom: South African Leaders on Religion and Politics*. Berkeley, CA: University of California Press, 1996.

Von Eschen, Penny M. *Race against Empire: Black Americans and Anticolonialism, 1937–1957*. Ithaca, NY: Cornell University Press, 1997.

Vorspan, Albert and David Saperstein. *Tough Choices: Jewish Perspectives on Social Justice*. New York: UAHC Press, 1992.

Walker, Cherryl. "'Freedom Does Not Come Walking to You—It Must Be Won': Sharpeville and the Decline of the FSAW." In *Women and Resistance in South Africa*, edited by Cherryl Walker, 267–278. London: Onyx Publishers, 1982.

Walker, Cherryl, ed. *Women and Resistance in South Africa*. London: Onyx Press, 1982.

———. *Women and Gender in Southern Africa to 1945*. Cape Town: David Philip Publishers, 1990.

Walton, Hanes, Jr. *Black Women at the United Nations*. San Bernadino, CA: Borgo Press, 1995.

Weisbord, Robert G. and Richard Kazarian, Jr. *Israel in the Black American Perspective*. Westport, CT: Greenwood Press, 1985.

Westad, Odd Arne. *The Global Cold War.* Cambridge, MA: Cambridge University Press, 2007.
Whitfield, Stephen, "Influence and Affluence, 1967–2000." In *The Columbia History of Jews and Judaism in America*, edited by Marc Lee Raphael, 142–166. New York: Columbia University Press, 2008.
Williams, Ian. "South Africa's Apartheid Experience Informs Israel-Palestine Discussion at Durban Racism Conference." *The Washington Report on Middle Eastern Affairs* (November 2001): 27–28.
Wolpe, AnnMarie. "Tribute to Ruth First." *Feminist Review* 13 (Spring 1983): 3–4.
Zayyad, Tawfik. "Israel's Setbacks in Africa." *Political Affairs* 52, no. 7 (July 1973): 58.
Zinsser, Judith P. "From Mexico to Copenhagen to Nairobi: The United Nations Decade for Women, 1975–1985." *Journal of World History* 13, no. 1 (Spring 2002): 139–168.

Unpublished Dissertations and Theses

Froman, Judy. "An Examination of the United Nations General Assembly Resolution 3379, 10 November 1975, Which Determines that Zionism is Racism and Racial Discrimination." Thesis, Professor Henry Steiner's Seminar on Human Rights, Harvard Law School, 1991.
Jackson, Nicole M. "Remembering Soweto: American College Students and International Social Justice, 1976–1988," Masters' Thesis, Ohio State University, 2009.
Mendelsohn, Adam. "Two Far South: The Responses of Southern and South African Jews to Apartheid and Racial Segregation in the 1950s and 1960s." Masters' Thesis, University of Cape Town, 2003.

Newspapers and Periodicals

Academe
Africa Today
American Jewish Committee Journal
Baltimore Jewish Times
Boston Globe
Caribbean Today (*Miami*)
Citizen (*South Africa*)
Columbia Daily Spectator
Commentary
Economic and Political Weekly
Economist
Forward
Gainesville Sun
Genesis (*Boston*)
Guardian
Haaretz
Hadassah
Israel Horizons

Jerusalem Post
Jewish Advocate (*Boston*)
Jewish Currents
Jewish Daily Forward
Jewish Frontier
Jewish Journal (*FL*)
Jewish News (*New York*)
Jewish News of Greater Phoenix
Jewish News Weekly of Northern California (*San Francisco*)
Jewish Press (*Omaha*)
Jewish Press (*Omaha, NE*)
Jewish Telegraphic Agency
Johns Hopkins News-Letter
The Justice (*Brandeis University*)
Labour Israel
Liberator Magazine
Lilith
Los Angeles Times
Michigan Citizen
Midstream Magazine
Middle East Research and Information Project
Modern Outlook
Mother Jones
Ms. Magazine
Nation
Near East Report
New Jersey Jewish News
New Outlook
New Pittsburgh Courier
New York Beacon
New York Daily News
New York Jewish Week
New York Post
New York Times
Newsweek
Northern California Jewish Bulletin (*San Francisco*)
Oakland Post
Ramparts
Reform Judaism
San Francisco Chronicle
Sentinel (*Chicago*)
Sun Reporter (*San Francisco*)
Tablet Magazine
Tikkun
Time Magazine
Tri-State Defender (*Memphis, TN*)
UN Chronicle
Washington Jewish Week
Washington Post
Washington Report on Middle East Affairs

Watch (Brandeis University)
Workers World
World Affairs
Xinhua News Agency

FILMS

Demme, Jonathan, dir. *Jimmy Carter: Man from Plains*. Sony Pictures Classic, 2007, DVD.
Rogosin, Lionel, dir. *Come Back, Africa*. Orig. 1959. Milestone Film, 2012, DVD.
Nogueira, Ana and Eron Davidson, dir. *Roadmap to Apartheid*.2012, DVD.

WEBSITES AND BLOGS

Anti-Defamation League. http://www.adl.org.
BDS Cookbook.http://www.stopbds.com.
Daily Beast Open Zion (blog). http://www.thedailybeast.com/openzion.html.
Electronic Intifada. http://electronicintifada.net.
Israel on Campus Coalition. http://israelcc.org.
Jewish Federation of North America Israel Action Network. http://israelactionnetwork.org.
Mondoweiss: The War of Ideas in the Middle East. http://mondoweiss.net.
New Jewish Agenda. http://newjewishagenda.net.
Palestinian BDS National Committee (BNC). http://www.bdsmovement.net.
Palestinian Campaign for the Academic and Cultural Boycott of Israel. http://www.pacbi.org.
Russell Tribunal on Palestine. http://www.russelltribunalonpalestine.com.
Shalom Center. http://theshalomcenter.org.
Tikkun Daily (blog). http://www.tikkun.org/tikkundaily.
United Nations. http://www.un.org
United Nations Information System on the Question of Palestine (UNISPAL). http://unispal.un.org.
World Jewish Congress.http://www.worldjewishcongress.org.

INTERNET ARCHIVES

African Activist Archive. Michigan State University.http://africanactivist.msu.edu.
Jewish Virtual Library. American-Israeli Cooperative Enterprise. http://www.jewishvirtuallibrary.org.
Jewish Women's Archive. http://jwa.org.

MANUSCRIPT COLLECTIONS

Records of the American Committee on Africa (ACOA), 1952–1985. Microfilm collection compiled by Randolph H. Boehm and Robert E. Lester. Bethesda, MD : University Publications of America, 1992. Original records housed at the Amistad Research Center, Tulane University.
American Jewish Congress Papers. Center for Jewish History, New York City.
Cleveland Robinson Papers. Tamiment Library, New York University.

David Belin/Jewish Outreach Papers. Special Collections, Harlan Hatcher Graduate Library, University of Michigan.
Gordon Fellman Papers, 1949–2006.Brandeis University Archives, Waltham, MA.
Hampshire College Archives. Hampshire College Library Center, Amherst, MA.
Jewish Labor Committee Papers. Tamiment Library, New York University.
Messinger, Ruth W. Oral History, May 20, 2008. Indiana University-Purdue University Indianapolis. Online at the IUPUI University Library Special Collections and Archives, http://hdl.handle.net/2450/5053.
National Jewish Community Relations Advisory Council Papers. Center for Jewish History, New York City.
National Jewish Community Relations Advisory Council Papers. Jewish Council for Public Affairs, New York City.
North American Jewish Students Appeal Papers. Center for Jewish History, New York.
Papers of the NAACP, Special Subject Files, 1966–1970. Microfilm collection edited by John H. Bracey, Jr, and Sharon Harley, Black Studies Research Sources (Bethesda, MD: University Publications of America, 2002), original records housed at the Library of Congress.
Provizer, Marlene. Oral History Library. American Jewish Committee: Irving M. Engel Collection on Civil Rights, Dorot Jewish Division, New York Public Library.
Reform Action Committee of the Union of American Hebrew Congregations Files. American Jewish Archives, Cincinnati, OH.
Religious Action Center Papers. American Jewish Archives, Cincinnati, Ohio.
Shad Polier Papers. Center for Jewish History, New York.
Swarthmore College Peace Collection. Swarthmore College, Swarthmore, PA.
Waskow, Rabbi Arthur. Interview, February 22, 2012. "Jews and Leftist Politics in Philadelphia Project." Feinstein Center for American Jewish History, Temple University, Philadelphia, PA.
World Jewish Congress Papers. American Jewish Archives, Cincinnati, OH.

Author Interviews and Correspondence

Diana Aviv, July 16, 2009.
Alison Bernstein, December 10, 2010.
Ellen Cantarow, May 15, 2013.
Leonard Fein, October 6, 2010.
Gordie Fellman, May 15, 2012.
Sharon Kleinbaum, May 13, 2011.
Sharon Kleinbaum, May 18, 2011.
Sharon Kleinbaum, January 26, 2011.
Sharon Kleinbaum, June 5, 2013.
Herb Magidson, February, 19, 2011.
Herb Magidson, April 22, 2011.
Ruth Messinger, January 6, 2011.
Marlene Provizer, June 7, 2013.
Eleanor Roffman, May 31, 2013.
Alisa Solomon, March 22, 2011.
Rabbi Brian Walt, May 30, 2013
Rabbi Arthur Waskow, February 21, 2013.

Cora Weiss, January 3, 2011.
Peter Weiss, July 27, 2009.
Peter Weiss, November 17, 2010.
Peter Weiss, January 23, 2013.
Peter Weiss, August 17, 2013.
Delores Wilkenfeld, March 28, 2011.

Index

1967 war. *See* Six-Day War
1973 war. *See* Yom Kippur War

Abramowitz, Yosef, 113–14
Abrams, Nathan, 172n13
Abudayyeh, Hatem, 152
Abunimah, Ali, 146, 151
Abzug, Bella, 91, 93
ACOA. *See* American Committee on Africa
AFL–CIO, 23, 69, 116, 129, 169n54
Africa Freedom Day, 22–9, 30, 31, 32, 38
Africa South, 25
African American Students Foundation (AASF), 23, 26
African National Congress (ANC), 9, 22, 25
 and Israel, 67, 95, 132, 136, 149–50
 repression of, 13, 25, 37
 South African Jews and, 49, 104, 114, 119, 150, 152, 200n10
 support for, in U.S., 18, 30, 133
 U.S. critics of, 111, 112, 129, 136
 see also Mandela, Nelson
Ahmadinejad, Mahmoud, 5, 140
AJC. *See* American Jewish Committee
Akuno, Kali, 140
Alexander, Edward, 126
Alexander, Ray, 104–5, 191n2, 192n93, 192n95
All-African People's Conference, 22
Alliance Against Women's Oppression (San Francisco), 93–4
Alperin, Mimi, 124–5
Amalgamated Clothing Workers of America, 30
Amampondo, 110

American Committee on Africa (ACOA), 18, 164–5n9
 Emergency Action Conference called by, 30–1
 founding of, 18, 164n9
 and frailty of Black/Jewish alliance, 56, 57–9
 and Israel, 28, 34, 56–9
 Jewish participation in, 18, 26, 53, 59, 175n55
 and Tom Mboya speaking tour, 22–3
American Federation of Teachers (AFT), 116
American Israel Public Affairs Committee (AIPAC), 142
American Jewish Committee (AJC), 122, 124, 135, 160–1n7
 and American Jewish Congress, 12, 160n7
 and apartheid, 117, 118, 120
 and South African Jewry, 120
 see also *Commentary* magazine
American Jewish Congress (AJCongress), 12–13, 42, 78, 125
 and American Jewish Committee, 12, 160n7
 and apartheid, 13, 27, 41, 42, 59–60, 69, 81, 117, 171n1
 founding of, 12
 and Israel–South Africa relationship, 77
 Peter Weiss and, 53, 54–5, 56, 59
 and World Jewish Congress, 12, 13, 15–16, 30
American Jewish World Service, 102–3
American Negro Leadership Conference on Africa (ANLCA), 36

American Society of African Culture (AMSAC), 30
American Studies Association (ASA), 146–7
American Zionist Federation, 85
Americans for Democratic Action (ADA), 30
Americans for Peace Now (APN), 56, 143, 148, 149
Americans for Progressive Israel, 120
Americans for South African Resistance (AFSAR), 164n9
Amin, Samir, 137–8
Amnesty International, 137
Anderson, Carol, 11
anticommunism, 23, 41, 69–70
  and U.S. South African policy, 9, 29, 163n37
  see also Cold War
Anti-Defamation League, 129, 142, 144
anti-Semitism, 14, 51, 108, 127, 194n20
  accusations of, 5, 25, 125, 140, 148; against BDS movement, 150; against Jewish liberals, 1, 113, 146; against Jimmy Carter, 143, 145; against NAACP, 169n54
  and Black Nationalism, 41, 51
  equating of anti-Israel attitudes with, 54, 113, 114, 125, 174n37, 182n49, 186n14
  linking of, to racism as similar evils, 12–13, 16, 27–8, 35, 105, 177n64, 196n50
  Mahmoud Ahmadinejad and, 5, 140
  Nazi, 162n25 (*see also* Holocaust)
  in New Left, 22, 42, 51
  in South Africa, 15, 16, 33, 106, 122, 170n62
  and Soviet Union, 73, 181n36 (*see also* Soviet Jewry)
  and UN conferences on racism, 136–7, 138, 139, 140
  and UN Resolution 3379, 73, 74, 75, 80
  and women's movement, 89, 91, 92, 96, 98
"apartheid" (word), 86, 199–200n44

broadening of, to include Israeli policies, 86, 107, 127, 136, 199–200n44
A. Philip Randolph Institute, 69, 116
APN. *See* Americans for Peace Now
Arab American Action Network, 152
Arab League, 76
Arafat, Yasser, 38, 78, 130
  demonization of, 1, 78, 126, 127–8
  and Nelson Mandela, 1, 130, 131, 155n2
  overtures to, 78–9, 128
Aronsfeld, C. C., 167n36
Aronson, Arnold, 118
Artists and Athletes against Apartheid, 56
Artists United Against Apartheid, 110
Ashe, Arthur, 56
Aviv, Diana, 122
Axelrad, Albert, 111–13, 125, 175n51, 195n34

Balka, Christie, 95, 97
Bandung conference of nonaligned nations (1955), 24, 26, 34, 138, 165–6n20
Barghouti, Omar, 143, 207n117
Barromi, Joel, 46–7
BASIC. *See* Black Americans to Support Israel Committee
Bates, Daisy, 24
Begin, Menachem, 84, 107
Beinart, Peter, 143, 150, 183n54
Belafonte, Harry, 23, 56, 110, 133, 165n16, 200n12
Bergman, Leslie, 121
Bernards, Reena, 95, 96
Berry, Mary Frances, 110
Bethune, Mary McLeod, 13
Biko, Stephen, 109
Black African nations, 72, 76
  early Israeli ties to, 24, 27, 32–4, 35, 46, 65–6, 67, 73, 75, 79, 82, 131
  shifting Israeli relationship to, 22, 24, 29, 65, 75, 76, 77
  in the United Nations, 24, 35, 67, 75, 77, 167n28
Black Americans to Support Israel Committee (BASIC), 69, 73, 77, 78

Black/Jewish alliance, 41, 45, 53–5, 69, 108–9, 115
and attitudes toward Israel, 4, 28–9, 56–9, 69–70, 78–9, 85–6, 125, 130
and Black Nationalism, 22, 41
and Cold War, 21–2, 64
complex factors affecting, 21–2, 41–2, 164n1
and labor movement, 31–2
Black Leadership Forum, 78
Black Nationalism, 22, 57
and anti-Semitism, 41, 51, 56
rise of, in 1960s, 4, 42, 43
Bloomberg, Michael, 142
B'nai B'rith, 36, 118. *See also* B'nai B'rith Hillel Foundation
B'nai B'rith Hillel Foundation, 109, 113
Boesak, Allan, 124
Bookbinder, Hyman, 117
Borstelmann, Thomas, 72
Boston Globe, 115, 150
Boston University, 109, 113
Boycott, Divestment, and Sanctions (BDS) movement, 5–6, 140–3, 146–7, 148, 151
African National Congress support for, 149–50
antiapartheid tactics as model for, 5, 140, 143, 151, 152
efforts to counter, 6, 141–3, 146–7
Jewish participation in, 141, 145, 146–7
boycotts, 31
of Israel, 125, 134, 138, 143 (*see also* Boycott, Divestment, and Sanctions movement)
of South Africa, 22, 29, 30, 31, 82, 110, 112, 120, 121
Brandeis University, 111–13, 144–7, 151, 175n51
Braude, Claudia, 105–6, 192n99, 192n101
Breira: A Project of Concern in Diaspora-Israel Relations, 67–8, 112, 145–6, 172n7
attacks on, 114, 123, 198n80
collapse of, 114, 123, 147

Brickner, Balfour, 53, 68, 69, 121, 124, 125, 132–3
Britain, 27, 33, 162n19
and Suez Canal conflict, 24–5, 47, 173–4n31
Brotherhood of Sleeping Car Porters, 23, 69
Brown v. Board of Education (1954), 12
Brutus, Dennis, 115
B'Tselem, the Israeli Information Center for Human Rights in the Occupied Territories, 151
Buhle, Paul, 42
Bunche, Ralph, 25
Bush (George W.) administration, 134
Bush, George H. W., 134

Cape Town University, 66
Carter, Jimmy, 5, 86, 150
controversial book by (*Palestine: Peace Not Apartheid*), 5, 143–5, 149
as president, 85, 95
Castro, Fidel, 130
Chase Manhattan Bank, 52
Chazan, Naomi, 96, 183n53, 188n48
Chicago Defender, 29, 70
Chomsky, Noam, 74, 146, 182n48
Cold War, 3, 21–2, 63–4, 67, 72
as barrier to condemnations of apartheid, 16, 60, 63, 81, 163n37
and Black Africans, 23, 33–4, 66
and divisions in U.S. Jewish community, 19, 21, 28–9, 44, 54–5, 109, 115, 123–4
Israel as U.S. ally in, 5, 50, 67, 72
and Israel–South Africa relations, 3, 33–4, 50, 76, 151
South Africa as U.S. ally in, 5, 9, 29, 38, 131
and Suez Canal conflict, 24, 25
and UN Resolution 3379, 63, 72, 75
Commentary magazine, 131, 143, 172n13
Commission on Social Action of Reform Judaism, 18, 130
communists, 18, 21, 23, 25, 79
in South Africa, 18, 104, 114, 179n9, 192n95
see also Soviet Union

Comprehensive Anti-Apartheid Act (1986), 116, 117–18
Conference of Independent African States (Accra, Ghana, 1958), 22, 31
Congregation Beit Simhat Torah, 101
Congressional Black Caucus, 70, 78, 108, 110, 135, 140
Cooper, Abraham, 137
Copenhagen conference. *See* World Conference of the UN Decade for Women
Council on African Affairs, 10, 158n26, 160n3
counterculture, Jewish, 42–3, 44, 50, 52, 89
Countess, Imani, 139

Daley, Margaret, 94
Davidson, Eron, 150–1
Davis, Miles, 110
Davis, Ossie, 55, 56, 177n64
De Gaulle, Charles, 49
Deborah, Golda, and Me (Pogrebin), 91
December 12th movement, 137, 202n43
Decter, Moshe, 75, 76
Dee, Ruby, 56, 177n64
Defiance Campaign, 11, 164n9
Dellums, Ron, 117
Demme, Jonathan, 144
Dershowitz, Alan, 144, 145
Diamond, Denis, 83
Diggs, Charles C., 59, 81
Diner, Hasia, 3, 164n2, 193n7
Dinkins, David, 133
Dire Straits, 110
divestment, 112
  in Israel, 134 (*see also* Boycott, Divestment, and Sanctions movement)
  in South Africa, 83, 100, 102, 109, 111–13, 120, 121, 134, 190n68, 191n86
Doron, Sara, 96
Du Bois, W. E. B., 46
Durban conference. *See* World Conference on Racism
Durban Review Conference (Geneva, 2009), 5, 138–40, 203n58

Eban, Abba, 66
Edelstein, Melville Leonard, 83
Egypt, 27, 34, 49
  and Soviet Union, 25, 29, 34, 44
  and Suez Canal conflict, 24–5, 47, 174n31
  in Yom Kippur War, 65
Eilan, Arieh, 35
Eisenhower, Dwight D. (and Eisenhower administration), 25, 29
Elath, Eliahu, 69
Electronic Intifada, 146, 151
Emergency Action Conference on South Africa (1960), 22, 30–1
Epril, Cecil, 131
Ethnic Labor Coalition, 116

Farber, David, 63, 178n1
Farmer, James, 36
Fauntroy, Walter, 78–9, 110
Federation of South African Women, 104
Fein, Leonard, 46, 54, 56, 68, 149, 176–7n63
Feldman, Kiera, 142
Feminist Arab Network, 96
Feminist Jews for Justice, 98
feminists, 87, 88, 192n102. *See also* Jewish feminists
First, Ruth, 104, 105, 114
Flesch, Fritz, 10, 16–18, 21, 28, 30, 35, 130
Flory, Ishmael, 79
Forward, the. See *Jewish Daily Forward*
Foundation for Ethnic Understanding, 135
Foxman, Abraham, 129
France, 162n19
  as colonial power, 24, 26, 27, 38, 167n28
  and Israel, 24, 26, 27, 38, 45, 47, 49
  and Suez Canal conflict, 24–5, 47, 173–4n31
Frankel, Glenn, 104
Free South Africa Movement (FSAM), 78, 110, 116, 117
Freedman, Samuel, 134, 138, 141
Freedom Seder (Waskow), 53
Friedman, Murray, 155n4
Friesel, Ofra, 181n36

INDEX

Front de Liberation Nationale (FLN, Algeria), 25–6, 28, 32
FSAM. *See* Free South Africa Movement
Fuchs, Lester, 200n10

Gabriel, Peter, 110
Galchinsky, Michael, 3, 43–4, 157n18, 159n2, 160n6, 160n7, 193n12
Ghanaian Times, 76
Glover, Danny, 138–9
Goldberg, Aleck, 119
Goldmann, Nahum, 14–15, 68, 280n20
Goldstein, Israel, 12, 17–18
Goldstone, Richard, 147–8, 152
  Gaza report by, 142, 147–8
Gordis, Daniel, 148
Gray, William, III, 116
Green, Nancy, 164n1
Greenberg, Cheryl, 21, 31
Greenberg, Irving, 152

Haaretz, 151–2
Hadassah Magazine, 83
Haddad, Carole, 96
Hammerskjold, Dag, 24
Hammerstein, David, 84–5, 125
Hampshire College, 109
Handler, Evelyn, 112
Harrington, Donald, 28, 164n9
Harris, David, 135
Harvard University, 102, 174n37
HaShomer Hatzair, 27–8, 33, 48–9, 54, 91. See also *Israel Horizons*
Hebrew Union College–Jewish Institute of Religion, 120–1
Height, Dorothy, 36
Hendessi, Mandana, 98, 189n56
Hertzberg, Arthur, 77, 78, 119, 133
Herzl, Theodor, 46, 133, 192n102
Herzog, Chaim, 75, 182n49
Heschel, Abraham Joshua, 48
Hightower, Charles, 57–8, 65
Himmelfarb, Milton, 56
Hines, Gregory, 56
Histadrut, 30, 69, 187n28
Hochstein, Philip, 81
Holocaust, 26, 77
  debates over lessons to be drawn from, 3, 45, 46, 106

  as inspiration for liberal ideals, 1, 3, 16–17, 21, 27–8, 33, 41, 53, 107, 111, 113, 133, 160–1n7, 164n2
  and Jewish unity, 2, 4, 14, 64
  memorial to, in Jerusalem (Yad Vashem), 75–6, 84
  and support for Israel, 2, 43, 71, 74, 75–6
  and support for Soviet Jewry, 60, 108
  survivors of, 26, 103, 125 (*see also* Flesch, Fritz)
homophobia, 99, 100, 196n50
Houser, George, 23, 164–5n9, 178n83
Houston, Whitney, 110
Hughes, Langston, 23
Human Rights Watch, 137
Hyman, Paula, 100, 186n11

Independence Day parade, 48–9
India, 10–11, 159n2
International Center for Peace in the Middle East, 56
International Confederation of Free Trade Unions (ICFTU), 31, 169n52
International Ladies' Garment Workers' Union (ILGWU), 30, 31, 116, 169n54
International Reform Movement, 121
International Women's Year, 87–8
Intifada (First), 122, 123
Isaac, Rael Jean, 123–4, 180n20, 198n80
Isaacson, Ben, 115, 124
Israel
  African American attitudes toward, 4, 56–9, 69–70, 78–9, 85–6, 125, 130 (*see also under* Rustin, Bayard; King, Martin Luther, Jr.)
  American Committee on Africa and, 28, 34, 56–9
  and Black African nations: early ties to, 24, 27, 32–4, 35, 46, 65–6, 67, 73, 75, 79, 82, 131; shifting relationship to, 22, 24, 29, 65, 75, 76, 77
  boycotting of, 125, 134, 138, 143 (*see also* Boycott, Divestment, and Sanctions movement)
  and France, 24, 26, 27, 38, 45, 47, 49

Israel—*Continued*
  and Palestinian territories
    (*see* Occupation)
  and South African government,
    33 (*see also* Israel–South
    Africa alliance)
  South African Jewry and, 30, 33, 35,
    104, 170n63
  in the United Nations, 24, 26, 33,
    34, 35, 67, 70–2, 75, 180n128
  as U.S. ally in Cold War, 5, 50, 67, 72
  see also Zionism
Israel Action Network (IAN), 6, 141–2,
  143, 146
Israel Apartheid Week (IAW), 5–6,
  140–1, 142, 146, 148, 151
Israel Horizons, 27–8, 49, 119–20, 123,
  169–70n62, 176–7n63
  on Israel–South Africa relations, 33,
    46–7, 123, 169–70
Israel–South Africa alliance, 65–6,
  71, 75
  American Jews' responses to, 67,
    75–6, 77–8, 79, 81–2, 83–6
  and Cold War, 3, 33–4, 50, 63,
    76, 151
  impact of, on Black/Jewish alliance,
    64–5, 76–7, 85–6
  origins of, 49, 65–6, 67, 75–6
  and Vorster visit to Israel, 63, 75–6,
    77, 79, 80, 84, 188n48

Jackson, Jesse, 135
Jacobson, Dan, 25
Jain, Devaki, 87, 93
Jaquette, Jane S., 181n41
Javits, Jacob, 17
Jewish Advocate (Boston), 145
Jewish Currents, 35, 77–8, 83, 85
Jewish Daily Forward, 152, 207n117
Jewish Federations of North America
  (JFNA), 6, 141. *See also* Israel
  Action Network
Jewish feminists, 52, 89, 99, 186n11
  and Cold War, 64, 92
  institutions built by, 89, 94–5, 98
  and patriarchy within Jewish
    community, 89, 94–5, 99, 101
  and UN women's conferences, 90–4,
    95–6, 98, 186n14, 192n102

  and Zionism, 52, 88, 91, 92, 93–4,
    98, 99–103
  see also Kleinbaum, Sharon;
    Messinger, Ruth; Pogrebin,
    Letty Cottin
Jewish Frontier, 107
Jewish Fund for Justice, 197n58
Jewish Labor Committee (JLC), 26
  and apartheid, 30, 31, 107,
    116–17, 118
  and domestic Civil Rights issues,
    31–2, 73–4, 169n54
  and Israel, 26–7, 28
  see also Magidson, Herbert
Jewish Radical, The, 84. *See also*
  Hammerstein, David
Jewish Renewal movement, 53
Jewish roots movement, 89, 91
Jewish Voice for Peace (JVP), 145–6
Jewish Women's Committee to End the
  Occupation (JWCEO), 98
Jews for Racial and Economic Justice
  (JFREJ), 102, 132–4, 201n26
JLC. *See* Jewish Labor Committee
Joftes, Saul, 36
Johns Hopkins University, 111
Jordan, Stanley, 110
Joseph, Helen, 104

Kasrils, Ronnie, 200n10
Kaye/Kantrowitz, Melanie, 159n28
Kelley, Robin D. G., 42
Kennedy, John F., 24, 165n16
Kenyatta, Margaret, 97
Kheel, Theodore, 23
Khrushchev, Nikita, 25, 166n23
Kinberg, Clare, 98
King, Martin Luther, Jr., 23, 38,
  47, 108–9
  on apartheid, 38, 155n1, 173n22
  death of, 53, 99
  on Israel, 36, 47, 48, 57, 174n37
Kissinger, Henry, 65, 190n67
Kjisane, Mlahleni, 30
Klapper, Melissa, 186n12
Klein, Morton, 145
Klein, Naomi, 136, 137, 141, 142,
  158n20
Kleinbaum, Sharon, 99–101, 105,
  143, 190n68, 190n69

Klepfisz, Irene, 98
Kraft, Gerald, 118
Krengel, Zev, 150
Kripke, Myer, 131
Kuper, Simon, 12

Labor Committee Against Apartheid (New York), 102
labor unions, 69, 130, 169n52, 169n54
　in apartheid protests, 30, 31, 102, 116, 130
　Israeli (see Histadrut)
　in South Africa, 116
　see also Jewish Labor Committee; specific unions
Lampert, Richard, 83
Laughlin, Kathleen A., 185n8
Laytner, Anson, 79–80, 134
Leadership Conference of National Jewish Women's Organizations, 94–5
Leadership Conference on Civil Rights (LCCR), 118
Lekach, Noam, 146
Lerner, Gail, 93
Lerner, Michael, 131–2, 148
Likud Party, 84, 96, 149
Lilith magazine, 92
Lipman, Eugene J., 18
Loeffler, James, 158n18, 160–1n7
Los Angeles Times, 96, 97
Love, Darlene, 110
Lovestone, Jay, 69–70
Lowery, Joseph, 78–9

Magidson, Herbert, 116–17, 129–30
Mahotella Queens, 110
Makeba, Miriam, 110, 194n16
Malan, Daniel F., 27–8
Mandela, Nelson, 11, 38, 82, 104, 153
　1990 U.S. visit by, 1, 2, 63, 102, 127–34, 155n2
　mourning of death of, 151–2
　and PLO, 1, 2, 126, 155n2
　as prisoner, 37, 110, 117
Mandela, Winnie, 129, 130
Matalon, Rolando, 132–3
Mays, Benjamin, 13
Mazower, Mark, 159n2, 160n3
Mbete, Baleka, 149–50

Mboya, Tom, 22–3, 24, 169n52
Meany, George, 69–70
Meir, Golda, 56, 67
　and Black Africa, 32, 34, 35, 46, 79, 81–2
Meister, Robert, 182n49
Mendelsohn, Adam, 45, 60, 107
Meretz Party, 46, 96, 183n53
Meriwether, James, 129, 165n9
Messinger, Ruth, 101–3, 105, 133
Mexico City conference. *See* United Nations World Conference on Women
Meyer, Marshall, 132–3
Michels, Tony, 31–2
Middle East Research and Information Project (MERIP), 76
Mkhize, Florence, 104
Mobilization for Peace and Justice, 115
Mokgoeboto, Zacharia, 115, 124
Moon, Henry Lee, 47–8
Morgan, Robin, 93
Moynihan, Daniel Patrick, 70, 71, 74, 77, 79–80
Mozambique, 72, 104
Ms. Magazine, 90, 91, 96
Muravchik, Joshua, 131
Muwamba, J. T. X., 78
Myeza, Lyndee, 187n28

Nairobi conference. *See* Third World Conference on Women
Namibia, 88, 98
Nasser, Gamal Abdel, 24, 25, 29, 34, 44
　as enemy of Israel, 24–5, 27, 34, 166n20, 167n36
Nation, The, 142
National Association for the Advancement of Colored People (NAACP), 23–4, 30, 56, 85–6, 160n3
　and apartheid, 29, 173n22
　and Jewish Labor Committee, 31, 169n54
　and Six-Day War, 47–8, 57
National Conference for New Politics (1967), 53
National Council of Jewish Women, 94, 118, 185n8

National Federation of Temple Sisterhoods (NFTS), 120
National Jewish Community Relations Advisory Council (NJCRAC), 36, 95, 141, 142
and apartheid, 36, 116–17, 118, 120, 121–2, 128
and concerns about younger Jews, 50–1, 115
and Mandela 1990 visit, 118, 155n2
see also Jewish Council for Public Affairs
National Jewish Students' Association (South Africa), 66
National Urban League, 23, 56
Negro American Labor Council, 29
Negro Trade Union Leadership Council, 116
Neimark, Marilyn Kleinberg, 132
Netanyahu, Benjamin, 147, 151–2
Neuer, Hillel, 136
Nevel, Donna, 132
New Jersey Jewish News, 103
New Jewish Agenda (NJA), 98, 107, 114–16, 133, 196n50
and apartheid, 107, 117
Arthur Waskow and, 53, 124
attacks on, 123–4
breaking apart of, 126, 128, 147
and Nairobi conference, 95, 96, 97
New Left, 44, 53
anti-Semitism in, 22, 42, 51
New Outlook, 77, 79–80
New York Times, 28, 76, 86, 97, 129, 132, 148
ads in, 1, 56–8, 59–60
letters to, 28, 47, 48, 65, 69, 73, 85
Ngoyi, Lilian, 104
Nixon, Richard, 24, 100
NJCRAC. *See* National Jewish Community Relations Advisory Council
Nogueira, Ana, 150–1
Norton, Eleanor Holmes, 110
Novak, Bill, 42, 172n7

Obama, Barack (and Obama administration), 138, 139, 140
Occupation, 53, 65, 67, 80, 149
growing criticisms of, 4, 57, 67, 68
likening of, to apartheid, 5, 67, 86, 92, 120, 127, 136, 143, 144, 150–1
protests against, 122, 140–1, 146, 149–50
Occupied Palestinian Territories. *See* Occupation
Organization of African Unity (OAU), 72, 76, 78
Organization of Nonaligned States, 70
Organization of Petroleum Exporting Countries (OPEC), 65, 73

Palestine Liberation Organization (PLO), 63, 68, 85
Andrew Young and, 85, 172n3
Nelson Mandela and, 127–8, 130, 131, 152
see also Arafat, Yasser
Palestine: Peace Not Apartheid (Carter), 5, 143–5, 149
Palestinians, 73, 137–8, 147, 148–9
and conflicts at international women's conferences, 92, 93, 96, 98–9, 189n56
identification of, with terrorism, 74
proposed one-state solution for, 141
proposed two-state solution for, 53, 68, 141, 143, 145, 172n7, 203n63
resistance movements of, 48, 122, 127 (*see also* Boycott, Divestment, and Sanctions movement; Palestine Liberation Organization)
support for, 4, 65, 68–9, 73, 123, 132; by African Americans, 85–6; by some Jewish activists, 45, 56, 68, 79, 80, 88, 98, 128, 132, 148–9; by Third World movement, 90, 127 (*see also* Boycott, Divestment, and Sanctions movement)
see also Occupation
Paley, Grace, 98
Pan African Congress, 22, 57
Pan American Airways, 80–1, 83, 84, 86
Pan-Africanist Congress (PAC), 13
Park Slope Food Cooperative (Brooklyn), 142–3
particularism. *See* universalism and particularism, balance between

Index

Patterson, William Lorenzo, 34
Perlzweig, Maurice, 12, 30, 60–1, 178n87
   attitude of, toward U.S. Jewish organizations, 14, 15, 16
   focus of, on Jewish unity, 12, 14, 15, 16, 30, 35, 60–1, 64
Petegorsky, David, 12, 13, 14, 42, 161n16
Peters, Joel, 181n41
Phillips, Channing, 53, 175–6n56
Pillay, Navi, 139–40
Podhoretz, Norman, 172n13
Pogrebin, Letty Cottin, 90–2, 148–9
   as critic of Occupation, 148–9
   and UN women's conferences, 91–2, 93, 95, 96, 97, 192n10
Pogrund, Benjamin, 158n22
Polakow-Suransky, Sasha, 3, 34, 84, 151
   on origins of Israel–South Africa alliance, 49, 65–6, 67, 75–6
Polier, Justine Wise, 102
postcolonial theory, 3
Powell, Colin, 135
Pravda, 76
Prinz, Joachim, 4, 15, 42, 68, 69
   and apartheid, 4, 15–16, 27, 35, 42, 59, 60, 68, 81
Provizer, Marlene, 95–6, 118, 197n58

Ramparts, 48, 53
Randall, Tony, 56
Randolph, A. Philip, 36, 47, 69, 108–9, 164n9
Ranz, Sheldon, 77, 78–9
Reagan, Maureen, 97
Reagan, Ronald (and Reagan administration), 63, 100, 109
   and Cold War, 63
   support of, for South Africa, 72, 110, 115, 116–17, 118
Reed, Lou, 110
Reform Judaism, 41, 120–1
   in South Africa, 82–3, 120–1, 191n86
   in the U.S., 130, 186n11;and apartheid, 18, 109, 113, 117, 193n11
Reilly, Niamh, 87
Response, 42

Rivonia trial (1963–1964), 37, 38, 170n62
Roadmap to Apartheid (film), 150–1
Robinson, Jackie, 23, 165n16
Robinson, Mary, 136
Robinson, Randall, 110
Roffman, Eleanor, 98, 130, 141
Roosevelt, Eleanor, 17, 23
Rosen, Rhoda, 105–6
Rubin, Sam, 68, 180n20
Russell, Bertrand, 148
Russell Tribunal on Palestine, 148
Rustin, Bayard, 34, 58, 108–9
   support of, for Israel, 34, 56–7, 69, 78, 108–9, 177n71

Safieh, Afif, 128
Said, Edward, 74, 131–2, 182n48
SAJBD. *See* South African Jewish Board of Deputies
Saperstein, David, 117, 193n11
Sarna, Jonathan, 43, 145–6, 161n15
Saron, Gus, 36–8, 50, 179n10
Saturday Review, 48
SAUPJ. *See* South African Union for Progressive Judaism
Schappes, Morris, 83–4, 133
Schneier, Marc, 135
Schwarzchild, Henry, 133
Scott-Heron, Gil, 110
Segal, Ronald M,. 25
Shalom Achshav, 56
Shamir, Yitzhak, 114
Sharon, Ariel, 138
Sharpeville Massacre (1960), 13, 25
   responses to, 29–30, 36, 52, 162
Sharpton, Al, 184–5n90
Shimoni, Gideon, 33, 67, 107
   on Israel–South Africa relations, 33, 67, 170n63
   on South African Jews, 105, 162n25, 163n34, 168n45, 170n63, 179n15, 192n99
Shlaim, Avi, 165n18
Silverman, Jerry, 141
Simon Wiesenthal Center, 137, 203n58
Simons, Ray. *See* Alexander, Ray
Sinai Peninsula, 49, 71, 165n18
sit-in movement, 13, 15, 16, 29

Six-Day War (1967), 24, 65, 170n63
  African Americans and, 47–8
  Black African nations and, 49, 65
  and generational divisions among U.S. Jews, 50
  and narrowed framework for U.S. Jewish opinion, 39, 43, 157n18, 172n13
Slomovitz, Philip, 81
Slovo, Joe, 104, 114, 152
Smythe, Hugh, 35
Solomon, Alisa, 132, 133, 201n23
Sommer, Evelyn, 95
South African Airways, 59, 117, 178n3
South African Jewish Board of Deputies (SAJBD), 11, 36, 83, 128, 150
  and American Jews, 36–8, 50, 59, 80–1, 119–20, 121–2
  and apartheid, 14, 15, 25, 36–7, 66–7, 82, 119, 121, 179n10, 191n86
  and World Jewish Congress, 11, 12, 15, 30, 60
  see also Saron, Gus
South African Jewry, 10, 11, 16, 29–30, 168n45
  divisions within, 37, 66–7, 106
  and Israel, 30, 33, 35, 104, 170n63
  and whiteness, 29, 200n9
  see also South African Jewish Board of Deputies
South African Tourist Bureau, 80
South African Union for Progressive Judaism (SAUPJ), 82–3, 120, 121, 191n86
Southern Christian Leadership Conference (SCLC), 78
Soviet Jewry (as issue in U.S.), 94–5, 107, 108–9
  counterposing of, to antiapartheid activism, 60, 112
Soviet Union, 76, 111, 166n23
  and Egypt, 25, 29, 34, 44
  and linking of Zionism to racism, 71, 72–3, 74, 75, 181n36
  and Middle East conflicts, 3, 25, 28–9, 34, 44, 65–6
  see also Soviet Jewry
Soweto massacre (1976), 82–3
Spiegler, Sam, 36
Springsteen, Bruce, 110

Staub, Michael, 3, 67–8, 158–9n27
  on marginalization of liberal/radical activists, 21, 43, 155n4, 198n80
Stein, Irwin, 82
Stephen Wise Free Synagogue, 125
Stern, Sol, 48
Stevens, Richard P., 58–9
Student Nonviolent Coordinating Committee (SNCC), 29, 173n22, 194n16
Students for a Democratic Society (SDS), 52
Suez Canal, 49–50
  1956 conflict over, 24–5, 47, 173–4n31
Sullivan Principles, 111
Sulzberger, Cyrus Leo, 50
Suzman, Helen, 33, 103, 114, 120–1, 131, 152
Svonkin, Stuart, 3, 21, 42, 51–2, 161n16, 164n5

Tambo, Oliver, 30, 104
Temple B'nai Jeshurun (Manhattan), 132–3
Theodor Herzl Institute of the Jewish Agency, 34–5
Third World Conference on Women (Nairobi, 1985), 94–8, 189n56
Third World movement, 38, 44, 64, 90
Thorn, Hakan, 162n20
Tikkun magazine, 131–2, 148
Time Magazine, 76–7, 85–6, 173n31
TransAfrica, 82, 86, 110, 117, 120, 138–9
Tri-State Defender, 77
Troy, Gil, 74, 135, 192n102
Tutu, Desmond, 63, 82, 102, 125, 128
  criticisms of Israel by, 125, 126, 142, 148
Twersky, David, 107

Ullstead, Neal, 110
UN Decade for Women (1975–1985), 87, 93. *See also* Third World Conference on Women; United Nations World Conference on Women; World Conference of the UN Decade for Women
UN Resolution 3379 (1975), 63, 72–5, 80, 88, 93, 135
  African Americans and, 73–4
  Black African states and, 75, 77

INDEX

and Cold War, 63, 72, 75
impact of, 74–5, 88, 113–14
impetus for, 72–3, 90, 180n30, 181n36
protests against, 4, 73–5, 77, 79–80, 94–5, 100, 118–19, 182n48, 182n49
repeal of (1991), 134, 135
UN Watch, 136
Ungar, Andre, 34–5, 69
Union of American Hebrew Congregations, 113, 118
United Auto Workers (UAW), 17, 18, 30, 31, 168n40
United Democratic Front, 104, 109, 119
United Nations (UN), 10, 24, 159n2, 193n12
and apartheid, 10–12, 13, 17, 33, 60, 109, 110
Black African nations and, 24, 35, 67, 75, 77, 167n28
conferences on racism held by, 5, 135–40
conferences on status of women held by, 4, 87–93, 94–8, 192n102
General Assembly of, 10, 70, 71–2, 160n3, 181n41 (see also UN Resolution 3379)
Israel in, 24, 26, 33, 34, 35, 67, 70–2, 75, 180n128
and Universal Declaration of Human Rights, 11, 160n7
U.S. role in, 79, 85, 181n41 (see also Moynihan, Daniel Patrick)
U.S. support for South Africa in, 9, 29, 110, 160n3
World Jewish Congress and, 5, 10, 11–12, 60, 135, 139, 140
United Nations Educational, Scientific, and Cultural Organization (UNESCO), 10
United Nations World Conference on Women (Mexico City, 1975), 72, 87–9, 91–2, 94, 97, 186n14
follow-up conferences to (see Third World Conference on Women; World Conference of the UN Decade for Women)
universalism and particularism, balance between, 19, 58, 92, 103, 132, 151, 153
in 1950s and early 1960s, 13, 21, 41

and apartheid, 52, 64, 66, 69, 106, 112, 114
and attitudes toward Israel, 46, 143, 149, 150
in Jewish labor movement, 18–19, 31–2
shifting, toward particularism, 16, 19, 22, 41, 43, 50, 172n13
in South Africa, 37, 150
University of California Berkeley, 84, 114, 142
University of California Davis, 114
University of Pennsylvania, 114
Unna, Yitzhak, 81–2, 84, 150

Vietnam War, 44, 47, 73
American Jews and, 3, 43, 48–9, 54–5
Vilakazi, Absalom, 30
Vorspan, Albert, 130
Vorster, John, 67, 86, 92
1976 visit of, to Israel, 63, 75–6, 77, 79, 80, 84, 188n48
as former Nazi supporter, 63

Walker, Alice, 142, 148, 151
Walt, Brian, 122, 179n9
Wang, Samuel, 59–60
Washington Jewish Week, 141
Washington Office on Africa, 124
Waskow, Arthur, 52–3, 59, 124, 133, 175n54, 175–6n56
Wedgwood, Ruth, 136–7
Weinberger, Andrew, 47
Weiner, Richard, 196n50
Weiss, Cora, 23, 26, 68, 109, 165n16
Weiss, Peter, 23, 53–6, 57–8, 68, 109, 133, 149, 203n63
and American Committee on Africa, 23, 56, 57–8, 65
and American Jewish Congress, 53, 54–5, 56, 59
as critic of Cold War rigidity, 54–5, 63, 123, 176n62
West, Cornel, 131–2
Westad, Odd Arne, 44, 167n28
whiteness, 29, 159n28, 200n9
Wiesel, Elie, 125, 142
Wiesenthal Center (Simon Wiesenthal Center), 137, 203n58
Wilkenfeld, Delores, 120
Wilkins, Roy, 36, 47, 108–9
Williams, G. Mennen, 23

Women's International Zionist
  Organization, 95
World Conference of the UN Decade
  for Women (Copenhagen, 1980),
  91–2, 93, 95, 97
World Conference on Racism (Durban,
  2001), 5, 73, 135–8. *See also*
  Durban Review Conference
World Jewish Congress (WJC), 4, 9,
  108, 119
  and apartheid, 4, 10, 11–12, 15–16,
    29, 35, 60–1, 119
  founding of, 9
  priority given by, to Jewish unity, 4,
    9, 10, 11–12, 14–15, 60–1, 139
  and United Nations, 5, 10, 11–12,
    60, 135, 139, 140
  and U.S. Jewish organizations,
    12–13, 15–16, 30, 35, 38
  see also Perlzweig, Maurice
World Union for Progressive Judaism,
  41. *See also* South African Union
  for Progressive Unionsim
World Zionist Organization (WZO),
  68, 108
Wyler, Marjorie, 101–2

Yad Vashem, 75–6, 84
Yazid, M'Hammed, 26
Yom Kippur War (1973), 24, 65–6, 67–8
  and founding of Breira, 68, 146–7,
    172n7
  and Israel–South Africa alliance,
    65–6, 67, 82
Yomekpe, Hope, 33

Young, Andrew, 85, 172n3
Young, Whitney, 36, 108–9
Young Conservative Foundation, 112

Zimbabwe, 65, 72
Zinsser, Judith, 93
Zionism, 28, 42, 46, 172n13
  African Americans and, 34, 48,
    55–9, 76–7, 79, 108, 174n37
  and anticolonialism, 22, 29, 32, 38,
    44, 46–7, 78
  conflicting views of, 79–80, 88,
    134; as a form of racism, 5, 71–2,
    75, 76, 87–90, 91–8, 135 (*see
    also* UN Resolution 3379); as a
    liberatory ideology, 1, 27, 28,
    32, 43, 46–7, 52, 55, 86, 91,
    133, 141, 152
  controversies over: on college
    campuses, 113–14, 142; at UN
    women's conferences, 87–90,
    91–8, 99
  efforts to divide, from Israeli
    policies, 56, 79–80, 182n48
  Jewish feminists and, 52, 88, 91, 92,
    93–4, 98, 99–103
  Jewish opponents of, 26, 29, 104,
    114, 122
  and radical left, 44, 48–9, 51
  socialist, 49 (*see also* Hashomer
    Hatzair)
  South African Jews and, 30, 33,
    37, 49, 58, 66, 83, 104, 114,
    122, 150
Zionist Organization of America, 145

Made in the USA
Coppell, TX
09 January 2022